Housing, Citizenship, and Communities for People with Serious Mental Illness

Books in the Series

Principles of Social Change
Leonard A. Jason

Community Psychology and Community Mental Health: Towards Transformative Change
Edited by Geoffrey Nelson, Bret Kloos, and José Ornelas

Influencing Social Policy: Applied Psychology Serving the Public Interest
Kenneth I. Maton

Housing, Citizenship, and Communities for People with Serious Mental Illness: Theory, Research, Practice, and Policy Perspectives
Edited by John Sylvestre, Geoffrey Nelson, and Tim Aubry

Forthcoming Books in the Series

Diverse Careers in Community Psychology
Edited by Judah J. Viola and Olya Glantsman

The Return of the Sun: Suicide and Social Transformation Among Inuit in Arctic Canada
Michael J. Kral

Community Power and Empowerment
Brian D. Christens

A Guidebook for Community Consultants
Susan M. Wolfe and Ann Webb Price

Rethinking American Indian Mental Health: Perspectives from Community Psychology
Joseph P. Gone

Housing, Citizenship, and Communities for People with Serious Mental Illness

Theory, Research, Practice, and Policy Perspectives

EDITED BY
JOHN SYLVESTRE
GEOFFREY NELSON
and
TIM AUBRY

OXFORD
UNIVERSITY PRESS

OXFORD
UNIVERSITY PRESS

Oxford University Press is a department of the University of Oxford. It furthers
the University's objective of excellence in research, scholarship, and education
by publishing worldwide. Oxford is a registered trade mark of Oxford University
Press in the UK and certain other countries.

Published in the United States of America by Oxford University Press
198 Madison Avenue, New York, NY 10016, United States of America.

CIP data is on file at the Library of Congress
ISBN 978–0–19–026560–1

1 3 5 7 9 8 6 4 2
Printed by Webcom Inc., Canada

CONTENTS

SERIES FOREWORD

The Society for Community Research and Action (SCRA), Division 27 of the American Psychological Association, is an international and interdisciplinary organization that supports the development of theory, research, and social action. Members share a common interest in promoting empowerment, health, and well-being, with special attention to multiple levels of analysis including the individual, group, organizational, community, cultural, and societal. Division members focus on an array of pressing social issues within national and global contexts (such as violence, mental health, HIV/AIDS, poverty, racism) and have developed effective social interventions to address seemingly intractable issues using a continuum of approaches from prevention to intervention to social change. These approaches to change involve diverse strategies, including, for example, advocacy, citizen participation, collaboration, community organizing, economic development, prevention education, self-help/mutual-help, socio-political development, social movements, and policy change. These change strategies typically share the goal of challenging and altering underlying power structures in the pursuit of social justice and community and individual well-being.

This book series, Advances in Community Psychology, is sponsored by the SCRA and aims to aid in the dissemination of theory, research, and social action as developed by SCRA members as well as nonmembers working in allied disciplines. The overarching mission of the series to create a publication venue that (1) highlights the contributions of the fields of community psychology and, more generally, community action, research, and practice; (2) integrates current knowledge regarding pressing topics and priorities for the field; and (3) offers the foundations for future directions.

This volume in the Series, *Housing, Citizenship, and Communities for People with Serious Mental Illness: Theory, Research, Practice, and Policy Perspectives*, addresses complex issues related to the intersection of homelessness and mental illness. This edited book provides a comprehensive overview of prominent models in the response to homelessness and highlights various theories of and tensions in the provision of housing support to those living with mental illness. Importantly, this volume begins with a historical perspective with attention to details that serve to encourage coherent discourse in the field. For example, the editors and authors discuss evolving terminology in the field and define the current terms used in the field ("single-site" versus "scattered-site") and how they refer to distinct practices. The volume incorporates a thorough review of the current state of empirical support for different approaches to homelessness and emphasizes the centrality of combining support (in varied forms) and housing for individuals with serious mental illness. Importantly, the volume offers a contextual view and addresses social and systemic environments in which interventions occur. Scholars and practitioners who desire thorough coverage and perspectives on best practices in response to homelessness will find this an invaluable volume. We are grateful that the editors and authors made this exceptional contribution to the Series.

Nicole E. Allen and Bradley Olson

ACKNOWLEDGMENTS

We thank Nicole Allen and Brad Olson, Editors of the Society for Community Research and Action (SCRA) book series, for their helpful guidance and encouragement for the preparation of this book.

ABOUT THE EDITORS

John Sylvestre, PhD, is associate professor in the School of Psychology and director of the Centre for Research on Educational and Community Services at the University of Ottawa. He was formerly senior editor of the *Canadian Journal of Community Mental Health*. He earned his BA from the University of Ottawa, and his MA and PhD from the University of Guelph. His interests lie in the study and the evaluation of community mental health programs and systems, with a focus on housing for people with serious mental illness. He is a member of the Society for Community Research and Action (Division 27 of the American Psychological Association), the Canadian Evaluation Society, and American Evaluation Association.

Geoffrey Nelson, PhD, is professor of psychology and a former faculty member in the graduate program in Community Psychology at Wilfrid Laurier University, Waterloo, Ontario. His research and practice has focused on community mental health programs and supports for people with serious mental illness and community-based prevention programs for children and families. Underlying his work is an emphasis on working in partnership with disadvantaged people, community-based participatory action research approaches using both quantitative and qualitative methods, and value-based critical perspectives that challenge the status quo and that are oriented toward social change. In 2013 he received the award for Distinguished Contributions to Theory and Research in Community Psychology from the Society for Community Research and Action, Division 27 (Community Psychology) of the American Psychological Association.

Tim Aubry, PhD, is professor in the School of Psychology and senior researcher at the Centre for Research on Educational and Community Services at the University of Ottawa. He currently holds the Faculty of Social Sciences Research Chair in Community Mental Health and Homelessness. Over the course of his career, Dr. Aubry has collaborated on research projects with community organizations and government at all levels, contributing to the development of effective social programs and policies. He received the Contribution to Evaluation Award from the Canadian Evaluation Society in 2013. He has also been named a fellow of the Canadian Psychological Association and the Society for Community Research and Action (Division 27 of the American Psychological Association).

ABOUT THE CONTRIBUTORS

Amandeep Bassi

Amandeep Bassi is a PhD candidate in experimental psychology at the University of Ottawa. She holds a bachelor of arts honors degree in psychology from Kwantlen Polytechnic University. Her research interest is aligned with understanding community living for persons with co-occuring mental illness and substance abuse disorders. She has gained direct experience with working on program evaluations in the areas of youth intensive case management and a multiagency evaluation of supportive housing in Ottawa, Ontario.

Katherine Bendell

Dr. Katie Bendell, C Psych (supervised practice) earned her PhD in clinical psychology from the University of Ottawa. She provides psychological services to individuals with a wide variety of issues, including depression, anxiety, posttraumatic stress disorder, substance use, relationship problems, and adjustment to life transitions. Dr. Bendell has a particular clinical interest in providing trauma-focused treatment to adults and older adults with lived experiences of trauma. In her work with the Royal's Operational Stress Injury (OSI) Clinic, Dr. Bendell provides psychological services to veterans who are experiencing psychological distress as a result of operational trauma. Her research interests focus on using participatory action research methods to understand experiences of living in supportive housing with serious and persistent mental illness.

Lorraine Bentley

Lorraine Bentley has a masters degree in urban planning from the University of Waterloo and has extensive experience in housing and social planning. She has both Canadian and international experience in researching, planning, and implementing housing and community support services for the most vulnerable populations. She is the executive director of Options Bytown Non-Profit Housing Corporation, in Ottawa, an organization that provides housing and support services to people with a history of homelessness, addictions, and mental illness. As the chairperson of Housing Plus: The Ottawa Supportive Housing Network, she is an advocate for supportive and affordable housing solutions to help end homelessness.

Joanne Bretherton

Joanne Bretherton joined the Centre for Housing Policy at the University of York in 2005. Her research interests center on evaluation, evidenced-based policy, and comparative research. Her particular focus is on homelessness and housing poverty. Joanne is codirector of the Women's Homelessness in Europe Network (WHEN), which includes leading academics in the fields of homelessness and housing poverty from 12 European countries. A Japanese speaker, her comparative homelessness research has included a visiting scholarship to Japan. Joanne has directed and worked on multiple research projects on homelessness and Housing First in the UK and she has also led homelessness research in Ireland.

Rachel Caplan

Rachel Caplan received her MA in early childhood studies from Ryerson University, and is currently a PhD student in community psychology at Wilfrid Laurier University. Her research interests are in child, family, and community mental health and homelessness as well as early childhood education, health, and equitable access to high-quality social services.

Rebecca Cherner

Rebecca Cherner is a postdoctoral fellow at the Centre for Research on Educational and Community Services at the University of Ottawa. Her research focuses on the mental health, physical health, and housing of vulnerable populations, particularly individuals who are homeless or at risk of homelessness. She is also involved in program evaluation with community organizations.

Susan Eckerle Curwood

Susan Eckerle Curwood has a PhD in community psychology and has led research studies on poverty reduction, housing and mental health, and youth homelessness. She is currently a knowledge broker at the Centre for Addiction and Mental Health in Toronto.

Henri Dorvil

Henri Dorvil, PhD, is a full professor in the School of Social Work at l'Université du Québec à Montréal (UQÀM). In 2014, he was named emeritus member of l'Ordre des Travailleurs Sociaux et des Thérapeutes Conjugaux et Familiaux du Québec. For over 20 years, he was a researcher with the Groupe de Recherche sur les Aspects Sociaux de la Santé et de la Prévention (GRASP-FCAR) at l'Université de Montréal and is currently an adjunct researcher with the social psychiatry division of the Centre de Recherche de l'Institut Universitaire en Santé Mentale de Montréal (IUSMM).

John Ecker

John Ecker, PhD, recently graduated from the experimental psychology program at the University of Ottawa. His doctoral research focused on community integration among homeless and vulnerably housed adults. He is currently a research associate at the Centre for Research on Educational and Community Services at the University of Ottawa. His research interests include homelessness, housing, mental health, and the LGBTQ community.

Benjamin F. Henwood

Benjamin Henwood, PhD, is a licensed clinical social worker whose practice and research has focused on adults who have experienced homelessness and serious health conditions, including mental illness, physical disease, and addiction. Dr. Henwood served as the clinical director of a Housing First agency in Philadelphia and has conducted research on frontline provider perspectives. Dr. Henwood is currently an assistant professor of social work at the University of Southern California.

Jonathan Jetté

Jonathan Jetté is a PhD candidate in the clinical psychology program at the University of Ottawa. His doctoral research focuses on the cost and cost efficacy of a Housing First intervention targeting homeless people with substance use disorder. He is currently doing a clinical internship at the University of Manitoba. His research interests include program evaluation, cost of services, homelessness, housing, mental health, and rural community.

Nick Kerman

Nick Kerman is a PhD student in clinical psychology at the University of Ottawa and formerly worked at the Centre for Addiction and Mental Health in Toronto as a research analyst. His areas of research focus on homelessness and housing, mental health, and support services.

Timothy MacLeod

Timothy MacLeod is a PhD in community psychology from Wilfrid Laurier University. His research is on Housing First and community integration for adults who have psychiatric disabilities.

Philip Mangano

Philip F. Mangano is founder and president of the American Round Table to Abolish Homelessness. Prior to his work with the Round Table, Mangano was appointed by President George W. Bush to be the executive director of the White House United States Interagency Council on Homelessness. In that role, he shaped and led the national strategy to prevent and end homelessness from 2002 to 2009, including in the transitional phase of the Obama administration. During that time, the first documented decrease in homelessness, a 37% decrease in street and chronic homelessness, was achieved. Mangano has been recognized for his strategic leadership in applying

business principles and practices to the issue of homelessness, including the application of cost-benefit analysis to policy considerations. He has been recognized for
his work with numerous awards and honors from a variety of public and private sector entities, including the US Conference of Mayors, *TIME* magazine, International
Downtown Association, the first International Homelessness Research Conference,
and state and local organizations. Over the past three decades, he has forwarded the
cause of the abolition of homelessness across the world, invited to speak in Canada,
England, Scotland, Australia, New Zealand, Germany, and Denmark, at United
Nations and European Union sponsored events at national meetings in a number of
countries, and at Harvard, Oxford, and a number of university campuses in the United
States and abroad.

Scott McCullough

Scott McCullough MCP is a senior research associate at the Institute of Urban
Studies (IUS), the University of Winnipeg. Scott's work at the IUS covers a wide
range of housing and urban issues including housing and housing market dynamics,
neighborhood analysis, Aboriginal community development, urban core change,
immigration settlement needs, and urban poverty. Recent work has focused on best
practices in eviction prevention for those at risk of homelessness, and helping to
coordinate Winnipeg's first Street Census of people experiencing homelessness.

Shannon McDermott

Shannon McDermott has 10 years of experience working on applied and theoretical research projects in the fields of mental health, homelessness, and aging.
Her research aims to understand how policy and practice can be structured to
deliver the best care for people in the community. Shannon began her career as a
social worker with Meals on Wheels in San Francisco before completing her PhD
at UNSW Australia in 2007. She worked at UNSW Australia as a lecturer in the
School of Social Sciences before joining the Cognitive Decline Partnership Centre
at the University of Sydney as a research fellow.

Patricia O'Campo

Dr. Patricia O'Campo is professor of epidemiology at the Dalla Lana School of
Public Health Sciences at the University of Toronto and an adjunct professor at
the Johns Hopkins Bloomberg School of Public Health and holds the Chair of
Intersectoral Solutions to Urban Health Problems. She is co-lead on the University
of Toronto's Healthier Cities Hub, a research and education unit dedicated to work
in partnership with community organizations to improve the health of those residing in urban settings. As a social epidemiologist she has been conducting research
on the social determinants of health and health inequalities for over 25 years.
Dr. O'Campo's research focuses on upstream determinants of health, quantifying
the impacts of structural issues and social programs, and working to propose concrete solutions.

Nicholas Pleace

Nicholas Pleace has been based at the Centre for Housing Policy at the University of York since 1991. Since 2010, he has been part of the European Observatory on Homelessness, operating under the auspices of FEANTSA, the European Federation of Homelessness Organisations. He has written widely on homelessness and directed homelessness research for the Finnish, French, and UK governments, along with multiple projects for homelessness charities in the UK, Ireland, and France and work for the European Commission and OECD. With Joanne Bretherton, Nicholas undertook some of the initial research on Housing First in the UK and he has led systematic reviews on the use of Housing First models in the European contexts. He is the author of the forthcoming pan-EU guidance on Housing First, titled *Housing First Europe*.

Jennifer Rae

Jennifer Rae is a PhD student in experimental psychology at the University of Ottawa. Her research interests include community mental health and homelessness. Her doctoral research is focused on an outcome evaluation of a community-based intervention program for marginalized youth.

Reena Sirohi

Reena Sirohi is a registered social worker with an MSW who works at the Centre for Addiction and Mental Health in Toronto in community engagement, education, and research focusing on housing, homelessness, poverty, and their intersectionality with mental health.

Emmy Tiderington

Emmy Tiderington, PhD, is a licensed social worker with over a decade of direct practice experience in housing and case management services for individuals with serious mental illness. Her research examines "street level" implementation of best practices in mental health and housing services. Dr. Tiderington is an assistant professor in the School of Social Work at Rutgers, The State University of New Jersey.

John Trainor

John Trainor was a program director at the Centre for Addiction and Mental Health in Toronto and worked in the areas of housing, income, and work. He retired in 2013. He is an adjunct professor in the Department of Psychiatry at the University of Toronto, and in 2015 was appointed as chairman of the Ontario Mental Health Foundation. He is active internationally in the Open Society Foundations (OSF) and chairs the Advisory Committee of the Mental Health Initiative and is a member of the Global Health Advisory Committee for OSF.

Ken Wireman

Ken Wireman, MSW, is the founding executive director of Main Street Housing, Inc. He received his masters in social work from the University of Maryland, and has worked in the mental health field in various capacities for over 25 years. With a long history of providing and overseeing mental health services in many different capacities, he has a well-rounded perspective on public mental health services delivery systems and the needs of the people they serve. Ken has been a landlord at various times in his life since the age of 16, and has an understanding of the mission and goals of affordable housing systems. Main Street Housing, Inc., interacts with both housing and mental health administrations in order to acquire properties and help folks with mental illness successfully. Ken also serves as an adjunct professor for the University of Southern New Hampshire.

Stephanie Yamin

Stephanie Yamin, PhD, is an assistant professor at Saint Paul University in the counseling program. She graduated from the clinical psychology program at the University of Ottawa. She worked for 2 years as a research associate at the Centre for Research on Educational and Community Services at the University of Ottawa, where she developed an interest in program evaluation. Her main research interests include vulnerable populations (i.e., homelessness and the older adult population) and examining specific programs that aim to increase quality of life and well-being.

INTRODUCTION

Housing is finally receiving recognition as a fundamental element of community mental health systems 50 years after the beginning of deinstitutionalization in North America. Unless people are well housed, they will not form the relationships, join the communities, and participate in the meaningful activities that are essential for healthy and satisfying lives. This growing recognition comes as a result of a number of contributions. One contribution has been encouraging research findings showing that good-quality housing with support can help people, even those with histories of homelessness, to remain stably housed. Progress has also come from the tireless advocacy of people with lived experience, their families, and supporters; from key political and policy decisions; and from the efforts of housing and support providers who commit themselves daily to ensure that people who are vulnerable are well housed.

But the goal is more than housing. Whereas housing is a start, the key concern is how it leads to social integration, community participation, recovery, and citizenship. This is the central question that this book considers. In considering this question we realized that a comprehensive treatment of the subject of housing was needed. Remarkably, despite being a topic of interest, debate, policy, and research for many years, there has never been a comprehensive book-length examination of housing in the community mental health field. Therefore, we sought to provide a comprehensive overview of the field that examined its history, to clarify vague and confusing terminology, to document recent research advances, to point to new avenues for research, and to bring theory to bear on a field that has long been empirically rather than conceptually driven. Recognizing that the field encompasses a variety of aspects and perspectives, and has grown to become an international concern, we have also included other contributors to ensure that the book could lay claim to adequately covering this broad field.

Community Psychology and Housing for People with Serious Mental Illness

In many countries, community psychology has its roots in community mental health (Reich, Riemer, Prilleltensky, & Montero, 2007). For example, at the Swampscott conference, where community psychology was founded in the United States, there was an explicit focus on educating community psychologists who work in the field of community mental health (Bennett et al., 1966). The field of community mental health began to emerge in the 1960s in the wake of deinstitutionalization. As the deinstitutionalization process unfolded, the problem of where to house former patients of psychiatric hospitals became a pressing issue for community mental health professionals.

Community psychologists stepped in to help address this problem and have made sustained contributions to housing people who have experienced serious mental illness over the past 50 years since the Swampscott conference was held. In the 1960s, George Fairweather and colleagues (Fairweather, Sanders, Maynard, & Cressler, 1969) developed the Lodge program in a Veteran's Administration hospital as an alternative to standard care of hospitalization and discharge for people experiencing mental illness. The Lodge program was based in community psychology principles (e.g., mutual aid), used community psychology approaches (e.g., program innovation, consultation, and dissemination), and was an early example of what is now known as "evidence-based practice." Fairweather et al. (1969) conducted a rigorous randomized controlled trial (RCT) of the Lodge that demonstrated its effectiveness over a follow-up period of several years.

Fast-forward to the 1980s and 1990s, when another psychologist, Paul Carling (1995), articulated a new approach to housing for people experiencing mental health issues that he called "supported housing." Supported housing was based on the principles of consumer choice and self-determination and community integration, which squarely align with community psychology principles of empowerment and community. Unlike Fairweather's Lodge, which preceded it, supported housing helped people to live in normal housing in the community through the support of portable rent supplements and mental health support services.

Later, the community psychologist Sam Tsemberis, a winner of the Society for Community Research and Action Practice Award, expanded supported housing to the ever-growing population of homeless people with serious mental illness and addictions. This model, called Housing First, was designed to rapidly end homelessness for people who had been chronically homeless (Tsemberis, 2010). Like Fairweather before, Tsemberis based Housing First in community psychology principles (e.g., choice, empowerment, and social justice) and rigorous quasi-experimental and RCT studies that he has conducted with other community psychologists. From its roots in New York City, Housing First is now being implemented and transforming mental health services in countries across the world.

While there have been recent books on housing for people with mental illness, these books have focused more on the homeless population and specific types of housing programs (e.g., Padgett, Henwood, & Tsemberis, 2015). However, there has not been a book that provides a comprehensive review of housing and serious mental illness, particularly from the vantage point of community psychology. Moreover, we believe that with its long-standing contributions to housing and community mental health that community psychology is uniquely positioned to provide such a review. Thus, we embarked on this book to fill that gap. We review housing theory and research that is comprehensive, current, and historical. We also include contributions from experts in housing and mental illness who examine housing programs and policies in other countries.

Overview of the Book

The book is divided into four sections. The first section lays a foundation by providing a historical overview of the field and providing important clarifications of terminology. Approaches to community-based housing have continued to evolve since their introduction in the 1960s, coinciding with deinstitutionalization. Over the years, innovations in these approaches have brought new terminology and new practices based on different core values. Chapter 1 by Nelson and MacLeod clarifies both this history and terms that have been introduced to describe different housing approaches. To further help dissipate common confusion in the distinctions between the different approaches, this chapter introduces new terminology (single-site versus scatter-site) to better distinguish among them. This terminology is adopted throughout the rest of the book. Building on chapter 1, chapter 2 by Nelson and Caplan distinguishes among various housing models using a three-step process. The chapter addresses the confusing terminology and a lack of clarity in the important distinctions between different housing models that has characterized this field.

Support is a critical component of successful housing programs. Chapter 3 by Aubry, Cherner, Ecker, and Yamin reviews the research on the effectiveness of different forms of professional support that have been combined with housing, particularly in terms of their potential to enable people with histories of institutionalization, homelessness, or unstable housing, to remain stably housed. Chapter 4 by Aubry, Rae, and Jetté reviews current evidence of the economic value and contributions of these programs. Housing programs compete with other social programs for limited funds from government. Notably, arguments about citizenship, compassion, or basic human rights have not been sufficient to ensure that these programs are appropriately funded and that there is a sufficient supply. Consequently economic analyses have been an important tool to justify expenditures on these programs.

Section II of the book provides a more forward-looking examination of housing theory and research methods. It includes chapters that aim to integrate theory more strongly into housing research as well as an overview of the concept of citizenship, and its implication for research, policy, and practice. The chapters in this section also point to the diversity of additional methods and techniques that could be employed in the study of housing. Chapter 5, by Nelson and MacLeod, describes the implicit or explicit theories that inform different housing approaches. Like all interventions, housing programs are also informed by theory—assumptions about how different program components work together to produce specific changes for people who participate in these programs. Whereas these assumptions may be explicitly stated, they may also be implicit in the program design. Chapter 6, also by Nelson and MacLeod, is also on housing theory, but this time is concerned with the context that surrounds housing programs. Individual housing programs operate in complex social and systemic environments. The outcomes envisioned for people who participate in these programs, highlighted in the previous chapter, can be facilitated or thwarted by factors that are external to these programs. Therefore, it is important to understand them and their potential impact on housing programs and tenants.

What should be the end goal of the provision of housing to people with serious mental illness who have been marginalized by society? Chapter 7 by Sylvestre contends that too often the focus has narrowly been on individual-level therapeutic outcomes. It argues that housing and support providers, and policy makers, must strive to provide housing and support that promote the full citizenship of tenants. The chapter distinguishes between different perspectives on citizenship and points to actions that can be taken at different levels to work toward this goal.

A goal of this book is to provide a comprehensive understanding of the current state of theory, research, and intervention concerning housing. Chapter 8, by Sylvestre, Bassi, and Bendell, discusses how this knowledge has been produced, and explores alternatives for the production of knowledge about housing. Though we typically think of the term "social science" as referring to the topic of study, this chapter emphasizes that science itself is a social process. It claims, in part, that a greater attention to the social process of science can produce a more comprehensive understanding of this topic.

Section III of the book considers policy, with historical and current perspectives from the United States, Canada, the European Union, and Australia. The chapters describe the policy and historical contexts for the shift toward Housing First, as well as point to lingering challenges and new opportunities. Chapter 9, by Mangano, provides a firsthand account of federal-level efforts in the United States that supported a shift toward Housing First. It describes how the adoption of different values and principles was critical for identifying the change that needed to occur and ensuring that the required changes happened. Chapter 10, by Trainor, Eckerle Curwood, Sirohi, and Kerman, describes the long road traveled to develop a modern and effective community mental health system in Canada, with housing as a cornerstone—a journey that continues to this day. It challenges us to evaluate policy in terms of its actual impact on people's lives, rather than only in terms of its written form. With its historical perspective, the chapter provides a context for the emergence of the Mental Health Commission of Canada, and the groundbreaking At Home/Chez Soi study—the largest Housing First experiment in the world. Chapter 11, by Pleace and Bretherton, demonstrates that Housing First is not only a North American phenomenon. While highlighting the adoption of Housing First in the European Union, the chapter also points to areas of resistance and ways in which the model has been adapted to fit within prevailing assumptions and mental health systems in the European Union. The chapter provides a critical examination of the notion and importance of fidelity in the importation of the Housing First model into diverse contexts. Chapter 12 by McDermott tracks the evolution of housing in Australia—from deinstitutionalization to the present day. It highlights the diversity of forms of housing that have evolved as well as the differences that emerged across the various states that are primarily responsible for housing. It highlights more recent national-level efforts to develop a national vision for housing and to ensure that it is a foundation of community mental health systems.

Section IV of the book is concerned with the delivery of housing and support services. Consumer-led housing has been around for some time. However, it has not received the same amount of attention as have other types of housing. Growing out of the consumer/survivor movement, it is informed by a distinct history and set of values. Chapter 13 by Wireman describes how one consumer-led housing program in Maryland evolved directly from and was informed by the consumer/survivor movement, and highlights peer support as an integral program element. Chapter 14, by Bentley and Sylvestre, examines the challenges facing providers of single-site supportive housing. It also makes a case for the role of this type of housing in local housing systems to meet the full range of preferences and needs of individuals. Drawing on qualitative research and case examples, chapter 15, by Henwood and Tiderington, provides a critical examination of the day-to-day challenges in providing Housing First. As this chapter highlights, the provision of Housing First is informed by key values or principles. Though in the abstract it is easy to clearly state these principles, when faced with the complexities of real-world service provision, it is less clear how to act on them. Drawing on multisite research from the At Home/Chez Soi project in Canada, chapter 16, by MacLeod, Aubry, Nelson, Dorvil, McCullough, and O'Campo, highlights some of the challenges and opportunities for working with private-market landlords. As stakeholders in the program, landlords have particular perspectives, skills, and needs that must be understood and addressed.

The fifth section of the book concludes with an overview by Sylvestre of what we have learned from the book. We believe that this book points to a field that is coalescing around some core values and practices, though some debate remains about how local housing systems can be configured with a range of housing options and approaches. We point to solid evidence that vulnerable people, including those with serious mental illness and complicated histories of homelessness and substance abuse, can be stably housed. However, we have found that there is still much work to be done. If the goal is for housing to facilitate social integration, community, recovery, and citizenship, then it is still elusive for many. New research, new practices, and new policies are needed to build on the gains that come from good housing and ensure that the lives we want for all our citizens are secured.

References

Bennett, C.C., Anderson, L., Cooper, S., Hassol, L., Klein, D.C., & Rosenblum, G. (1966). *Community psychology: A report of the Boston conference on the education of psychologists for community mental health.* Boston: Department of Psychology, Boston University Press.

Carling, P.J. (1995). *Return to community: Building support systems for people with psychiatric disabilities.* New York: Guilford Press.

Fairweather, G.W., Sanders, D.H., Maynard, H., & Cressler, D.L. (1969). *Community life for the mentally ill.* Chicago: Aldine.

Padgett, D., Henwood, B., & Tsemberis, S. (2015). *Housing First: Ending homelessness, transforming systems, and changing lives.* New York: Oxford University Press.

Reich, S.M., Riemer, M., Prilleltensky, I., & Montero, M. (Eds.). (2007). *International community psychology: History and theories.* New York: Springer.

Tsemberis, S. (2010). *Housing First: The Pathways model to end homelessness for people with mental illness and addiction.* Center City, MN: Hazelden.

OVERVIEW OF HISTORY AND HOUSING APPROACHES FOR PEOPLE WITH SERIOUS MENTAL ILLNESS

1

The Evolution of Housing for People with Serious Mental Illness

GEOFFREY NELSON AND TIMOTHY MACLEOD

In this chapter, we provide an overview of the recent history of housing for people with serious mental illness, with an emphasis on developments in North America. We identify approaches to community housing in the early years of deinstitutionalization in the 1960s through the 1980s. We then go on to review subsequent developments in housing, beginning in the 1990s to the present day, including key programmatic initiatives that have emerged. In our review of housing during these two time periods (1960s–1980s, 1990s to today), we use a framework that we have adapted from Prilleltensky (1997) that includes the following elements: (1) context, (2) assumptions, (3) values, and (4) practices (see Table 1.1). Our purpose is to understand not only the practices in housing for people with serious mental illness during these two time periods but also the assumptions and values that underlie them and the context in which they developed. In so doing, our review is focused more on the historical, contextual, and moral aspects of housing discourse and action for this population than on the effectiveness of different approaches.

We argue that housing during the 1960s–1980s was driven by deinstitutionalization of people with serious mental illness from mental hospitals that were downsized or closed. The practices that emerged in community housing replicated those seen in psychiatric hospitals that were oriented either toward custodial care or active treatment. The assumptions and values on which community housing were based mirrored those of mental hospitals. Beginning in the 1990s, the growing problem of homelessness, coupled with the continuing consequences of deinstitutionalization, led to the development of supported housing and the Housing First movement. The assumptions and values on which this approach are based differ fundamentally from those of previous approaches to community housing. Like others before us (e.g., Ridgway & Zipple, 1990), we argue that Housing First represents a paradigm shift in housing for people with serious mental illness in its emphasis on assumptions

Table 1.1 **Framework for the Examination of Historical and Current Approaches to Housing for People with Serious Mental Illness**

Framework Elements	Time Period	
	1960s–1980s	*1990s–today*
Context	• Deinstitutionalization	• Homelessness
Assumptions	• Professional as expert, consumer as chronic patient	• Consumer as expert, professional as facilitator
Values	• Care vs. rehabilitation • Illness management vs. skill building • Segregation • Lack of consumer self-determination • Lack of collaboration and participation in treatment planning • Inattention to citizenship rights and resources	• Citizenship and rehabilitation • Recovery orientation • Community integration • Consumer self-determination • Collaboration with professionals (therapeutic alliance) and among consumers (peer support and self-help) • Housing as a right of citizenship • Attention to other resources (e.g., employment, education, meaningful activity)
Practices	• Custodial vs. therapeutic housing (e.g., board-and-care homes vs. halfway houses) • Residential continuum	• Scattered-site housing delinked from support (e.g., Assertive Community Treatment, Intensive Case Management) • Rent supplements

and values of citizenship, recovery, self-determination, collaboration, community integration, rights, and resources.

In constructing this analysis, we rely primarily on reviews of the literature on housing for people with serious mental illness that were conducted during the 1970s and 1980s (Arce & Vergare, 1985; Brozost, 1978; Carpenter, 1978; Colten, 1978; Cometa, Morrison, & Ziskoven, 1979; Cutler, 1986; Hall, Nelson, & Smith Fowler, 1987; Nelson & Smith Fowler, 1987; Rog & Raush, 1975) and from the 1990s to the present (Aubry, Ecker, & Jetté, 2014; Benston, 2015; Chilvers, MacDonald, & Hayes, 2002; Fakhoury, Murray, Shepherd, & Priebe, 2002; Fitzpatrick-Lewis et al., 2011; Frankish, Hwang, & Quantz, 2005; Groton, 2013; Hwang, Tolomiczenko, Kouyoumdjian, & Garner, 2005; Kyle & Dunn, 2008; Leff et al., 2009; MacPherson, Shepherd, & Edwards, 2004; Nelson, Aubry, & Lafrance, 2007; Newman, 2001;

O'Campo et al., 2009; Ogilvie, 1997; Parkinson, Nelson, & Horgan, 1999; Rog, 2004; Rog et al., 2014; Rogers et al., 2008; Rosenheck, 2000; Schiff & Rook, 2012; Schiff, Schiff, & Schneider, 2010). These reviews provide important windows into the context, assumptions, values, and practices of housing for people with serious mental illness during the times that they were written. We also use previous work that has traced the evolution of housing for people with serious mental illness (Nelson, 2010; Parkinson et al., 1999; Schiff et al., 2010; Trainor, Morrell-Bellai, Ballantyne, & Boydell, 1993). Finally, we concentrate primarily on the North American context in our review, as most of the literature on housing and mental health has focused on North America.

Backdrop: Mental Hospitals

Beginning in the mid-1800s, mental hospitals were created to care for people with serious mental illness. In the United States and Canada, Dorothea Dix, a retired schoolteacher, learned that people with mental illness lived in poorhouses and jails. Like the European reformers Phillipe Pinel in France and William Tuke in Britain who preceded her, Dix began a campaign to ensure that people with mental illness were treated in settings that were specifically designed for them. However, whereas the moral treatment era spearheaded earlier by Pinel and Tuke focused on small retreats and personalized care, Dix called for a medical model of treatment in hospitals. Dix was successful in persuading US state governments to construct 30 mental hospitals (Rochefort, 1996), and after her death, more mental hospitals were built and others expanded. In spite of Dix's best intentions, these hospitals became overcrowded and understaffed and were used to warehouse poor people, immigrants, and others who did not fit into mainstream society. Many people who were admitted lived in mental hospitals for the remainder of their lives. Some hospitals even had their own cemeteries with graves marked with stones with patients' hospital identification numbers rather than their names—anonymous in death, just as they had been anonymous in life.

In these institutions, operated by medical superintendents and the emerging medical specialty of psychiatry, some patients were subjected to primitive and deplorable "treatments" like lobotomy and insulin coma therapy. Institutional abuses occurred because patients had no rights and little to no power (McCubbin, 2009). Goffman (1961) wrote about how the culture of mental hospitals led to demoralization and disculturation in patients. Key aspects of the culture included rigid routines, block treatment (e.g., eating together, lining up for medications), depersonalization of residents, and social distance between the staff and residents. Goffman described the patients as "inmates," because they had no power, and the hospitals as "total institutions," because they existed as a separate social space designed to meet all the basic needs of patients—shelter, food, and clothing.

Because inmates were forced to adopt "the sick role," a culture of dependency, passivity, and chronicity was fostered among patients.

There were periodic cycles of exposé of the scandalous conditions of mental hospitals and attempts at reform (Rochefort, 1996). However, most of these reforms were either short-lived or occurred only in selected locales. In the 1960s, some mental health professionals began to introduce active, evidence-based rehabilitation programs as an alternative to the custodial care that existed in most hospitals. More specifically, some hospitals began to employ milieu therapy, based on therapeutic community principles, or token economies, based on social learning principles (Paul & Lentz, 1977). The theme of custodial care versus rehabilitation is one that continued into community residences for former patients in the era of deinstitutionalization, to which we now turn.

The 1960s to the 1980s
Context

Deinstitutionalization, which refers to a process of mental hospital bed reductions and hospital closures, started as early as the 1950s, but was in full swing in the 1960s (Bachrach, 1976). In the United States, the resident population of state and county mental hospitals dropped from 558,922 in 1955 to 70,402 in 1989, an 82% reduction (Rochefort, 1996). Moreover, the median length of hospital stay dropped from 41 days in 1970 to 23 days in 1980. In Canada the number of beds in provincial mental hospitals declined from 69,128 in 1965 to 20,301 in 1981, a 70% reduction (Sealy & Whitehead, 2004). Deinstitutionalization occurred for several reasons: (1) Psychiatric hospitals were becoming expensive to maintain; (2) the public welfare system provided financial support for discharged patients, albeit at a poverty level; (3) psychotropic medications were developed and quickly became widely used; (4) the limitations of hospitals had become visible and unacceptable; (5) there was a new focus on patients' rights; and (6) a progressive vision of a new system of community mental health services was emerging (Nelson, 2012).

Unfortunately, in the early days of deinstitutionalization, the funding did not follow patients into the community. There was increased funding for general hospital psychiatric units (Wasylenki, Goering, & Macnaughton, 1994), but funding was not systematically reallocated from the hospitals to housing in the community or community support services. As a result, many discharged patients ended up living in boarding homes, in single room occupancy hotels (SROs), in nursing homes, with foster families, or in other poor quality housing, or they became homeless (Rochefort, 1996). While many of the problems discharged patients faced in the community were social, economic, or interpersonal, they were given medication but little else (Harris, Hilton, & Rice, 1993). Evidence-based programs like assertive community treatment (ACT) and intensive case management (ICM) were in their early stages of development and were not widely available (Mueser, Bond, Drake, & Resnick, 1998). Goering, Wasylenki, Farkas, Lancee, and Freeman (1984) found that 6 months after discharge from psychiatric facilities in Toronto, 33% were readmitted to hospital; 68% reported moderate to severe difficulties in social functioning; and 20% lived in substandard housing. The situation became even more dire at a 2-year follow-up.

In summary, in the wake of deinstitutionalization, housing and support became major issues of concern. In the past, mental hospitals functioned as "total institutions," providing housing and staff to meet patients' basic needs. Without this infrastructure, the questions of where and how discharged patients should live came to the fore.

Assumptions

Regardless of whether former patients were viewed as needing custodial care or treatment/rehabilitation, an implicit assumption of housing programs from the 1960s to the 1980s was that the mental health professional is the expert who knows what is best for the patient. This is reflected in the language used to describe the population being served. Terms like "chronic psychiatric patient" (Carpenter, 1978), "chronically mentally ill" (Cutler, 1986), and "chronically mental disabled" (Nelson & Smith Fowler, 1987) were commonly used. Rather than using people-first language, this professional discourse focuses on individuals' "patienthood," and the supposed "chronic" nature of their illness. Individuals have no agency or voice in these writings about housing in the new era of deinstitutionalization. Rather being viewed as citizens or community members with rights, patients were seen as the objects of custodial care or professional intervention. Thus, the historical legacy of institutional care followed discharged patients into the community through the creation of mini-institutions or institutions without walls. Patients were still viewed as sick and as in need of lifelong care or treatment that would be administered by mental health professionals.

Values

The values of care versus rehabilitation that became evident in mental hospitals when active treatment programs were introduced as an alternative to custodial care continued to compete with one another in the early days of deinstitutionalization. It is important to note that many custodial care facilities in the community, such as board-and-care homes, were and continue to be profit-oriented. Therefore, owners and operators of such facilities, who typically have no training in mental health and rehabilitation, have a vested interest in maintaining a stable and docile group of residents. Based on a study of 100 residents of 10 board-and-care homes, Blake (1985/1986) concluded that "instead of being empowered as consumers, residents have become commodities; instead of gaining additional freedoms, dein-stitutionalized persons have been abandoned" (p. 75). While there were efforts to provide rehabilitation services to residents of board-and-care homes (Pulier & Hubbard, 2001) and SRO hotels (Linhorst, 1991), many of these facilities repli-cated features of mental hospitals in providing housing, meals, and medications, and functioned like mini-institutions in the community (Segal & Aviram, 1978; Trainor et al., 1993). In contrast, community residential treatment programs were developed during this time period to improve the functioning and well-being of dis-charged patients (Carpenter, 1978; Colten, 1978). These programs included tran-sitional programs (e.g., halfway houses), group homes, and supportive apartments, all of which provided active treatment and rehabilitation.

A related set of competing values is that of illness management versus skill-building. Custodial facilities in the community tended to provide medication to manage psychiatric symptoms, but little in the way of rehabilitation. In a study of 200 patients living in residential care facilities (80% with a diagnosis of schizophre-nia or other psychotic disorder), all received medication, but more than 60% did not receive any rehabilitation or mental health services (Anderson, Lyons, & West, 2001). On the other hand, rehabilitation-oriented housing programs, such as those mentioned above, have focused on developing skills, like social skills, life skills, employment competencies, and so forth (Nelson & Smith Fowler, 1987).

While custodial and rehabilitation approaches to housing differ in the ways mentioned above, they also share some values. Rather than promoting inte-gration into normal community settings with people who do not have serious mental illness, residents are congregated in one facility. Such congregate settings often evoke negative responses from others in the community or their siting is restricted by zoning lows, both of which serve to exclude rather than include peo-ple with serious mental illness from participating as citizens in the normal life of the community (Aviram & Segal, 1973; Hall et al., 1987). "Not in My Back Yard" is a familiar refrain that planners have heard in locating congregate facilities in different neighborhoods.

There is also a lack of consumer self-determination regarding housing and sup-port. This value is evident in the discourse of "residential placement" (Carpenter, 1978), in which professionals assign or place patients in different types of com-munity housing, rather than consumers having a voice and choice about where and with whom they want to live. Similarly, the value of collaboration is de-emphasized, especially in custodial housing. Since it is assumed that professionals know what is best for people with serious mental illness, little attention is paid to consumer strengths and collaboration in treatment planning (Nelson, Lord, & Ochocka, 2001). Brozost (1978) illustrates these values well in the following quote:

> Older, more disabled and chronically inept persons should be referred only into long-term custodial care, relatively low-expectation homes;

generally, younger and less chronic former mental patients with rehabilitation should be referred only to transitional rehabilitation-oriented high-expectation residences. (p. 260)

This quote shows the prevailing view that professionals know what is best for patients and the belief of professionals that older, "inept" people have little to no potential for rehabilitation. Finally, both custodial housing and group homes that provide rehabilitation fail to attend to citizenship rights and resources. Consumers are commodities or cases to be managed rather than citizens with rights, responsibilities, and resources. Therapeutic values, as opposed to citizenship values, are emphasized in rehabilitation-oriented housing programs (Sylvestre, Nelson, Sabloff, & Peddle, 2007).

Practices

The housing practices that emerged during the 1960s through the 1980s have been referred to as custodial housing (e.g., board-and-care homes, SRO hotels) and supportive housing (e.g., halfway houses, group homes, supervised apartments) (Nelson, 2010; Parkinson et al., 1999; Trainor et al., 1993). One important difference between these two types of housing is that custodial housing is often a for-profit business, while supportive housing, either scattered-site or single-site, is typically operated by nonprofit agencies. A second difference is that supportive housing typically has staff trained in mental health and rehabilitation, while custodial housing does not. Finally, as we noted earlier, supportive housing typically involves psychiatric rehabilitation, whereas this is not the norm with custodial housing.

Research on custodial housing does not show beneficial outcomes for residents (Parkinson et al., 1999). For example, in a 10-year follow-up study of 360 residents of sheltered care facilities in California, Segal and Kotler (1993) found that while these facilities were able to achieve low rates of recidivism to mental hospitals, residents experienced significantly poorer health, more psychiatric symptoms, lower levels of independent social functioning, and no changes in community integration over time. A few studies have compared custodial and supportive housing. For example, Lamb and Goertzel (1972) found in a randomized study that long-stay patients living in "high expectations" halfway houses had significantly better outcomes in terms of employment rates and social functioning than those living in board-and-care homes. Similarly, Nelson, Hall, and Walsh-Bowers (1997) found in a quasi-experiment that residents of board-and-care homes reported significantly lower levels of resident control, less improvement in staff-rated independent functioning, and lower rates of community involvement over time than those residing in supportive apartments or group homes.

In supportive housing, both single-site and scattered-site programs were organized along a residential continuum or staircase model with increasing levels of patient autonomy, coupled with decreasing levels of staff support (Carling, 1995; Ridgway & Zipple, 1990). The assumption of this model is that discharged patients are not ready to live independently. Rather, mental health staff decides what type of setting is best for the individual, according to the amount of structure and support provided and the functioning level of the patient. Once the patient progresses, he or she can then move up the staircase to a more independent setting. So after discharge, a person might first live in a group home, then be moved to a halfway house, then to a supervised apartment, and finally to independent living. At each step in the staircase, the goal is to prepare the patient to move to the next level. The person must be "ready" to live more autonomously.

The 1990s to Today

Context

"Supported housing" emerged—following the lead of consumer advocates—with the work of Ridgway and Zipple (1990) and Paul Carling (1995) in the United States and their critique of the residential continuum model. Some of these criticisms were: (1) frequent moves were counterproductive (Aubry et al., 2014); (2) housing was still segregated and thus socially isolating (Nelson, 2010); (3) program participants lacked choice and control over their lives (Leff et al., 2009); and (4) the end of the continuum, independent living, is typically challenging because of the lack of affordable housing in the community (Parkinson et al., 1999). Wong and Solomon (2002) contend that three factors preceded the development of supported housing: (1) criticism of the continuum and supportive housing; (2) the overrepresentation of individuals diagnosed with a mental illness who are concurrently homeless; and (3) the development of ACT and ICM as effective community-based supports.

Supported housing, or what is now more commonly known as scattered-site supportive housing, consists of the provision of normal housing provided independently of flexible community-based supports, underscored by consumer choice (Carling, 1995). A number of consumer preference studies conducted in the United States (Tanzman, 1993) and Canada (Nelson, Hall, & Forchuk, 2003; Piat et al., 2008) have found that 75%–80% of mental health consumers want to live in their own apartments with off-site support. In the United States, federal Section 8 certificates provided through the Department of Housing and Urban Development provide a rent supplement so that individuals pay no more than 30% of their income on housing. These certificates became the mechanism that enabled the development of the scattered-site approach. The development of scattered-site housing was also accompanied by the growth of the consumer/survivor movement and a new emphasis on recovery, consumer empowerment, and community integration (Carling, 1995; Nelson, 2012).

While the type of housing that consumers choose depends on their preferences, scattered-site supportive housing is typically characterized by apartments that are dispersed in the community and that have no more than 20% of the residents in an apartment building with a mental illness. In contrast, supportive single-site housing is characterized by all of the available units in a building being reserved for people with mental illness.

In addition to the development of supportive scattered-site housing, the growth of homelessness in the 1980s compounded the problem of deinstitutionalization for people with serious mental illness (Schiff et al., 2010). While there are not good longitudinal data on the prevalence of homelessness over time, there are some data that indicate that homelessness, in general, as determined by shelter admission rates, increased during the late 1980s and early 1990s (Burt, 1996). Moreover, there is evidence to suggest that the percentage of the homeless population with chronic mental illness increased from about 20% to 33% during the 1980s (Burt, 1993). Hopper (2003) asserts that "by the mid-1980s, the numbers of homeless poor in the United States had outstripped anything seen since the Great Depression" (p. 176) and that "local coalitions to fight homelessness began to proliferate in the early 1980s" (p. 179). As well, the work of Kuhn and Culhane (1998) employed cluster analysis to show that the majority of shelter usage came from a small subset of the homeless population, the so-called chronically or episodically homeless. Moreover, this group accounted for an inordinate amount of costly shelter and emergency services, as was popularized in Malcolm Gladwell's (2006) story of the "Million Dollar Murray."

Nelson and Saegert (2009) have attributed this growth in homelessness to neoliberal policies that cut income supports and social housing for low-income citizens. They report that in Canada, the federal government created more than 25,000 units of social housing in the year 1980, but between 1993 and 2000, fewer than 1,000 units were created. This resulted because of cutbacks in federal funding for housing by the Mulroney government beginning in the 1980s, the downloading of responsibility for social housing to the provinces in the 1990s, and, in some provinces, the downloading of housing to the municipalities.

Supportive scattered-site housing and homelessness came together in the 1990s with the McKinney research demonstration projects for homeless adults with mental illness in a few US cities (Shern et al., 1997). In 1992, Sam Tsemberis founded the Pathways to Housing program in New York City. While Tsemberis and Eisenberg (2000) initially used the term "supported housing," he later coined the term "Housing First" to describe the Pathways program (Tsemberis, Gulcur, & Nakae, 2004). Housing First is based on the concept of supportive scattered-site housing, but it explicitly focuses on homeless adults with mental illness, often with co-occurring addictions, not just people with mental illness as was the case when "supported housing" was introduced.

While the language of "supported housing" is sometimes still used (e.g., Tabol, Drebing, & Rosenheck, 2010), it has largely given way to the term "Housing First."

This change in language has occurred partly because many people in the field find the distinction between supported and supportive housing confusing. Moreover, the development of a solid research base for Housing First and its widespread dissemination and adoption (Stanhope & Dunn, 2011) have also led to the shift in language away from "supported housing" to "Housing First." It is important to keep in mind, however, that while Housing First is typically associated with, scattered-site housing (e.g., apartments), it can and does include other types of housing, even custodial housing, if that is the consumer's choice.

Assumptions

Housing First diverges sharply from continuum-based housing and services in its assumptions about homeless adults who are diagnosed with a mental illness. Where the continuum tends to organize service and housing along a support-based continuum that seeks to produce housing readiness, Housing First dramatically reorders this chronology. This divergence drives at the normative shift to framing homeless adults diagnosed with a mental illness as citizens or tenants as opposed to clients or patients and reflects the assumption that it is possible to both house and treat mentally ill individuals in the community (Aubry et al., 2014; Leff et al., 2009; Nelson, 2010; Nelson, Goering, & Tsemberis, 2012; Ogilvie, 1997; Tabol et al., 2010). Congruent with this assumption is the idea that consumers are experts in their own process of recovery (Nelson et al., 2012). This assumption is often accompanied by presenting housing as an important determinant of both health and mental health from the vantage point of both researchers and consumers (Fakhoury et al., 2002; Hwang et al., 2005; Kyle & Dunn, 2008; Nelson & Saegert, 2009; Nelson et al., 2012; MHCC, 2011).

Perhaps the most telling indicator of assumptions regarding supportive scattered-site housing is the outcomes used to assess its merits in literature reviews. Across these reviews, outcomes can be divided into three areas: (1) housing stability (Aubry et al., 2014; Benston, 2015; Fitzpatrick-Lewis et al., 2011; Leff et al. 2009, Nelson et al., 2007; Newman, 2001; Rog, 2004; Rog et al., 2014; Schiff & Rook, 2012; Tabol et al., 2010); (2) hospitalization/use of emergency services (Aubry et al., 2014; Leff et al., 2009; Rog, 2004; Rog et al., 2014; Tabol et al., 2010); and (3) health and mental health outcomes (Aubry et al., 2014; Benston, 2015; Fitzpatrick-Lewis et al., 2011; Hwang et al., 2005; Kyle & Dunn 2008; Newman, 2001). It should be noted that cost, housing choice, and community integration are emerging as outcomes of interest in current research on scattered-site housing (Aubry et al., 2014). From these broad indicators it is reasonable to surmise that service provision for homeless individuals diagnosed with a mental illness ought to seek to ensure housing stability which is, in most cases, linked to health and mental health outcomes and decreased use of emergency services and inpatient hospitalizations. These outcomes speak to new constellations of housing and service provision—novel to the Housing First model—that encourage a broader under-standing of homelessness away from individual behavior toward more systems-level processes. In this regard, Housing First seeks to transform the mental health system (Nelson, 2010). This is increasingly reflected in foregrounding the importance of coordinated delivery of housing and services across professional and governmen-tal domains (Fakhoury et al., 2002; Hwang et al., 2005; Macpherson et al., 2004; MHCC, 2011).

Values

Housing First has a distinctive set of values that are divergent from the values of both custodial housing and the residential continuum. The values underpinning Housing First include (1) citizenship and rehabilitation, (2) recovery orientation, (3) community integration, (4) consumer self-determination, (5) collaboration with professionals and among consumers, (6) housing as a right of citizenship, and (7) attention to other resources (e.g., employment, education, meaningful activity).

Stemming from the disability rights movement, citizenship and rehabilitation are central values in Housing First. It might be helpful to think of citizenship and rehabilitation as a meta-value encompassing recovery, and self-determination and housing as a right. Citizenship and rehabilitation foreground the importance of inclusion of individuals with mental illness within civil society and their right to participate in their own communities (Rowe, Kloos, Chinman, Davidson, & Cross, 2001). Research by Rowe et al. (2012) has found that mental health consumers believe that citizenship includes personal responsibilities, government and infra-structure, caring for self and others, civil rights, legal rights, choices, and world stewardship. It is in supporting program participants in actualizing these rights that Housing First has value.

The value of recovery in Housing First places emphasis on successful community living consistent with the quality of life for those persons not diagnosed with a men-tal illness (Aubry et al., 2014). Positioning consumers as "experts" as opposed to clients or patients is central to the operationalization of recovery in Housing First. The provision of flexible community-based supports and housing that seek to "nor-malize" are central to recovery values and related to the value of community integra-tion (Leff et al., 2009).

Community integration hinges on the inclusion of individuals who are formerly homeless and are diagnosed with a mental illness within community life (Carling, 1995). Writing in the context of scattered-site housing, Wong and Solomon (2002) asserted that community integration has three main dimensions: (1) physical integration (i.e., participation in community settings, (2) social integration (i.e., interaction with community members and social network members), and (3) psy-chological integration (i.e., experience of a psychological sense of community). The value of community integration might best be contextualized within the progression of treatment of mental illness that has been defined by segregation. Community integration is salient insofar as it allows consumers to build meaningful and important long-term community relationships, which are deemed important in the recovery process (Aubry et al., 2014; Leff et al., 2009; Nelson, 2010). Community integration is accomplished through the use of scattered-site housing (Nelson et al., 2012) and the inclusion of "natural supports"—unpaid nonclinical supports such as landlords—as partners in recovery (Kloos, Zimmerman, Scrimenti, & Crusto, 2002). Community integration is a core value of Housing First (Tabol et al., 2010; Tsemberis et al., 2004; Wong & Solomon, 2002). For people leaving institutions, the process of community integration must often start from scratch, because people who have had lengthy stays in institutions have often become disconnected from their communities. But for homeless people with mental illness and addictions, community integration often involves breaking ties with nonsupportive peers, as well as developing new relationships and/or rekindling estranged family relationships.

The value of consumer self-determination means that consumers "choose, get, and keep" housing, which is provided independently of services (Carling, 1995). This separation of housing and services is crucial in maintaining the ability of consumers to choose which services and supports have value for them. Importantly, it is the fact that there are no preconditions for access to housing that ensures that self-determination is preserved. The emergence of community-based support delivery systems, like ACT and ICM, has been central to ensuring that supports remain flexible so as to respect consumer preferences.

The value of collaboration with professionals and among consumers is important in providing effective care to homeless adults diagnosed with a mental illness (O'Campo et al., 2009). Self-help and mutual aid are important supports for consumers that can serve to validate the lived experience of individuals and communities (Brown & Wituk, 2010).

Housing as a citizenship right is a central value to Housing First (Aubry et al., 2014; Fakhoury et al., 2002; Kyle & Dunn, 2008; Macpherson et al., 2004; Nelson, 2010; Nelson et al., 2012; Ogilvie, 1997). This value foregrounds the sociolegal dimension of mental illness to assert that individuals diagnosed with a mental illness have a right to be housed and receive treatment. Citizenship rights are most clearly enacted through rent subsidies in which Housing First program tenants are given legal title to their property. This gives program tenants a degree of legal protection and control over their lives and living situations unparalleled in custodial housing or the residential continuum.

Finally, Housing First values the importance of other resources such as employment and education. Aubry et al. (2014) highlight the importance of outcomes outside of the standard barometers of care that reflect participation in the broader community. By moving away from a deficit- to a strengths-based approach, Housing First strives to provide opportunities that encourage participation in mainstream society.

Practices

Housing First is marked by the provision of normal housing—usually through rent supplements—independent of flexible community-based support services. Throughout the literature, and in practice, there is difficulty in differentiating supportive housing from Housing First, as the lines between these service delivery systems can become blurred (Aubry et al., 2014; Fakhoury et al., 2002; Macpherson et al., 2004; Nelson, 2010; Ogilvie, 1997; Rog, 2004; Tabol et al., 2010). There is a widespread consensus that it is important to move toward a uniform notion of key components that will allow comparison across programs. Moreover, clarifying key program elements should be helpful in determining program fidelity, which can ensure that interventions purporting to be Housing First are adhering to the tenets of that model.

The Pathways Housing First model has made strides toward concretely defining the principles and key components that constitute markers of program fidelity (Aubry, Nelson, & Tsemberis, 2015; Stefancic, Tsemberis, Messeri, Drake, & Goering, 2013). These principles and program components are noted in Table 1.2. Housing choice is a key principle of Housing First. This principle is operationalized through the availability of rent supplements that enable participants to access normal market housing, scattered throughout the community, with leases with private landlords. The second principle of citizenship reflects that participants' clinical status is in no way linked with their housing status. That is, participants don't have to demonstrate any criteria of "readiness to be housed," nor do they have to participate in treatment for mental illness or addictions to stay in housing. Furthermore, clinical services are "delinked" or separated so that there are no live-in staff in the person's housing. Rather staff support is portable and services can consist of home visits or meetings in other community settings. The third principle of recovery-oriented, individualized treatment services has three program components: (1) service philosophy, (2) service array, and (3) program structure. The service philosophy component again focuses on choice in treatment, harm reduction, and consumer independence. Service array refers to a menu of treatment approaches to meet the needs identified by the individual. Finally, program structure includes low consumer/staff ratios, a team approach, and the inclusion of peer support workers.

In a realist review of community-based interventions for homeless adults with both a mental illness and substance use disorders, O'Campo and colleagues (2009) found six promising strategies for addressing both mental health challenges and substance use disorders: (1) consumer choice in treatment decision-making, (2) positive interpersonal relationships with service-providers, (3) ACT approaches, (4) Housing First, (5) supports for instrumental needs, and (6) nonrestrictive program approaches. These strategies are quite in line with principles and activities of the Housing First model.

Table 1.2 **Pathways Housing First Theoretical Principles and Program Components/Fidelity Indicators**

Theoretical Principles	*Program Components/Fidelity Indicators*
Housing choice and community integration	Housing choice and structure 1. Consumers have choice in the location and other features of their housing 2. Program helps participants move quickly into units of their choosing 3. Housing is assumed to be permanent 4. Consumers pay less than 30% of their income for housing costs 5. Consumers live in scattered-site private market housing 6. Consumers are not expected to share any living areas with other tenants
Citizenship	Separation of housing and clinical services 1. Consumers are not required to demonstrate housing readiness 2. Tenancy is not linked with adherence to clinical treatment 3. Consumers have legal rights to the unit 4. Program offers new housing to those who have lost their housing 5. Consumers continue to receive services even if they lose housing 6. Program staff are mobile and not located at consumers' residences
Recovery-oriented, individualized treatment approach	Service philosophy 1. Consumers choose the type, sequence, and intensity of services 2. Consumers are not required to take medication or participate in treatment 3. Consumers with substance use disorders are not required to participate in treatment 4. Program uses a harm-reduction approach to substance use 5. Staff use motivational interviewing 6. Staff uses an array of techniques to engage participants 7. Staff does not use coercive approaches 8. Staff uses person-centered planning 9. Staff use specific interventions focusing on a range of life areas 10. Staff advocate for consumer self-determination and independence in daily life

Table 1.2 **Continued**

Theoretical Principles	Program Components/Fidelity Indicators
	Service array
	1. Program offers services for consumer to maintain housing
	2. Psychiatric services are provided
	3. Substance use treatment is provided
	4. Supported employment is provided
	5. Nursing services are provided
	6. Social integration services are provided
	7. Program provides 24 hour crisis services
	8. Program works with in-patient treatment services
	Program structure
	1. Program gives priority to individuals with multiple obstacles to housing stability
	2. Program has low consumer-to-staff ratio (e.g., 10:1 for Assertive Community Treatment, 15:1 for Intensive Case Management)
	3. Program has minimum threshold of contact with consumers
	4. Program staff functions as a team
	5. Program staff meets frequently
	6. Program uses daily meeting to review consumers
	7. Program has a peer specialist
	8. Program offers consumers opportunities for representation and input in program operations

Source: Compiled from Aubry et al., 2015; Stefancic et al., 2013; and Tsemberis, 2010.

In summary, the Housing First approach has gained much prominence over the past two decades as a potential solution to the twin problems of deinstitutionalization of people with serious mental illness, which began in the 1960s, and homelessness, which began to grow in the 1980s. Indeed, many of the applications of Housing First have been conducted with homeless people with serious mental illness (Aubry et al., 2014; Fitzpatrick et al., 2011; Hwang et al., 2005; Nelson et al., 2007; O'Campo et al., 2009).

Conclusion

In this chapter, we described the evolution of housing for people with serious mental illness. There has been a progression from institutions to housing to homes. For a century, people with serious mental illness were housed in mental hospitals. During the early days of deinsitutionalization from the 1960s to the 1980s, the locus of housing shifted to a variety of housing options in the community. Two broad approaches, custodial housing and supportive housing, emerged. We believe that the move to supportive housing, either single-site or scattered-site, was ameliorative (Nelson, 2010); certainly rehabilitation-oriented housing was an improvement over institutional and custodial housing approaches. However, the linear continuum of housing retained many of the assumptions, values, and practices of the medical model. Residents were still patients, with little voice, choice, or citizenship rights.

Beginning in the 1990s, supported housing and Housing First emerged and began to gain momentum. Based on different assumptions and values, such as recovery, self-determination, and citizenship, the Housing First represented a fundamental departure from institutional, custodial, and single-site supportive housing approaches. Housing First can be described as a transformative change or a paradigm shift in the way housing for people with serious mental illness is conceptualized and practiced (Nelson, 2010; Nelson et al., 2001). As well, there is a body of controlled research on supportive scattered-site housing that attests to its effectiveness (Aubry et al., 2014; Rog et al., 2014). While there are efforts underway to disseminate and scale-up the Housing First approach (McGraw et al., 2010), it is important to bear in mind that the practice of housing has not caught up with the evolution in thinking about housing for homeless people with serious mental illness. In a US national survey of 1,446 persons diagnosed with schizophrenia, Tsai, Stroupe, and Rosenheck (2011) found that "46% of participants were living with family members and loved ones, 5% were living with other nonrelatives, 18% were living alone independently, 17% were in an institution, and 14% were not stably housed" (p. 76). These findings show that most people with serious mental illness do not live in permanent, scattered-site housing.

References

Anderson, R.L., Lyons, J.S., & West, C. (2001). The prediction of mental health service use in residential care. *Community Mental Health Journal*, 37, 313–322.

Arce, A.A., & Vergare, M. (1985). An overview of community residences as alternatives to hospitalization. *Psychiatric Clinics of North America*, 8, 423–436.

Aubry, T., Ecker, J., & Jetté, J. (2014). Supported housing as a promising Housing First approach for people with severe and persistent mental illness. In M. Guirguis-Younger, R. McNeil, & S.W. Hwang (Eds.), *Homelessness and health* (pp. 155–188). Ottawa: University of Ottawa Press.

Aubry, T., Nelson, G., & Tsemberis, S. (2015). Housing First for people with severe mental illness who are homeless: A review of the research and findings from the At Home/Chez Soi demonstration project. *Canadian Journal of Psychiatry*, 60, 467–474.

Aviram, U., & Segal, S.P. (1973). Exclusion of the mentally ill: Reflection of an old problem in a new context. *Archives of General Psychiatry*, 29, 126–131.

Bachrach, L. (1976). *Deinstitutionalization: An analytic review and sociological perspective*. Rockville, MD: National Institute of Mental Health.

Benston, E.A. (2015). Housing programs for homeless individuals with mental illness: Effects on housing and mental health outcomes. *Psychiatric Services*, 66, 806–816.

Blake, R. (1985/1986). Normalization and boarding homes: An examination of paradoxes. *Social Work in Health Care*, 11, 75–86.

Brown, L.D., & Wituk, S. (Eds.). (2010). *Mental health self-help: Consumer and family initiatives*. New York: Springer.

Brozost, B.A. (1978). Psychiatric community residences: A review of past experiences. *Psychiatric Quarterly*, 50, 253–263.

Burt, M.R. (1993). *Over the edge: The growth of homelessness in the 1980s*. New York: Russell Sage Foundation.

Burt, M.R. (1996). Homelessness: Definitions and counts. In J. Baumohl, (Ed.), *Homelessness in America* (pp. 15–23). Westport, CT: Greenwood.

Carling, P.J. (1995). *Return to community: Building support systems for people with psychiatric disabilities*. New York: Guilford Press.

Carpenter, M.D. (1978). Residential placement for the chronic psychiatric patient: A review and evaluation of the literature. *Schizophrenia Bulletin*, 4, 384–398.

Chilvers, R., MacDonald, G.M., & Hayes, A.A. (2002). Supported housing for people with severe mental disorders. *Cochrane Library*, Issue 4. Art. No.: CD000453. DOI: 10.1002/14651858. CD000453.pub2

Colten, S.I. (1978). Community residential treatment strategies. *Community Mental Health Review*, 3(5/6), 1, 16–21.

Cometa, M.S., Morrison, J.K., & Ziskoven, M. (1979). Halfway to where? A critique of research on psychiatric halfway houses. *Journal of Community Psychology*, 25, 167–188.

Cutler, D.L. (1986). Community residential options for the chronically mentally ill. *Community Mental Health Journal*, 22, 61–73.

Fakhoury, A., Murray, G., Shepherd, S., & Priebe, S. (2002). Research in supported housing. *Social Psychiatry and Psychiatric Epidemiology*, 37, 301–315.

Fitzpatrick-Lewis, D., Ganann, R., Krishnaratne, S., Ciliska, D., Kouyoumdijan, F., & Hwang, S.W. (2011). Effectiveness of interventions to improve the health and housing status of homeless people: A rapid systematic review. *BMC Public Health*, 11, 638, Open access.

Frankish, C.J., Hwang, S.W., & Quantz, D. (2005, March/April). Homelessness and health in Canada. *Canadian Journal of Public Health*, 96, S23–S29.

Gladwell, M. (2006, February 13). Million dollar Murray: Why problems like homelessness may be easier to solve than to manage. *The New Yorker*. http://www.newyorker.com/archive/2006/02/13/060213fa_fact

Goering, P., Wasylenki, D., Farkas, M., Lancee, W., & Freeman, S.J.J. (1984). From hospital to community: Six-month and two-year outcomes for 505 patients. *Journal of Nervous and Mental Disease*, 172, 667–673.

Goffman, E. (1961). *Asylums: Essays on the social situation of mental patients and other inmates*. New York: Doubleday.

Groton, D. (2013). Are Housing First programs effective? A research note. *Journal of Sociology and Social Welfare*, 40, 51–63.

Hall, G.B., Nelson, G., & Smith Fowler, H. (1987). Housing for the chronically mentally disabled: Part I—Conceptual framework and social context. *Canadian Journal of Community Mental Health*, 6(2), 65–78.

Harris, G.T., Hilton, N.Z., & Rice, M.E. (1993). Patients admitted to psychiatric hospital: Presenting problems and resolution at discharge. *Canadian Journal of Behavioural Science*, 25, 267–285.

Hopper, K. (2003). *Reckoning with homelessness*. Ithaca: Cornell University Press.

Hwang, S.W., Tolomiczenko, G., Kouyoumdjian, F., & Garner, R. (2005). Interventions to improve the health of the homeless: A systematic review. *American Journal of Preventive Medicine, 29*, 311.e1–75.

Kloos, B., Zimmerman, S., Scrimenti, K., & Crusto, C. (2002). Landlords as partners for promoting success in supported housing: "It takes more than a lease and a key." *Psychiatric Rehabilitation Journal, 25*, 235–244.

Kuhn, R., & Culhane, D.P. (1998). Applying cluster analysis to test a typology of homelessness by pattern of shelter utilization: Results from the analysis of administrative data. *American Journal of Community Psychology, 26*, 207–232.

Kyle, T., & Dunn, J.R. (2008). Effects of housing circumstances on health, quality of life, and health care use for people with severe mental illness: A review. *Health and Social Care in the Community, 16*, 1–15.

Lamb, H.R., & Goertzel, V. (1972). High expectations of long-term ex-state hospital patients. *American Journal of Psychiatry, 129*, 131–135.

Leff, H.S., Chow, C.M., Pepin, R., Conley, J., Allen, I.E., & Seaman, C.A. (2009). Does one size fit all? What we can and can't learn from a meta-analysis of housing models for persons with mental illness. *Psychiatric Services, 60*, 473–482.

Linhorst, D.M. (1991). The use of single room occupancy (SRO) housing as a residential alternative for persons with chronic mental illness. *Community Mental Health Journal, 27*, 135–144.

Macpherson, R., Shepherd, G., & Edwards, T. (2004). Supported accommodation for people with severe mental illness: A review. *Advances in Psychiatric Treatment, 10*, 180–188.

McCubbin, M. (2009). Oppression and empowerment: The genesis of a critical analysis of mental health. In D. Fox, I. Prilleltensky, & S. Austin (Eds.), *Critical psychology: An introduction* (2nd ed., pp. 300–316). Los Angeles: Sage.

McGraw, S.A., Larson, M.J., Foster, S.E., Kresky-Wolff, M., Botelho, E.M., Elstad, E.A., ... Tsemberis, S. (2010). Adopting best practices: Lessons learned in the collaborative initiative to help end chronic homelessness (CICH). *Journal of Behavioral Health Services and Research, 37*, 197–212.

Mental Health Commission of Canada. (2011). *Turning the key: Assessing housing an related supports for mental health problems and illnesses.* http://www.mentalhealthcommission.ca/SiteCollectionDocuments/service%20systems/Turning_the_Key_FINAL.pdf.

Mueser, K.T., Bond, G.R., Drake, R.E., & Resnick, S.G. (1998). Models of community care for severe mental illness: A review of research on case management. *Schizophrenia Bulletin, 24*, 37–74.

Nelson, G. (2010). Housing for people with serious mental illness: Approaches, evidence, and transformative change. *Journal of Sociology and Social Welfare, 37*, 123–146.

Nelson, G. (2012). Mental health policy in Canada. In A. Westhues & B. Wharf (Eds.), *Canadian social policy* (5th ed., pp. 229–252). Waterloo, ON: Wilfrid Laurier University Press.

Nelson, G., Aubry, T., & Lafrance, A. (2007). A review of the literature on the effectiveness of housing and support, assertive community treatment, and intensive case management for persons with mental illness who have been homeless. *American Journal of Orthopsychiatry, 77*, 350–361.

Nelson, G., Goering, P., & Tsemberis, S. (2012). Housing for people with lived experience of mental health issues: Housing First as a strategy to improve quality of life. In C.J. Walker, K. Johnson, & E. Cunningham (Eds.), *Community psychology and the socio-economics of mental distress: International perspectives* (pp. 191–205). Basingstoke, UK: Palgrave Macmillan.

Nelson, G., Hall, G.B., & Forchuk, C. (2011). Current and preferred housing of mental health consumer-survivors. In C. Forchuk, R. Csiernik, & E. Jensen (Eds.), *Homelessness, housing, and mental health: Finding truths—creating change* (pp. 107–121). Toronto: Canadian Scholars' Press.

Nelson, G., Hall, G.B., & Walsh-Bowers, R. (1997). A comparative evaluation of supportive apartments, group homes, and board-and-care homes for psychiatric consumer/survivors. *Journal of Community Psychology, 25*, 167–188.

Nelson, G., Lord, J., & Ochocka, J. (2001). *Shifting the paradigm in community mental health: Towards empowerment and community.* Toronto: University of Toronto Press.

Nelson, G., & Saegert, S. (2009). Housing and quality of life: An ecological perspective. In V.R. Preedy & R.R. Watson (Eds.), *Handbook of disease burdens and quality of life measures* (pp. 3363–3382). Heidelberg, Germany: Springer-Verlag.

Nelson, G., & Smith Fowler, H. (1987). Housing for the chronically mentally disabled: Part II. Process and outcome. *Canadian Journal of Community Mental Health, 6*(2), 79–91.

Newman, S.J. (2001). Housing attributes and serious mental illness: Implications for research and practice. *Psychiatric Services, 52,* 1309–1317.

O'Campo, P., Kirst, M., Schaefer-McDaniel, N., Firestone, M., Scott, A., & McShane, K. (2009). Community-based services for homeless adults experiencing concurrent mental health and substance use disorders: A realist approach to synthesizing evidence. *Journal of Urban Health: Bulletin of the New York Academy of Medicine, 86,* 965–989.

Ogilvie, R. (1997). The state of supported housing for mental health consumers: Literature review. *Psychiatric Rehabilitation Journal, 21,* 122–131.

Parkinson, S., Nelson, G., & Horgan, S. (1999). From housing to homes: A review of the literature on housing approaches for psychiatric consumer/survivors. *Canadian Journal of Community Mental Health, 18,* 145–163.

Paul, G.L., & Lentz, R.J. (1977). *Psychosocial treatment of chronic mental patients: Milieu vs. social-learning programs.* Cambridge, MA: Harvard University Press.

Piat, M., Lesage, A., Boyer, R., Dorvil, H., Couture, A., Grenier, G., & Bloom, D. (2008). Housing for persons with serious mental illness: Consumer and service provider preferences. *Psychiatric Services, 59,* 1011–1017.

Prilleltensky, I. (1997). Values, assumptions, and practices: Assessing the moral implications of psychological discourse and action. *American Psychologist, 52,* 517–535.

Pulier, M.L., & Hubbard, W.T. (2001). Psychiatric rehabilitation principles for re-engineering board and care facilities. *Psychiatric Rehabilitation Journal, 24,* 266–274.

Ridgway, P., & Zipple, A.M. (1990). The paradigm shift in residential services: From the linear continuum to supported housing approaches. *Psychosocial Rehabilitation Journal, 13,* 11–31.

Rochefort, D.A. (1996). *From poorhouses to homelessness: Policy analysis and mental health care* (2nd ed.). Westport, CT: Greenwood.

Rog, D.J. (2004). The evidence on supported housing. *Psychiatric Rehabilitation Journal, 27,* 334–344.

Rog, D.J., Marshall, T., Dougherty, R.H., George, P., Daniels, A.S., Ghose, S.S., & Delphin-Rittmon, M.E. (2014). Permanent supportive housing: Assessing the evidence. *Psychiatric Services, 65,* 287–294.

Rog, D.J., & Raush, H.L. (1975). The halfway house: How is it measuring up? *Community Mental Health Journal, 11,* 155–162.

Rogers, E.S., Farkas, M., Anthony, A., Kash, M., Harding, C., & Olschewski, A. (2008). *Systematic review of supported housing literature, 1993–2008.* Boston: Center for Psychiatric Rehabilitation.

Rosenheck, R. (2000). Cost-effectiveness of services for mentally ill homeless people: The application of research to policy and practice. *American Journal of Psychiatry, 157,* 1563–1570.

Rowe, M., Clayton, A., Benedict, P., Bellamy, C., Antunes, K., Miller, R., . . . O'Connell, M. (2012). Going to the source: Creating a citizenship outcome measure by community-based participatory research methods. *Psychiatric Services, 63,* 445–450.

Rowe, M., Kloos, B., Chinman, M., Davidson, L., & Cross, A.B. (2001). Homelessness, mental illness, and citizenship. *Social Policy and Administration, 35,* 14–31.

Schiff, J.W., & Rook, J. (2012). *Housing First: Where is the evidence?* Toronto: Homeless Hub.

Schiff, R., Schiff, J.W., & Schneider, B. (2010). Housing for the disabled mentally ill: Moving beyond homogeneity. *Canadian Journal of Urban Research, 19,* 108–128.

Sealy, P., & Whitehead, P.C. (2004). Forty years of deinstitutionalization of psychiatric services in Canada: An empirical assessment. *Canadian Journal of Psychiatry, 49,* 249–257.

Segal, S.P., & Aviram, U. (1978) *The mentally ill in community-based sheltered care: A study of community care and social integration.* New York: Wiley.

Segal, S.P., & Kotler, P.L. (1993) Sheltered care residence: Ten-year personal outcomes. *American Journal of Orthopsychiatry, 63,* 80–91.

Shern, D.L., Felton, C.J., Hough, R.L., Lehman, A.F., Goldfinger, S., Valencia, E., . . . Wood, P.A. (1997). Housing outcomes for homeless adults with mental illness: Results from the second-round McKinney program. *Psychiatric Services, 48,* 239–241.

Stanhope, V., & Dunn, K. (2011). The curious case of Housing First: The limits of evidence based policy. *International Journal of Law and Psychiatry, 34,* 275–282.

Stefancic, A., Tsemberis, S., Messeri, P., Drake, R., & Goering, P. (2013). The Pathways Housing First fidelity scale for individuals with psychiatric disabilities. *American Journal of Psychiatric Rehabilitation, 16,* 240–261.

Sylvestre, J., Nelson, G., Sabloff, A., & Peddle, S. (2007). Housing for people with serious mental illness: A comparison of values and research. *American Journal of Community Psychology, 40,* 125–137.

Tabol, C., Drebing, C., & Rosenheck, R.A. (2010). Studies of "supported" and "supportive" housing: A comprehensive review of model descriptions and measurement. *Evaluation and Program Planning, 33,* 446–456.

Tanzman, B. (1993). Researching the preferences for housing and supports: An overview of consumer preference surveys. *Hospital and Community Psychiatry, 44,* 40–50.

Trainor, J., Morrell-Bellai, T.L., Ballantyne, R., & Boydell, K.A. (1993). Housing for people with mental illness: A comparison of models and an examination of the growth of alternative housing in Canada. *Canadian Journal of Psychiatry, 38,* 494–501.

Tsai, J., Stroup, T.C., & Rosenheck, R.A. (2011). Housing arrangements among a national sample of adults with chronic schizophrenia living in the United States: A descriptive study. *Journal of Community Psychology, 39,* 76–88.

Tsemberis, S., & Eisenberg, R. F. (2000). Pathways to housing: Supported housing for street-dwelling homeless individuals. *Psychiatric Services, 51,* 487–493.

Tsemberis, S., Gulcur, L., & Nakae, M. (2004). Housing first, consumer choice, and harm reduction for homeless individuals with a dual diagnosis. *American Journal of Public Health, 94,* 651–656.

Wasylenki, D., Goering, P., & MacNaughton, E. (1994). Planning mental health services: Background and key issues. In L.L. Bachrach, P. Goering, & D. Wasylenki (Eds.), *Mental health care in Canada* (pp. 21–29). San Francisco: Jossey-Bass.

Wong, Y.I., & Solomon, P.L. (2002). Community integration of persons with psychiatric disabilities in supportive independent housing: A conceptual model and methodological considerations. *Mental Health Services Research, 4,* 13–28.

2

Housing Models for People with Serious Mental Illness

Unpacking Custodial and Supportive Housing Models

GEOFFREY NELSON AND RACHEL CAPLAN

It is difficult to differentiate housing models for people with serious mental illness. Previous reviews have made distinctions between custodial, supportive, and supported housing (Parkinson, Nelson, & Horgan, 1999; Tabol, Drebing, & Rosenheck, 2010; Trainor, Morrell-Bellai, Ballantyne, & Boydell, 1993) and between residential care and treatment, the residential continuum, permanent supported housing, and nonmodel housing (Leff et al., 2009). Attempting to sort programs into categories entails distinguishing housing models based on particular characteristics that are presumed to be shared by programs following a particular model and different from the characteristics of other models. However, making distinctions between different types of housing models is not always clear-cut (McHugo et al., 2004; Tabol et al., 2010). Housing models can change over time, and there is often overlap between different models, as new, hybrid approaches develop. Moreover, newer models like Housing First have influenced the way other types of housing operate, with some of the key principles and components of Housing First being incorporated into single-site supportive housing programs (Patterson et al., 2013; Pearson, Montgomery, & Locke, 2009).

As noted in chapter 1, the key principles and program components of the Pathways Housing First program in New York City have been well articulated (Nelson, Goering, & Tsemberis, 2012; Tsemberis, 2010). Moreover, these key principles and components have been incorporated into a theory of change for Housing First, along with intended short-term and long-term outcomes (Aubry, Nelson, & Tsemberis, 2015; Tsemberis & Asmussen, 1999). Finally, a measure of program fidelity has been developed that operationalizes the degree to which a given program adheres to the core principles and components of the Pathways model (Stefancic, Tsemberis, Messeri, Drake, & Goering, 2013; Tsemberis, 2010). The development of a fidelity measure for Pathways introduces a dimensional approach, as opposed to a categorical approach, to understand housing models. Whereas a categorical approach seeks to identify whether or not a particular program is part of a specific housing model, the dimensional approach seeks to understand how well a particular program adheres to the core principles and components of a particular model.

The purpose of this chapter is to describe housing models for people with serious mental illness. We propose a three-step process for understanding different housing models that combines categorical and dimensional approaches. We first introduce the three steps in the process, and then we use this process to examine past and present housing models. Our goal is to clearly delineate the key components of different housing models.

A Three-Step Process for Understanding Housing Models

The first two steps in the proposed decision-making process retain the categorical approach, but they introduce key criteria for differentiating housing models. The third step introduces a dimensional approach for better understanding the current wide range of housing models. The goal of this approach is to clearly differentiate between types of housing, especially within two main types of housing: single-site supportive housing and scattered-site supportive housing. The three-step decision tree is depicted in Table 2.1.

First Step

The first step differentiates custodial housing from supportive housing. We propose that two criteria be used to make this distinction: profit orientation and presence of recovery-oriented psychosocial rehabilitation services. If either of these characteristics is absent, then the housing is custodial. Both profit orientation and the absence of psychosocial rehabilitation are integral characteristics of custodial housing and suggest a community-based analogue of psychiatric hospitals, that differ only nominally in terms of for-profit community-based provision of room, board, and medical services (Community Support and Research Unit, 2012). Examples of custodial housing include board-and-care homes, rooming houses, nursing homes, single-room occupancy (SRO) hotel rooms, and foster family care. All other housing is supportive, providing psychosocial rehabilitation services under the auspices of nonprofit housing or mental health organizations. If the housing is determined to be supportive at this step, one proceeds to the second step. If it is custodial, one does not proceed further.

Table 2.1 **Three-Step Decision Tree for Understanding Housing Models**

Step 1—Is the housing custodial or supportive?	
Custodial—Housing is for profit or does not offer psychosocial rehabilitation.	**Supportive**—Housing is operated by a nonprofit organization and offers psychosocial rehabilitation.

*Step 2 (if housing is **Supportive**)—Does the housing offer choice and a rent subsidy?*

Single-site—Housing choice is limited because no rent subsidy is available.

OR

Scattered-site—Housing choice is enabled through the provision of a rent subsidy.

Step 3—To what extent does the program demonstrate fidelity to key components that are related to positive outcomes?

Housing Choice and Structure—includes choice, rapid housing, permanent, affordable (no more than 30% of income spent on rent), scattered site

Separation of Housing and Clinical Services—no preconditions, tenancy not linked to participation in treatment, standard lease, new housing offered to those who have lost housing, services continue to be offered if tenant loses housing, no staff on site

Service Philosophy—consumers choose services, no requirements for treatment adherence, harm reduction approach, motivational interviewing, individualized planning, etc.

Service Array—services provided to maintain housing, psychiatric services, substance use treatment, nursing services, etc.

Program Structure—priority given to individuals with multiple obstacles to housing, low consumer-to-staff ratio, minimum threshold of contact, staff functions as a team, peer specialist

Second Step

The second step differentiates single-site supportive housing from scattered-site supportive housing. Building on previous work that has strived to differentiate supportive and supported housing (Parkinson et al., 2009; Pauly, Carlson, & Perkin, 2012; Tabol et al., 2010), we propose that two criteria be used to make this differentiation: consumer choice and the availability of a rent subsidy to enable choice. Consumer choice and rent subsidies are key elements of Housing First, which is a prime exemplar of supportive scattered-site housing (Tsemberis, 2010). If consumers have the choice as to where and with whom they live, and if they have a rent subsidy that enables them to select an apartment in the community of their choice, or any other type of housing that they prefer, then the program is scattered-site supportive housing. On the other hand, if consumers have very limited choice over their housing or do not have a rent subsidy, then the program is single-site supportive housing.

Third Step

The dimensional approach is introduced in the third step, and this applies to both single-site and scattered-site supportive housing. We argue that there are five key components that are important for any type of supportive housing for people with serious mental illness: (1) housing choice and structure, (2) separation of housing and clinical services, (3) service philosophy, (4) service array, and (5) and program structure. These components are taken from Stefancic, Tsemberis, et al.'s (2013) Pathways fidelity measure, described in chapter 1. While this scale was developed specifically to examine adherence to the Housing First model, many, but not all, of the elements included in the scale could pertain to practices in single-site support- ive housing, and it would be valuable to understand how components of Housing First have been incorporated into practices in single-site housing.

The first component, housing choice and structure, includes choice over one's housing, rapid housing, permanency of housing, a rent supplement so that the person pays no more than 30% of her or his income on housing, and scattered or geographically dispersed apartments that have an appearance of fitting with neigh- borhood norms. Consumers are integrated with nonconsumers and have privacy over access to their apartment, and there are no shared living spaces. While single- site supportive housing typically does not include a rent supplement, scattered-site housing, or living with nonconsumers, single-site housing may include rapid, perma- nent housing.

Regarding the second component, separation of housing and clinical services, housing is provided irrespective of behavioral requirements that constitute "hous- ing readiness" (e.g., being sober, participating in treatment), and tenancy is not linked with adherence to treatment. Single-site supportive housing programs may also operate on these principles. The separation of housing and clinical services also means that the consumer holds a lease, that no staff members work in the person's housing, that consumers continue to receive services if they lose housing, and that new housing is offered to those who lose housing. These conditions are more likely to be met in scattered-site supportive housing than in single-site sup- portive housing.

Finally, the components of service philosophy, service array, and program struc- ture are less dependent on housing arrangements and more related to the service model. Clinical services can include evidence-based approaches like assertive com- munity treatment (ACT) or intensive case management (ICM) models (Mueser, Bond, Drake, & Resnick, 1998). These components can be practiced in either sin- gle-site or scattered-site housing. For example, ACT was used both in a large single- site setting (an old hotel) and in the typical scattered-site apartments of Housing First in Vancouver (Patterson et al., 2013).

There are several reasons for adopting this dimensional approach in step three of the decision tree. First, the Housing First approach is clearly based on a number of progressive values/principles, including choice, a recovery orientation, and a focus on community integration (Tsemberis, 2010). Second, these principles have been translated into program components that are part of a theory of change of housing for people with serious mental illness (Tsemberis & Asmussen, 1999). Third, specific program components have been operationalized in the fidelity scale that assesses the degree to which the Housing First components have been implemented. Fourth, research has demonstrated that program fidelity matters. The level of fidelity to the Housing First model that programs achieve has been shown to be directly related to program outcomes (Davidson et al., 2014; Gilmer et al., 2014; Goering et al., 2016).

Review of the Literature on Housing Program Models

In this section, we describe different housing program models. We begin by describing the criteria that we used for the selection of articles that describe program models.

Criteria for Selection of Studies

An electronic literature search was conducted of the databases of published articles from January 2008 to July 2014, using MEDLINE and PsycINFO, and by entering the following keywords: "community residences," "halfway houses," "group homes," "permanent supported housing," "homelessness," "housing first," "homeless mentally ill," and "supported housing." To locate articles published prior to 2008, we examined several literature reviews on housing for people with serious mental illness (Arce & Vergare, 1985; Aubry, Ecker, & Jetté, 2014; Benston, 2015; Brozost, 1978; Carpenter, 1978; Chilvers, MacDonald, & Hayes, 2002; Colten, 1978; Cometa, Morrison, & Ziskoven, 1979; Fakhoury, Murray, Shepherd, & Priebe, 2002; Fitzpatrick-Lewis et al., 2011; Groton, 2013; Hall, Nelson, & Smith Fowler, 1987; Hwang, Tolomiczenko, Kouyoumdjian, & Garner, 2005; Kyle & Dunn, 2008; Leff et al., 2009; Macpherson, Shepherd, & Edwards, 2004; Macpherson, Shepherd, & Thyarappa, 2012; Nelson, Aubry, & Lafrance, 2007; Nelson & Smith Fowler, 1987; Newman, 2001; O'Campo et al., 2009; Ogilvie, 1997; Parkinson et al., 1999; Pauly et al., 2012; Rog, 2004; Rog et al., 2014; Rog & Raush, 1975; Rogers et al., 2008; Rosenheck, 2000; Schiff & Rook, 2012; Schiff, Schiff, & Schneider, 2010). The selection of eligible articles emerging from our literature search was based on the following criteria: (1) the article was published in a refereed journal in English; (2) the article focused on housing for adults with mental illness; and (3) the article described research that examined a housing program model.

Housing Models

Custodial Housing

While there has been progress in the development of single-site and scattered-site supportive housing in recent years (Priebe et al., 2008; Trainor et al., 1993), as many as half a million people in Canada with mental illness are estimated to be inadequately housed (Trainor, Tallion, & Pandalangat, 2012). Many of these individuals live in some form of custodial housing. For example, more than 6,000 units of custodial housing in Ontario and nearly 7,000 units in New Brunswick are dedicated to mental health consumers (Community Support and Research Unit, 2012; Sylvestre et al., 2006). Using the first step of the decision-making model in the previous section, we describe two examples of housing that can be classified as custodial in that they operate for profit and do not provide rehabilitation services. These two examples are board-and-care homes and foster families.

Board-and-Care Homes

Boarding homes, homes for special care, sheltered care, lodging homes, long-term care, and nursing homes are some of the names associated with single-site living facilities that vary in size and are owned by private operators who have a contract with the state to provide a set of services—room, meals, medication, recreation— to a group of clients. Since such facilities are privately owned, there is no incentive for owners to promote consumer independence and rehabilitation. On the contrary, the incentive is to keep a stable population of residents for as long as possible (Blake, 1986).

Foster Families

A similar type of arrangement is provided by foster families, who have a contract with the state to provide care services for people with mental illness. In Montreal, it has been estimated that foster care makes up more than half of the subsidized housing for people with mental illness (Piat, Wallace, Wohl, Minc, & Hatton, 2002). Again, the number of clients served by foster families can vary, and independence and rehabilitation are de-emphasized as these goals are at odds with the profit incentive.

Single-Site Supportive Housing

In this section, we review housing that is determined to be supportive (from the first step in the decision-making model) and single-site (from the second step in the decision-making model). We provide illustrations of these types of housing with attention to some of the key components we outlined in the third step of the decision-making model (see Table 2.2). We do not provide an exhaustive review of all single-site supportive housing programs. Rather we illustrate each type of

Table 2.2 **Different Models of Single-Site Supportive Housing Programs and Their Key Components**

Program Types	Consumer Choice	Preconditions	Permanency	Type of Housing	Separation of Housing and Clinical Services	Nature of Clinical Services
Residential Treatment Programs						
Soteria House (Mosher & Menn, 1978)	No	No unknown visitors	No	Community residence (six residents)	No	Nonmedical, psychosocial program
Horizon House (Blankertz & Cnaan, 1994)	No	No	No	Community residence (28 residents)	No	Psychosocial rehabilitation
Residential treatment (Burnam et al., 1995)	No	Yes, abstinence	Yes	Community residence	No	Case management, AA, group treatment
Transitional Housing						
High expectations halfway houses (Budson et al., 1977; Lamb & Goertzel, 1972; Wilder et al., 1968)	No	Yes	No	Townhouse (23 residents)	Yes	"High expectations" for improvement and community participation
Residential Continuum						
New York City continuum (Lipton et al., 2000)	No	Yes	No for high intensity; yes for low intensity	Varies from large facilities to scattered-site apartments	No, with some exceptions	Range of psychosocial and medical services

(continued)

Table 2.2 **Continued**

Program Types	Consumer Choice	Preconditions	Permanency	Type of Housing	Separation of Housing and Clinical Services	Nature of Clinical Services
Group Living						
Fairweather Lodge (Fairweather et al., 1969)	No	Yes, must participate in work activities	Yes	Community residence (4–8 residents)	Yes	Assistance with group problem-solving
Evolving Consumer Households (Schutt, 2011)	No	Yes, must participate in weekly house meetings	Yes	Community residence (6–10 residents)	Some on-site staff assistance provided	Assistance with group problem-solving
Integrated Housing and Services						
Collaborative Initiatives to End Chronic Homelessness (Mares & Rosenheck, 2011)	No	?	Yes	Varied, but included subsidized apartments and SRO hotels	No	A variety of on-site supportive services
Downtown Emergency Service Center (DESC)—1811 East Lake (Pearson et al., 2009)	No	No	Yes	Apartment block with individual units	No	Case management and harm reduction
Bosman Hotel (Patterson et al., 2013)	No	No	Yes	Hotel with individual units	No	ACT

single-site supportive housing with a few examples. While we use the same language that the authors used to describe the different program types, we note that there is considerable overlap in these types of single-site supportive housing. Moreover, we use six indicators to more clearly describe these programs: (1) consumer choice, (2) preconditions, (3) permanency, (4), type of housing, (5) separation of housing and clinical services, and (6) the nature of clinical services.

Residential Treatment

As we noted in chapter 1, in the early days of deinstitutionalization, there were efforts to shift the locus of psychiatric treatment from the hospital to residential settings in the community (Brozost, 1978; Carpenter, 1978; Colten, 1978). While practices in these community residences often replicated institutional treatment, there were some exceptions.

SOTERIA HOUSE This program de-emphasizes medical treatment, with minimal use of psychotropic drugs, and instead uses an existential, phenomenological approach to assist individuals experiencing early episodes of schizophrenia (Mosher & Bola, 2000; Mosher & Menn, 1978). The residence is staffed by nonprofessionals and uses a treatment approach in which staff emphasizes personal growth, nonhierarchical relationships between staff and residents, and a family-like atmosphere. While Soteria House is often held up as a radical alternative to mainstream supportive housing, it does not incorporate the principles of choice or permanency of housing.

HORIZON HOUSE A more recent residential treatment program is provided by Blankertz and Cnaan (1999). Both 24-hour on-site rehabilitation services and off-site services were provided to homeless people with mental illness and addictions by professional staff. Participants could stay in the program for up to 2 years. While this program does not require housing readiness, like Soteria House, consumers have no choice over where they live and housing is time limited.

A similar residential treatment program for dually diagnosed homeless individuals requires that residents be abstinent (Burnam et al., 1995). Residential treatment programs remain common today. Zippay and Thompson (2007) identified 227 of these programs in seven states. The majority of these (71%) are group settings, housing an average of eight persons with mental illness. In the UK, Macpherson et al. (2012) describe these settings as "24-hour nursed care units."

Transitional Housing

Transitional programs, initially called halfway houses or quarterway houses, were designed for people released from institutions who were believed to need some preparation for community living (Cometa et al., 1979; Dickey, Cannon, McGuire, & Gudeman, 1986; Rog & Raush, 1975).

HIGH EXPECTATIONS HALFWAY HOUSES Early reports on halfway houses used the language of "high expectations" to characterize the psychosocial environments of these settings and to contrast them with "low expectations" custodial housing (Budson, Grob, & Singer, 1977; Lamb & Goertzel, 1972; Wilder, Kessel, & Caulfield, 1968). Budson et al. described a "high expectations" halfway house—Berkeley House—in which residents lived in a townhouse with a married couple as house managers. A family-like atmosphere is emphasized with high expectations for participation in school or work, mutual support, and learning of problem-solving skills.

Lamb and Goertzel (1972) randomly assigned long-stay mental hospital patients to either a "high expectations" halfway house ($n = 48$) or "low expectations" board-and-care homes ($n = 43$). At 6-, 12-, 18-, and 24-month follow-up periods, the "high expectations" group had significantly better outcomes in terms of employment rates and social functioning.

Wilder et al. (1968) described a "high expectations" halfway house—the Overing apartments—that consisted of two semidetached townhouses, each with two three-bedroom apartments and recreation rooms. These halfway houses stipulated some conditions for placement. For example, at Berkeley House, tenants were required to participate in weekly house meetings and daily activities (Budson et al., 1977), and tenants at the Overing apartments were expected to be active during the day in terms of work or education (Wilder et al., 1968). Moreover, the Overing apartments program excluded participants with substance use issues and (sic) "overt homosexuals" (p. 104). Generally, clinical services were separated from housing in these settings, but consumers had no choice over their housing, which was time-limited.

Residential Continuum
The residential continuum or "staircase" model emphasizes a range of supportive housing programs that vary in terms of the intensity of support provided and the degree of autonomy afforded to residents. While the continuum model was initially meant to have residents begin in high-intensity treatment programs and move to supervised apartments, today there is more flexibility in most staircase models. For example, Bebout, Drake, Xie, McHugo, and Harris (1997) stated that in Washington, DC, "movement with the continuum was fluid rather than linear, which permitted individuals to enter and exit from component housing settings as needed while maintaining continuous involvement with core services" (p. 937). "Placement" of residents on the continuum by treatment staff or matching residents' needs with program intensity remains central to the continuum approach.

NEW YORK CITY CONTINUUM Lipton, Siegel, Hannigan, Samuels, and Baker (2000) have described the residential continuum in New York that has been the focus of contrast with New York's Pathways Housing First program. They categorized housing programs as high, medium, or low in intensity. High-intensity settings exclusively serve people with mental illness, and often co-occurring addictions, and most are transitional in nature. As well, most of the high-intensity settings are single-site in nature, include on-site staff, provide meals, have many rules and restrictions, and do not have a rental agreement or lease with residents. In moderate-intensity settings, residents have their own rooms or apartments and share cooking facilities, with an average of 50 units per building. Services are offered on-site; there are rules and restrictions, but they are less rigid than those in high-intensity settings; and residents have leases or rental agreements. Low-intensity settings vary from scattered-site apartments to up to 650 units in a large hotel. Services are provided on or off-site, and all residents have leases. Supportive housing in other locales is often organized according to this type of continuum model, with programs varying in intensity (Brunt & Hansson, 2004; de Heer-Wunderink, Visser, Caro-Nienhuis, Sytema, & Wiersma, 2012; Piat, Sabetti, Fleury, Boyer, & Lesage, 2011).

Group Living
While residential treatment, transitional housing, and many settings in the residential continuum typically provide single-site supportive housing, there are other group-living models that are more unique and offer permanent housing.

FAIRWEATHER LODGE Fairweather, Sanders, Maynard, and Cressler (1969) developed an innovative program for men with mental illness about to be discharged from a Veterans' Administration hospital—the Lodge program. The participants moved into a residence and started their own business (janitorial and yard work), functioning as a mutually supportive community. Professional support was provided to aid in the transition to the community, but was gradually faded out so that participants could function as an autonomous group. While the Lodge program was developed some time ago, it does incorporate many of the principles of Housing First, including the separation of housing and services, permanency of housing, and ongoing support if requested.

EVOLVING CONSUMER HOUSEHOLDS Schutt (2011) has described a program that is similar in theory to the Lodge program. Evolving consumer households are based on the principle that consumer-tenants should be responsible for operating their group residence, with the goal of withdrawing staff support. Staff empowerment coordinators held weekly meetings, encouraging residents to assume greater and greater responsibility for the home. However, this process was fraught with conflict, and staff members were not able to withdraw their support over an 18-month period to people with mental illness with a history of homelessness.

Integrated Housing and Services
Another approach emphasizes the link between housing and services, often with services being provided on-site in a single setting, such as a hotel or an apartment

building (Hodgins, Cyr, & Gaston, 1990). McHugo et al. (2004) have called this approach "integrated" housing to contrast it with "parallel" housing, in which housing and services are delinked, as is the approach in the Pathways Housing First model. This approach has also been termed "comprehensive" housing (Clark & Rich, 2003; Mares & Rosenheck, 2011).

Collaborative Initiatives to End Chronic Homelessness
Mares and Rosenheck (2011) have described a multi-site Collaborative Initiatives to End Chronic Homelessness (CICH) program. The sites varied in their approaches. For example, the Chattanooga site appeared to follow the Pathways Housing First model, but the other four sites provided individual units in large SRO hotels or apartments with on-site support services.

DOWNTOWN EMERGENCY SERVICE CENTER—1811 EAST LAKE The Downtown Emergency Service Center (DESC) in Seattle explicitly espouses Housing First principles in a single-site setting. The DESC owns four buildings with individual units that consumers rent. The DESC serves people with serious mental illness and substance use problems (Larimer et al., 2009; Pearson et al., 2009). There are no preconditions for housing; case management and a harm reduction approach are used; housing is permanent; and residents have a lease. Consumers do not have choice over where they live, and housing and clinical services are not separated.

BOSMAN HOTEL This hotel in the downtown east end of Vancouver was another single-site supportive housing program based on Housing First principles. This program was part of the Canadian At Home/Chez Soi initiative (Patterson et al., 2013) and was closed at the end of the project. Like the DESC, the Bosman served people with serious mental illness and substance use problems. There were no preconditions; ACT with harm reduction was used; housing was permanent; and residents had a lease. Also like the DESC, residents had no choice over where they lived, and there was no separation of housing and clinical services.

Summary

Several points emerge from this review of single-site supportive housing models. First, many of the different models were developed 30–40 years ago. For example, while the original Fairweather Lodge was developed in the 1960s, there are 90 lodges in 16 US states today (http://www.theccl.org/Fairweather.htm). Second, while there are some exceptions (e.g., Fairweather et al., 1969), few of the models have a clearly articulated theory of change that specifies program principles, components, and intended short-, medium-, and long-term outcomes, and few provide a rationale that links program principles and components with intended outcomes (Chen, 2005). Thus, many single-site supportive housing models do not have a set of standards to which they must adhere. Third, there is a great deal of diversity within the different types of single-site supportive housing. Fourth, while we have grouped programs into some larger types here, there is considerable overlap between these types. Fifth, there is no single model of single-site supportive housing that enjoys widespread popularity.

Finally, some single-site programs have explicitly incorporated some Housing First principles (Pearson et al., 2009; Patterson et al., 2013), and thus are likely to demonstrate greater fidelity to some components of the Housing First model. Gilmer, Katz, Stefancic, and Palinkas (2013) conducted a study of the implementation of 93 Full Service Partnership programs in California. Using the Housing First fidelity assessment measure that they developed, they found substantial variation in fidelity to Housing First principles. While many programs provided a rich array of services, they tended to be low in fidelity to the domains of housing choice and service philosophy. Given these findings, it is important to evaluate the fidelity of housing programs using the dimensional approach that we have described.

Scattered-site Housing

In this section, we review housing that is determined to be supportive (from the first step in the decision-making model) and scattered-site (from the second step in the decision-making model). We provide illustrations of scattered-site supportive housing with attention to some of the key components we outlined in the third step of the decision-making model (see Table 2.3). We do not provide an exhaustive review of all Housing First programs. Rather we illustrate different scattered-site supportive housing programs, some of which vary in terms of extent to which the qualities in Table 2.1 are evident.

McKinney Project

In the early 1990s, the National Institute of Mental Health funded a multisite McKinney Research Demonstration Project for homeless people with mental illness (Schutt, 2011). In Boston, the McKinney Research Demonstration Project was developed in response to the wishes of people with serious mental illness to have increased personal autonomy (Dickey, Latimer, Powers, Gonzalez, & Goldfinger, 1997). The project was a randomized controlled trial that compared various housing options for homeless adults with severe mental illness (Seidman et al., 2003). At this site, the Boston Housing Authority provided consumers with one- or two-bedroom single apartments in public housing, as well as various support services through ICM. Income supports were provided for consumers, and they were required to pay rent no more than 30% of their income support subsidy. Off-site project staff was on call during all hours, and consumers were encouraged, but not required to engage in mental health center programs (Goldfinger et al., 1999).

Table 2.3 Scattered-Site Supportive Housing Programs and Their Key Components

Program	Consumer Choice	Preconditions	Permanency	Type of Housing	Separation of Housing and Clinical Services	Nature of Clinical Services
McKinney Project (Schutt, 2011)—Boston (Seidman et al., 2003) and San Diego (Hurlburt et al., 1996)	Yes	Boston: Yes, cannot be deemed dangerous to self or others San Diego: no history of violent crime, drug dealing, substance abuse problems, unless committed to treatment	Yes	Single-occupancy units owned by public housing authority	Yes	ICM
Pathways to Housing—New York City (Tsemberis & Asmussen, 1999)	Yes	No	Yes	Scattered-site apartments	Yes	ACT
HUD-VASH Supported Housing Program—Multiple US sites (O'Connell et al., 2009; Rosenheck et al., 2003)	Yes	No	Yes	Scattered-site apartments	Yes	ICM
At Home/Chez Soi—5 Canadian sites (Goering et al., 2011; Goering et al., 2014)	Yes	No	Yes	Scattered-site apartments	Yes	ACT or ICM

The San Diego McKinney Homeless Research Demonstration Project aimed to integrate homeless adults with severe mental illness into the community, by "providing access to normal community housing with appropriate support" and "comprehensive case management" (Wood, Hurlburt, Hough, & Hofstetter, 1998, p. 329). This aim was based on certain principles indicating that scattered-site housing should minimize linkages between housing and mental health services, allow for client choice with respect to housing selection and treatment services, and provide immediate support in helping individuals learn the skills necessary to integrate effectively within their community (Hurlburt, Wood, & Hough, 1996). Based on these principles, this randomized controlled trial evaluated the outcomes of case management outcomes and Section 8 subsidies (Hurlburt et al., 1996; Wood et al., 1998).

Pathways to Housing

In 1992, Pathways to Housing ("Pathways") was created to provide immediate access to scattered-site supportive housing for people with psychiatric and co-occurring substance use disorders, and living on the streets and in public places (e.g., in parks) in New York City. This intervention was based on the principles of Housing First, which proposes that permanent housing is a basic right of all people without having preconditions (e.g., abstinence or medical adherence) placed on them. Additionally, beliefs that people should have control over where and with whom they live; that housing and clinical services should be functionally and legally separate entities; and that consumers should hold standard tenancy agreements with landlords are fundamental to this program. Furthermore, Pathways includes a harm reduction approach to substance use and provides clinical, rehabilitation, and support services for consumers through ACT teams offered 24 hours a day, 7 days per week (Kirsh, Gewurtz, & Bakewell, 2011; Tsemberis & Asmussen, 1999). Based on promising evidence-based housing outcomes achieved through the Pathways program, this program was expanded first to suburban Westchester County, then to Washington, DC, Philadelphia, and rural Vermont (Padgett, Henwood, & Tsemberis, 2016; Stefancic & Tsemberis, 2007; Stefancic, Henwood, et al., 2013; Tsemberis, Kent, & Respress, 2012). These programs, as well, demonstrated promising outcomes for consumers and communities, through scattered-site housing solutions based on a Housing First approach. Pathways has since been implemented in multiple cities across the United States (Tsemberis, 2010), as well as in the province of Alberta, Canada (Gaetz, Scott, & Gulliver, 2013); five other Canadian provinces (Goering et al., 2011); and in Europe (Greenwood, Stefancic, Tsemberis, & Busch-Geertsema, 2013).

HUD-VASH

From 1992 to 2006, the US Department of Housing and Urban Development (HUD) along with the US Department of Veteran Affairs offered the HUD-VASH scattered-site housing program for homeless veterans experiencing mental illness and/or substance use disorders in multiple sites across the United States. The HUD-VASH program was developed to offer immediate access to rent subsidies (through Section 8 certificates), ICM, and immediate, scattered-site supportive housing, where residents were not required to pay more than 30% of their income to rent (O'Connell, Kasprow, & Rosenheck, 2009; Rosenheck, Kasprow, Frisman, & Liu-Mares, 2003), nor did they have to abide by any preconditions to obtain housing (O'Connell, Kasprow, & Rosenheck, 2010). Multiple studies have looked at the outcomes of the HUD-VASH program (e.g., Cheng, Lin, Kasprow, & Rosenheck, 2007; Kasprow, Rosenheck, Frisman, & DiLella, 2000; Mares & Rosenheck, 2011; Tsai, Kasprow, & Rosenheck, 2011).

At Home/Chez Soi

In November 2009, the 4-year At Home/Chez Soi research demonstration project began in five Canadian cities: Vancouver, British Columbia; Winnipeg, Manitoba; Toronto, Ontario; Montreal, Quebec; and Moncton, New Brunswick. Using a mixed-methods approach in a randomized controlled trial, the Housing First approach (based on the Pathways program, emphasizing consumer choice and providing a rent supplement) was compared to treatment as usual (TAU) for chronically homeless individuals with serious mental illness. For individuals with high needs, the Housing First approach in conjunction with ACT was compared to TAU. For individuals with moderate psychiatric needs, the Housing First approach in conjunction with ICM was compared to TAU (Goering et al., 2011). Furthermore, due to the diverse nature of varying Canadian cities, each site was given the option to include a third-arm comparison group. For example, Vancouver's third-arm intervention included a variation on Housing First that has demonstrated efficacy with participants who use substances. Winnipeg's third-arm intervention included an Aboriginal peer-support model, while Toronto's third-arm intervention included ICM for ethnoracial minorities (Goering et al., 2011). The At Home/Chez Soi project examined consumer outcomes, costs, and implementation fidelity. Some of the outcomes of interest were: housing stability, quality of life, health status (mental, physical, emotional), employment, social functioning, and community integration (Goering et al., 2014).

Summary

A number of points emerge from this review of scattered-site housing programs. First, in contrast to single-site supportive housing programs, scattered-site supportive housing programs are more current. All of these scattered-site supportive housing programs emerged within the last 20 years and many of them continue to operate and expand today. Second, in contrast to many single-site supportive housing models, all of the scattered-site supportive housing programs have a clear theory of change that specify program principles, components, and outcomes (Tabol et al., 2010). Furthermore, through the recently articulated key principles and components of the Pathways program, as well as fidelity measures created to determine adherence to these principles (Gilmer, Stefancic, et al., 2013; Stefancic, Tsemberis, et al., 2013), it has become much easier to determine the degree to which a program is in fact a Housing First program. In addition, less variability (and in turn greater fidelity) exists in terms of implementation when programs are based on specific principles and components. Finally, based on the literature reviewed, the Pathways Housing First program model appears to be the "gold standard" of scattered-site supportive housing models.

Conclusion

The purpose of this chapter was to describe housing models for people with serious mental illness based on a review of the published literature. We proposed a three-step process for understanding different housing models that combined both categorical and dimensional approaches. The first two steps include distinguishing custodial housing from supportive housing (with respect to profit orientation and presence of recovery-oriented psychosocial rehabilitation services), and then differentiating between single-site supportive housing and scattered-site supportive housing (with respect to consumer choice and rent subsidy availability). The third step includes examining the extent to which either single-site supportive housing or scattered-site supportive housing programs adhere to key components of the Housing First model. We hope that this process allows for the differentiation between housing models that have been developed and implemented over the last 40 years for people with serious mental illness.

References

Arce, A.A., & Vergare, M. (1985). An overview of community residences as alternatives to hospitalization. *Psychiatric Clinics of North America, 8*, 423–436.

Aubry, T., Ecker, J., & Jetté, J. (2014). Supported housing as a promising Housing First approach for people with severe and persistent mental illness. In M. Guirguis-Younger, R. McNeil, & S.W. Hwang (Eds.), *Homelessness and health* (pp. 155–188). Ottawa: University of Ottawa Press.

Aubry, T., Nelson, G., & Tsemberis, S. (2015). Housing First for people with severe mental illness who are homeless: A review of the research and findings from the At Home/Chez Soi demonstration project. *Canadian Journal of Psychiatry, 60*, 467–474.

Bebout, R.R., Drake, R.E., Xie, H., McHugo, G.J., & Harris, M. (1997). Housing status among formerly homeless dually diagnosed adults. *Psychiatric Services, 48*, 936–941.

Benston, E.A. (2015). Housing programs for homeless individuals with mental illness: Effects on housing and mental health outcomes. *Psychiatric Services, 66*, 806–816.

Blake, R. (1986). Normalization and boarding homes: An examination of paradoxes. *Social Work in Health Care, 11*, 75–86.

Blankertz, L.E., & Cnaan, R.A. (1994). Assessing the impact of two residential programs for dually diagnosed individuals. *Social Service Review, 68,* 536–560.

Brozost, B.A. (1978). Psychiatric community residences: A review of past experiences. *Psychiatric Quarterly, 50,* 253–263.

Brunt, D., & Hansson, L. (2004). The quality of life of persons with severe mental illness across housing settings. *Nordic Journal of Psychiatry, 58,* 293–298.

Budson, R.D., Grob, M.C., & Singer, J.E. (1977). A follow-up study of Berkeley House—A psychiatric halfway house. *International Journal of Social Psychiatry, 23,* 120–131.

Burnam, M.A., Morton, S.C., McGlynn, E.A., Petersen, L.P., Stecher, B.M., Hayes, C., & Vaccaro, J.V. (1995). An experimental evaluation of residential and nonresidential treatment for dually diagnosed homeless adults. *Journal of Addictive Diseases, 14,* 111–134.

Carpenter, M.D. (1978). Residential placement for the chronic psychiatric patient: A review and evaluation of the literature. *Schizophrenia Bulletin, 4,* 384–398.

Chen, H.-T. (2005). *Practical program evaluation: Assessing and improving planning, implementation, and effectiveness.* Newbury Park, CA: Sage.

Cheng, A.-L., Lin, H., Kasprow, W., & Rosenheck, R.A. (2007). Impact of supported housing on clinical outcomes: Analysis of a randomized trial using multiple imputation technique. *Journal of Nervous and Mental Disease, 195,* 83–88.

Chilvers, R., Macdonald, G.M., & Hayes, A.A. (2002). Supported housing for people with severe mental disorders. *Cochrane Library,* Issue 4. Art. No.: CD000453. DOI: 10.1002/14651858. CD000453.pub2.

Clark, C., & Rich, A.R. (2003). Outcomes of homeless adults with mental illness in a housing program and in case management only. *Psychiatric Services, 54,* 78–83.

Colten, S.I. (1978). Community residential treatment strategies. *Community Mental Health Review, 3*(5/6), 1, 16–21.

Cometa, M.S., Morrison, J.K., & Ziskoven, M. (1979). Halfway to where? A critique of research on psychiatric halfway houses. *Journal of Community Psychology, 25,* 167–188.

Community Support and Research Unit. (2012). *From this point forward: Ending custodial housing for people with mental illness in Canada.* Toronto: Centre for Addiction and Mental Health. https://knowledgex.camh.net/csru/Pages/publications.aspx

Davidson, C., Neighbors, C., Hall, G., Hogue, A., Cho, R., Kutner, B., & Morganstern, J. (2014). Association of Housing First implementation and key outcomes among homeless persons with problematic substance abuse. *Psychiatric Services, 65,* 1318–1324.

de Heer-Wunderink, C., Visser, E., Caro-Nienhuis, A., Sytema, S., & Wiersma, D. (2012). Supported housing and supported independent living in the Netherlands, with a comparison with England. *Community Mental Health Journal, 48,* 321–327.

Dickey, B., Cannon, N.L., McGuire, T.G., & Gudeman, J.E. (1986). The quarterway house: A two-year cost study of an experimental residential program. *Hospital and Community Psychiatry, 37,* 1136–1143.

Dickey, B., Latimer, E., Powers, K., Gonzalez, O., & Goldfinger, S.M. (1997). Housing costs for adults who are mentally ill and formerly homeless. *Journal of Mental Health Administration, 24,* 291–305.

Fairweather, G.W., Sanders, D.H., Maynard, H., & Cressler, D.L. (1969). *Community life for the mentally ill.* Chicago: Aldine.

Fakhoury, A., Murray, G., Shepherd, S., & Priebe, S. (2002). Research in supported housing. *Social Psychiatry and Psychiatric Epidemiology, 37,* 301–315.

Fitzpatrick-Lewis, D., Ganann, R., Krishnaratne, S., Ciliska, D., Kouyoumdijan, F., & Hwang, S.W. (2011). Effectiveness of interventions to improve the health and housing status of homeless people: A rapid systematic review. *BMC Public Health, 11,* 638. Open access.

Gaetz, S., Scott, F., & Gulliver, T. (2013). *Housing First in Canada: Supporting communities to end homelessness.* Toronto: Canadian Homelessness Research Network Press.

Gilmer, T.P., Katz, M.L., Stefancic, A., & Palinkas, L.A. (2013). Variation in implementation of California's Full Services Partnership for persons with serious mental illness. *Health Services Research, 48*, 2245–2267.

Gilmer, T.P., Stefancic, A., Katz, M.L., Sklar, M., Tsemberis, S., & Palinkas, L.A. (2014). Fidelity to the Housing First model and effectiveness of supported housing. *Psychiatric Services, 65*, 1311–1317.

Gilmer, T.P., Stefancic, A., Sklar, M., & Tsemberis, S. (2013). Development and validation of a Housing First fidelity survey. *Psychiatric Services, 64*, 911–914.

Goering, P.N., Streiner, D.L., Adair, C., Aubry, T., Barker, J., Distasio, J., . . . Zabkiewicz, D.M. (2011). The At Home/Chez Soi trial protocol: A pragmatic, multi-site, randomized controlled trial of Housing First in five Canadian cities. *BMJ Open*, 1–18. http://bmjopen.bmj.com/content/1/2/e000323.full

Goering, P., Veldhuizen, S., Nelson, G., Stefancic, A., Tsemberis, S., Adair, C., . . . Streiner, D. (2016). Further validation of the Pathways Housing First fidelity scale. *Psychiatric Services, 67*, 111–114.

Goering, P., Veldhuizen, S., Watson, A., Adair, C., Kopp, B., Latimer, E., . . . Aubry, T. (2014). *National final report: Cross-site At Home/Chez Soi project.* Calgary, AB: Mental Health Commission of Canada.

Goldfinger, S.M., Schutt, R.K., Tolomiczenko, G.S., Seidman, L.J., Penk, W.E., Turner, W.M., & Caplan, B. (1999). Housing placement and subsequent days homeless among formerly homeless adults with mental illness. *Psychiatric Services, 50*, 674–679.

Greenwood, R.M., Stefancic, A., Tsemberis, S., & Busch-Geertsema, V. (2013). Implementation of Housing First in Europe: Successes and challenges in maintaining model fidelity. *American Journal of Psychiatric Rehabilitation, 16*, 290–312.

Groton, D. (2013). Are Housing First programs effective? A research note. *Journal of Sociology and Social Welfare, 40*, 51–63.

Hall, G.B., Nelson, G., & Smith Fowler, H. (1987). Housing for the chronically mentally disabled: Part I. Conceptual framework and social context. *Canadian Journal of Community Mental Health, 6*(2), 65–78.

Hodgins, S., Cyr, M., & Gaston, L. (1990). Impact of supervised apartments on the functioning of mentally disordered adults. *Community Mental Health Journal, 26*, 507–516.

Hurlburt, M.S., Wood, P.A., & Hough, R.L. (1996). Providing independent housing for the homeless mentally ill: A novel approach to evaluating long-term longitudinal housing patterns. *Journal of Community Psychology, 24*, 291–310.

Hwang, S.W., Tolomiczenko, G., Kouyoumdjian, F., & Garner, R. (2005). Interventions to improve the health of the homeless: A systematic review. *American Journal of Preventive Medicine, 29*, 311.e1–75.

Kasprow, W.J., Rosenheck, R.A., Frisman, L., & DiLella, D. (2000). Referral and housing processes in a long-term supported housing program for homeless veterans. *Psychiatric Services, 51*, 1017–1023.

Kirsh, B., Gewurtz, R., & Bakewell, R.A. (2011). Critical characteristics of supported housing: Resident and service provider perspectives. *Canadian Journal of Community Mental Health, 30*, 15–30.

Kyle, T., & Dunn, J.R. (2008). Effects of housing circumstances on health, quality of life, and health care use for people with severe mental illness: A review. *Health and Social Care in the Community, 16*, 1–15.

Lamb, H.R., & Goertzel, V. (1972). High expectations of long-term ex-state hospital patients. *American Journal of Psychiatry, 129*, 131–135.

Larimer, M.E., Malone, D.K., Garner, M.D., Atkins, D.C., Burlingham, B., Lonczak, H.S., . . . Marlatt, G.A. (2009). Health care and public service use and costs before and after provision of housing for chronically homeless persons with severe alcohol problems. *Journal of the American Medical Association, 301*, 1349–1357.

Leff, H.S., Chow, C.M., Pepin, R., Conley, J., Allen, I.E., & Seaman, C.A. (2009). Does one size fit all? What we can and can't learn from a meta-analysis of housing models for consumers with mental illness. *Psychiatric Services, 60*, 473–482.

Lipton, F.R., Siegel, C., Hannigan, A., Samuels, J., & Baker, S. (2000). Tenure in supportive housing for homeless persons with severe mental illness. *Psychiatric Services, 51*, 479–486.

Macpherson, R., Shepherd, G., & Edwards, T. (2004). Supported accommodation for people with severe mental illness: A review. *Advances in Psychiatric Treatment, 10*, 180–188.

Macpherson, R., Shepherd, G., & Thyarappa, P. (2012). Supported accommodation for people with severe mental illness: An update. *Advances in Psychiatric Treatment, 18*, 381–391.

Mares, A.S., & Rosenheck, R.A. (2011). A comparison of treatment outcomes among chronically homeless adults receiving comprehensive housing and health care services versus usual local care. *Administration and Policy in Mental Health, 38*, 459–478.

McHugo, G.J., Bebout, R.R., Harris, M., Cleghorn, S., Herring, G., Xie, H., . . . Drake, R.E. (2004). A randomized controlled trial of integrated versus parallel housing services for homeless adults with severe mental illness. *Schizophrenia Bulletin, 30*, 969–982.

Mosher, L.R., & Bola, J.R. (2000). The Soteria project: Twenty five years of swimming upriver. *Complexity and Change, 9*, 68–74.

Mosher, L.R., & Menn, A.Z. (1978). Community residential treatment for schizophrenia: Two-year follow-up. *Hospital and Community Psychiatry, 29*, 715–722.

Mueser, K.T., Bond, G.R., Drake, R.E., & Resnick, S.G. (1998). Models of community care for severe mental illness: A review of research on case management. *Schizophrenia Bulletin, 24*, 37–74.

Nelson, G., Aubry, T., & Lafrance, A. (2007). A review of the literature on the effectiveness of housing and support, assertive community treatment, and intensive case management for persons with mental illness who have been homeless. *American Journal of Orthopsychiatry, 77*, 350–361.

Nelson, G., Goering, P., & Tsemberis, S. (2012). Housing for people with lived experience of mental health issues: Housing First as a strategy to improve quality of life. In C.J. Walker, K. Johnson, & E. Cunningham (Eds.), *Community psychology and the socio-economics of mental distress: International perspectives* (pp. 191–205). Basingstoke, UK: Palgrave Macmillan.

Nelson, G., & Smith Fowler, H. (1987). Housing for the chronically mentally disabled: Part II—Process and outcome. *Canadian Journal of Community Mental Health, 6*(2), 79–91.

Newman, S.J. (2001). Housing attributes and serious mental illness: Implications for research and practice. *Psychiatric Services, 52*, 1309–1317.

O'Campo, P., Kirst, M., Schaefer-McDaniel, N., Firestone, M., Scott, A., & McShane, K. (2009). Community-based services for homeless adults experiencing concurrent mental health and substance use disorders: A realist approach to synthesizing evidence. *Journal of Urban Health: Bulletin of the New York Academy of Medicine, 86*, 965–989.

O'Connell, M.J., Kasprow, W., & Rosenheck, R. (2009). Direct placement versus multistage models of supported housing in a population of veterans who are homeless. *Psychological Services, 6*, 190–201.

O'Connell, M., Kasprow, W., & Rosenheck, R.A. (2010). National dissemination of supported housing in the VA: Model of adherence versus model modification. *Psychiatric Rehabilitation Journal, 33*, 308–319.

Ogilvie, R. (1997). The state of supported housing for mental health consumers: Literature review. *Psychiatric Rehabilitation Journal, 21*, 122–131.

Padgett, D.K., Henwood, B.F., & Tsemberis, S. (2016). *Housing First: Ending homelessness, transforming systems, and changing lives.* New York: Oxford University Press.

Parkinson, S., Nelson, G., & Horgan, S. (1999). From housing to homes: A review of the literature on housing approaches for psychiatric consumer/ survivors. *Canadian Journal of Community Mental Health, 18*, 145–163.

Patterson, M., Moniruzzaman, A., Palepu, A., Zabkiewicz, D., Frankish, C.J., Krausz, M., & Somers, J. (2013). Housing First improves subjective quality of life among homeless adults with mental illness: 12-month findings from a randomized controlled trial in Vancouver, British Columbia. *Social Psychiatry and Psychiatric Epidemiology, 48*, 1245–1259.

Pauly, B., Carlson, E., & Perkin, K. (2012): *Strategies to end homelessness: Current approaches to evaluation.* Toronto: Canadian Homelessness Research Network Press. Available at the Homeless Hub, http://www.homelesshub.ca/

Pearson, C., Montgomery, A.E., & Locke, G. (2009). Housing stability among homeless individuals with serious mental illness participating in Housing First programs. *Journal of Community Psychology, 37*, 404–417.

Piat, M., Sabetti, J., Fleury, M.-J., Boyer, R., & Lesage, A. (2011). "Who believes most in me and my recovery?" The importance of families for persons with serious mental illness living in structured community housing. *Journal of Social Work in Disability and Rehabilitation, 10*, 49–65.

Piat, M., Wallace, T., Wohl, S., Minc, R., & Hatton, L. (2002). Developing housing for persons with severe mental illness: An innovative community foster home. *International Journal of Psychosocial Rehabilitation, 7*, 43–51.

Priebe, S., Frottier, P., Gaddini, A., Killian, R., Lauber, C., Martinez-Leal, R., . . . Wright, D. (2008). Mental health care institutions in nine European countries, 2002–2006. *Psychiatric Services, 59*, 570–573. doi: 10.1176/appi.ps.59.5.570

Rog, D.J. (2004). The evidence on supported housing. *Psychiatric Rehabilitation Journal, 27*, 334–344.

Rog, D.J., Marshall, T., Dougherty, R.H., George, P., Daniels, A.S., Ghose, S.S., & Delphin-Rittmon, M.E. (2014). Permanent supportive housing: Assessing the evidence. *Psychiatric Services, 65*, 287–294.

Rog, D.J., & Raush, H.L. (1975). The halfway house: How is it measuring up? *Community Mental Health Journal, 11*, 155–162.

Rogers, E.S., Farkas, M., Anthony, A., Kash, M., Harding, C., & Olschewski, A. (2008). *Systematic review of supported housing literature, 1993–2008.* Boston: Center for Psychiatric Rehabilitation.

Rosenheck, R. (2000). Cost-effectiveness of services for mentally ill homeless people: The application of research to policy and practice. *American Journal of Psychiatry, 157*, 1563–1570.

Rosenheck, R.A., Kasprow, W., Frisman, L., & Liu-Mares, W. (2003). Cost-effectiveness of supported housing for homeless persons with mental illness. *Archives of General Psychiatry, 60*, 940–951.

Schiff, J.W., & Rook, J. (2012). *Housing First: Where is the evidence?* Toronto: Homeless Hub. http://www.homelesshub.ca/Library/Housing-first---Where-is-the-evidence-54120.aspx

Schiff, R., Schiff, J.W., & Schneider, B. (2010). Housing for the disabled mentally ill: Moving beyond homogeneity. *Canadian Journal of Urban Research, 19*, 108–128.

Schutt, R.K. (2011). *Homelessness, housing and mental illness.* Cambridge, MA: Harvard University Press.

Seidman, L.J., Schutt, R.K., Caplan, B., Tolomiczenko, G.S., Turner, W.M., & Goldfinger, S.M. (2003). Effects of housing interventions on neuropsychological function in homeless mentally ill individuals. *Psychiatric Services, 54*, 905–908.

Stefancic, A., Henwood, B.F., Melton, H., Shin, S.-M., Lawrence-Gomez, R., & Tsemberis, S. (2013). Implementing Housing First in rural areas: Pathways Vermont. *American Journal of Public Health, 103*(S2), S206–S209.

Stefancic, A., & Tsemberis, S. (2007). Housing First for long-term shelter dwellers with psychiatric disabilities in a suburban county: A four-year study of housing access and retention. *Journal of Primary Prevention, 28*, 265–279.

Stefancic, A., Tsemberis, S., Messeri, P., Drake, R., & Goering, P. (2013). The Pathways Housing First fidelity scale for individuals with psychiatric disabilities. *American Journal of Psychiatric Rehabilitation, 16*, 240–261.

Sylvestre, J., Nelson, G., Durbin, J., George, L., Aubry, T., & Ollenberg, M. (2006). Housing for people with serious mental illness: Challenges for system-level community development. *Journal of the Community Development Society, 37*, 35–45.

Tabol, C., Drebing, C., & Rosenheck, R.A. (2010). Studies of "supported" and "supportive" housing: A comprehensive review of model descriptions and measurement. *Evaluation and Program Planning*, 33, 446–456.

Trainor, J., Morrell-Bellai, T.L., Ballantyne, R., & Boydell, K.A. (1993). Housing for people with mental illness: A comparison of models and an examination of the growth of alternative housing in Canada. *Canadian Journal of Psychiatry*, 38, 494–501.

Trainor, J., Tallion, P., & Pandalangat, M. (2012). *Turning the key: Assessing housing and related supports for persons living with mental health problems and illnesses.* Calgary: Mental Health Commission of Canada. http://www.mentalhealthcommission.ca/english/pages/default. aspx

Tsai, J., Kasprow, W., & Rosenheck, R.A. (2011). Exiting homelessness without a voucher: A comparison of independently housed and other homeless veterans. *Psychological Services, 8*, 114–122.

Tsemberis, S. (2010). *Housing First: The Pathways model to end homelessness for people with mental illness and addiction.* Center City, MN: Hazelden Press.

Tsemberis, S., & Asmussen, S. (1999). From streets to homes: The Pathways to Housing consumer preference supported housing model. *Alcoholism Treatment Quarterly, 17*, 113–131.

Tsemberis, S., Kent, D., & Respress, C. (2012). Housing stability and recovery among chronically homeless persons with co-occurring disorders in Washington, DC. *American Journal of Public Health, 102*, 13–16.

Wilder, J.F., Kessel, M., & Caulfield, S.C. (1968). Follow-up of a "high-expectations" halfway house. *American Journal of Psychiatry, 124*, 103–109.

Wood, P.A., Hurlburt, M.S., Hough, R.L., & Hofstetter, C.R. (1998). Longitudinal assessment of family support among homeless mentally ill participants in a supported housing program. *Journal of Community Psychology, 26*, 327–344.

Zippay, A., & Thompson, A. (2007). Psychiatric housing: Locational patterns and choices. *American Journal of Orthopsychiatry, 77*, 392–401.

3

Community-Based Support in the Context of Housing

A Review of Models and Evidence

TIM AUBRY, REBECCA CHERNER, JOHN ECKER, AND STEPHANIE YAMIN

Introduction

This chapter focuses on the effectiveness of community-based support available to people with severe mental illness living in various forms of housing. The chapter distinguishes among professional forms of support such as assertive community treatment (ACT) and intensive case management (ICM) that are offered to individuals with, but are separate from housing. This includes other forms of support that are integrated into single-site housing (formerly termed "supportive housing"). This chapter reviews the research on the effectiveness of these different kinds of community-based supports associated with both single-site and scattered-site supportive housing.

Supportive Housing with On-Site Support

In response to deinstitutionalization, the earliest form of housing, established in the 1980s and 1990s, that included some form of community support was termed "supportive housing" (Aubry, Ecker, & Jetté, 2014; Nelson, 2010; Parkinson, Nelson, & Horgan, 1999; Trainor, 2008; Trainor, Morrell Bellai, Ballantyne, & Boydell, 1993). For the purpose of this review and in line with the terminology used in this book, "supportive housing" is referred to as "single-site supportive housing." In this type of housing, support is integrated into the housing and offered on-site, focusing on rehabilitation (Ridgway & Zipple, 1990). Although the level of training of staff in these housing programs is quite variable, the focus of their support, which is also variable, can include counseling, social and life skills training, and case management (Parkinson et al., 1999).

A range of single-site supportive housing programs were created in communities with the intent of putting into place a residential continuum (e.g., quarterway houses, halfway houses, group homes, apartment programs) that would provide different levels of intensity of support depending on an individual's needs and abilities (Blanch, Carling, & Ridgway, 1988; Parkinson et al., 1999). Ultimately, it was expected that individuals would progress along a continuum of different levels of support integrated into housing until they would eventually live on their own in regular housing (Ridgway & Zipple, 1990).

Criticisms of single-site supportive housing included the limited housing options in many communities such that a continuum failed to exist, the disruption for consumers associated with moving in and out this type of housing because of its transitional nature, and the fact that they typically failed to achieve independent living (Blanch et al., 1988; Ridgway & Zipple, 1990).

Supported Housing with Portable Community Support

In response to these criticisms, a new model of housing, known as "supported housing" (or scattered-site supportive housing) was proposed, wherein support would be separate from housing and be of sufficient intensity to enable individuals to live in regular housing as tenants (Blanch et al., 1988; Carling, 1993, 1995; Ridgway & Zipple, 1990). The location of the housing was intended to be scattered and thereby expected to optimize community integration. For the purpose of this review and in line with the terminology used in the rest of the book, "supported housing" is referred to as "scattered-site supportive housing."

The approach to support that has been typically provided in scattered-site supportive housing programs has involved some form of case management (Tabol, Drebing, & Rosenheck, 2010). Although Carling (1993, 1995) and Ridgway and Zipple (1990) proposed that this kind of housing include a focus on both housing and support that were provided separately, it was ultimately the development of Housing First programs by Pathways to Housing in New York City that operationalized and tested the approach (Tsemberis, 1999).

The term "case management" covers a broad range of services and programs that share the common purpose of coordinating and providing services and supports for persons with severe mental illness living in the community (Intagliata, 1982). A number of case management approaches are described in the literature. These include assertive community treatment (ACT) (Olfson, 1990), the psychosocial rehabilitation model (e.g., Goering, Wasylenki, Farkas, Lancee, & Ballantyne, 1988), the strengths or developmental acquisition model (Modrcin, Rapp, & Poertner, 1988), and the brokerage model (Franklin, Solovitz, Mason, Clemons, & Miller, 1987). A difficulty encountered in examining the literature is being able to differentiate programs based on these more specific approaches.

A less fine-grained distinction that has been made to describe the different case management approaches and that is used to organize our review of the research on housing-related community support is whether or not clients receive services from a multidisciplinary team of service providers or from an individual case manager (Bond, McDonel, Miller, & Pensec, 1991). Programs described and examined in the empirical literature can usually be differentiated along these lines.

Assertive Community Treatment

The multidisciplinary team approach is commonly referred to as ACT (Stein & Test, 1980). The team is typically made up of psychiatrists, nurses, social workers, and occupational therapists, with the responsibility for clients shared among team members. The client to staff ratio is typically 10:1, and the intent is to provide wrap-around services including 24-hour coverage by the treatment team (Monroe-Devita, Teague, & Moser, 2011). Initially ACT was established as a response to deinstitutionalization, but over time, with the creation of scattered-site supportive housing, it has been used as a form of community support to address homelessness (Coldwell & Bender, 2007). Assertive community treatment is the most-developed and researched approach to community support in the mental health field, as reflected by the development of ACT fidelity scales that identify what are considered its critical ingredients (McGrew, Bond, Dietzen & Salyers, 1994; Monroe-Devita et al., 2011; Teague, Bond, & Drake, 1998).

Intensive Case Management

The approach using individual case managers who support individually a specific group of clients in the community is often referred to as ICM. Case managers usually have small caseloads (i.e., less than 20), see clients in the community, focus on every-day problems, perform advocacy functions, and follow clients on a long-term basis (Dieterich, Irving, Park, & Marshall, 2010). Intensive case management includes direct services such as counseling, life skills training, and crisis intervention as well as indirect services intended to coordinate their clients' access to and use of community resources. Recent work has focused on defining standards for ICM (Ontario Ministry of Health and Long-Term Care, 2005) and the development of a fidelity scale as it applies to implementing ICM in combination with housing for people who are homeless (Nelson et al., 2014).

Overview of Chapter

In the following sections in this chapter we provide reviews of effectiveness studies on the different types of housing approaches defined by whether or not they entail scattered-site supportive housing, single-site supportive housing, or transitional housing. In these studies, the approaches are compared to different housing and support approaches or to simply different forms of support without housing. The outcomes examined in the studies have been grouped into housing, service use, clinical functioning, and community adaptation outcomes. These reviews are followed by a synthesis of the findings across the different types of community support, limitations of the research to date, and future directions for research.

Search Strategy

For the review, we conducted a literature search of effectiveness studies on ACT and ICM as a housing-related support in PsycINFO (American Psychological Association) and MEDLINE. The subsequent criteria were used to select the appropriate studies for this review: (1) participants in one of the conditions in the study received a combination of scattered-site supportive housing and ACT or ICM; (2) the study used either an experimental design or a quasi-experimental design with a comparison group; (3) the reporting of the study's findings were peer-reviewed; (4) the study participants were individuals with mental illness; (e) the study examined participant outcomes (cost-effectiveness studies are reviewed in a subsequent chapter). Search terms included combinations of "supported housing," "homelessness," "Housing First," "assertive community treatment," and "intensive case management."

A slightly different set of keywords was used for locating studies on single-site housing and transitional housing with on-site support. The same selection criteria used for the ACT and ICM studies were retained. The following key words were used to select the studies on single-site housing and transitional housing with on-site support: "homeless," "supportive housing," "congregate housing," "second stage housing," "transitional housing," and "residential care."

Scattered-Site Supportive Housing with ACT or ICM
Versus ACT or ICM Without Housing

The following section describes the research findings that compared the outcomes of scattered-site supportive housing with ACT or ICM with those of ACT or ICM without housing.

Study Characteristics

Table 3.1 describes the nine published articles reporting findings from four separate studies comparing scattered-site supportive housing with ACT or ICM to ACT or ICM without housing. All were conducted in the United States. Two adopted

Table 3.1 **Characteristics of Effectiveness Studies Comparing Scattered-Site Supportive Housing with ACT or ICM to ACT or ICM Without Housing**

Study	Location	Sample	Comparison Group(s)	Experimental Group	Study Type	Follow-up
Hurlburt, Wood, et al. (1996); Hurlburt, Hough, et al. (1996); Wood et al. (1998)	San Diego, CA	C1: 90 C2: 91 E1: 90 E2: 91	No Section 8 certificate with comprehensive (caseload of 1:22) (C1) or traditional case management (caseload of 1:40) (C2)	Scattered-site supportive housing: Section 8 certificate with either comprehensive case management (caseload of 1:22) (E1) or traditional case management (1:40) (E2)	Experimental	24 mos. (Hurlburt, Hough, et al., 1996; Hurlburt, Wood, et al., 1996); 36 mos. (Wood et al., 1998)
Clark & Rich (2003)	Florida	C: 69 E: 83	Case management only (C)	Comprehensive housing programs (E); "guaranteed access to housing," housing support, and case management	Quasi-experimental	12 mos.
Rosenheck et al. (2003); Cheng et al. (2007); O'Connell et al. (2008); O'Connell et al. (2012)	San Francisco, CA; San Diego, CA; New Orleans, LA; Cleveland, OH	C1: 90 E: 182	No Section 8 certificate with intensive case management (C1) (caseload of 1:25)	Scattered-site supportive housing: Section 8 certificate with intensive case management (E) (caseload of 1:25)	Experimental	24 mos. (O'Connell et al., 2012); 36 mos. (Rosenheck et al., 2003; Cheng et al., 2007); 60 mos. (O'Connell et al., 2008)
Montgomery et al. (2013)	Major metropolitan area	C: 70 E: 107	Standard case HUD-VASH management (C) (no mention of caseload numbers)	Housing voucher with ACT (E)	Quasi-experimental	12 mos.

a true experimental design (i.e., participants were randomly assigned to different treatment conditions) (Hurlburt, Hough, & Wood, 1996; Rosenheck, Kasprow, Frisman, & Liu-Mares, 2003) and two used a quasi-experimental design (i.e., participants of different groups were not randomly assigned but were matched on key variables instead) (Clark & Rich, 2003; Montgomery, Hill, Kane, & Culhane, 2013). Table 3.1 presents a detailed description of the comparison groups used.

The participants in the studies fell into two groups: homeless military veterans (Montgomery et al., 2013; Rosenheck et al., 2003) and homeless adults (Clark & Rich, 2003; Hurlburt, Hough, et al., 1996). The samples of military veterans were slightly older and had larger proportions of males compared with the adult samples (Clark & Rich, 2003; Hurlburt, Hough, et al., 1996). For ethnicity, the studies with homeless adults had predominantly White samples, whereas the military veteran studies had predominantly African American samples.

All of the studies targeted a population of individuals that was homeless or at-risk of homelessness and had severe and persistent mental illnesses. There was a relatively high prevalence of schizophrenia and mood disorders (Clark & Rich, 2003; Hurlburt, Hough, et al., 1996). Rosenheck et al. (2003) reported that their sample was "diagnostically heterogeneous," as 9.7% had serious psychiatric diagnoses, 35.2% had dual diagnoses, and 4.7% had other psychiatric disorders. Substance use disorders were also common across the studies.

Outcomes

Table 3.2 presents the outcomes of the studies grouped into the areas of housing, service use, clinical functioning, and community adaptation.

Housing

Overall, individuals placed in scattered-site supportive housing with ACT or ICM had better housing outcomes than those receiving only ACT or ICM. In particular, scattered-site supportive housing with ACT or ICM resulted in superior outcomes in terms of acquiring and remaining in independent housing (Hurlburt, Hough, et al., 1996; Hurlburt, Wood, & Hough, 1996), remaining in independent housing longer (Cheng et al., 2007; Clark & Rich, 2003; Montgomery et al., 2013; O'Connell, Kasprow, & Rosenheck, 2012; Rosenheck et al., 2003), experiencing fewer days of homelessness (Clark & Rich, 2003; O'Connell et al., 2012; Rosenheck et al., 2003), and having a lower risk of returning to homelessness (O'Connell, Kasprow, & Rosenheck, 2008). Individuals living in scattered-site supportive housing with ICM also reported higher levels of satisfaction with their housing and experienced fewer problems related to their housing than individuals receiving just ICM (Cheng et al., 2007; Rosenheck et al., 2003).

Table 3.2 Findings of Effectiveness Studies on Scattered-Site Supportive Housing with ACT or ICM Compared with ACT or ICM Without Housing

Studies	Housing	Service Use Outcomes	Clinical Outcomes	Community Adaptation
Hurlburt, Hough, et al. (1996)	(+) achieve stability in independent housing (subsidy compared to no subsidy; case management type not significant)			
Hurlburt, Wood, et al. (1996)	(+) shorter amount of time to being independently housed (+) obtaining stable independent housing	(+) less likely to drop out of program		
Wood et al. (1998)	(+) % independent living at 2 yrs			ND interaction with family, satisfaction with family, perceived availability of family
Rosenheck et al. (2003)	(+) days housed at 36 mos. (+) fewer days homeless (+) housing satisfaction and fewer housing problems ND housing quality	(+) fewer days institutionalized	ND alcohol use, substance use, and psychiatric symptoms	(+) social network size, quality of life ND employment, income, and legal involvement
Cheng et al. (2007)	(+) days housed at 36 mos. (+) fewer negative housing characteristics ND positive housing characteristics	(+) fewer days institutionalized	(+) fewer days of alcohol use; ND fewer days intoxicated, days using drugs (+) lower alcohol index score ND lower drug index score	ND social network size and employment, (+) overall quality of life

(continued)

Table 3.2 Continued

Studies	Housing	Service Use Outcomes	Clinical Outcomes	Community Adaptation
O'Connell, et al. (2008)	(+) lower risk of returning to homelessness (+) fewer days between baseline interview and first day housed		ND reduced expenditure on substances ND psychiatric symptoms	ND social network, employment, income, and legal involvement (+) overall quality of life
O'Connell et al. (2012)	(+) more days housed at 24 mos. (+) fewer days homeless at 24 mos.	(+) fewer days institutionalized	(+) reduced alcohol and drug index score (+) reduced expenditure on substances ND reduced alcohol and drug index score, days intoxicated, days of drug use	ND quality of life, social contacts, and days worked
Clark & Rich (2003)	(+) proportion of time housed (high-impairment) (+) reduction in proportion of time spent homeless (high-impairment) ND proportion of time housed and reduction in time spent homeless (low-to-medium impairment)		ND psychiatric symptoms, days of alcohol and drug use (high-, medium-, and low-impairment)	
Montgomery et al. (2013)	(+) reduced amount of time from initial program assessment to moving into permanent housing (+) housing retention after 12 mos.	both groups had decreases in urgent care visits both groups had decreases in inpatient mental health treatment days		

(+) outcomes in favor of scattered-site supportive housing group, (−) outcomes in favor of comparison group, ND = no group difference.

Some of the housing outcomes were contingent on certain conditions. Receiving a housing subsidy, regardless of the type of support received, resulted in better housing outcomes compared to not receiving a housing subsidy (Hurlburt, Hough, et al., 1996). Clark and Rich (2003) stratified their participants based on psychiatric impairment and found that their high-impairment group benefited the most from scattered-site supportive housing and ICM. Their low- and medium-impairment experimental groups demonstrated similar housing outcomes as low- and medium-impairment participants in the comparison group who were receiving ICM alone.

Service Use

Service use outcomes showed mixed results among the reviewed studies. Hurlburt, Wood, et al. (1996) report that tenants living in scattered-site housing with ICM were more likely to stay in the program compared with individuals receiving just case management services. Two of the studies found that individuals in scattered-site supportive housing with ICM experienced less time in institutions compared with individuals receiving just ICM (Cheng et al., 2007; O'Connell et al., 2012), unlike previously reported findings from the study in which there was no group difference in time spent in institutions (Rosenheck et al., 2003). Although the papers analyzed data from the same original source (Rosenheck et al., 2003), differences were found as a result of Cheng et al. (2007) replacing missing data and O'Connell et al. (2012) examining a shorter follow-up period.

Montgomery et al. (2013) did not find that scattered-site supportive housing with ACT reduced service use compared with standard case management. Individuals in the scattered-site supportive housing with ACT demonstrated comparable rates of reduction in urgent care visits as the individuals receiving standard case management. However, in terms of mental health treatment, individuals receiving only standard case management exhibited a significantly greater reduction in inpatient mental health treatment days compared with the individuals in scattered-site supportive housing with ACT.

Clinical Functioning

Of the studies evaluating clinical outcomes, mixed results were again found. Individuals receiving scattered-site supportive housing with ICM had significantly fewer days of alcohol use (Cheng et al., 2007), lower scores on a composite alcohol problem index (Cheng et al., 2007; O'Connell et al., 2008), lower scores on a composite drug problem scale (O'Connell et al., 2008), and less money spent on substances (O'Connell et al., 2008) than the ICM only group. No group differences were found for a reduction in the number of days intoxicated and days using drugs (Cheng et al., 2007; Clark & Rich, 2003; O'Connell et al., 2012), amount of money spent on substances (Cheng et al., 2007), and severity of psychiatric symptoms (Cheng et al., 2007; Clark & Rich, 2003).

Community Adaptation

The studies assessing community adaptation outcomes also yielded mixed results, with some finding that scattered-site supportive housing produced superior outcomes in this area and others finding no improved outcomes. Scattered-site supportive housing with ICM tenants reported fewer housing problems (Rosenheck et al., 2003), larger social networks (Rosenheck et al., 2003), and greater quality of life (Cheng et al., 2007; O'Connell et al., 2008; Rosenheck et al., 2003) in comparison with consumers receiving ICM only. On the other hand, there were no differences found between consumers in scattered-site supportive housing with ICM and consumers receiving only ICM with regard to improvements in family relations (Wood, Hurlburt, Hough, & Hofstetter, 1998), or size of social networks (Cheng et al., 2007; O'Connell et al., 2008, 2012).

In terms of employment and legal involvement, individuals living in scattered-site supportive housing with ICM showed no differences in outcomes compared with individuals receiving ICM only (Rosenheck et al., 2003; O'Connell et al., 2008).

Summary

In general, housing outcomes were better for those who received scattered-site supportive housing in combination with ACT or ICM, than for people who received ACT or ICM alone. In contrast, mixed results were found on nonhousing outcomes in the areas of service use, clinical functioning, and community adaptation, with scattered-site supportive housing with ACT or ICM yielding either better outcomes in some studies or no better outcomes in other studies when compared with ACT or ICM alone.

Scattered-Site Supportive Housing with ACT or ICM Versus Single-Site Supportive Housing with ACT or ICM

The following section discusses the research findings that compare the outcomes of scattered-site supportive housing with ACT or ICM to those of single-site supportive housing with ACT or ICM.

Study Characteristics

Table 3.3 describes the six published articles reporting findings from three separate studies comparing scattered-site supportive housing with ACT or ICM to single-site housing with ACT or ICM. All of the studies were conducted in the United States. Two studies adopted a true experimental design (i.e., participants were

Table 3.3 Findings of Effectiveness Studies Comparing Scattered-Site Supportive Housing with ACT or ICM to Single Site Supportive Housing with ACT or ICM

Study	Location	Sample	Comparison Group(s)	Experimental Group	Study Type	Follow-up
Dickey et al. (1996); Goldfinger et al. (1999); Seidman et al. (2003); Caplan et al. (2006)	Boston, MA	C:63 E: 55	Evolving consumer households with congregate living and intensive case management (C); housing subsidized	Scattered-site supportive housing, independent living and intensive case management (E); housing subsidized	Experimental	18 mos. (Dickey et al., 1996; Goldfinger et al., 1999; Seidman et al., 2003); 48 mos. (Caplan et al., 2006)
Pearson et al. (2009)	Seattle, WA (DESC); San Diego, CA (REACH); New York, NY (Pathways)	C1 (DESC): 25 C2 (REACH): 29 E (Pathways): 26	Single-site supportive housing with modified ACT (C1); Multisite housing with modified ACT (C2)	Pathways scattered-site supportive housing with ACT (E)	Quasi-experimental	12 mos.
McHugo et al. (2004)	Washington, DC	C: 61 E: 60	Single-site housing with ICM (C); assumed housing subsidy	Scattered-site supportive housing with ACT (E); assumed housing subsidy	Experimental	18 mos.

randomly assigned to different treatment conditions) (Dickey, Gonzalez, Latimer, & Powers, 1996; McHugo et al., 2004) and one used a quasi-experimental design (i.e., participants of different groups were not randomly assigned but were matched on key variables instead) (Pearson, Montgomery, & Locke, 2009).

The samples in the selected studies displayed some similarities. The studies generally had middle-aged participants. Two of the studies had primarily male participants (Dickey et al., 1996; Pearson et al., 2009), and one study had almost equal representation of males and females (McHugo et al., 2004). One of the studies had predominantly African American participants (McHugo et al., 2004), whereas one had more equal distributions of African American and White participants (Dickey et al., 1999). For Pearson et al. (2009), the race of the participants was contingent on the three study locations. One of the sites reported a much higher representation of African American participants compared with the other two sites.

All of the studies targeted individuals who were homeless or at risk of homelessness and had a severe and persistent mental illness. McHugo et al. (2004) and Pearson et al. (2009) reported a high prevalence of schizophrenia within their samples. The participants in the Dickey et al. (1996) set of studies all met criteria for a major mental illness, but they did not report the specific disorders. The presence of substance use disorders was also common across the studies.

Outcomes

Table 3.4 presents a summary of client outcomes related to housing, service use, clinical functioning, and community adaptation from the three studies.

Housing

Housing outcomes varied among the three studies. A similarly high proportion of tenants in scattered-site supportive housing with ACT or ICM were housed as tenants in single-site supportive housing with ACT or ICM (Dickey et al., 1996; Pearson et al., 2009). There were also no differences between tenants in scattered-site supportive housing with ACT and single-site supportive housing and ICM in terms of housing and neighborhood satisfaction (McHugo et al., 2004) and the proportion of days spent living in one's apartment (McHugo et al., 2004); however, tenants in single-site supportive housing with ICM did have significantly longer stays in stable housing (McHugo et al., 2004) and fewer days spent homeless (Goldfinger et al., 1999; McHugo et al., 2004) than tenants in scattered-site supportive housing with ACT. Lastly, tenants in scattered-site supportive housing with ACT reported significantly fewer housing problems than tenants in single-site supportive housing with ACT (Pearson et al., 2009).

Table 3.4 Findings of Effectiveness Studies Comparing Scattered-Site Supportive Housing with ACT or ICM to Single-Site Supportive Housing with ACT or ICM

Studies	Housing	Service Use Outcomes	Clinical Outcomes	Community Adaptation
Dickey et al. (1996)	ND % housed at 18 mos.	ND hospitalizations ND use of mental health and addiction services ND time spent with case manager		
Goldfinger et al. (1999)	(−) fewer % experiencing homelessness, mean # of days homeless			
Seidman et al. (2003)			ND neuropsychological functioning over time (−) executive functioning over time	
Caplan et al. (2006)			(−) executive functioning over time for non-substance abusers; ND for substance abusers ND logical memory and auditory attention over time for non-substance abusers and substance abusers	
Pearson et al. (2009)	ND % housed at 12 mos. (+) fewer housing problems			

(continued)

Table 3.4 **Continued**

Studies	Housing	Service Use Outcomes	Clinical Outcomes	Community Adaptation
McHugo et al. (2004)	(−) increased time in stable housing (−) decreased functional homelessness ND proportion of days in one's own apartment ND housing satisfaction ND neighborhood satisfaction	ND decreases in institutional stays, medical or dental care, treatment for alcohol and drug use, psychiatric services	(−) fewer psychiatric symptoms over time ND days of alcohol use & days of drug use	ND reduced exposure to community violence ND increased life satisfaction over time (−) lower life satisfaction for men in scattered-site housing vs. women in scattered-site, and women and men in single-site housing

(+) outcomes in favor of scattered-site supportive housing group, (−) outcomes in favor of single-site supportive housing, ND = no group difference.

Service Use

No differences were reported for tenants of scattered-site supportive housing and single-site supportive housing in their amounts of overall use of health services or institutional stays (Dickey et al., 1996; McHugo et al., 2004).

Clinical Outcomes

Tenants in scattered-site supportive housing with ACT reported similar levels of improvement in the severity of psychiatric symptoms as tenants in single-site supportive housing with ICM (McHugo et al., 2004). No differences were reported in terms of alcohol use and days of drug use between the groups over the course of the study (McHugo et al., 2004).

In their comparison of tenants in scattered-site supportive housing with ICM and single-site supportive housing with ICM, Seidman et al. (2003) and Caplan, Schutt, Turner, Goldfinger, and Seidman (2006) examined different clinical outcomes than the other studies. In particular, they assessed changes in neuropsychological functioning over time. Overall, neuropsychological functioning improved significantly across both groups from baseline to 18 months. However, the executive functioning (i.e., an umbrella term for skills involving mental control and self-regulation) of the tenants in scattered-site supportive housing had a significant decline across this study period, while single-site supportive housing tenants had a slight, but nonsignificant, improvement in their executive functioning (Seidman et al., 2003). This trend was similar in Caplan et al. (2006) over a 48-month period; however only for tenants with no substance abuse problems, as tenants with substance abuse problems reported similar executive functioning regardless of program participation. Caplan et al. (2006) also found improvements in logical memory and auditory attention across the two types of housing programs and substance use profiles.

Community Adaptation

Only one of the studies assessed community adaptation. Male tenants in scattered-site supportive housing with ACT were found to have lower rates of general life satisfaction compared with female tenants in scattered-site supportive housing with ACT and male and female tenants in single-site supportive housing with ICM (McHugo et al., 2004). No differences emerged between single-site supportive housing with ACT or ICM and scattered-site supportive housing with ACT or ICM with both groups reporting similar levels of increase in life satisfaction over time. There were also no differences between the groups in terms of exposure to community violence, as both groups experienced similar levels of decrease in exposure.

Summary

The three studies comparing scattered-site supportive housing with single-site supportive housing found that tenants in both types of housing experienced similar outcomes. Notably, tenants in both types of housing programs achieved similar levels of housing stability and similar improvements in life satisfaction. One study reported deterioration in executive functioning (i.e., skills related to mental control and self-regulation) of tenants of scattered-site supportive housing, while no change in this area was found for tenants of single-site supportive housing (Seidman et al., 2003).

Scattered-Site Supportive Housing with ACT or ICM Versus Standard Care

The following section describes the research findings comparing the outcomes of scattered-site supportive housing with ACT or ICM to those of standard care.

Study Characteristics

Table 3.5 describes 16 published articles reporting findings from seven separate studies that explored the outcomes for individuals who received scattered-site supportive housing along with case management, ACT, or ICM, in comparison with a control group that received standard care (i.e., access to usual services in the community).

The majority of studies comparing scattered-site supportive housing with standard care were conducted in large American cities. There was also a national Canadian study (At Home/Chez Soi) in five cities with different population size and composition. Five of the studies were single-site (Appel, Tsemberis, Joseph, Stefancic, & Lambert-Wacey, 2012; Basu, Kee, Buchanan, & Sadowski, 2012; Gabrielian, Yuan, Andersen, Rubenstein, & Gelberg, 2014; Gilmer, Stefancic, Ettner, Manning, & Tsemberis, 2010; Sadowski, Kee, VanderWeele, & Buchanan, 2009; Stefancic & Tsemberis, 2007). Four papers reviewed a multisite study in four American cities at different time points (Cheng et al., 2007; O'Connell et al., 2008, 2012; Rosenheck et al., 2003). Findings from the At Home/Chez Soi study are presented in papers that present the findings from one site (Patterson et al., 2013; Patterson, Moniruzzaman, & Somers, 2014; Somers, Rezansoff, Moniruzzaman, Palepu, & Patterson, 2013), four sites (Stergiopoulos et al., 2015), and all five sites (Aubry et al., 2015; Aubry et al., 2016). Four studies adopted an experimental design (Aubry et al., 2015; Aubry et al., 2016; Basu et al., 2012; Cheng et al., 2007; O'Connell et al., 2008, 2012; Rosenheck et al., 2003; Sadowski et al., 2009; Stefancic & Tsemberis, 2007; Stergiopoulos et al., 2015) and

Table 3.5 **Characteristics of Effectiveness Studies Comparing Scattered-Site Supportive Housing with ICM or ACT to Standard Care**

Study		Location	Sample	Comparison Group(s)	Experimental Group	Study Type	Follow-up
Rosenheck et al. (2003); Cheng et al. (2007); O'Connell et al. (2008); O'Connell et al. (2012)	1	San Francisco, CA; San Diego, CA; New Orleans, LA; Cleveland, OH	C: 188 E: 182	Standard treatment (C)	Subsidized housing (Section 8 certificate) with ICM (E) (caseload of 1:25)	Experimental	24 mos. (O'Connell et al., 2012); 36 mos. (Rosenheck et al., 2003; Cheng et al., 2007); 60 mos. (O'Connell et al., 2008)
Stefancic & Tsemberis (2007)	2	New York, NY	C: 51 E1: 131; E2: approx. 210	Standard care (C)	ACT and subsidized housing (Pathways) (E1); Subsidized housing and ACT (Consortium of treatment and housing agencies) (E2)	Experimental	20 mos. (E1, E2, & C); 47 mos. (E1, E2)
Gilmer et al. (2010)	3	San Diego County, CA	C: 154 E: 209	Outpatient public mental health services (C)	Subsidized housing with ACT (E)	Quasi-experimental	12 mos.

Table 3.5 Continued

Study	Location		Sample	Comparison Group(s)	Experimental Group	Study Type	Follow-up
Sadowski et al. (2009); Basu et al. (2012)	Chicago, IL	4	C: 206 E: 201	Usual care (C)	Transitional housing, subsequent placement in stable housing, and case management (E); housing subsidy	Experimental	18 mos.
Appel et al. (2012)	New York, NY	5	C: 30 E: 31	Standard methadone maintenance treatment (C)	Subsidized housing with ACT; methadone maintenance treatment (E)	Quasi-experimental	3 yrs. post-implementation
Patterson et al. (2013); Patterson et al. (2014); Somers et al. (2013)	Vancouver, Canada	6.a	C1: 100 C2: 100 E1: 90 E2: 100	Standard care (high needs) (C1); Standard care (moderate needs) (C2)	Subsidized housing with ACT (E1); Subsidized housing with ICM (caseload 1:16) (E2)	Experimental	12 mos. (Patterson et al., 2013; Patterson et al., 2014); Up to 2 yrs. post randomization (range 9 mos. to 24 mos.; Somers et al., 2013)

Study	Location		Sample	Comparison (C)	Intervention (E)	Design	Follow-up
Stergiopoulos et al. (2015)	Vancouver, Winnipeg, Toronto, Montreal, Canada	6.b	C: 689 E: 509	Standard care (C)	Subsidized housing with ICM (E)	Experimental	24 mos.
Aubry et al. (2015); Aubry et al. (2016)	Vancouver, Winnipeg, Toronto, Montreal, Moncton, Canada	6.c	E: 469 C: 481	Standard care (C)	Subsidized housing with ACT (E)	Experimental	12 mos. (Aubry et al., 2015); 24 mos. (Aubry et al., 2016)
Gabrielian et al. (2014)	Los Angeles, CA	7	C1: 1760; C2: 21,862; C3: 37,020; E: 1997	Standard care: Currently homeless veterans (C1); Housed, low-income veterans (C2); Housed, not low-income veterans (C3)	Formerly homeless veterans in subsidized housing (Section 8 certificate) with case management (E)	Quasi-experimental	12 mos.

three were quasi-experimental (Appel et al., 2012; Gabrielian et al., 2014; Gilmer et al., 2010).

All intervention groups had access to subsidized housing. In addition to housing, the intervention groups received ACT in four of the studies (Appel et al., 2012; Aubry et al., 2015; Aubry et al., 2016; Gilmer et al., 2010; Patterson et al., 2013; Patterson et al., 2014; Somers et al., 2013; Stefancic & Tsemberis, 2007) and ICM in two studies (Cheng et al., 2007; O'Connell et al., 2008, 2012; Patterson et al., 2013; Patterson et al., 2014; Rosenheck et al., 2003; Stergiopoulos et al., 2015). In two studies it was unclear whether or not the case management was intensive (Basu et al., 2012; Gabrielian et al., 2014; Sadowski et al., 2009). In all studies the control groups received standard care. In one study the control group also received methadone maintenance treatment (Appel et al., 2012), and in another it also received outpatient public mental health services (Gilmer et al., 2010).

Outcomes

Table 3.6 presents the outcomes from the studies grouped into the areas of housing, service use, clinical functioning, and community adaptation.

Housing

Housing outcomes were examined in five of the seven studies. Individuals in scattered-site supportive housing who received ACT or ICM had better housing outcomes than individuals who received standard care. A study comparing scattered-site supportive housing with ICM to treatment as usual found that participants with scattered-site housing and ICM had more days housed, fewer days homeless, greater housing satisfaction, higher quality housing, and a lower risk of returning to homelessness (Cheng et al., 2007; O'Connell et al., 2008, 2012; Rosenheck et al., 2003). Another study of individuals in transitional housing who were subsequently placed in scattered-site supportive housing with case management found that this intervention group had more days in stable housing than the participants who received standard care in the community subsequent to seeing a social worker for discharge planning from the transitional housing (Basu et al., 2012).

Both ACT and ICM appear to be effective in helping individuals remain in their scattered-site supportive housing, in comparison with those receiving standard care (Aubry et al., 2015; Aubry et al., 2016; Stefancic & Tsemberis, 2007; Stergiopoulos et al., 2015). Moreover, methadone maintenance treatment in addition to scattered-site supportive housing with ACT helped significantly more people with substance abuse issues to remain independently housed for up to 3 years, in comparison with those receiving solely methadone treatment (Appel et al., 2012).

Table 3.6 **Findings of Effectiveness Studies Comparing Scattered-Site Housing with ICM or ACT to Standard Care**

	Studies	Housing	Service Use	Clinical Functioning	Community Adaptation
1.i.	Rosenheck et al. (2003)	(+) days housed at 36 mos. (+) fewer days homeless (+) housing satisfaction, housing quality, and fewer housing problems	Fewer days institutionalized	ND substance use, psychiatric symptoms	(+) social network size, satisfaction with family relations ND employment, income, and legal involvement
1.ii	Cheng et al. (2007)	(+) days housed at 36 mos. (+) more positive housing characteristics (+) fewer negative housing characteristics	Fewer days institutionalized	(+) fewer days of alcohol use, days intoxicated (+) fewer days using drugs (+) reduced drug index score (+) reduced expenditure on substances ND alcohol index score ND psychiatric symptoms	ND social network size and employment, overall quality of life
1.iii	O'Connell et al. (2008)	(+) lower risk of returning to homelessness (+) fewer days between baseline interview and being housed		ND on alcohol and drug index scores, days used drugs or intoxicated, expenditures on substances	ND social network, employment, income, and legal involvement
1.iv	O'Connell et al. (2012)	(+) more days housed at 24 mos. (+) fewer days homeless at 24 mos.	Fewer days institutionalized	ND alcohol and drug index scores, days intoxicated, days of drug use	ND quality of life, social contacts, days worked

(*continued*)

Table 3.6 Continued

	Studies	Housing	Service Use	Clinical Functioning	Community Adaptation
2	Stefancic & Tsemberis (2007)	(+) living in permanent housing at 20 mos. 84% of E1 and E2 housed at 2 yrs; 68% housed at 4 yrs.			
3	Gilmer et al. (2010)		Increased case management, medication management, therapy/rehabilitation, total visits Decreased probability of using inpatient, emergency, justice system services		(+) quality of life (living situation, safety, daily activities, leisure, health, general life satisfaction, social relationships, family relationships)
4.i	Sadowski et al. (2009)		Fewer hospitalizations Fewer days hospitalized Fewer emergency department visits (adjusted for baseline characteristics)		ND quality of life (physical and mental health)

4.ii	Basu et al. (2012)	(+) days in stable housing	ND prison days
		ND hospitalized days, nursing home days	
		Fewer emergency room visits	
		Fewer days in residential substance abuse treatment	
		Increased outpatient days	
		Increased days in respite care	
		Increased case management services	
5	Appel et al. (2012)	(+) independently housed 3 yrs. after start of program	Greater retention in methadone maintenance treatment
6.a.i.	Patterson et al. (2013)		(+) quality of life (total score, safety, living situation at 6 and 12 mos.; global life satisfaction at 6 mos.; leisure satisfaction at 12 mos.) for E1 and C1

(continued)

Table 3.6 Continued

Studies	Housing	Service Use	Clinical Functioning	Community Adaptation
				ND quality of life (family, finances, and social at 6 and 12 mos.; leisure 6 mos.; global at 12 mos.) for E1 and C1
				(+) quality of life (living situation, safety 6 and 12 mos.) for C2 and E2
				ND quality of life (total score, family, finances, leisure, social, global at 6 or 12 mos.) for E2 and C2
6.a.ii. Somers et al. (2013)				(+) convicted offenses for E1 vs C1
6.a.iii. Patterson et al. (2014)				ND physical integration for all groups
				ND psychological integration for C1, E1
				(+) psychological integration for E2 vs. C2

6.b	Stergiopoulos et al. (2015)	(+) more days stably housed (−) fewer participants never housed	ND number of emergency department visits	ND mental illness symptom severity, physical health, mental health, recovery, severity of substance use problems	ND quality of health functioning (+) quality of life (total score, leisure, living situation, safety) ND quality of life (finances, social, overall), community functioning, psychological community integration, physical community integration, number of arrests
6.c	Aubry et al. (2015)	(+) more likely to have stable housing (+) more days housed		ND severity of psychiatric symptoms, substance use problems	(+) quality of life (total score, living situation, safety, leisure); community functioning (total score, social skills, behavior) ND quality of life (finances, family relations, social relations), community functioning (health, adaptation)

(continued)

Table 3.6 Continued

Studies	Housing	Service Use	Clinical Functioning	Community Adaptation
6. d Aubry et al. (2016)	(+) rapidly housed (+) more likely to be stably housed (+) more days housed over the course of the study (+) more days consecutively housed at end of study (+) better rating of quality of housing	ND days in hospital, emergency room visits, arrests	ND severity of psychiatric symptoms, physical health, substance use problems	ND quality of life; community functioning; psychological integration
7 Gabrielian et al. (2014)		More medical/ surgical admissions (E vs. C1, C2, C3) More outpatient surgery visits (E, C2 vs. C1, C3) More outpatient specialty services (E vs. C1, C2, C3)		

More emergency
department visits
(E, C1 vs. C2, C3)

More individual
mental health visits
(E, C1 vs. C2, C3)

More group mental
health visits
(E, C1 vs. C2, C3)

More psychiatric
admissions
(E vs. C2, C3)

ND psychiatric
admission (E vs C1)

More psychiatric
readmissions
(C1 vs. E)

ND number
of preventable
admissions across
groups

Note: (+) outcomes in favor of scattered-site supportive housing, (−) outcomes in favor of standard care, ND = no group difference.

Service Use

Only three studies compared the service use of those in scattered-site supportive housing with ACT to those receiving standard care. Significantly more of those in scattered-site supportive housing receiving ACT and methadone maintenance treatment remained in methadone maintenance treatment compared with individuals who solely received the standard methadone treatment (Appel et al., 2012).

Gilmer et al. (2010) compared service use in the year prior to the start of services with service use in the year following the initiation of services for individuals in scattered-site supportive housing with ACT and individuals receiving outpatient public mental health services. The scattered-site supportive housing with ACT group reported significantly greater increases in the number of case management visits, medication management visits, therapy/rehabilitation visits, and total visits compared with the group receiving outpatient services (Gilmer et al., 2010). The scattered-site supportive housing with ACT group also showed a greater decrease in the use of inpatient, emergency, and justice system services compared with the group of patients receiving outpatient services (Gilmer et al., 2010).

Finally, Aubry et al. (2016) found individuals in scattered-site supportive housing with ACT showed similar levels of decrease in emergency room visits and days in hospital as individuals receiving treatment as usual in the community.

For the most part, individuals receiving scattered-site supportive housing with ICM had better service use outcomes than those receiving only standard care. These individuals had fewer days institutionalized at 2-year follow-up (O'Connell et al., 2012) and 3-year follow-up (Cheng et al., 2007; Rosenheck et al., 2003). Another study found fewer emergency room visits for individuals in scattered-site supportive housing with ICM as well as fewer days in residential substance abuse treatment, and more days in respite care compared with individuals in a standard care condition (Basu et al., 2012). Further, in this same study, individuals living in scattered-site supportive housing with ICM had fewer hospitalizations and a lower number of hospital days compared with those receiving standard care (Sadowski et al., 2009). However, there were no differences between groups found in the number of days hospitalized or the number of days in nursing homes (Basu et al., 2012). Another study, however, found no change for either of the groups in the number of emergency room visits over 2 years (Stergiopoulos et al., 2015).

In contrast, Gabrielian et al. (2014) found that veterans in scattered-site supportive housing with ICM had higher rates of inpatient and outpatient use than currently homeless veterans. The rates of psychiatric admission were greater for the scattered-site supportive housing with ICM group compared with housed, low-income and not-low-income veterans, but similar to the rate of homeless veterans. However, after adjusting for demographic and service use need indicators, as well as primary care usage, veterans in scattered-site supportive housing with ICM used less specialty medical and surgical services compared with the housed, not-low-income veterans, but still had more outpatient mental health visits and emergency department visits than housed, not-low-income veterans (Gabrielian et al., 2013). It was not known how long veterans in the Gabrielian et al. (2013) study were in scattered-site supportive housing with ICM prior to their entry into the study.

In terms of outpatient services, individuals in scattered-site supportive housing with ICM had more outpatient days and increased use of case management services compared with usual care (Basu et al., 2012). Gabrielian et al. (2014) also found more outpatient medical service use and more mental health visits for veterans in scattered-site supportive housing with ICM compared with homeless veterans.

Clinical Functioning

Findings were inconsistent in studies comparing the clinical functioning outcomes of individuals in scattered-site supportive housing, with ACT or ICM, with those receiving only standard care. O'Connell et al. (2012), Rosenheck et al. (2003), and O'Connell et al. (2008) found no differences in substance use outcomes between individuals living in scattered-site supportive housing with ICM and those receiving standard care at 2 years, 3 years, and 5 years. However, Cheng et al. (2007), who reanalyzed data from Rosenheck (2003) using multiple imputation for missing data, found that scattered-site supportive housing with ICM led to significantly fewer days of alcohol and drug use, fewer days with drinking to intoxication, reduced expenditure on substances, and lower scores on a composite drug problem index.

Two papers from the At Home/Chez Soi study found no difference in the severity of substance use problems between the scattered-site supportive housing and the standard care group for those receiving ACT at 12 or 24 months (Aubry et al., 2015; Aubry et al., 2016) or ICM at 24 months (Stergiopoulos et al., 2015). Both groups had an improvement in their substance use problems over time. Similar findings were also reported for psychiatric symptoms both in the At Home/Chez Soi study (Aubry et al., 2016; Stergiopoulos et al., 2015) and the Rosenheck et al. (2003) study. The scattered-site supportive housing with ACT and ICM and standard care groups in the At Home/Chez Soi project also experienced similar levels of improvement in mental health functioning and no changes in physical health functioning over the course of the study (Aubry, et al., 2016; Stergiopoulos et al., 2015).

Community Adaptation

The studies assessing community adaptation outcomes also yielded mixed results. Whereas in some studies, tenants in scattered-site supportive housing with ICM reported superior outcomes in this area, in others no differences were identified in comparison with individuals receiving standard care. Rosenheck et al. (2003) reported that, after 3 years, tenants in scattered-site supportive housing with ICM had larger social networks, and greater satisfaction with their family relationships in comparison with consumers receiving standard care. However, two other papers from this study reported no group differences on social network size after 3 years and after 5 years (Cheng et al., 2007; O'Connell et al., 2008) and no difference in social contacts after 2 years (O'Connell et al., 2012).

Scattered-site supportive housing with ACT or ICM appears to produce greater improvements in quality of life than standard care. Tenants in scattered-site supportive housing with ICM reported significantly larger improvements in global quality of life compared with individuals receiving treatment as usual (Stergiopoulos et al., 2015). As well, tenants in scattered-site supportive housing with ICM reported greater improvement in their quality life in life domains related to their safety and living situation in comparison with individuals receiving treatment as usual (Patterson et al., 2013; Stergiopoulos et al., 2015). On the other hand, no differences were found in the domains of finances and social relations (Patterson et al., 2013; Stergiopoulos et al., 2015). Patterson also reported no differences in improvement in quality of life in the areas of leisure and family relations. However, Stergiopoulos et al. (2015) reported greater improvements in quality of life in relation to leisure activities for the scattered-site supportive housing and ICM group compared with the standard care group.

Scattered-site supportive housing with ACT was associated with improvements in quality of life (Aubry et al., 2015; Gilmer et al., 2010; Patterson et al., 2014). In particular, individuals in scattered-site supportive housing with ACT reported greater improvements in all life domains than individuals receiving standard care, including (beginning with the domains with the largest difference between the groups) living situation, safety, daily activities, leisure, health, general life satisfaction, social relationships, and family relationships (Gilmer et al., 2010).

Across the five sites of the At Home/Chez Soi study in Canada, after 1 year individuals who received scattered-site supportive housing with ACT showed greater improvements than individuals receiving standard care on overall quality of life and in the specific areas of leisure, living situation, and safety (Aubry et al., 2015). However, at 24 months, differences between the two groups had attenuated, with participants receiving standard care catching up to individuals receiving scattered-site supportive housing with ACT (Aubry et al., 2016).

Generally, research findings have also been mixed in terms of the effects of housing and support on improvements in community functioning and community integration. After a period of 1 year, individuals in the scattered-site supportive housing with ACT group from the five sites of the At Home/Chez Soi study demonstrated greater improvements in overall community functioning and more specifically in areas such as social abilities and independent living and treatment engagement behaviors (Aubry et al., 2015). However, these improvements were no longer apparent after 2 years, when there were no differences between individuals in the scattered-site supportive housing with ACT condition and those only receiving standard care (Aubry et al., 2016). Similarly, no differences in level of improvement were found for individuals receiving scattered-site supportive housing with

·ICM compared with those receiving standard care (Stergiopoulos et al., 2015). Additionally, no differences were identified in levels of improvements in participation in activities in the communities and psychological integration in the neighborhood at either 1 or 2 years.

An exception was identified at the Vancouver site of the At Home/Chez Soi project, where improvements in community integration were identified at 6 months and 1 year for individuals in scattered-site supportive housing with ICM in comparison with individuals receiving standard care (Patterson et al., 2014). The scattered-site supportive housing with ICM group was more likely to feel at home where they lived and to feel like they belonged where they lived compared with the standard care group.

Across the studies reviewed here, scattered-site supportive housing and ICM or ACT have not produced better legal involvement outcomes than standard care (Basu et al., 2012; O'Connell et al., 2008; Rosenheck et al., 2003; Stergiopoulos et al., 2015). Only at the Vancouver site in the Canadian *At Home/Chez Soi* project was it found that individuals with housing and ACT had fewer convicted offenses up to 2 years post randomization compared with those receiving standard care (Somers et al., 2013).

The one study that compared employment and income outcomes between scattered-site supportive housing with ICM and standard care found no group differences at any time point (Cheng et al., 2007; O'Connell et al., 2008, 2012; Rosenheck et al., 2003).

Summary

Overall, the weight of the evidence favors the combination of scattered-site supportive housing with ACT or ICM over standard care in producing better housing outcomes. Although it is less clear for nonhousing outcomes, findings show scattered-site supportive housing with ACT or ICM either producing better outcomes relative to standard care or no differences. A greater proportion of individuals in scattered-site supportive housing with ACT or ICM exited homelessness and achieved housing stability than individuals receiving standard care. As well, individuals in scattered-site supportive housing with ACT or ICM spent more time housed and less time homeless than individuals receiving standard care. As well, individuals in scattered-site supportive housing with ACT or ICM showed greater engagement in treatment and decreased use of acute care services. There were no group differences on clinical functioning outcomes for substance use or psychiatric symptoms, except for one study reporting better substance use outcomes for the scattered-site supportive housing group compared with the standard care group. Overall, the outcomes in the area of community adaptation were either better for scattered-site supportive housing combined with ACT or ICM, or there were no differences.

Scattered-Site Supportive Housing Versus Residential Continuum Housing

The following section describes the research findings that compare the outcomes of scattered-site supportive housing to those of residential continuum housing.

Study Characteristics

Table 3.7 provides a description of the four studies that compare the outcomes of individuals who received scattered-site supportive housing with ACT or ICM to the outcomes of individuals in a residential continuum model. The studies were conducted in single-site, large American cities, predominantly in New York, with the exception of one that included 15 sites across the United States (O'Connell, Kasprow, & Rosenheck, 2009). One study had an experimental design (Greenwood, Schaefer-McDaniel, Winkel, & Tsemberis, 2005; Gulcur, Stefancic, Shinn, Tsemberis, & Fischer, 2003; Gulcur, Tsemberis, Stefancic, & Greenwood, 2007; Padgett, Gulcur, & Tsemberis, 2006; Tsemberis, Gulcur, & Nakae, 2004; Tsemberis, Moran, Sinn, Asmussen, & Shern, 2003), and three had a quasi-experimental design (Tsemberis, 1999; Tsemberis & Eisenberg, 2000; Padgett, Stanhope, Henwood, & Stefancic, 2011). All of the studies examined the provision of scattered-site supportive housing with ACT for homeless adults, except O'Connell et al. (2009), which provided ICM rather than ACT.

The services received by the comparison groups included single-site housing with on-site support configured in a residential continuum model (Greenwood et al., 2005; Gulcur et al., 2003; Gulcur et al., 2007; Padgett et al., 2006; Tsemberis, 1999; Tsemberis & Eisenberg, 2000; Tsemberis et al., 2004; Tsemberis et al., 2003), single-site housing with on-site support leading to independent housing (Padgett et al., 2011), and subsidized multistage housing with ICM (O'Connell et al., 2009).

Outcomes

Table 3.8 presents the outcomes of the studies grouped into the areas of housing, service use, clinical functioning, and community adaptation.

Housing

Housing outcomes were explored in all four studies. Two studies compared scattered-site supportive housing with ACT to single-site supportive housing with on-site support configured in a residential continuum, and both reported more positive housing outcomes for the participants receiving scattered-site supportive

Table 3.7 **Characteristics of Effectiveness Studies Comparing Scattered-Site Supportive Housing with ACT or ICM and Residential Continuum**

Study	Location		Sample	Comparison Group(s)	Experimental Group	Study Type	Follow-up
Tsemberis (1999); Tsemberis & Eisenberg (2000)	New York, NY	1	C: 3,811 E: 139 (Tsemberis, 1999); C: 1,600 E: 241 (Tsemberis & Eisenberg, 2000)	Residential continuum model (linear residential treatment—range of residential settings leading to independent housing) (C)	Pathways scattered-site supportive housing with ACT (E); housing subsidized	Quasi-experimental	36 mos. (Tsemberis, 1999); 60 mos. (Tsemberis & Eisenberg, 2000)
Gulcur et al. (2003); Tsemberis et al., (2003); Tsemberis et al. (2004); Greenwood et al. (2005); Padgett et al. (2006); Gulcur et al. (2007)	New York, NY	2	C: 126 E: 99	Residential continuum model (starts with lower demand programs and moves through congregate settings to finally independent housing) (C)	Pathways scattered-site supportive housing with ACT (E); housing subsidized	Experimental	6 mos. (Tsemberis et al., 2003); 24 mos. (Gulcur et al., 2003; Tsemberis et al., 2003; Tsemberis et al., 2004); 36 mos. (Greenwood et al., 2005); 48 mos. (Gulcur et al., 2007; Padgett et al., 2006)

(continued)

Table 3.7 Continued

Study	Location		Sample	Comparison Group(s)	Experimental Group	Study Type	Follow-up
O'Connell et al. (2009)	15 sites across the United States	3	C: 183 E: 139	Section 8 voucher with multistage housing and intensive case management (C)	Section 8 voucher with direct placement into independent housing and ICM (E)	Quasi-experimental	24 mos.
Padgett et al. (2011)	New York, NY	4	C: 48 E: 27	Continuum approach leading to housing readiness (congregate housing leading to independent housing) (C)	Pathways scattered-site supportive housing with ACT (E); housing subsidized	Quasi-experimental	12 mos.

Table 3.8 Findings of Effectiveness Studies Comparing Scattered-Site Supportive Housing with ICM/ACT and Residential Continuum

	Studies	Housing	Service Use	Clinical Functioning	Community Adaptation
1.i	Tsemberis (1999)	(+) housing retention at 2 yrs.			
1.ii	Tsemberis & Eisenberg (2000)	(+) housing retention at 5 yrs.			
2.i	Gulcur et al. (2003)	(+) less time homeless	Fewer days in psychiatric hospitals		
2.ii	Tsemberis et al. (2003)	(+) time stably housed (+) less time in institutional & transitional placements (+) less time homeless			
2.iii	Tsemberis et al. (2004)	(+) housed earlier (+) time stably housed (+) less time homeless	Less use of substance abuse treatment	ND drug use, alcohol use, psychiatric symptoms	(+) perceived choice
2.iv	Greenwood et al. (2005)	(+) less time homeless		ND psychiatric symptoms, mastery	(+) perceived choice
2.v	Padgett et al. (2006)		Less use of substance abuse treatment Less mental health treatment at 4 yrs.	ND drug use, alcohol use	

(continued)

Table 3.8 Continued

Studies	Housing	Service Use	Clinical Functioning	Community Adaptation
2.vi. Gulcur et al. (2007)				(+) social integration ND physical, psychological integration, self-actualization
3 O'Connell et al. (2009)	(−) days homeless (+) greater decrease in days homeless over time ND days housed	Fewer days institutionalized More days of outpatient services Fewer days of inpatient and residential care	ND psychiatric symptoms, substance abuse and medical problems (except increase in days of drug use)	ND, quality of life, income, social network ND decreased minor and major crimes over time ND incarceration days (−) fewer days worked, lower employment index score over time, more of income from benefits
4 Padgett et al. (2011)		Less use of substance abuse treatment More ACT and housing clients remain in housing program	(+) substance use	

Note: (+) outcomes in favor of scattered-site supportive housing, (−) outcomes in favor of residential continuum housing, ND = no group difference.

housing with ACT (Greenwood et al., 2005; Gulcur et al., 2003; Tsemberis, 1999; Tsemberis & Eisenberg, 2000; Tsemberis et al., 2004; Tsemberis et al., 2003).

Specifically, housing retention was greater in the scattered-site supportive housing with ACT group at 2 years (Tsemberis, 1999) and at 5 years (Tsemberis & Eisenberg, 2000). The findings from the other study with a residential continuum comparison group found the scattered-site supportive housing with ACT group being housed earlier (Tsemberis et al., 2004) and spending more time stably housed (Tsemberis et al., 2004; Tsemberis et al., 2003), less time in institutional and transitional placements (Tsemberis et al., 2003), and less time homeless (Greenwood et al., 2005; Gulcur et al., 2003; Tsemberis et al., 2004; Tsemberis et al., 2003).

One study had mixed findings, as individuals who were directly placed into scattered-site supportive housing with ICM had more days homeless than individuals in multistage housing also with ICM (O'Connell et al., 2009). However, the study design was quasi-experimental in nature, with differences in housing status between the groups at the outset. Specifically, at the beginning of the study, the direct-placement group was homeless while the multistage housing group was already housed; moreover, it took several months for the direct-placement group to be housed, so differences in housing outcomes may be due to differences in housing status at the beginning of the study.

Service Use

Overall, living in scattered-site supportive housing with ACT was associated with less institutionalization, but also less substance abuse treatment than residential continuum housing. Individuals living in scattered-site supportive housing with ACT also spent fewer days in a psychiatric hospital compared with those who received on-site support through the residential continuum model (Gulcur et al., 2003). Individuals receiving ICM with direct placement into scattered-site supportive housing had fewer days of institutionalization and fewer days of inpatient and residential care than those in multistage housing with ICM (O'Connell et al., 2009). Clients placed in scattered-site supportive housing with ACT were also more likely to remain in the program compared with those who entered a residential continuum program intended to eventually lead to "housing readiness" (Padgett et al., 2011).

Two studies found greater use of substance abuse treatment by individuals in residential continuum programs compared with individuals in scattered-site supportive housing with ACT programs (Padgett et al., 2006; Padgett et al., 2011; Tsemberis et al., 2004). As well, individuals in scattered-site supportive housing with ACT were found to make less use of mental health services at the 4-year time point than individuals participating in a residential continuum program (Padgett et al., 2006). However, in another study, those who had direct placement into scattered-site supportive housing with ICM had more days of outpatient services than those living in multistage housing (O'Connell et al., 2009).

Clinical Functioning

Only three studies compared scattered-site supportive housing to residential continuum programs in terms of clinical functioning outcomes (Greenwood et al., 2005; O'Connell et al., 2009; Padgett et al., 2006; Padgett et al., 2011; Tsemberis et al., 2004). Of these, only one study reported that housing with ACT was associated with more positive clinical functioning outcomes as it related to substance use compared with residential continuum programs (Padgett et al., 2011). In this study, the residential continuum group was 3.4 times more likely to use drugs or abuse alcohol than the group receiving scattered housing with ACT (Padgett et al., 2011).

In contrast, another study found no differences between the individuals in scattered-site supportive housing programs with ACT versus individuals in residential continuum programs on drug and alcohol use at any follow-up time points, up to 48 months after the initiation of services, and there was no change in substance use by either group over time (Padgett et al., 2006; Tsemberis et al., 2004). As well, in this study, no group differences were found on reduction in psychiatric symptoms (Greenwood et al., 2005; Tsemberis et al., 2004). Although the 24-month follow-up for this study found no change in psychiatric symptoms over time (Tsemberis et al., 2004), the 36-month follow-up reported an overall decrease in psychiatric symptoms for both groups (Greenwood et al., 2005). Level of *mastery* (personal control) did not differ between groups and did not change over time (Greenwood et al., 2005).

A comparison of direct placement in scattered-site supportive housing with ICM and multistage housing groups found no differences between the groups on psychiatric symptoms, substance abuse, or medical problems at 24 months and both groups showed improvement over time in these areas; however, days of drug use had a small increase over time in both groups (O'Connell et al., 2009).

Community Adaptation

Two studies investigated outcomes related to community adaptation and the findings were mixed. The perception of how many choices individuals had related to the housing and services, such as choice of residence, was greater for those individuals in scattered-site supportive housing with ACT compared with individuals in a residential continuum program (Greenwood et al., 2005; Tsemberis et al., 2004). Findings from the same study examining community integration at 48 months showed that membership in the experimental group receiving scattered-site supportive housing and ACT (vs. in a control group receiving residential continuum services) was related to having higher levels of social integration (Gulcur et al., 2007). However, experimental or control group membership did not predict physical or psychological integration or self-actualization, as no differences between the two groups emerged (Gulcur et al., 2007).

In the other study, individuals placed directly in scattered-site supportive housing with ICM and individuals in multistage housing groups showed similar levels of improvement in quality of life, income, size of social network, and the number of minor and major crimes and no differences in the number of days incarcerated over a 24-month period (O'Connell et al., 2009). However, the direct placement to scattered-site supportive housing group had fewer days worked and a lower employment index score, and received more income from benefits over the 24-month period compared with the multistage housing group (O'Connell et al., 2009).

Summary

Generally, the housing outcomes were better for individuals in scattered-site supportive housing with support compared with individuals placed in residential continuum type housing. Service use outcomes were mixed, with less institutionalization for the scattered-site supportive housing, but also less participation in substance use treatment and mixed findings on outpatient service use. Clinical outcomes were similar between the scattered-site supportive housing and the residential continuum group, with both groups showing improvements in severity of psychiatric symptoms or no change, except for one study that reported better outcomes in line with decreases in substance use for individuals in scattered-site supportive housing with ACT. Generally, the outcomes for community adaptation were either better for scattered site supportive housing combined with ACT compared to residential continuum programs, or there were no differences. Overall, the weight of the evidence favors the combination of scattered-site supportive housing and ACT over the residential continuum model in producing better housing outcomes, while it is less clear for other nonhousing outcomes.

Single-Site Supportive Housing Versus Other Housing and/or Support Programs

In the following section, studies comparing the outcomes of single-site supportive housing to other housing and/or support are reviewed. Single-site supportive housing can be transitional or permanent in nature in which individuals with severe mental illness and/or substance abuse live either together in a housing unit or in their satellite apartment in an apartment block combined with on-site support services. In all of these studies, on-site services were provided but did not include ICM or ACT, which have been reviewed in the previous two sections. Various forms of on-site services were offered, including but not limited to case management, permanent housing support, vocational services, social support, addictions treatment, mental health support, and crisis management.

Study Characteristics

Table 3.9 presents descriptive information on the studies comparing the outcomes of single-site supportive housing to other housing and/or support. Of the eight studies, six were conducted in the United States, one was conducted in Canada, and one was conducted in Australia. Five adopted a true experimental design (i.e., participants were randomly assigned to different treatment conditions) (Burnam et al., 1995; Conrad et al., 1998; Schinka, Francis, Hughes, LaLone, & Flynn, 1998; Stecher et al., 1994; Wright & Devine, 1995), two used a quasi-experimental design (i.e., participants of different groups were not randomly assigned but were matched on key variables instead) (Hwang et al., 2011; Siskind et al., 2014), and one used a retrospective cohort design (i.e., participants of different groups were not randomly assigned and the data was collected from past records) (Kessell, Bhatia, Bamberger, & Kushel, 2006).

Demographic and clinical characteristics demonstrated some similarities as well as some variability. Study participants were often male or exclusively male (Conrad et al., 1998), Caucasian (Burnam et al., 1995; Siskind et al., 2014; Stecher et al. 1994) or African American (Conrad et al., 1998; Kessell et al., 2006; Wright & Devine 1995), middle-aged, and diagnosed with mood disorders (Burnam et al., 1995; Kessell et al., 2006; Stecher et al., 1994), or with comorbid disorders when the presence of mental health problems was included as a recruitment criteria (Kessell et al., 2006; Siskind et al., 2014). The majority of participants had lengthy histories of homelessness, but some studies included individuals with shorter histories of homelessness (Wright & Devine, 1995).

Outcomes

Table 3.10 presents a summary of outcomes related to housing, service use, clinical functioning, and community adaptation.

Housing

For many housing outcomes, individuals living in single-site supportive housing and those receiving nonresidential treatment (Burnam et al., 1995; Conrad et al., 1998; Schinka et al., 1998; Stecher et al., 1994), time-limited residential treatment (Wright & Devine, 1995), or standard care (Hwang et al., 2011; Kessell et al., 2006; Siskind et al., 2014) displayed similar positive housing trajectories over time. No group differences emerged in terms of length of time spent in independent housing (Burnam et al., 1995; Hwang et al., 2011). One study did find that single-site supportive housing residents were more likely to move from transitional housing into permanent independent living arrangements after a period of 6 months compared to participating in a detox program followed by a 12-step program, counseling, and case management (Wright & Devine, 1995).

Table 3.9 **Characteristics of Effectiveness Studies Comparing Single Site Housing with On-Site Support to Other Services**

Study	Location	Sample	Comparison Group(s)	Experimental Group(s)	Study Type	Follow-up
Burnam et al. (1995)	Los Angeles, CA	People with serious mental illness and addictions; E1: 67; E2: 144; C1:65	Standard available community services (C)	E1: Residential abstinence-based treatment with psychoed. groups, 12 step programs, process groups, individual counseling and case management; E2: Day program during the week with same treatment elements at E1 but applying harm reduction services & more case management	Experimental	9 mos.
Conrad et al. (1998)	Hines, IL	Homeless veterans with addictions; E: 178 C: 180	Inpatient hospital treatment for up to 21 days that included psychoed. groups and individual therapy with a focus on abstinence. Followed by community services including community halfway houses (C)	Transitional residential care with social treatment and CBT interventions & 12-step program for up to 6 mos. followed by 6 mos. of case management & 12-step program (E)	Experimental	24 mos.

(continued)

Table 3.9 Continued

Study	Location	Sample	Comparison Group(s)	Experimental Group(s)	Study Type	Follow-up
Stecher et al. (1994)	Los Angeles, CA	Dually diagnosed individuals who were homeless; E: 67 C: 144	Nonresidential treatment comprising all the same interventions as residential treatment (C)	Residential treatment for 3 mos. focusing on abstinence and relapse prevention. Included psychoed. groups, individual counseling, 12-step program, and social/ recreational activities. After 3 mos., individuals received nonresidential treatment (E)	Experimental	24 mos.
Wright & Devine (1995)	New Orleans, LA	Homeless individuals with addictions and physical and mental health problems; E: 505; C1 and C2: 165	Detox program for 7 days that included introduction to 12-step programs, counseling, and case management (C)	E1: Detox program for 7 days (as described in comparison group); transitional residential program with case management, addiction treatment groups E2: Detox program and residential treatment followed by extended independent living for 12 mos. while continuing interventions from residential placement	Experimental	6 mos.
Kessell et al. (2006)	San Francisco, CA	Chronically homeless people; E: 114 C: 135	Usual services in the community that can include housing other than supportive housing under study (C)	Supportive housing with on-site case management, benefits counseling, and referral to community services (E)	Retrospective cohort study	24 mos.

Author	Location	Population	Intervention (E) / Comparison (C)	Intervention (E)	Design	Duration
Hwang et al. (2011)	Toronto, Canada	Homeless and vulnerably housed people with and without severe mental illness; E: 46 C: 66	Wait-listed applicants who received usual care in the community (C)	Satellite self-sufficient subsidized apartments with some common areas, drop-in center, on-site life skills support and counseling, and medical and dental clinic (E)	Prospective quasi-experimental design	18 mos.
Schinka et al. (1998)	Tampa, FL	VA patients with addictions and psychiatric comorbidity; E: 36 C: 62	Intensive 3-week inpatient program that includes psychoeducation, individual counseling, group therapy, family therapy, AA & NA meetings (C)	Satellite transitional apartments with participation in same therapeutic activities as inpatients during the day in hospital, attendance at AA or NA meetings, and group meetings at residence (E)	Experimental	2 mos.
Siskind et al. (2014)	Brisbane, Australia	Patients with severe and persistent mental illness and a history of homelessness; E: 113 C: 139	Usual community mental health services (C)	Shared two-bedroom apartments for period of 6 mos. that could be extended; 12 hrs per week support that included living skills training, crisis management, and linkage to community services, abstinence was expected; also received usual community mental health services similar to comparison group (E)	Retrospective quasi-experimental design	12 mos.

Table 3.10 Findings of Effectiveness Studies Comparing Single Site Housing with On-Site Support to Other Services

Studies	Housing	Service Use	Clinical Functioning	Community Adaptation
Burnam et al. (1995)	ND % time on streets ND % time in independent housing		(+) days used alcohol (3 mos.) (−) severity of drug use (6 mos.) ND days used alcohol (6, 9 mos.) ND level of alcohol use ND days used drugs ND severity of drug use (3, 9 mos.). ND depression and anxiety ND psychotic symptoms ND mania ND self-esteem	
Conrad et al. (1998);	(+) nights spent homeless (overall) (+) nights spent homeless (3, 12 mos.) (−) nights spent homeless (24 mos.) (E had more)		(+) alcohol abuse (overall) (+) alcohol abuse (3, 9 mos.) ND alcohol abuse (6, 12, 18, 24 mos.) (+) medical problems (overall)	(+) employment (overall) (+) employment (6, 9, 12, 18 mos.)

ND nights spent homeless (6, 9, 18 mos.)

(+) medical problems (6 mos.)

ND medical problems (3, 9, 12, 18, 24 mos.)

ND drug use (overall)

(+) drug use (3, 6, 9 mos.)

ND drug use (12, 18, 24 mos.)

ND psychiatric problems (overall and each month)

ND legal problems (overall and each month)

Stecher et al. (1994)

(+) more psychiatric appointments (E had more)

(−) coordination of care services contacts

(+) discharge planning contacts

(−) housing contacts

(−) employment contacts

(+) level of program engagement

(continued)

Table 3.10 Continued

Studies	Housing	Service Use	Clinical Functioning	Community Adaptation
Wright & Devine (1995)	(+) fewer returns to homelessness (+) independent living arrangements	ND service utilization	(+) alcohol relapse ND drug relapse ND emotional well-being ND physical health	ND family and social relationships ND legal problems
Hwang et al. (2011)	(+) satisfaction with housing (group × time) (+) days spent on the street ND residential stability ND days spent in own place ND days spent staying with friends or family ND days spent in a shelter ND days spent in an institution	ND, NC healthcare utilization	ND physical health ND mental health ND alcohol use ND drug use	ND general life satisfaction ND satisfaction with finances ND satisfaction with safety
Schinka et al. (1998)			ND alcohol and drug use	

Kessell et al. (2006)		ND medical services
		ND ambulatory generalist care
		ND primary care provider
		ND ambulance services
		ND emergency department visits
		ND inpatient hospitalizations
		ND outpatient substance abuse service use
		ND outpatient mental health service use
Siskind et al. (2014)	(+) reduction in problems with living conditions	(+) reduction in hospital bed-days
		ND emergency department visits
		ND total illness acuity
		ND nonaccidental self-injury
		ND substance abuse

Note: (+) outcomes in favor of scattered-site supportive housing, (−) outcomes in favor of standard care, ND = no group difference.

Three studies demonstrated that single-site supportive housing residents were less likely to spend time homeless (Conrad et al., 1998; Hwang et al., 2011) or return to homelessness (Wright & Devine, 1995) than individuals receiving standard care. Burnam et al. (1995) reported no group differences in time spent homeless between individuals living in single-site supportive housing and individuals accessing standard care services.

Lastly, individuals living in single-site supportive housing were found to have significantly higher satisfaction with their housing (Hwang et al., 2011) and individuals in shared transitional housing reported fewer problems with their living conditions (Siskind et al., 2014) compared with individuals receiving standard care.

Service Use

Studies that examined service use outcomes found few group differences and few reductions in service use for both individuals in single-site supportive housing and individuals receiving standard care. No group differences were reported in terms of decreased service use (Wright & Devine, 1995), healthcare use (Hwang et al., 2011), emergency department visits (Siskind et al., 2014), and use of specific services (e.g., ambulatory generalist care, primary care, ambulance services, inpatient hospitalizations, outpatient substance abuse services, and outpatient mental health services) (Kessell et al., 2006). Siskind et al. (2014) did find, however, that individuals living in single-site supportive housing of a transitional nature had a reduction in hospital bed-days compared with individuals receiving regular community mental health services.

Stecher et al. (1994) found that individuals in single-site supportive housing of a transitional nature for a period of 3 months were more likely to have psychiatric appointments, more discharge planning contacts, and a greater level of program engagement than individuals receiving nonresidential treatment services. On the other hand, individuals in nonresidential services were more likely to have a greater number of contacts with a housing worker, an employment worker, and a coordination of care service worker.

Clinical Functioning

Studies comparing the clinical functioning outcomes of participants in single-site supportive housing programs and nonresidential treatment in the community have produced mixed results. Two studies found similar levels of improvement in severity of psychiatric symptoms between individuals living in single-site supportive housing of a transitional nature and individuals receiving inpatient treatment followed by community services (Conrad et al., 1998) and individuals receiving standard care (Burnam et al., 1995). Other studies found no improvements in physical and mental health functioning associated with transitional single-site supportive housing, permanent single-site housing, or standard care (Hwang et al., 2011;

Siskind et al., 2014; Wright & Devine, 1995). In contrast, Conrad et al. (1998) found that individuals living in single-site supportive housing reported a reduction in medical problems overall compared with individuals receiving short-term inpatient treatment followed by community services including community halfway houses (Conrad et al., 1998).

In three studies, similar levels of improvement were apparent in reductions in alcohol and drug use over time between individuals living in transitional single-site supportive housing and those receiving standard care (Burnam et al., 1995; Schinka et al., 1998) or between individuals in permanent single-site supportive housing and standard care (Hwang et al., 2011). Conrad et al. (1998) found that individuals living in single-site supportive housing of a transitional nature had greater reductions in drug use than individuals receiving short-term inpatient treatment followed by community treatment. Other studies found no significant group differences when comparing improvement in drug use over time in single-site supportive housing versus usual care in the community (Hwang et al., 2011; Siskind et al., 2014), satellite transitional apartments with hospital treatment versus intensive 3 week inpatient program (Schinka et al., 1998) and detox program for 7 days and transitional residential treatment programs versus detox program and transitional residential treatment followed by extended independent living, and versus detox program with case management for 7 days (Wright & Devine, 1995).

Focusing on alcohol use, positive outcomes were reported regarding reductions in use for transitional residential care with a 12-step program and 6 months of case management in comparison with inpatient hospital treatment for 21 days (Conrad et al., 1998) and likelihood of relapse for previously described detox programs and transitional residential treatment compared to detox program alone (Wright & Devine, 1995). It should be noted that the significantly greater reductions in alcohol and drug use reported by Conrad et al. (1998) for the transitional residential care group compared with inpatient hospital treatment were only evident for the first 9 months, with these differences attenuated in subsequent follow-ups up to 24 months.

Community Adaptation

Overall single-site supportive housing was not associated with greater improvements in community adaptation, in comparison with nonresidential treatment or standard care. Studies examining legal issues (Conrad et al., 1998; Wright & Devine), life satisfaction (Hwang et al., 2011), and satisfaction with social relations (Hwang et al., 2011; Wright & Devine, 1995) all found no group differences between single-site supportive housing and nonresidential treatment or standard care. When considering employment, Conrad et al. (1998) reported that individuals living in transitional single-site housing had superior employment outcomes compared with individuals receiving inpatient treatment followed by community services, although both groups showed improvement on this outcome over time.

Summary

Overall, permanent single-site supportive housing and transitional single-site supportive housing produced similar levels of improvements in housing stability over time as nonresidential treatment or standard care. Differences in the reduction of homelessness and achievement of independent living favored single-site supportive housing in a couple of studies. No differences emerged in service use outcomes between single-site supportive housing and standard care, with either similar changes or no change with the exception of greater engagement in services in one study and a greater reduction in days in hospital over time in another study for individuals in single-site supportive housing.

Mixed results emerged in comparing the clinical functioning outcomes of single-site supportive housing and nonresidential treatment or standard care, with either both types of services showing improvement, notably in mental health functioning and substance use; single-site supportive housing demonstrating greater improvements in alcohol use; or no changes in this area and no improvements for either single-site supportive housing and comparison services across the full range of clinical functioning outcomes. Finally, comparison of single-site supportive housing with other nonresidential services or standard care yielded either similar levels of improvement or no change in terms of community adaptation outcomes.

Synthesized Summary of Findings

Overall, housing outcomes (in terms of the ability to get and keep housing) were consistently better for individuals in scattered-site supportive housing with ICM or ACT when compared with individuals who were receiving ICM or ACT without housing. When they were examined, mixed results were found on nonhousing outcomes in the areas of service use, clinical functioning, and community adaptation. In particular, either individuals in scattered-site supportive housing combined with ICM or ACT showed better outcomes in these areas compared with individuals receiving ICM or ACT alone or there were no differences.

For the most part, studies found tenants in scattered-site supportive housing with ICM or ACT and tenants in single-site housing with on-site support showing similar outcomes. Tenants in both types of housing programs achieved similar housing outcomes and reported similar improvements in life satisfaction.

Research has found that the combination of scattered-site supportive housing with ICM or ACT yields better housing outcomes than standard care in the community or residential continuum housing. However, mixed findings are evident for nonhousing outcomes, with either no differences in level of improvement over time or results that favor scattered-site supportive housing with ICM or ACT over standard care and residential continuum housing in terms of clinical functioning and community adaptation outcomes.

Finally, single-site supportive housing, whether permanent or transitional in nature, showed similar housing and nonhousing outcomes as nonresidential treatment or standard care, with findings from two studies favoring single-site supportive housing over comparison groups in terms of housing outcomes and service use outcomes.

Limitations of the Research

Although there is growing body of research literature on the outcomes of combining housing with various forms of support, a number of limitations characterize the research that has been conducted. A significant limitation is the range of program models that have been studied (Tabol et al., 2010). As a result of this variation, it is difficult to compare study findings. This is particularly the case with the research on single-site supportive housing. Related to this variation is the lack of any assessment of program fidelity in most of the research that has been conducted. It is only very recently that a fidelity tool for the combination of scattered-site supportive housing with ACT or ICM has been developed (Stefancic, Tsemberis, Messeri, Drake, & Goering, 2013).

A further limitation to the research conducted to date is the wide range of services to which the combination of housing and support is compared in the studies. Some of these services are termed "standard care" or "residential continuum services"; however, they are not described in much detail and it can be expected that they will vary greatly depending on the services that have been developed and are available in different contexts. This limitation makes it difficult comparing the findings of studies and interpreting where there are differences in outcomes.

The narrow range of outcomes in the studies to date with a heavy focus on housing outcomes is also a limitation. Although housing outcomes can be considered a primary outcome for most of programs combining housing and support, since they target the resolution of homelessness, there is a broader agenda attached to the support services that includes facilitating community integration and recovery and improving quality of life (Tsemberis, 2010). However, as detailed in this review, only a small number of studies have investigated these nonhousing outcomes and the findings that emerge are not clear or conclusive. A further issue related to interpreting the nonhousing outcomes is the relatively short period of follow-up of most of the studies (i.e., 24 months or less) when examining these outcomes.

Finally, there is only one study that compares scattered-site supportive housing and single-site supportive housing (McHugo et al., 2004), and the interpretability of its findings are complicated by the fact that individuals living in scattered-site supportive housing received ACT while those in single-site housing received ICM.

Future Research Directions

In line with these limitations, we propose a number of future research directions to advance the state of knowledge in this area. There is a need for future research to define the housing and support ingredients in a systematic way for single-site supportive housing. The development and testing of a fidelity scale for this purpose, similar to the recent fidelity scale created for scattered-site supportive housing (Stefancic et al., 2013), is recommended. Related to defining fidelity, it would be worthwhile to develop research examining the relationship of program fidelity to outcomes.

More generally, there is a need for more research on the effectiveness of single-site housing that offers on-site support. This should include future research comparing the outcomes of single-site supportive housing with scattered-site supportive housing as well as comparisons of single-site supportive housing with standard care in the community. As well, more research on the effectiveness of transitional single-site supportive housing relative to permanent single-site supportive housing is necessary.

It would also appear worthwhile for future research to specifically compare the effectiveness of scattered-site supportive housing with ACT and scattered-site supportive housing with ICM. As mentioned, the one study comparing the combination of housing with these two approaches to support examined scattered-site supportive housing with ACT and single-site supportive housing with ICM. Research suggests that combining housing with ACT yields larger effects on housing outcomes than housing with ICM (Nelson, Aubry, & LaFrance, 2007), but no single study has yet investigated this issue.

There is also a need for future research that examines support services that target specific nonhousing outcomes. To date, the support services have been generic, producing inconsistent and at best only modest positive nonhousing outcomes. This suggests that programs combining housing and support that specifically target issues like employment, education, addictions, and social support should be studied. Related to this issue, future research in the area should as much as possible include a wide range of what have become outcomes of interest in examining mental health programs such as community integration, quality of life, and recovery.

Future research examining the effectiveness of combined housing and support programs should also build in to its design longer follow-up periods. This would allow for an examination of longer-term housing outcomes as well as whether or not housing stability over time produces improvements in nonhousing outcomes such as community integration, quality of life, and recovery. Longer follow-up periods would also allow for developing a better understanding of nonresponders to combined housing and support approaches. Findings of research to date suggest that up to 20% of individuals receiving scattered-site supportive housing combined with either ACT or ICM fail to establish housing stability (e.g., O'Connell et al., 2008; Tsemberis & Eisenberg, 2000). However, it is unknown at this point what personal and situational factors play a role in these negative housing outcomes.

Finally, given that virtually all of the research on combined housing and support approaches has been conducted in the United States, there is a need for more international research. The recently completed multicity trial in Canada, of which the results are reported in this review, and a multicity trial currently being conducted in France, both on combined scattered-site supportive housing and support, will provide important new knowledge on its effectiveness in different contexts (Goering et al., 2012).

Conclusion

Findings on the effectiveness of the combination of scattered-site supportive housing with ACT or ICM in helping individuals exit homelessness over the past 10 years are producing a paradigm shift across North America and in Europe (Busch-Geertsema, 2014; Gaetz, 2010; Stanhope & Dunn, 2011). In particular, they are moving mental health and social service systems to adopt "Housing First" approaches as opposed to "Treatment First" before individuals with severe mental illness can leave homelessness to enter independent regular housing in the community. There is a clear need to develop more of these programs given that they represent the type of housing and support that a majority of consumers prefer (Nelson, Hall, & Forchuk, 2003; Piat et al., 2008; Tanzman, 1993).

At the same time, single-site supportive housing with on-site support remains the most common type of supportive housing because of the lengthier history of this model, with its origin beginning shortly after deinstitutionalization. It is also an option that some consumers prefer because of the social contact, structure, and security associated with it (Nelson et al., 2003; Piat et al., 2008; see also chapter 6, this volume). As well, both transitional and permanent housing with on-site support are needed to complement scattered-site supportive housing for individuals who are unable to manage the demands associated with this latter approach. At this point, it is difficult to predict which individuals will encounter trouble living in scattered-site supportive housing with support (Volk et al., 2016).

References

Appel, P.W., Tsemberis, S., Joseph, H., Stefancic, A., & Lambert-Wacey, D. (2012). Housing First for severely mentally ill homeless methadone patients. *Journal of Addictive Diseases, 31*, 270–277.

Aubry, T., Ecker, J., & Jetté, J. (2014). Supported housing as a promising Housing First approach for people with severe and persistent mental illness. In M. Guirguis, R. MacNeil, &

S. Hwang (Eds.), *Homelessness and health in Canada* (pp. 155–188). Ottawa, ON: University of Ottawa Press.

Aubry, T., Goering, P., Veldhuizen, S., Adair, C.E., Bourque, J., Distasio, J., . . . Tsemberis, S. (2016). A multiple-city RCT of Housing First with assertive community treatment for homeless Canadians with serious mental illness. *Psychiatric Services, 67,* 275–281.

Aubry, T., Tsemberis, S., Adair, C.E., Veldhuizen, S., Streiner, D., Latimer, E., . . . Goering, P. (2015). One-year outcomes of a randomized controlled trial of Housing First with ACT in five Canadian cities. *Psychiatric Services, 66,* 463–469.

Basu, A., Kee, R., Buchanan, D., & Sadowski, L.S. (2012). Comparative cost analysis of housing and case management program for chronically ill homeless adults compared to usual care. *Health Services Research, 47,* 523–543.

Blanch, A.K., Carling, P., & Ridgway, P. (1988). Normal housing with specialized supports: A psychiatric rehabilitation approach to living in the community. *Rehabilitation Psychology, 33,* 47–55.

Bond, G.R., McDonel, E.C., Miller, L.D., & Pensec, M. (1991). Assertive community treatment and reference groups: An evaluation of their effectiveness for young adults with serious mental illness and substance abuse problems. *Psychosocial Rehabilitation Journal, 15,* 31–43.

Burnam, M.A., Morton, S.C., McGlynn, E.A., Petersen, L.P., Stecher, B.M., Hayes, C., & Vaccaro, J.V. (1995). An experimental evaluation of residential and nonresidential treatment for dually diagnosed homeless adults. *Journal of Addictive Diseases, 14,* 111–134.

Busch-Geertsema, V. (2014). Housing first Europe: Results of a European social experimentation project. *European Journal of Homelessness, 8,* 13–28.

Caplan, B., Schutt, R.K., Turner, W.M., Goldfinger, S.M., & Seidman, L.J. (2006). Change in neuro-cognition by housing type and substance abuse among formerly homeless seriously mentally ill persons. *Schizophrenia Research, 83,* 77–86.

Carling, P.J. (1993). Housing and supports for persons with mental illness: Emerging approaches to research and practice. *Hospital and Community Psychiatry, 44,* 439–449.

Carling, P.J. (1995). *Return to community: Building support systems for people with psychiatric disabilities.* New York: Guilford Press.

Cheng, A., Lin, H., Kasprow, W., & Rosenheck, R.A. (2007). Impact of supported housing on clinical outcomes: Analysis of a randomized trial using multiple imputation technique. *Journal of Nervous and Mental Disease, 195,* 83–88.

Clark, C., & Rich, A.R. (2003). Outcomes of homeless adults with mental illness in a housing program and in case management only. *Psychiatric Services, 54,* 78–83.

Coldwell, C.M., & Bender, W.S. (2007). The effectiveness of assertive community treatment for homeless populations with severe mental illness: A meta-analysis. *American Journal of Psychiatry, 164,* 393–399.

Conrad, K.J., Hultman, C.I., Pope, A.R., Lyons, J.S., Baxter, W.C., Daghestani, A.N., . . . Manheim, L.M. (1998). Case managed residential care for homeless addicted veterans: Results of a true experiment. *Medical Care, 36,* 40–53.

Dickey, B., Gonzalez, O., Latimer, E., & Powers, K. (1996). Use of mental health services by formerly homeless adults residing in group and independent housing. *Psychiatric Services, 47,* 152–158.

Dieterich, M., Irving, C.B., Park, B., & Marshall, M. (2010). Intensive case management for severe mental illness. *Cochrane Database of Systematic Reviews, 10.*

Franklin, J.L., Solovitz, B., Mason, M., Clemons, J.R., & Miller, G.E. (1987). An evaluation of case management. *American Journal of Public Health, 77,* 674–678.

Gabrielian, S., Yuan, A., Andersen, R.M., Rubenstein, L.V., & Gelberg, L. (2014). VA health service utilization for homeless and low-income veterans: A spotlight on the VA Supportive Housing (VASH) program in greater Los Angeles. *Medical Care, 52,* 454–461.

Gaetz, S. (2010). The struggle to end homelessness in Canada: How we created the crisis, and how we can end it. *Open Health Services and Policy Journal, 3*, 21–26.

Gilmer, T.P., Stefancic, A., Ettner, S.L., Manning, W.G., & Tsemberis, S. (2010). Effect of full-service partnerships on homelessness, use and costs of mental health services, and quality of life among adults with serious mental illness. *Archives of General Psychiatry, 67*, 645–652.

Goering, P., Girard, V., Aubry, T., Barker, J., Fortanier, C., Latimer, E., ... Tinland, A. (2012). Conduite d'essais relatifs aux politiques qui soutiennent le modèle d'intervention accordant la priorité au logement: L'histoire de deux pays. *Lien Social et Politique, 67*, 161–182.

Goering, P.N., Wasylenki, D.A., Farkas, M., Lancee, W.J., & Ballantyne, R. (1988). What difference does case management make? *Hospital and Community Psychiatry, 39*, 272–276.

Goldfinger, S.M., Schutt, R.K., Tolomiczenko, G.S., Seidman, L., Penk, W.E., Turner, W., & Caplan, B. (1999). Housing placement and subsequent days homeless among formerly homeless adults with mental illness. *Psychiatric Services, 50*, 674–679.

Greenwood, R.M., Schaefer-McDaniel, N.J., Winkel, G., & Tsemberis, S.J. (2005). Decreasing psychiatric symptoms by increasing choice in services for adults with histories of homelessness. *American Journal of Community Psychology, 36*, 223–238.

Gulcur, L., Stefancic, A., Shinn, M., Tsemberis, S., & Fischer, S.N. (2003). Housing, hospitalization, and cost outcomes for homeless individuals with psychiatric disabilities participating in continuum of care and Housing First programmes. *Journal of Community and Applied Social Psychology, 13*, 171–186.

Gulcur, L., Tsemberis, S., Stefancic, A., & Greenwood, R.M. (2007). Community integration of adults with psychiatric disabilities and histories of homelessness. *Community Mental Health Journal, 43*, 211–228.

Hurlburt, M.S., Hough, R.L., & Wood, P.A. (1996). Effects of substance abuse on housing stability of homeless mentally ill persons in supported housing. *Psychiatric Services, 47*, 731–736.

Hurlburt, M.S., Wood. P.A., & Hough, R.L. (1996). Providing independent housing for the homeless mentally ill: A novel approach to evaluating long-term longitudinal housing patterns. *Journal of Community Psychology, 24*, 291–310.

Hwang, S.W., Gogosis, E., Chambers, C., Dunn, J.R., Hoch, J.S., & Aubry, T. (2011). Health status, quality of life, residential stability, substance use, and health care utilization among adults applying to a supportive housing program. *Journal of Urban Health: Bulletin of the New York Academy of Medicine, 88*, 1076–1090.

Intagliata, J. (1982). Improving the quality of community care for the chronically mentally disabled: The role of case management. *Schizophrenia Bulletin, 8*, 655–674.

Kessell, E.R., Bhatia, R., Bamberger, J.D., & Kushel, M.B. (2006). Public health care utilization in a cohort of homeless adult applicants to a supportive housing program. *Journal of Urban Health: Bulletin of the New York Academy of Medicine, 83*, 860–873.

McGrew, J.H., Bond, G.R., Dietzen, L., & Salyers, M. (1994). Measuring the fidelity of implementation of a mental health program model. *Journal of Consulting and Clinical Psychology, 62*, 670–678.

McHugo, G.J., Bebout, R.R., Harris, M., Cleghorn, S., Herring, G., Xie, H., ... Drake, R.E. (2004). A randomized controlled trial of integrated versus parallel housing services for homeless adults with severe mental illness. *Schizophrenia Bulletin, 30*, 969–982.

Modrcin, M., Rapp, C., & Poertner, J. (1988). The evaluation of case management services with the chronically mentally ill. *Evaluation and Program Planning, 11*, 307–314.

Monroe-DeVita, M., Teague, G.B., & Moser, L.L. (2011). The TMACT: A new tool for measuring fidelity to assertive community treatment. *Journal of the American Psychiatric Nurses Association, 17*, 17–29.

Montgomery, A.E., Hill, L.L., Kane, V., & Culhane, D.P. (2013). Housing chronically homeless veterans: Evaluating the efficacy of a housing first approach to HUD-VASH. *Journal of Community Psychology, 41*, 505–514.

Nelson, G. (2010). Housing for people with serious mental illness: Approaches, evidence, and transformative change. *Journal of Sociology and Social Welfare, 37,* 123–146.

Nelson, G., Aubry, T., & Lafrance, A. (2007). A review of the literature on the effectiveness of housing and support, assertive community treatment, and intensive case management interventions for persons with mental illness who have been homeless. *American Journal of Orthopsychiatry, 77,* 350–361.

Nelson, G., Hall, G.B., & Forchuk, C. (2003). Current and preferred housing of psychiatric consumer/survivors. *Canadian Journal of Community Mental Health, 22,* 5–19.

Nelson, G., Stefancic, A., Rae, J., Townley, G., Tsemberis, S., McNaughton, E., & Goering, P. (2014). Early implementation evaluation of a multi-site housing first intervention for homeless people with mental illness: A mixed methods approach. *Evaluation and Program Planning, 43,* 16–26.

O'Connell, M.J., Kasprow, W., & Rosenheck, R.A. (2008). Rates and risk factors for homelessness after successful housing in a sample of formerly homeless veterans. *Psychiatric Services, 59,* 268–275.

O'Connell, M.J., Kasprow, W., & Rosenheck, R. (2009). Direct placement versus multistage models of supported housing in a population of veterans who are homeless. *Psychological Services, 6,* 190–201.

O'Connell, M.J., Kasprow, W., & Rosenheck, R.A. (2012). Differential impact of supported housing on selected subgroups of homeless veterans with substance abuse histories. *Psychiatric Services, 63,* 1195–1205.

Olfson, M. (1990). Assertive community treatment: An evaluation of the experimental evidence. *Hospital and Community Psychiatry, 41,* 649–651.

Ontario Ministry of Health and Long-Term Care. (2005). *Intensive case management standards for mental health services and supports.* Toronto, ON: Authors.

Padgett, D.K., Gulcur, L., & Tsemberis, S. (2006). Housing First services for people who are homeless with co-occurring serious mental illness and substance use. *Research on Social Work Practice, 16,* 74–83.

Padgett, D.K., Stanhope, V., Henwood, B.F., & Stefancic, A. (2011). Substance use outcomes among homeless clients with serious mental illness: Comparing Housing First with Treatment First programs. *Community Mental Health Journal, 47,* 227–232.

Parkinson, S., Nelson, G., & Horgan, S. (1999). From housing to homes: A review of the literature on housing approaches for psychiatric consumers/survivors. *Canadian Journal of Community Mental Health, 18,* 145–164.

Patterson, M., Moniruzzaman, A., Palepu, A., Zabkiewicz, D., Frankish, C.J., Krausz, M., & Somers, J.M. (2013). Housing First improves subjective quality of life among homeless adults with mental illness: 12-month findings from a randomized controlled trial in Vancouver, British Columbia. *Social Psychiatry and Psychiatric Epidemiology, 48,* 1245–1259.

Patterson, M.L., Moniruzzaman, A., & Somers, J.M. (2014). Community participation and belonging among formerly homeless adults with mental illness after 12 months of Housing First in Vancouver, British Columbia: A randomized controlled trial. *Community Mental Health Journal, 50,* 604–611.

Pearson, C., Montgomery, A.E., & Locke, G. (2009). Housing stability among homeless individuals with serious mental illness participating in Housing First programs. *Journal of Community Psychology, 37,* 404–417.

Piat, M., Lesage, A., Boyer, R., Dorvil, H., Courure, A., Grenier, G., & Bloom D. (2008). Housing for persons with serious mental illness: Consumer and service provider preferences. *Psychiatric Services, 59,* 1011–1017.

Ridgway, P., & Zipple, A.M. (1990). Challenges and strategies for implementing supported housing. *Psychosocial Rehabilitation Journal, 13,* 115–120.

Rosenheck, R., Kasprow, W., Frisman, L., & Liu-Mares, W. (2003). Cost-effectiveness of supported housing for homeless persons with mental illness. *Archives of General Psychiatry, 60,* 940–951.

Sadowski, L.S., Kee, R.A., VanderWeele, T.J., & Buchanan, D. (2009). Effect of a housing and case management program on emergency department visits and hospitalizations among chronically ill homeless adults: A randomized trial. *Journal of the American Medical Association, 301,* 1771–1778.

Schinka, J.A., Francis, E., Hughes, P., LaLone, L., & Flynn, C. (1998). Comparative outcomes and costs of inpatient care and supportive housing for substance-dependent veterans. *Psychiatric Services, 49,* 946–950.

Seidman, L.J., Schutt, R.K., Caplan, B., Tolomiczenko, G.S., Turner, W.M., & Goldfinger, S.M. (2003). The effect of housing interventions on neuropsychological functioning among homeless persons with mental illness. *Psychiatric Services, 54,* 905–908.

Siskind, D., Harris, M., Kisely, S., Siskind, V., Brogan, J., Pirkis, J., . . . Whiteford, H. (2014). A retrospective quasi-experimental study of a transitional housing program for patients with severe and persistent mental illness. *Community Mental Health Journal, 50,* 538–547.

Somers, J.M., Rezansoff, S.N., Moniruzzaman, A., Palepu, A., & Patterson, M. (2013). Housing First reduces re-offending among formerly homeless adults with mental disorders: Results of a randomized controlled trial. *PLoS ONE, 8,* e72946.

Stanhope, V., & Dunn, K. (2011). The curious case of Housing First: The limits of evidence based policy. *International Journal of Law and Psychiatry, 34,* 275–282.

Stecher, B.M., Andrews, C.A., McDonald, L., Morton, S.C., McGlynn, E.A., Petersen, L.P., . . . Vaccaro, J.V. (1994). Implementation of residential and nonresidential treatment for the dually diagnosed homeless. *Evaluation Review, 18,* 689–717.

Stefancic, A., & Tsemberis, S. (2007). Housing First for long-term shelter dwellers with psychiatric disabilities in a suburban county: A four-year study of housing access and retention. *Journal of Primary Prevention, 28,* 265–279.

Stefancic, A., Tsemberis, S., Messeri, P., Drake, R., & Goering, P. (2013). The Pathways housing first fidelity scale for individuals with psychiatric disabilities. *American Journal of Psychiatric Rehabilitation, 16,* 240–261.

Stein, L.I., & Test, M.A. (1980). An alternative to mental heath treatment: I. Conceptual model, treatment program, and clinical evaluation. *Archives of General Psychiatry, 37,* 392–397.

Stergiopoulos, V., Hwang, S.W., Gozdzik, A., Nisenbaum, R., Latimer, E., Rabouin, D., . . . Goering, P.N. (2015). Effect of scattered-site housing using rent supplements and intensive case management on housing stability among homeless adults with mental illness: A randomized trial. *Journal of the American Medical Association, 313,* 905–915.

Tabol, C., Drebing, C., & Rosenheck, R. (2010). Studies of "supported" and "supportive" housing: A comprehensive review of model descriptions and measurement. *Evaluation and Program Planning, 33,* 446–456.

Tanzman, B. (1993). An overview of surveys of mental health consumers' preferences for housing and support services. *Hospital and Community Psychiatry, 44,* 450–455.

Teague, G.B., Bond, G.R., & Drake, R.E. (1998). Program fidelity in assertive community treatment: Development and use of a measure. *American Journal of Orthopsychiatry, 68,* 216–232.

Trainor, J.N. (2008). Housing and the development of a personal resource base. In J.F. Pelletier, M. Piat, S. Côte, & H. Dorvil (Eds.), *Hébergement, logement et rétablissement en santé mental* (pp. 33–51). Boisbriand, QC: Prologue.

Trainor, J.N., Morrell Bellai, T.L., Ballantyne, R., & Boydell, K.M. (1993). Housing for people with mental illnesses: A comparison of models and an examination of the growth of alternative housing in Canada. *Canadian Journal of Psychiatry/La Revue Canadienne De Psychiatrie, 38,* 494–501.

Tsemberis, S. (1999). From streets to homes: An innovative approach to supported housing for homeless adults with psychiatric disabilities. *Journal of Community Psychology, 27,* 225–241.

Tsemberis, S. (2010). *Housing First: The Pathways model to end homelessness for people with mental illness and addiction.* Center City, MN: Hazelden.

Tsemberis, S., & Eisenberg, R.F. (2000). Pathways to housing: Supported housing for street-dwelling homeless individuals with psychiatric disabilities. *Psychiatric Services, 51,* 487–493.

Tsemberis, S., Gulcur, L., & Nakae, M. (2004). Housing First, consumer choice, and harm reduction for homeless individuals with a dual diagnosis. *American Journal of Public Health, 94,* 651–656.

Tsemberis, S.J., Moran, L., Sinn, M., Asmussen, S.M., & Shern, D.L. (2003). Consumer preference programs for individuals who are homeless and have psychiatric disabilities: A drop-in center and a supported housing program. *American Journal of Community Psychology, 32,* 305–317.

Volk, J., Aubry, T., Goering, P., Adair, C.E., Distasio, J., Jette, J., . . . Tsemberis, S. (2016). Tenants with additional needs: When Housing First does not solve homelessness. *Journal of Mental Health, 25,* 169–175.

Wood, P.A., Hurlburt, M.S., Hough, R.L., & Hofstetter, C.R. (1998). Longitudinal assessment of family support among homeless mentally ill participants in a supported housing program. *Journal of Community Psychology, 26,* 327–344.

Wright, J.D., & Devine, J.A. (1995). Factors that interact with treatment to predict outcomes in substance abuse programs for the homeless. *Journal of Addictive Diseases, 14,* 169–181.

4

Economic Analysis of Housing Interventions for People with Serious Mental Illness Who Are Homeless

A Review of the Literature

TIM AUBRY, JENNIFER RAE, AND JONATHAN JETTÉ

Economic analysis is especially important when demand for services is large and resources are limited. This is certainly the case for healthcare in general and community mental health services more specifically, including as it applies to housing and support services. Given the scarcity of available resources for community mental health services, difficult decisions often have to be made about where to allocate funds.

As outlined by Drummond, Sculpher, Torrance, O'Brien, and Stoddart (2005), when determining which housing and support programs to invest in, economic analysis is useful for three reasons. First, economic evaluation involves a useful analysis of a range of programs and services. When a new program is under consideration, the economic costs and benefits are not simply evaluated in isolation, but instead are systematically compared to relevant alternative programs, offering a more rigorous standard against which the new program is compared before being considered economically worthwhile. Second, economic evaluation is useful because it can be conducted from a variety of different analytic viewpoints. Costs and outcomes can be examined from perspectives ranging from the individual to the societal, and anything in between, allowing for a more comprehensive understanding of a given program based on the inclusion or exclusion of various costing components. Third, economic evaluation is useful because it reduces the uncertainty around the value for money that a program provides. This is accomplished by examining the real cost of a program, including not only the dollars spent on the program but also the value of benefits achieved by the program in comparison to the foregone benefits that could have been achieved by other programs had they been invested in to a similar extent.

In the field of community mental health, agencies have been tasked with demonstrating that community-based services are more cost-effective than traditional institutional-based services. To do so, comprehensive costing methods have been used. It is not enough to simply measure direct service costs. The work of Knapp and Beecham (1990) suggests that indirect program costs must also be considered, including agency costs, costs to the client, costs to the family, and costs to society. Indirect program contributions, such as a client's volunteer work or employment, should be considered as well.

In the case of housing interventions, a comprehensive costing analysis includes the consideration of the health, social, and economic impacts associated with poor housing, poverty, and homelessness. The cost of a housing intervention may be contrasted with the cost of crisis and emergency services, including day programs, emergency shelters, policing, jails, ambulance trips, and hospital beds (Gaetz, 2012; Shapcott, 2007). Economic analysis may be particularly relevant for housing interventions because of the sheer amount of money being spent. Housing interventions are expensive: Yearly costs per person for supportive and transitional housing are usually in the tens of thousands of dollars (Pomeroy, 2005).

In the interest of fiscal responsibility, it is understandable that funders wish to be prudent about where to spend such significant amounts of money. Of course, the cost of doing nothing is no small matter: In Canada for example, the annual cost of homelessness is estimated at $7 billion (Gaetz, Donaldson, Richter, & Gulliver, 2013). In this high-stakes context, economic analysis can provide guidance as to how best to allocate limited resources to produce the best possible outcomes.

In this chapter, we examine the economic evidence pertaining to housing interventions as a component of the community mental health system. We review a body of research that addresses the economic impact of providing stable, high-quality housing for people with severe and persistent mental illness. To set the context for the review of the literature, we first provide a brief primer on costing and economic analysis in healthcare. Subsequently, we describe the method we used for the review of the literature on housing interventions for people with severe and persistent mental illness. Finally, we present a synthesized summary of the findings emerging from the literature, including a discussion of limitations, implications, and directions for future research.

Overview of Economic Analysis

We begin by introducing some of the basic concepts of economic analysis. We first present the various economic perspectives that can be adopted, then describe the ways in which costs can be estimated, and finally, we provide a brief overview of some of the different types of economic analysis available. A more comprehensive examination of economic analysis in the field of health has been previously presented by Drummond and his colleagues (2005).

Economic Perspectives

When an economic analysis of an intervention is undertaken, it is essential to first define the economic perspective being used. Different perspectives include different costing components, depending on the interests of the stakeholders involved. For example, stakeholders from a particular agency offering a supportive housing intervention could be interested in a narrow, program-level perspective. This perspective would include only those costs of the intervention that are directly related to the agency itself, such as salary, overhead, and capital cost. A broader, more inclusive perspective would be a healthcare system-level perspective, which would account for intervention-related costs like hospital stays, emergency room visits, ambulance use, and visits with health professionals like doctors, nurses, and dentists. A societal-level perspective would be broader still, and would theoretically include all possible costs and savings related to the intervention. In summary, the economic perspective serves as a guideline used to determine which different costing components should be included in the calculation.

Estimating Costs

Program costs can be calculated in terms of inputs and opportunity costs. The inputs are the different resources used by the program to produce outputs and, ultimately, outcomes. A unit refers to a single way to calculate the important results achieved by a program. For example, a unit could be one night of shelter, one meal served at a soup kitchen, or one visit to an emergency room. There are two main approaches to calculating unit costs: the bottom-up approach and the top-down approach (Chapko, Liu, Perkins, Li Fortney, & Maciejewski, 2009). The simplest scenario in the top-down approach consists of an organization that provides only one type of service (such as emergency shelter). In this scenario, the organization's total budget is divided by the total number of units it provides. When an organization provides more than one type of service, the total budget can be divided by areas of service, and then divided by the number of units provided under each of these areas (Chapko et al., 2009). In the bottom-up approach (also called activity-based costing) costs are estimated by first assessing the amount of resources that are used to deliver a particular service—known as a unit cost—and then assigning costs to the amount of services provided by multiplying the number of services by the unit cost (e.g., number of emergency room visits multiplied by cost per emergency room visit) (Chapko et al., 2009). In a recent study, Chapko and his colleagues (2009) calculated various costs using both top-down and bottom-up methodologies. They found that the Pearson correlation between the two approaches was $r = .85$ for total annual healthcare-related costs.

Types of Economic Analysis

The various types of economic analysis differ in two key ways: (1) whether the analysis involves a comparison of two or more alternative programs, and (2) whether both cost (inputs) and consequences (outputs) of alternative programs are examined.

Cost Comparison Analysis

The cost analysis type of economic analysis is also called cost-saving, cost offset, or cost comparison analysis. For the purpose of this chapter, we use the term "cost comparison analysis." This type of analysis presents the cost differences between two different programs. The total costs of the program of interest are compared with those of another program, or with treatment as usual in the community. In addition to comparing direct program-related costs, this analysis may include a comparison of the cost of services used by participants beyond the program itself. For example, these outside service costs could include court costs, healthcare costs, or funding transfer costs.

Cost-Effectiveness Analysis

In cost-effectiveness analysis, the inputs and outcomes of the program are linked together (Drummond et al., 2005). In other words, cost-effectiveness studies account for both the costs and the outcomes of more than one treatment option, and make comparisons between the two. Cost-effectiveness analysis involves calculating a cost-effectiveness ratio comparing a treatment group (intervention) to a comparison group (different intervention or treatment as usual). The ratio is calculated by comparing the difference in costs of both interventions and dividing this result by any differences in their level of effectiveness in terms of a particular standardized outcome. For example, in the case of the cost-effectiveness of a housing program, a standard care program could cost $100 and produce 10 nights of stable housing. In contrast, the comparison treatment program could cost $200 and produce 15 nights of stable housing. In this example, the incremental cost to produce one additional night of stable housing would be $20 [($200–$100)/(15–10)].

Literature Search Method

We conducted an electronic literature search using the PsycINFO and MEDLINE databases. We used the keywords "homeless" or "housing," "supported" or "supportive," and "cost" or "economic." We expanded our search by examining the references of each article, as well as a list of any other authors citing it. Only peer-reviewed, published studies were considered eligible: gray literature was not examined.

The selection of eligible studies emerging from the literature search was based on the following criteria: (1) The study focused on individuals who received some form of housing and support, (2) the study reported at least some findings related to costs, (3) the study involved a comparison of two groups of individuals receiving different forms of housing and/or support services.

Through our review of the literature, we identified 16 studies matching our inclusion criteria. We summarize the findings of studies comparing scattered-site supportive housing to treatment as usual or to other types of services ($n = 6$), single-site supportive housing to treatment as usual ($n = 2$), and cost studies on other combinations of housing and support ($n = 8$). We further organize the studies according to the different costing perspectives they adopted, which was dependent on the costing components the authors included in their calculations. Table 4.1 details the different perspectives, all of the potential costing components that could be included under each perspective, and the minimum number of costing components that a study had to include in order for us to consider it to have adopted each perspective.

Findings

The findings of our literature review are presented below. The Appendix to this chapter presents detailed information about the reviewed studies, including the costing findings. The studies are grouped according to the types of programs that were compared.

Cost Comparisons of Scattered-Site Supportive Housing and Treatment as Usual

We begin by presenting our review of six studies comparing scattered-site supportive housing and treatment as usual or other types of services.

Description of Studies

Table 4.2 presents those studies that report the findings of economic analyses comparing scattered-site supportive housing to treatment as usual (Aubry et al., 2016; Gilmer et al., 2010; Gulcur, Stefancic, Shinn, Tsemberis, & Fischer, 2003; Rosenheck, Kasprow, Frisman, & Liu-Mares, 2003; Siskind et al., 2014; Stergiopoulos et al., 2015). Four of the studies used an experimental design (Aubry et al., 2016, Gulcur et al., 2003; Rosenheck et al., 2003; Stergiopoulos et al., 2015), while two studies used a quasi-experimental design (Gilmer et al., 2010; Siskind et al., 2014). Of this group, one study included a cost-effectiveness analysis (Rosenheck et al., 2003), while the remainder involved cost comparison analyses. The costing perspectives in the studies ranged from narrow program-level costing (Siskind et al., 2014) to

Table 4.1 **Different Costing Perspectives Used in Economic Analysis Research**

Perspective	Potential Costing Components Included	Minimum Costing Components Included to Be Considered of That Perspective
Program Perspective	• Program costs	• Program costs
Physical Healthcare System Perspective	• Hospitalization • Emergency visit • Outpatient services and treatment • Medical services and treatment in community • Surgical intervention • Supportive housing • Group home • Nursing home	• Emergency room visits • Outpatient services and treatment • Hospitalization
Mental Healthcare System Perspective	• Mental health treatment • Substance use treatment • Mental health hospitalization • Psychiatric emergency services • Mobile crisis services	• Mental health treatment • Substance use treatment
Governmental Perspective[1]	• Jail • Mental health treatment in jail • Rent supplement • Residential treatment • Emergency shelter	• Jail • Emergency shelter
Societal Perspective[1]	• Transfer payments • Earnings from employment	• Earnings from employment

[1]Includes components from above costing perspectives.

comprehensive societal-level costing (Aubry et al., 2016; Rosenheck et al., 2003; Stergiopoulos et al., 2015). All of the studies compared scattered-site supportive housing to treatment as usual with the exception of Siskind and his colleagues (2014), who compared scattered-site supportive housing to inpatient mental healthcare.

Table 4.2 Descriptive Characteristics and Findings of Costing Studies Comparing Scattered-Site Supportive Housing vs. Treatment as Usual or Other Types of Services (N = 6)

Authors & Year	Study Design & Intervention	Type of Costing, Perspective, & Source of Service Use Data	Statistically Significant Findings
Aubry et al. (2016)	Experimental (Randomized Controlled Trial) *Group A:* (N = 469) Scattered site supportive housing with Assertive Community Treatment (ACT) support *Group B:* (N = 481) Treatment as Usual *Inclusion Criteria:* Serious mental illness, absolutely homeless or precariously housed, with high needs	Cost Comparison Analysis, Societal Perspective Client Self-Report	Statistical comparisons of costs not reported *Summary Statement:* "On average, Housing First with ACT services [Group A] cost CAD $22,257 per participant annually. Taking into account use of health, social, and justice services, Housing First produced an average net cost offset of CAD $21,367 per participant per year, or 96% of the cost of the intervention. The most important cost offsets were office visits, hospitalizations for physical health conditions, emergency shelter, home visits, and incarceration."
Gilmer et al. (2010)	Quasi-Experimental *Group A* (N = 209) Scattered site supportive housing with ACT support *Group B* (N = 154) Treatment As Usual	Cost Comparison Analysis, Physical Health Care & Mental Health Care Systems Perspective Program Staff Self-Report, Administrative Records	*Significantly Higher Costs:* (Group A) Outpatient mental health costs, housing costs *Significantly Lower Costs:* (Group A) Inpatient mental health costs, emergency mental health service costs, jail mental health service costs

(continued)

Table 4.2 Continued

Authors & Year	Study Design & Intervention	Type of Costing, Perspective, & Source of Service Use Data	Statistically Significant Findings
	Inclusion Criteria: Homeless, Severe Mental Illness		*Summary Statement*: "[Among FSP participants (Group A)] Outpatient costs increased by $9180; inpatient costs declined by $6882; emergency service costs declined by $1721; jail mental health services costs declined by $1641; and housing costs increased by $3180 (p. 003 each)." Overall difference found supportive housing consuming $2,116 more per year of mental health services than treatment as usual (not significantly different).
Gulcur et al. (2003)	Experimental (Randomized Controlled Trial) *Group A*: (*N* = 99) Scattered site supportive housing with ACT support *Group B*: (*N* = 126) Treatment As Usual (Continuum of Care) *Inclusion Criteria*: Homeless (shelter or hospitalization), Axis I diagnosis of mental illness (except personality disorders and developmental disability)	Cost Comparison Analysis, Housing Perspective, Client Self-Report	*Significantly Lower Costs*: (Group A) Housing costs *Summary Statement*: "Participants randomly assigned to the experimental condition [Group A] spent significantly less time homeless and in psychiatric hospitals, and incurred fewer [housing] costs than controls."

Study	Design / Groups / Inclusion Criteria	Method	Findings
Rosenheck et al. (2003)	Experimental (Randomized Controlled Trial) *Group A:* ($N = 182$) Scattered-site supportive housing with Intensive Case Management (ICM) support *Group B:* ($N = 90$) ICM support *Group C:* ($N = 188$) Treatment As Usual *Inclusion Criteria:* Veteran; Literally homeless for 1 month or longer; Diagnosis of a major psychiatric disorder or an alcohol or drug abuse disorder or both	Cost Comparison Analysis/Cost Effectiveness, Societal Perspective, Administrative Records, Client Self-Report	*Significantly Higher Costs:* (Group A) Mental healthcare costs, total outpatient costs (mental healthcare, medical surgical care, and case management) *Summary Statement:* "From the societal perspective, HUD-VASH [Group A] was $6200 (15%) more costly than standard care [Group C]. Incremental cost-effectiveness ratios suggest that HUD-VASH cost $45 more than standard care for each additional day housed (95% confidence interval, $−19 to $108)."
Siskind et al. (2014)	Quasi-Experimental *Group A:* ($N = 113$) Supportive transitional housing with 12 hours of support from interdisciplinary team of off-site staff, case management, and assistance finding housing upon discharge *Group B:* ($N = 139$) Inpatient mental healthcare *Inclusion Criteria:* Severe and persistent mental illness and homelessness	Cost Comparison Analysis, Program Perspective, Administrative Records	Statistical comparisons of costs not reported *Summary Statement:* "There was a statistically significant difference-in-difference favouring THT participants [Group A] for bed days (mean difference in difference -20.76 days, S.E. 9.59, $p = .031$) and living conditions (HoNOS Q11 mean difference in difference -0.93, S.E. 0.23, $p < .001$). THT cost less per participant (I$14,024) than the bed-days averted (I$17,348)."

(continued)

Table 4.2 Continued

Authors & Year	Study Design & Intervention	Type of Costing, Perspective, & Source of Service Use Data	Statistically Significant Findings
Stergiopoulos et al. (2015)	Experimental (Randomized Controlled Trial) *Group A:* (*N* = 689) Scattered-site supportive housing with ICM support *Group B:* (*N* = 509) Treatment as Usual *Inclusion Criteria:* Serious mental illness, absolutely homeless or precariously housed, with moderate needs	Cost Comparison Analysis, Societal Perspective, Client Self-Report	Statistical comparisons of costs not reported *Summary Statement:* "On average, the cost of supportive housing with ICM services [Group A] was CAD $14 177 per participant annually, approximately 30% less than the cost of supportive housing with ACT (CAD $22 257) [offered to high-needs participants in the same study], and resulted in an average net cost offset of CAD $4849 per participant per year, or 34% of the cost of the intervention. The most important cost offsets emerged from reduced use of emergency shelters and single-room occupancy with support, whereas the costs of office visits with other non-study medical (physicians) and clinical community (eg, social workers and nurses) providers rose."

Study Findings

We review the studies in the order of program, housing, and societal perspectives.

Program Perspective

Siskind and his colleagues (2014) investigated the cost offset related to inpatient mental health treatment for individuals with severe mental illness who were homeless or at risk of homelessness who received transitional scattered-site housing with intensive case management (ICM) for a period of 12 months. The costs of the scattered-site housing program, along with costs associated with inpatient mental health hospitalizations for program participants, were compared to the costs of inpatient mental healthcare for a matched comparison group (i.e., matched on gender, period of discharge from hospital, and diagnosis) receiving treatment as usual in the community. The program costs of $14,024 USD (2009 dollars) per participant produced cost savings in inpatient bed-days averted of $17,348 USD (2009 dollars) per participant. The researchers concluded that participation in the program resulted in $3,324 USD (2009 dollars) in savings related to hospitalizations.

Housing Perspective

In a randomized controlled trial comparing individuals receiving scattered-site supportive housing and individuals accessing treatment as usual (i.e., described as a residential continuum model), Gulcur and her colleagues (2003) examined the costs associated with different residential situations (e.g., supportive housing, hospital, other types of residential treatment) over a 2-year period. Their findings showed that individuals in scattered-site supportive housing had significantly lower housing or residential costs per day over the course of the study than individuals consuming treatment as usual. Differences in costs between the two groups were primarily the result of individuals in the treatment-as-usual group spending significantly more time in hospital.

Mental Healthcare System Perspective

In a quasi-experimental retrospective study using administrative data, Gilmer and his colleagues (2010), compared the costs associated with public mental health service use among people with severe mental illness who are chronically homeless receiving either subsidized scattered-site or single-site supportive housing with Assertive Community Treatment (ACT) and a sample of similar individuals matched on history of homelessness and demographic and clinical characteristics. Cost comparisons were conducted 1 year prior to study entry (and into the supportive housing program) and 1 year after study entry.

Findings showed individuals living in scattered-site and single-site supportive housing had significantly higher costs associated with their subsidized housing and outpatient services (including those associated with receiving ACT) than individuals in the treatment as usual group. On the other hand, individuals in the scattered-site and single-site supportive housing group had significantly lower costs associated with their use of inpatient services, emergency services, and mental health services used in the correctional system. Although individuals in scattered-site supportive housing used $2,116 USD (2007 dollars) more mental health services than individuals accessing treatment as usual, the difference between the two groups was not statistically significant. Overall, the amount of offset represented 82% of the cost of the subsidized housing with ACT.

Societal Perspective

Three studies conducted a cost comparison analysis from a societal perspective with comprehensive costing of services, transfer payments, and employment conducted using administrative data and client self-report data.

Two published papers from the At Home/Chez Soi Demonstration Project, a large randomized controlled trial conducted in five cities in Canada and reviewed in chapter 5 of this book, reported findings from a cost comparison analysis using a societal perspective (i.e., costing health, social, and legal/judicial/correctional services) from self-report data of individuals and receiving scattered-site supportive housing with ACT and individuals receiving treatment as usual. The findings suggest that cost offsets associated with scattered-site supportive housing vary depending on the level of need of the individuals receiving the services.

Aubry and his colleagues (2016) reported that on average scattered-site supportive housing with ACT cost $22,257 CAD (2011 dollars) per participant. This cost was almost completely offset by a reduced consumption of health, social, and legal/judicial/correctional services by these individuals relative to individuals receiving treatment as usual. Most notable were reductions in office visits for mental healthcare, hospitalizations for physical health problems, emergency shelter use, and incarceration. This reduced consumption totaled $21,367 CAD (2011 dollars) or 96% of the cost of the intervention.

In contrast to these findings that showed scattered-site supportive housing to be cost-neutral after taking into account cost savings, Stergiopoulos and her colleagues (2015) found the costs of scattered-site supportive housing with ICM for individuals with a moderate level of need to be only partially offset by the reduction in use of services when compared with the use of services by individuals receiving treatment as usual. In particular, the cost of scattered-site supportive housing with ICM was $14,177 CAD (2011 dollars) per participant per year, and it was found to produce an average net cost offset of $4,849 CAD (2011 dollars), representing 34% of the cost of the housing program. Cost savings were the result of reduced use of emergency shelters and single room occupancy with support. On the other hand, costs associated with treatment received from medical and other healthcare providers in the community for physical health issues increased.

In the third study, also involving a randomized controlled trial, Rosenheck and his colleagues (2003) compared costs associated with these service areas of three groups of veterans who were homeless in five American cities: (1) veterans receiving scattered-site supportive housing group with ICM, (2) veterans accessing case management only, and (3) veterans receiving standard services for homeless individuals.

From a societal perspective, veterans in scattered-site supportive housing with ICM consumed $6,200 USD (1996 dollars) more of services than veterans accessing treatment as usual. However, these costs did not include housing subsidies or other transfer payments such as shelter and incarceration. The inclusion of these costs in calculating government cost estimates found that veterans in scattered-site supportive housing consumed $10,295 USD (1996 dollars) more of services than individuals in standard care. Veterans in scattered-site supportive housing had significantly higher costs associated with outpatient services (medical surgical care and case management) and mental health services.

To date, this study is also the only costing study on mental health housing to calculate incremental cost-effectiveness ratios related to each additional day housed. Rosenheck and his colleagues (2003) found that each additional day housed among veterans receiving scattered-site supportive housing cost $50 USD (1996 dollars) from the perspective of the health system, $74 USD (1996 dollars) from the perspective of governmental agencies, and $45 USD (1996 dollars) from a societal perspective.

Summary of Findings

To date only a small number of cost comparison studies have been conducted on scattered-site supportive housing. These studies have adopted a range of costing perspectives, making it difficult to make comparisons and draw conclusions. Moreover, only one cost-effectiveness study has been completed (Rosenheck et al., 2003). Overall, cost comparison analyses yielded a range of findings that showed the cost of scattered-site supportive housing to be either completely offset and yielding cost savings or to be only partially offset by cost savings. The results of the three studies that have used more comprehensive costing perspectives at societal levels suggest that the modest cost of delivering scattered-site supportive housing is only partially offset by cost savings associated with a reduction of service use (Aubry et al., 2016, Rosenheck et al., 2003; Stergiopoulos et al., 2015). Notably, Aubry and his colleagues (2016) did find that for people with a high level of needs, scattered-site supportive housing offset almost all program costs (96%) through the reduction of service use.

Cost Comparisons of Single-Site Housing and Treatment as Usual

We now present our review of two studies comparing single-site housing and treatment as usual.

Description of Studies

Table 4.3 presents the costing studies in which single-site housing was compared with treatment as usual. Only two of these types of costing studies have been conducted (Larimer et al., 2009; Srebnik, Connor, & Sylla, 2013). Both studies were conducted in Seattle and used a quasi-experimental design, collected service use data from administrative databases, and adopted a broad governmental costing perspective that included costing healthcare, addictions treatment, and correctional services. The inclusion criteria in both studies targeted individuals with severe alcohol use problems who were high service users. In the case of the study conducted by Larimer and his colleagues (2009), individuals with high total costs associated with use of emergency services, sobering center stays, and jail time were recruited. Srebnik and her colleagues (2013) recruited individuals with medical illnesses who had extensive hospital stays in the year preceding admission to the study.

Study Findings

Both studies found a greater reduction in service use for individuals accessing single-site supportive housing compared with individuals receiving treatment as usual, such that cost savings exceeded the cost of single-site housing programs. In particular, Larimer and his colleagues (2009) reported significantly lower costs related to reduced use of emergency services, inpatient hospital stays, sobering center stays, and jail time. After 1 year in the program, cost savings related to reduced service use totaled $42,964 USD (year not specified) per person compared with $13,440 USD (year not specified) per person for delivery of the housing program. This represented an overall cost saving of $29,524 USD (year not specified) per person per year.

In line with Larimer's findings, Srebnik and her colleagues (2013) reported that individuals receiving single-site supportive housing with on-site support from a comprehensive team of case managers, chemical dependency specialists, and a registered nurse showed a significantly greater reduction in emergency department and sobering center use compared with individuals receiving treatment as usual. As well, individuals in single-site housing had greater reductions in hospital admissions and jail bookings. From a costing perspective, individuals in single-site supportive housing had an overall reduction in estimated costs of $62,504 USD (year not specified) per person per year compared with a reduction of $25,925 USD (year not specified) for individuals receiving treatment as usual. The difference between the two groups amounted to $36,579 USD (year not specified), indicating a saving associated with single-site supportive housing above and beyond its cost of $18,600 USD (year not specified) per year. However, it is important to note that Srebnik and her colleagues (2013) did not report the differences in costs as being statistically significant.

Table 4.3 **Descriptive Characteristics and Findings of Costing Studies Comparing Single-Site Supportive Housing and Treatment as Usual (N = 2)**

Authors & Year	Study Design & Intervention	Type of Costing & Perspective	Findings
Larimer et al. (2009)	Quasi-Experimental *Group A:* (N = 95) Single site supportive housing with on-site case management support, meals, and on-site healthcare services *Group B:* (N = 39) Treatment As Usual *Inclusion Criteria:* Chronically homeless, severe alcohol problems with highest total costs for use of alcohol-related hospital emergency services, the sobering center, and jail stays	Cost Comparison Analysis, Governmental Perspective Administrative Records	*Significantly Lower Costs:* (Group A) Total costs (including emergency department services; inpatient hospital admissions; sobering center use; jail use) *Summary Statement:* "Total cost offsets for Housing First participants [Group A] relative to controls averaged $2449 per person per month after accounting for housing program costs."
Srebnik, Connor, & Sylla (2013)	Quasi-Experimental *Group A:* (N = 29) Single-site supportive housing with case management support, additional support from housing case managers, chemical dependency specialists, and a registered nurse *Group B:* (N = 31) Treatment As Usual *Inclusion Criteria:* Chronically homeless, Very high inpatient hospital users in past year	Cost Comparison Analysis, Governmental Perspective Administrative Records	Statistical comparisons of costs not reported *Summary Statement:* "Participants showed a significantly greater reduction in emergency department and sobering center use relative to the comparison group. At a trend level, participants had greater reductions in hospital admissions and jail bookings. Reductions in estimated costs for participants and comparison group members were $62504 and $25925 per person per year—a difference of $36579, far outweighing program costs of $18600 per person per year."

Summary of Findings

Both studies show similar results with single-site supportive housing yielding cost savings from a governmental perspective that exceed the total cost of the program. These are certainly promising findings. However, it is important to note that both programs targeted heavy users of services and it is quite possible that this targeting played a role in the amount of cost savings that was accrued. Similar to the outcomes of these two studies, Goering and her colleagues (2014) reported in a technical report that individuals receiving scattered-site supportive housing, who represented the top 10% of users of health, social, and legal/judicial/correctional services prior to entry in the study, showed reductions in overall costs related to these services that were over two times the costs of supportive housing programs (i.e., $10 CAD invested in scattered-site supportive housing produced $21.72 CAD in cost savings).

Cost Comparisons of Scattered- and Single-Site Supportive Housing and Treatment as Usual

We now present our review of four studies comparing scattered- and single-site supportive housing and treatment.

Description of the Studies

Table 4.4 presents the studies in which scattered-site supportive housing or single-site supportive housing taken together were compared with treatment as usual. Our literature review identified four of these kinds of studies (Basu, Kee, Buchanan, & Sadowski, 2012; Culhane, Metraux, & Hadley, 2002; Galster, Champney, & Williams, 1994; Gilmer, Manning, & Ettner, 2009; Mares & Rosenheck, 2011). Participants in all of the studies were individuals with severe mental illness or a disabling health condition who were homeless. Costing perspectives used in the studies ranged from a physical and mental health services perspective to a governmental perspective.

Study Findings

Studies drawing comparisons between the combination of scattered-site and single-site supportive housing programs to treatment as usual are presented in order from the narrowest costing perspective undertaken (i.e., mental healthcare system) to the broadest (i.e., governmental perspective).

Mental Healthcare System Perspective
In a quasi-experimental retrospective study using administrative data, Gilmer and his colleagues (2009) compared mental health service costs of individuals with

Table 4.4 **Description and Costing Findings of Scattered-Site and Single-Site Supportive Housing Studies** (*N* = 4)

Authors & Year	Study Sample, Design & Intervention	Type of Costing, Costing Perspective, Data Source	Findings
Basu et al. (2012)	Experimental (Randomized Controlled Trial) *Group A:* (*N* = 201) Supportive housing (scattered site or single site) *Group B:* (*N* = 204) Treatment as Usual *Inclusion Criteria:* Homeless at hospital discharge, Chronic medical condition	Cost Comparison Analysis, Governmental Perspective Administrative Records, Client Self-Report	*Significantly Higher Costs:* (Group A) Outpatient visits, housing and respite care, case management *Significantly Lower Costs:* (Group A) Residential substance abuse treatment days *Summary Statement:* "Compared to usual care, the intervention group [Group A] generated an average annual cost savings of − $6,307 per person (95 percent CI: -16,616, 4,002; *p* = .23)".
Culhane, Metraux, & Hadley (2002)	Quasi-Experimental *Group A* (*N* = 4,679) Supportive housing (scattered site or single site) *Group B:* (*N* = 3,365) Treatment As Usual *Inclusion Criteria:* Homeless, Severe Mental Illness	Cost Comparison Analysis, Governmental Perspective Administrative Records	*Significant C* *Summary Statement:* "Before placement, homeless people with severe mental illness used about $40,451 per person per year in services (1999 dollars). Placement was associated with a reduction in services use of $16,281 per housing unit per year. Annual unit costs are estimated at $17,277 for a net cost of $995 per unit per year over the first two years."

(continued)

Table 4.4 Continued

Authors & Year	Study Sample, Design & Intervention	Type of Costing, Costing Perspective, Data Source	Findings
Gilmer et al. (2009)	Quasi-Experimental Group A: (N = 177) Supportive housing (single site or scattered site) with ACT Group B: (N = 161) Treatment As Usual Inclusion Criteria: Homeless, Serious Mental Illness	Cost Comparison Analysis, Mental Healthcare System Perspective Administrative Records	Significantly Higher Costs: (Group A) Case Management Significantly Lower Costs: (Group A) Mental health inpatient & emergency services, mental health services provided by the criminal justice system Summary Statement: "Participation in REACH [Group A] was associated with substantial increases in outpatient services as well as cost offsets in inpatient and emergency services and criminal justice system services. The net cost of services, $417 over two years, was substantially lower than the total cost of services ($20,241)."
Mares & Rosenheck (2011)	Quasi-Experimental Group A: (N = 281) Supportive Housing (Scattered-Site or Single Site) Group B: (N = 104) Treatment As Usual Inclusion Criteria: Chronically homeless, Unaccompanied, Disabling condition	Cost Comparison Analysis, Physical Healthcare & Mental Healthcare Systems Perspective Client Self-Report	Significantly Higher Costs: (Group A) Total healthcare services, outpatient mental health services, substance abuse services Summary Statement: "Total quarterly healthcare costs were significantly higher for CICH clients [Group A] than comparison subjects ($4,544 vs. $3,326) due to increased use of outpatient mental health and substance abuse services."

serious mental illness in a housing program that offered subsidized scattered- or single-site housing with case management support to a group of individuals matched on demographic and clinical characteristics receiving treatment as usual. Prior to placement in supportive housing, individuals were housed in a transitional housing program for 4 to 6 months while they applied for social benefits. Administrative records of mental health service use (i.e., case management, outpatient services, inpatient services, emergency services, criminal justice system services) were used to calculate the costs of services consumed by individuals in the housing program for a period of 2 years prior to and 2 years after program entry. A comparable period was used for individuals receiving treatment as usual.

Overall, findings showed no differences between the two groups in the change in costs associated with the use of mental health services from pre- to post-intervention. In fact, the supportive housing group showed an increase in consumption of mental health services compared with the treatment as usual group amounting to only $417 USD (year not specified) over the 2-year period. Specifically, individuals in supportive housing consumed $4,907 USD (year not specified) more mental health services once in the housing program compared with individuals receiving treatment as usual consuming $4,491 USD (year not specified) more services.

An examination of specific areas demonstrating change found that costs of specific mental health services for individuals in supportive housing increased significantly for outpatient services and case management, and decreased significantly for inpatient, emergency, and criminal justice system services. Gilmer and his colleagues (2009) concluded that a significant proportion of the costs of the supportive housing programs accessed in the study were offset by differences in mental health service use relative to individuals receiving treatment as usual.

Physical and Mental Healthcare Systems Perspective
In a prospective quasi-experimental study using self-report data, Mares and Rosenheck (2011) compared the costs associated with receiving physical and mental health services among individuals with a history of chronic homelessness placed in scattered-site and single-site supportive housing combined with comprehensive healthcare and individuals with similar chronic histories of homelessness receiving treatment as usual in five American cities. Findings showed individuals in scattered-site and single-site supportive housing consumed more healthcare services that in total were significantly more costly than individuals accessing treatment as usual. In particular, individuals in supportive housing consumed $4,544 USD (year not specified) in healthcare costs in the last 3 months of the study compared with $3,326 USD (year not specified) consumed by individuals receiving treatment as usual. A comparison of the use of specific services found individuals in supportive housing had significantly higher costs associated with their use of outpatient mental health services and substance use treatment.

Governmental Perspective

Culhane and his colleagues (2002) conducted a retrospective quasi-experimental study using administrative records that compared costs associated with healthcare, emergency shelter services, and correctional services of individuals in scattered-site and single-site housing with either community-based or on-site support services and individuals receiving treatment as usual matched on demographic and clinical characteristics and on history of homelessness. The period of observation in the study was for 2 years prior to individuals receiving supportive housing and for 2 years after receiving supportive housing.

Prior to placement in supportive housing, individuals with severe mental illness and a history of homelessness averaged $40,451 USD (1999 dollars). Subsequent to placement in supportive housing, individuals in supportive housing showed a reduction of $16,281 USD (1999 dollars) more per housing unit per year in service relative to individuals receiving treatment as usual. This cost offset resulted in a saving that represented on average 94% of the cost of supportive housing per year ($17,277 USD, 1999 dollars). Approximately 95% of the cost reductions were related to reductions in healthcare and emergency shelter services. Half of the cost reductions were the result of reduced use of state psychiatric inpatient services. One-quarter of the cost reductions were associated with reduced use of emergency shelter services.

In a randomized controlled trial that used administrative and client self-report data, Basu and his colleagues (2012) conducted a comprehensive cost comparison study of individuals with chronic medical illness who are homeless and discharged from hospital who received subsidized scattered-site or single-site supportive housing with case management or treatment as usual. Data on use of health services, social services, and correctional services occurring 1 year prior to the study entry and 6 months post study entry were costed. Compared with individuals receiving treatment as usual, individuals placed in supportive housing demonstrated an overall reduction in service use that yielded cost savings of $6,307 USD (2010 dollars) per person per year. These savings were the result of reduced costs (nonsignificant) for hospitalizations, emergency room visits, residential substance abuse treatment, nursing home days, and legal costs. Subgroup analyses found cost savings of $3,484 USD (2010 dollars) for people who had drug use in the past 30 days, of $6,622 USD (2010 dollars) for people diagnosed with HIV, and of $9,809 USD (2010 dollars) for people diagnosed with a chronic history of homelessness who were housed in scattered-site supportive housing.

Summary of Findings

Overall, similar to studies comparing scattered-site supportive housing to treatment as usual, the research that compares supportive housing (whether scattered-site or single-site) to treatment as usual shows that supportive housing programs produce costs savings associated with service use that either offsets a major proportion of the cost of supportive housing (Culhane et al., 2002; Gilmer, 2009; Mares & Rosenheck, 2011) or yields costs savings above and beyond the cost of supportive housing (Basu et al., 2012). It is important to note that Basu and his colleagues (2012) had the most rigorous research design (i.e., RCT) and used the broadest perspective in costing services.

Costs Comparisons Involving Other Types of Housing

We now present our review of four studies comparing other types of housing.

Description of the Studies

Table 4.5 presents the descriptive characteristics and findings of studies that focused on cost comparisons of other types of housing. In particular, these studies compared different types of scattered-site and single-site supportive housing (Galster et al., 1994), different types of single-site supportive housing programs (Dickey, Latimer, Powers, Gonzalez, & Goldfinger, 1997), different types of supportive housing and housing without support (Jarbrink, Hallam, & Knapp, 2001), and immediate placement into scattered-site or single-site supportive housing versus placement initially in residential treatment/transitional housing followed by placement into scattered-site or single-site supportive housing (Tsai, Mares, & Rosenheck, 2010).

Study Findings

Using a combination of administrative data, self-report data, and data from case managers, Dickey and her colleagues (1997) conducted a randomized controlled trial and compared the costs associated with housing and mental healthcare of individuals with mental illness who were homeless assigned to scattered-site supportive housing with ICM and a comparable group of individuals assigned to single-site supportive housing with on-site support, an approach known as evolving consumer households (ECH). The ECH approach entailed a shared housing arrangement that was permanent and did not require treatment compliance. Individuals from both groups had a case manager and received a housing subsidy.

The total annual costs associated with housing, case management, and other mental health treatment were found to be significantly greater for the individuals in the single-site supportive housing group ($56,434 USD, 1994 dollars) than for individuals living in scattered-site supportive housing ($29,838 USD, 1994 dollars). A significant portion of the difference between the two groups was related to the greater costs of housing and notably the on-site support for the ECH group. In fact, mean housing expenditures for individuals in the ECH group were more than three times those in the scattered-site supportive housing group. These findings were counter to those predicted, as it was thought that the additional peer support

Table 4.5 Descriptive Characteristics and Findings of Costing Studies on Other Types of Housing (N = 4)

Study	Design	Analysis & Perspective	Data Sources	Findings
Dickey et al. (1997)	Experimental (Randomized Controlled Trial) *Group A:* (N = 51) Scattered-Site Supportive Housing (with on-site and on-call support, plus ICM support) *Group B:* (N = 61) Single Site Supportive Housing (shared housing with on-site and on-call support, plus ICM support) *Inclusion Criteria:* Homeless (in shelter); Mental illness; Not a danger to self or others; No prior convictions for violence	Cost Comparison Analysis, Governmental Perspective	Administrative Records, Client Self-Report, Case Manager Self-Report	*Significantly Lower Costs:* (Group A) Housing, total annual expenditures *Summary Statement:* "The authors found that treatment and case management costs did not vary by housing type, but housing costs were significantly higher for those assigned to Evolving Consumer Households [Group B]."
Galster, Champney, & Williams (1994)	Quasi-Experimental *Group A:* (N = 16) Supportive housing (single site or scattered site) with ICM *Group B:* (N = 24) Supportive housing (single site or scattered site) *Group C:* (N = 11) Nonsubsidized private housing plus ICM support *Group D:* (N = 11) Nonsubsidized private housing plus nonintensive case management support	Cost Comparison Analysis, Physical Healthcare & Mental Healthcare Systems Perspective	Administrative Records, Client Self-Report	*Significantly Higher Costs:* (Group A) Housing Services, (Group B) Housing services, (Group E) Mental health services, Total Operating Costs *Significantly Lower Costs:* (Group D) Total operating costs, housing services, (Group C) Housing services, Personal Consumption, Total Operating Costs

	Group E: (N = 11) Single-site supportive public housing (with extraordinarily intensive Community Services Team support) or scattered-site supportive housing (with extraordinarily intensive Community Services Team support)		*Summary Statement:* "Results indicated that in the areas of housing costs, mental health costs, personal-consumption costs, and total costs, there were statistically significant differences among the five community-based groups."
	Inclusion Criteria: State-certified severely mentally disabled; Bearing some form of financial responsibility for a rental dwelling unit but not a property owner; Receiving gov't income assistance; Receiving mental health services from a local, publicly funded, mental health service agency; Not in a nursing home		
Jarbrink, Hallam, & Knapp (2001)	Quasi-Experimental	Cost Comparison Analysis, Program Perspective	*Significantly Higher Costs:* (Group A) Aids and adaptations, informal care; (Group C) Mortgage, maintenance and staffing, total cost of accommodation, day center visits, total services
	Group A: (N = 25) Scattered-site housing with no formal support	Administrative Records, Client Self-Report	
	Group B: (N = 132) Supportive housing (single site or scattered site) with regular visits from housing officers or community care workers		*Significantly Lower Costs:* (Group B) Total cost of nonaccommodation service use
	Group C: (N = 76) Group/residential homes plus on-site staff support		

(continued)

Table 4.5 **Continued**

	Inclusion Criteria: Living in some form of accommodation received from a housing provider for a minimum of 9 months; Designated by housing provider as "vulnerable"		*Summary Statement:* "When the costs of accommodation and non-accommodation services are combined, costs for tenants in group/residential homes [Group C] were significantly higher than for tenants in the other two categories (Scheffe, $p < .05$ both comparisons)."
Tsai, Mares, & Rosenheck (2010)	Quasi-Experimental *Group A:* ($N = 578$) Immediate scattered-site housing and healthcare services *Group B:* ($N = 131$) Residential treatment or transitional housing *Inclusion Criteria:* Chronically homeless, Unaccompanied, Disabling condition	Cost Comparison Analysis, Physical Healthcare & Mental Healthcare Systems Perspective Client Self-Report	*Significantly Higher Costs:* (Group B) Total healthcare costs, mental health services, substance abuse services *Summary Statement:* "There were no clinical advantages for clients who had residential treatment or transitional housing prior to entry into community housing [Group B], but they incurred higher substance abuse service costs."

in the single-site shared accommodations would produce the need for less on-site support. There were no differences between the two groups on treatment and case management costs.

In the earliest costing study conducted on housing combined with support for people with mental health difficulties, Galster and his colleagues (1994) used administrative and self-report data to compare the governmental costs associated with five different combinations of housing and support: (1) subsidized private scattered-site housing or public single-site housing with ICM, (2) nonsubsidized private scattered-site housing or public single-site housing with nonintensive case management, (3) nonsubsidized private scattered-site housing with ICM, (4) subsidized private scattered-site housing with nonintensive case management, and (5) private scattered-site housing or public single-site housing with very intensive support provided by a multidisciplinary team.

Findings showed that total monthly operating costs that included costs of housing, mental health and medical services, dental treatment, and personal consumption (out-of-pocket spending) was lowest for individuals without housing subsidies and receiving nonintensive case management ($741 USD, 1990 dollars) and highest for individuals receiving very intensive support from a multidisciplinary team ($1,782 USD, 1990 dollars). The total operating costs for these two groups were significantly different from those of the other groups.

Individuals receiving a housing subsidy and ICM had the next highest level of monthly operating costs ($1,421USD, 1990 dollars), followed by the other two groups, which had similar levels of total monthly operating costs ($1093 USD [1990 dollars] for subsidized private scattered-site housing or public single-site housing with nonintensive case management; $1062.44 USD [1990 dollars] for nonsubsidized private scattered-site housing with ICM). Differences among these three groups were not significant. Not surprisingly, differences among the groups were strongly related to housing costs (i.e., whether or not they received a subsidy for housing) and mental health services (i.e., the intensity of the community support they received).

Jarbrink and his colleagues (2001) compared the costs of housing and mental health services of individuals with severe mental illness living in three types of housing with varying levels of care and support, namely general scattered-site housing with no formal support, scattered-site supported housing that included regular visits from a support worker, and single-site group/residential housing that included on-site support. Service use was determined through governmental administrative records and client self-report. The data was collected at one time point, and the research design entailed an observational retrospective quasi-experimental study.

Their results found the total cost of housing and mental healthcare per month (£390.28 GBP, 1998 pounds) was significantly greater for individuals in group/residential homes with on-site support compared with individuals in scattered-site supportive housing (£212.01 GBP, 1998 pounds) or individuals in scattered-site general housing with no formal support (£233.66 GBP, 1998 pounds). The costs for aids, home adaptations, and informal care were significantly higher for individuals in general housing compared with the other two types of housing. On the other hand, the cost for mental health services accessed in the community was significantly less for individuals living in supportive housing receiving support through home visits.

Finally, Tsai and his colleagues (2010) used a quasi-experimental retrospective observational design to compare the costs of healthcare incurred by individuals with a disabling condition and a chronic history of homelessness placed immediately in scattered-site housing versus individuals who are placed initially in single-site residential treatment or transitional housing for a period of at least 2 weeks before moving into scattered-site supportive housing. Costs for healthcare consumption were estimated from self-report data on service use for 3-month periods over the course of the 2-year study.

Tsai and his colleagues (2010) reported that total health service costs were not significantly different for individuals who initially accessed single-site residential treatment/transitional housing compared with individuals moving immediately into scattered-site supportive housing. An examination of types of services showed significant differences between the groups on costs of substance abuse services with individuals initially in residential/transitional housing incurring significantly greater costs.

Summary of Findings

The two studies comparing the costs of housing and mental health services consumed by individuals in scattered-site supportive housing versus individuals in single-site supportive housing reported similar findings with costs of services consumed by individuals placed in single-site supportive housing being significantly greater than those of individuals in scattered-site supportive housing (Dickey et al., 1997; Jarbrink et al., 2001).

Conclusion

The 16 studies included in our review offer only moderate insight into the economic implications of housing interventions for people with severe and persistent mental illness. It is clear that, like the research on effectiveness of mental health housing programs, the body of literature in this area remains at an early stage, with much of the costing research having been conducted only in the last 10 years. We can expect that this knowledge base will continue to grow, particularly in the current context of increased research on the effectiveness of different types of housing programs.

Implications of Findings

Despite the small number of studies and their methodological limitations, we can make some tentative conclusions from the findings of this research at this point:

1. When compared with treatment as usual, either all or a large proportion of the added costs of delivering supportive housing programs, whether scattered-site or single-site, are offset by cost savings in healthcare, social services, and correctional services. The modest costs associated with delivering supportive housing programs (e.g., $45 USD per night of stable housing; Rosenheck et al., 2003) and the consistently large effects achieved in helping individuals leave homelessness and achieve stable housing (as documented in chapter 5 of this book) suggest that these programs are a wise investment of public dollars.

2. At the same time, supportive housing programs do not yield major cost savings associated with a reduced use of health and social services. The business case for ending homelessness, that has been argued and advocated for as a primary justification for supportive housing programs (Gaetz, 2012; Gladwell, 2006; Patterson, Somers, McIntosh, Shell, & Frankish, 2008; Shapcott, 2007) is not supported by the extant literature. However, it is worth noting that the concept of cost savings is somewhat problematic in and of itself. In the health and social service system, even if a program is shown to yield cost savings (e.g., reductions in hospital bed stays), we know that money is not really being saved, as those costs will usually be accrued by other patients in the system (i.e., hospital beds will still be filled). Thus, cost savings can be illusory, and it may be more meaningful to consider questions of efficiencies (i.e., reduction of waiting times) or appropriate use of services (refer to our third conclusion below). In this context, these so-called cost savings are not sufficient on their own to guide policy decisions but need to be combined with noneconomic outcomes to build a persuasive case for diffusing programs that yield cost savings. Further, as Culhane (2008) argues, we must acknowledge that homelessness is associated with significant "moral costs" that include dehumanization, inability to access basic rights, and susceptibility to victimization. Although these dire consequences of homelessness are not easily monetized, they represent very real costs to individuals and to communities. Moreover, Culhane (2008) argues that the cost accounting methodology that has been applied in this area of research fails to include the economic value of having stable housing, and improved health, family relations, and community integration.

3. Some of the studies showed shifts in costs that reflected a decrease in use of acute focused services (i.e., inpatient hospitalizations, emergency room visits, jail) and an increase in outpatient and case management services (Basu et al., 2012; Culhane et al., 2002; Gilmer et al., 2010; Mares & Rosenheck, 2011). These

findings suggest that moving into supportive housing leads to individuals receiving more appropriate services that can properly address their healthcare needs.

4. Individuals who use the most services while they are homeless will yield the greatest cost savings after they move into supportive housing. However, it can also be expected that individuals who have been disengaged from services while homeless will use more services once they move into supportive housing, contributing to greater costs rather than cost savings. The range of service use among individuals with severe mental illness who are homeless likely contributes to the research findings that fail to show large costs savings associated with receiving supportive housing.

5. Although it has not been extensively studied, the evidence to date from two studies suggest that the costs of housing and support associated with scattered-site housing are significantly less than those associated with single-site housing (Dickey et al., 1997; Jarbrink et al., 2001). These findings, when combined with research showing scattered-site and single-site housing achieving similar outcomes (as reviewed in chapter 5), argue for the scaling up of scattered-site supportive housing programs rather than building what appear to be more costly new single-site supportive housing programs. In fact, given the differences in cost, it would make sense for systems of care to reserve single-site supportive housing with on-site support for those individuals who encounter ongoing difficulties with living in scattered-site supportive housing.

Limitations

The existing literature is limited due to weaknesses in the methodology used, and inconsistencies in the specific program, population, and context studied. Many of the studies we reviewed are limited by a lack of rigorous methodology. Only six of the studies we reviewed used a randomized controlled trial design. The quasi-experimental nature of most studies raises concerns about the equivalency of the comparison groups used, and whether preexisting differences influenced study outcomes in important ways. Methodological gaps are also evidenced by the limited costing types and perspectives used. Few studies adopted a societal level costing perspective (Aubry et al., 2016; Rosenheck, et al., 2003; Stergiopoulos et al., 2015). As asserted by Knapp (1999) in his paper on mental health economics, "Mental health problems tend to impact upon many aspects of life and welfare, and not just for the person with the illness but also for their families and others. Evaluations should endeavour to address all of those dimensions" (p. 166). It is important for studies to examine a wide range of costs, or otherwise risk capturing only a narrow, incomplete picture of an intervention's consequences.

Further, Rosenheck and colleagues' (2003) study was the only study we reviewed that involved a cost-effectiveness analysis. In many of the other studies we reviewed, economic analysis was just one small component of an outcome study, rather than the main focus of the paper, and a very basic cost comparison analysis approach was the most widely used costing type. This type of analysis is much less informative than the more sophisticated cost-effectiveness analysis, which accounts for both the costs and the outcomes of a program. Notably, cost-effectiveness analysis can provide an estimate of the cost of a night of stable housing. This information is particularly useful for policy makers considering the allocation of funding for housing and support services.

It is also clear from our review that the various studies are quite different in terms of the specific program being studied, making it difficult to make meaningful comparisons and draw any overarching conclusions from their combined findings. One particular problem is that many of the studies do not include an adequate description of the program being implemented. We frequently found ambiguous, vague, or incomplete reports of important program elements like case management staff-to-client ratio, intensity of services, permanency of housing, readiness requirements, and degree of consumer choice and self-determination. All of these factors can have important implications for both costs and outcomes. Implementation evaluations or fidelity assessments were also rarely referenced, making it difficult to determine whether the program being described was actually delivered as intended.

Comparability across studies was further complicated by the wide variation in sample populations being studied and the lack of consistent inclusion/exclusion criteria. The definition of chronic homelessness varied across studies, as did the definition of mental illness. The specific subpopulations examined in different studies included veterans, high service users, people with chronic medical conditions, people with severe alcohol problems, and people receiving inpatient mental healthcare (Basu et al. 2012; Larimer et al., 2009; Rosenheck et al., 2003; Siskind et al., 2014; Srebnik, et al., 2013). It is questionable whether results are comparable across these unique subgroups, and/or comparable to the more general population of people who are homeless.

One last issue of comparability pertains to the particular context of the various studies. The studies are predominately American, and thus their findings may not be generalizable to other countries. Only four studies examined housing programs outside of the United States: one in London, England; one in Brisbane, Australia; and two based on the cross-Canada At Home/Chez Soi demonstration project (Aubry et al., 2016; Jarbrink, et al., 2001; Siskind et al., 2014; Stergiopoulos et al., 2015). Beyond the country in which the program is located, most studies do not contain an adequate description of the context of the program, such as city size, housing vacancy rate, local economy, demographics, or insurance coverage. More detail about community context is especially needed in the case of the 11 studies that compare a housing intervention to "treatment as usual." Treatment as usual, and associated service use costs, can vary drastically depending on the specific setting in question. Service use costs are inevitably higher in service-rich environments compared with service-poor environments, such as rural areas.

Future Directions for Research

The body of research on cost related to housing interventions is still in its early stages, providing the opportunity for additional quality research to be conducted. Future research in this area should overcome some of the methodological limitations we have highlighted in our review. We hope that future research will be conducted in different countries, not just the United States, and will be characterized by more randomized controlled trials, more comprehensive societal costing perspectives, more sophisticated types of costing analysis, more consistent inclusion/exclusion criteria, and more detailed descriptions of the specific intervention program, its implementation, and its context.

In particular, the importance of adopting more advanced costing perspectives and methods cannot be understated, as we currently have only one cost-effectiveness study to draw from, and few with a societal perspective (Aubry et al., 2016; Rosenheck et al., 2003; Stergiopoulos et al., 2015). The general trend of the existing literature suggests that housing interventions are more costly than, or just as costly as, nonhousing community-based interventions or treatment as usual. Yet the literature also suggests that housing interventions systematically result in superior housing outcomes (as documented in chapter 5 of this book). More comprehensive studies assessing the cost-effectiveness of housing interventions are needed to further expound these findings.

The existing body of literature has provided us with some useful data on scattered-site and mixed housing interventions in comparison with treatment as usual. It would now be beneficial for additional research to draw comparisons between different types of housing interventions. In the studies we reviewed, single-site and scattered-site interventions were frequently grouped together, and only two studies in our review compared single-site housing interventions with treatment as usual (neither of which used a societal perspective). It is important to better understand the economic implications of different housing interventions, given the difference in resource allocation that is needed for each intervention.

Another area of improvement for future research pertains to the length of the follow-up period used to assess the economic outcome of the intervention. Knapp (1999) commented on the length of the follow-up period used in mental health economics research, saying, "Questions about the adequacy of the standard short-term evaluation are raised by the chronicity of many mental health problems, together with their externality effects and their inter-generational transmission potential. Mental health problems are rarely short-term, one-off events, and economic and other evaluations should be designed with this in mind" (p. 166). The longest follow-up period of the studies we reviewed was 3 years post-intervention, and most studies used follow-up periods of 2 years or less.

Validity of data sources is another concern that needs to be addressed by future research. Studies are currently being done using either administrative or self-report data, but there is no clear direction on the accuracy of either source. For example, research conducted with seniors, and with patients accessing mental healthcare, has recorded large discrepancies between these two data sources (Palin, Goldner, Koehoorn, & Hertzman, 2011; Raina, Torrance-Rynard, Wong, & Woodward, 2002). Data collection with populations who have mental illness and/or are unstably housed presents its own data collection challenges such as recall/memory, and inconsistent patterns of accessing a wide range of services. Only one study on a homeless population looked at agreement between self-report data and administrative data. The authors obtained a level of agreement ranging from 78% to 82% depending on type of service used (Clifasefi, Collins, Burlingham, Hoang, & Larimer, 2011). Additional studies are needed in the field to assess the validity of the data sources.

Additional rigorous research on the economic implications of housing interventions would give policy makers and other stakeholders the appropriate tools they need to make informed decisions. Current research, though limited, suggests that housing interventions produce positive housing outcomes and some cost offsets. Future research will benefit from the use of stronger methodological approaches, comprehensive costing perspectives, and sophisticated costing analyses.

References

Aubry, T., Goering, P., Veldhuizen, S., Adair, C. E., Bourque, J., Distasio, J., . . . Tsemberis, S. (2016). A multiple-city RCT of Housing First with assertive community treatment for homeless Canadians with serious mental illness. *Psychiatric Services, 67*, 275–281.

Basu, A., Kee, R., Buchanan, D., & Sadowski, L.S. (2012). Comparative cost analysis of housing and case management program for chronically ill homeless adults compared to usual care. *Health Services Research, 47*, 523–543.

Chapko, K.M., Liu, C.-F., Perkins, M., Li, Y.-F., Fortney, C.J., & Maciejewski, L.M. (2009). Equivalence of two healthcare costing methods: Bottom-up and top-down. *Health Economics, 18*, 1188–1201.

Clifasefi L.S., Collins, E.S., Burlingham, B., Hoang, E.S., & Larimer, E.M. (2011). Agreement between self report and archival public service utilization data among chronically homeless individuals with severe alcohol problems. *Journal of Community Psychology, 39*, 631–644.

Culhane, P.D. (2008). The cost of homelessness: A perspective from the United States. *European Journal of Homelessness, 2*, 97–114.

Culhane, P.D., Metraux, S., & Hadley, T. (2002). Public service reductions associated with placement of homeless persons with severe mental illness in supportive housing. *Housing Policy Debate, 13*, 107–163.

Dickey, B., Latimer, E., Powers, K., Gonzalez, O., & Goldfinger, S.M. (1997). Housing costs for adults who are mentally ill and formerly homeless. *Journal of Mental Health Administration, 24*, 291–305.

Drummond, M.F., Sculpher, M.J., Torrance, G.W., O'Brien, B.J., & Stoddart, G.L. (2005). *Methods for the economic evaluation of health care programmes*. Oxford: Oxford University Press.

Gaetz, S. (2012). *The real cost of homelessness: Can we save money by doing the right thing?* Toronto, ON: Canadian Homelessness Research Network Press.

Gaetz, S., Donaldson, S., Richter, T., & Gulliver, T. (2013). *The state of homelessness in Canada*. Toronto, ON: Canadian Homelessness Research Network Press.

Galster, G.C., Champney, T.F., & Williams, Y. (1994). Costs of caring for persons with long-term mental illness in alternative residential settings. *Evaluation and Program Planning, 17,* 239–248.

Gilmer, T.P., Manning, G.W., & Ettner, L.S. (2009). A cost analysis of San Diego county's REACH program for homeless persons. *Psychiatric Services, 60,* 445–450.

Gilmer, T.P., Stefancic, A., Ettner, S.L., Willard, G., Manning, W.G., & Tsemberis, S. (2010). Effect of full-service partnerships on homelessness, use and costs of mental health services, and quality of life among adults with serious mental illness. *Archives of General Psychiatry, 67,* 645–652.

Gladwell, M. (2006, February 13). Department of Social Services Million Dollar Murray: Why problems like homelessness may be easier to solve than manage. *New Yorker,* 96–107.

Goering, P., Veldhuizen, S., Watson, A., Adair, C., Kopp, B., Latimer, . . . Aubry, T. (2014). *National At Home/Chez Soi final report*. Calgary, AB: Mental Health Commission of Canada.

Gulcur, L., Stefancic, A., Shinn, M., Tsemberis, S., & Fischer, S.N. (2003). Housing, hospitalization and cost outcomes for homeless individuals with psychiatric disabilities participating in continuum of care and Housing First programs. *Journal of Community and Applied Social Psychology, 13,* 171–186.

Jarbrink, K., Hallam, A., & Knapp, M.R.J. (2001). Costs and outcomes management in supported housing. *Journal of Mental Health, 10,* 99–108.

Knapp, M., (1999). Economic evaluation and mental health: Sparse past . . . fertile future? *Journal of Mental Health Policy and Economics, 2,* 163–167.

Knapp, M.R.J., & Beecham, J.K. (1990). Costing mental health services. *Psychological Medicine, 20,* 893–908.

Larimer, E.M., Malone, K.D., Garner, D.M., Atkins, C.D., Burlingham, S.B., Lonczak, S.H., . . . Marlatt, G.A. (2009). Health care and public service use and costs before and after provision of housing for chronically homeless persons with severe alcohol problems. *Journal of the American Medical Association, 301,* 1349–1357.

Mares, A.S., & Rosenheck, R.A. (2011). A comparison of treatment outcome among chronically homeless adults receiving comprehensive housing and health care services versus usual local care. *Administration Policy Mental Health, 38,* 459–475.

Palin, L.J., Goldner, M.E., Koehoorn, M., & Hertzman, C. (2011). Primary mental health care visits in self-reported data versus provincial administrative records. *Statistics Canada, Catalogue no. 82-003-XPE—Health Reports, 22,* 41–47.

Patterson, M., Somers, J., McIntosh, K., Sheill, A., & Frankish, J. (2008). *Housing and Support for adults with severe addictions and/or mental illness in British Columbia*. Vancouver, BC: Centre for Applied Research in Mental Health and Addiction and Simon Fraser University.

Pomeroy, S. (2005). *The cost of homelessness: Analysis of alternate responses in four Canadian cities*. Ottawa, ON: National Secretariat on Homelessness.

Raina, P., Torrance-Rynard, V., Wong, M., & Woodward, C. (2002). Agreement between self-reported and routinely collected health-care utilization data among seniors. *Health Services Research, 37,* 751–774.

Rosenheck, R.A, Kasprow, W., Frisman, L., & Liu-Mares, W. (2003). Cost-effectiveness of supported housing for homeless persons with mental illness. *Archives of General Psychiatry, 60,* 940–951.

Shapcott, M. (2007). *The blueprint to end homelessness in Toronto*. Toronto, ON: Wellesley Institute.

Siskind, D., Harris, M., Kisely, S., Siskind, V., Brogan, J., Pirkis, J., . . . Whiteford, H. (2014). A retrospective quasi-experimental study of a transitional housing program for patients with severe and persistent mental illness. *Community Mental Health Journal, 50,* 538–547.

Srebnik, D., Connor, T., & Sylla, L., (2013). A pilot study of the impact of Housing First–supported housing for intensive users of medical hospitalization and sobering services. *American Journal of Public Health, 103*, 316–323.

Stergiopoulos, V., Hwang, W. S., Gozdzik, A., Nisenbaum, R., Latimer, E., Rabouin, D., . . . Goering, N.P. (2015). Effect of scattered-site housing using rent supplements and intensive case management on housing stability among homeless adults with mental illness: A randomized trial. *Journal of the American Medical Association, 313*, 905–915.

Tsai, J., Mares, A.S., & Rosenheck, R.A., (2010). A multisite comparison of supported housing for chronically homeless adults: "Housing First" versus "Residential Treatment First." *Psychological Services, 7*, 219–232.

Appendix 4.A

Scattered-Site Supportive Housing vs. Treatment as Usual or Other Types of Services (N = 6)

Aubry et al. (2016)	Location	Five Canadian Cities: Vancouver, BC; Toronto, ON; Montreal, QC; Moncton, NB; Winnipeg, MB
	Study Design	Experimental (Randomized Controlled Trial), Prospective
	Sample Size	Overall N = 950, Intervention Group n = 469, Comparison Group n = 481
	Selection Criteria	Serious mental illness, absolutely homeless or precariously housed, with high needs
	Intervention Received by Comparison Group	Treatment as Usual
	Intervention Received by Intervention Group (s)	Scattered-site supportive housing with ACT support
	Length of Study	21–24 Months (0 month period preintervention, 21–24 month period postintervention)
	Source of Data	Client Self-Report
	Type of Costing	Cost Comparison Analysis
	Perspective	Societal
	Costs Assessed	Use of health, social, and justice services, including office visits, hospitalizations, inpatient and outpatient physical and mental healthcare, emergency shelter, home visits, and incarceration, arrests, police contact, court appearances, alternative justice service programs

	Statistically Significant Differences between Intervention and Comparison Group (Nonsignificant results not reported)	Statistical comparisons of costs not reported
Gilmer et al. (2010)	Location	San Diego County
	Study Design	Quasi-Experimental, Prospective
	Sample Size	Overall N = 363, Comparison Group n= 154, Intervention Group n = 209
	Selection Criteria	Homeless; Severe mental illness
	Intervention Received by Comparison Group	Treatment as Usual (Authors only report that comparison group participants initiated case management or outpatient services at the same time as intervention group clients)
	Intervention Received by Intervention Group (s)	ACT (one team per 100 clients), Scattered-site housing; Housing First
	Length of Study	24 months (12-month period preintervention,12-month period postintervention)
	Source of Data	Program Staff Self-Report, Administrative Data
	Type of Costing	Cost Comparison Analysis
	Perspective	Mental Healthcare System
	Costs Assessed	Mental health service use (use of outpatient, inpatient, emergency, and justice system services), and mental health services and housing costs from the perspective of the public mental health system
	Statistically Significant Differences between Intervention and Comparison Group (Nonsignificant results not reported)	The outpatient costs and housing costs incurred by the intervention group increased significantly compared to the comparison group. Intervention group inpatient costs, emergency service costs, and jail mental health services costs decreased significantly compared to the comparison group

Gulcur et al. (2003)	Location	New York
	Study Design	Experimental (Randomized Controlled Trial), Prospective
	Sample Size	Overall N =225, Comparison Group n = 126 Intervention Group n = 99
	Selection Criteria	Inclusion criteria for participants recruited from shelters (n = 157): Spent 15 out of the last 30 days on the street or in other public places (shelters were not included); Exhibited a period of housing instability over the past 6 months; Axis I diagnosis (any major mental illness, such as schizophrenia or bipolar disorder, except personality disorders and mental retardation)
		Inclusion criteria for participants recruited from state psychiatric hospitals (n = 68): Same as above prior to hospitalization
	Intervention Received by Comparison Group	Treatment as Usual (Consistent with a Continuum of Care approach)
	Intervention Received by Intervention Group (s)	Scattered-site housing, Pathways Housing First Model, ACT support (no indication of staff-to-client ratio)
	Length of Study	24 months (0-month period preintervention, 24-month period postintervention)
	Source of Data	Client Self-Report
	Type of Costing	Cost Comparison Analysis
	Perspective	Housing
	Costs Assessed	Costs of residential placements: own housing, shelter use, psychiatric institutional stays. (No costs assessed for nights spent on the street.)
	Statistically Significant Differences between Intervention and Comparison Group (Nonsignificant results not reported)	Intervention group cost significantly less than the comparison group

Rosenheck et al. (2003)	Location	San Francisco, San Diego, New Orleans, Cleveland
	Study Design	Experimental (Randomized Controlled Trial), Prospective
	Sample Size	Overall N = 460; Intervention Group n = 182; Comparison Group 1, n = 90; Comparison Group 2, n = 188
	Selection Criteria	Inclusion Criteria: Veteran; Literally homeless for 1 month or longer; Diagnosis of a major psychiatric disorder or an alcohol or drug abuse disorder or both
	Intervention Received by Comparison Group	1) ICM (maximum caseloads of 25:1) without special access to housing 2) Standard Veterans Affairs homeless services
	Intervention Received by Intervention Group(s)	Scattered-site housing vouchers; ICM (maximum caseloads of 25:1); Housing First approach
	Length of Study	36 months (0-month period preintervention, 36-month period postintervention)
	Source of Data	Administrative Records, Client Self-Report
	Type of Costing	Cost-Effectiveness Analysis
	Perspective	Societal
	Costs Assessed	Veterans Affairs health service utilization (inpatient care, outpatient care, residential treatment); Non–Veterans Affairs services (medical and mental health inpatient, residential, and nursing home care, medical-surgical outpatient care, mental health outpatient care), Non-healthcare costs (shelter beds, jail or prison, cash transfer payments like Veterans Affairs benefits, Supplemental Security Income, and Social Security disability); Earnings; Cost of subsidized housing vouchers offered to the Intervention group

	Statistically Significant Differences between Intervention and Comparison Group (Nonsignificant results not reported)	Mental healthcare costs and total outpatient costs (outpatient costs included mental healthcare, medical surgical care, and case management) were significantly higher than the Intervention group compared with the other two groups
Siskind et al. (2014)	Location	Brisbane, Australia
	Study Design	Quasi-Experimental, Retrospective
	Sample Size	Overall $N = 252$, Comparison Group $n = 139$, Intervention Group $n = 113$
	Selection Criteria	Inclusion Criteria: Severe and persistent mental illness
	Intervention Received by Comparison Group	Receiving inpatient mental healthcare
	Intervention Received by Intervention Group (s)	Received scattered-site, shared transitional social housing for approximately 6 months. Entered the program either from inpatient mental health care (63.7%), or directly from the community (36.3%). Received 12 hours of support from an interdisciplinary team of off-site staff (ratio not reported, included nurses, occupational therapists, and nonclinical support staff), as well as clinical case management (ratio of 1 staff to 25 clients) from a public mental health service during the program. Prior to discharge from the program, were given assistance finding permanent housing
	Length of Study	24 months (12-month period preintervention, 12-month period postintervention)
	Source of Data	Administrative Records
	Type of Costing	Cost Comparison Analysis
	Perspective	Program
	Costs Assessed	Inpatient bed days; Cost of transitional housing outpatient care

	Statistically Significant Differences between Intervention and Comparison Group (Nonsignificant results not reported)	Statistical comparisons not reported
Stergiopoulos et al. (2015)	Location	Four Canadian cities: Vancouver, BC; Winnipeg, MB; Toronto, ON; and Montreal, QC
	Study Design	Experimental (Randomized Controlled Trial)
	Sample Size	Overall $N = 1,198$, Intervention Group $n = 689$, Comparison Group $n = 509$
	Selection Criteria	Serious mental illness, absolutely homeless or precariously housed, with moderate needs
	Intervention Received by Comparison Group	Treatment as Usual
	Intervention Received by Intervention Group (s)	Scattered-site supportive housing with ICM support
	Length of Study	24 months (0-month period preintervention, 24-month period postintervention)
	Source of Data	Client Self-Report
	Type of Costing	Cost Comparison Analysis
	Perspective	Societal
	Costs Assessed	Income, services used, and housing, including arrests, emergency room visits, hospitalizations, emergency shelters and single-room occupancy with support, office visits
	Statistically Significant Differences between Intervention and Comparison Group (Nonsignificant results not reported)	Statistical comparisons of costs not reported

Single Site Supportive Housing vs. Treatment as Usual (N = 2)

Larimer et al. (2009)	Location	Seattle, Washington
	Study Design	Quasi-Experimental, Prospective
	Sample Size	Overall N = 134, Comparison Group n = 39, Intervention Group n = 95
	Selection Criteria	Inclusion Criteria: Chronically homeless individuals; Severe alcohol problems
	Intervention Received by Comparison Group	Treatment as Usual, On a wait-list for intervention (intervention assigned on a first-come, first-served basis)
	Intervention Received by Intervention Group (s)	Single-site housing with on-site case managers (staff-to-client ratio not reported), meals, and on-site healthcare services
		Housing First, no treatment requirements, allowed to drink in rooms.
	Length of Study	18–24 Months (For Intervention Group: 12-month period preintervention, 12-month period postintervention, For Comparison Group: 12-month period preintervention, 6-month period postintervention)
	Source of Data	Administrative Records
	Type of Costing	Cost Comparison Analysis
	Perspective	Governmental
	Costs Assessed	Hospital-based medical services; Emergency medical services; Sobering center use; Publicly funded alcohol and drug detoxification and treatment; Jail bookings; Days incarcerated; Shelter use; Medicaid-funded services
	Statistically Significant Differences between Intervention and Comparison Group (Non-Significant results not reported)	Intervention group had significantly lower total costs than comparison group, with those housed for the longest period of time experiencing the greatest cost reductions

Srebnik, Connor, & Sylla (2013)	Location	Seattle, Washington
	Study Design	Quasi-Experimental, Prospective
	Sample Size	Overall $N = 60$, Comparison Group $n = 31$, Intervention Group $n = 29$
	Selection Criteria	Inclusion Criteria: Chronically homeless (including 12 consecutive months of homelessness or 4 homeless episodes in the prior 3 years with significant disabling physical or psychiatric conditions); Referred from County Public Health's homeless outreach team with 60 or more sobering sleep-off center visits within the prior year or from medical respite with incurred inpatient paid claims of at least $10,000 within the prior year
	Intervention Received by Comparison Group	Treatment as Usual
	Intervention Received by Intervention Group (s)	Single-site housing, Housing first, Case management (ratio of 1 case manager to 21 clients), Additional support from a team of housing case managers, chemical dependency specialists, and a registered nurse
	Length of Study	24 months (12-month period preintervention, 12-month period postintervention)
	Source of Data	Administrative
	Type of Costing	Cost Comparison Analysis
	Perspective	Governmental
	Costs Assessed	Emergency department services; Inpatient hospital admissions; Sobering center use; Jail use
	Statistically Significant Differences between Intervention and Comparison Group (Nonsignificant results not reported)	Statistical comparisons not reported

Mixed/Other Housing (N = 8)		
Mixed (Scattered-Site & Single-Site Supportive Housing)		
Basu et al. (2012)	Location	Chicago, Illinois
	Study Design	Experimental (Randomized Controlled Trial), Prospective
	Sample Size	Overall N = 405, Comparison Group n = 204, Intervention Group n = 201
	Selection Criteria	Inclusion criteria: Homeless at hospital discharge (did not have stable housing during the 30 days prior to hospitalization); Chronic medical condition
	Intervention Received by Comparison Group	Treatment as Usual
	Intervention Received by Intervention Group (s)	Both Scattered-site and single-site housing; Case management (no ratio specified); Not Housing First (Housing choice absent)
	Length of Study	18 months (12-month period preintervention, 6-month period postintervention)
	Source of Data	Administrative Records, Client Self-Report
	Type of Costing	Cost Comparison Analysis
	Perspective	Governmental
	Costs Assessed	Hospitalization; Emergency room visits; Outpatient services; Residential substance abuse treatment; Nursing home; Legal; Housing and respite care; Case management
	Statistically Significant Differences between Intervention and Comparison Group (Nonsignificant results not reported)	Among intervention group participants, outpatient visit costs, housing and respite care costs, and case management costs all significantly increased from pre- to postintervention, compared with the comparison group
		Residential substance abuse treatment costs significantly decreased from pre- to postintervention, compared with the comparison group

Culhane, Metraux, & Hadley (2002)	Location	New York, NY
	Study Design	Quasi-Experimental, Retrospective
	Sample Size	Overall N = 8,044, Comparison Group n = 3,365, Intervention Group n = 4,679
	Selection Criteria	Inclusion Criteria: Severe mental illness; Homeless
	Intervention Received by Comparison Group	Treatment as Usual
	Intervention Received by Intervention Group (s)	Mix of different types of housing (both scattered-site and single-site housing) and different types of support interventions
	Length of Study	48 months, depending on data availability (24-month period preintervention, 24-month period postintervention)
	Source of Data	Administrative Records
	Type of Costing	Cost Comparison Analysis
	Perspective	Governmental
	Costs Assessed	Shelter use; Inpatient psychiatric hospital stays; Medicaid-reimbursed inpatient and outpatient healthcare; Inpatient stays at municipal hospitals; Inpatient stays in a VA hospital; prison and jail utilization
	Statistically Significant Differences between Intervention and Comparison Group (Nonsignificant results not reported)	Supportive housing group had significantly greater reductions in emergency shelter use and inpatient hospitalizations than the comparison group from pre- to postintervention. Supportive housing group had significantly greater increases in use of outpatient services from pre- to postintervention
Gilmer et al. (2009)	Location	San Diego County, California
	Study Design	Quasi-Experimental, Retrospective
	Sample Size	Overall N = 338, Comparison Group n = 161, Intervention Group n = 177
	Selection Criteria	Inclusion criteria: Homeless; Serious mental illness

Intervention Received by Comparison Group	Treatment as Usual (Authors only report that comparison group participants initiated case management or outpatient services at the same time as intervention group clients)
Intervention Received by Intervention Group (s)	Both scattered-site and single-site housing; Services are Housing First (but housing has strict rules on drug use); Assertive community treatment team–based case management (service intensity not reported)
Length of Study	48 months (24-month period preintervention, 24-month period postintervention)
Source of Data	Administrative Records
Type of Costing	Cost Comparison Analysis
Perspective	Mental Healthcare Systems Perspective
Costs Assessed	Case management; Mental health outpatient; Mental health inpatient plus emergency room visits (included hospitalizations, stays at crisis residential facilities, emergency psychiatric unit services, and psychiatric emergency response team services); Mental health services provided in the criminal justice system (i.e., the County Jail)
Statistically Significant Differences between Intervention and Comparison Group (Nonsignificant results not reported)	Among intervention group participants, case management costs significantly increased from pre- to post intervention, compared to the comparison group. Mental health inpatient plus emergency services costs significantly decreased, and mental health services provided by the criminal justice system costs significantly decreased from pre- to postintervention, compared with the comparison group

Mares & Rosenheck (2011)	Location	Chattanooga, TN; Los Angeles, CA; Martinez, CA; New York, NY; Portland, OR
	Study Design	Quasi-Experimental, Prospective
	Sample Size	Overall N = 385, Comparison Group n = 104, Intervention Group n = 281
	Selection Criteria	Inclusion criteria: Chronically homeless (continuously homeless for 1 year or more or has had at least four episodes of homelessness in the past 3 years); Unaccompanied; Disabling condition.
	Intervention Received by Comparison Group	Treatment as Usual
	Intervention Received by Intervention Group (s)	Received comprehensive housing and healthcare services through a federal program. Specific intervention varied across the five sites
	Length of Study	24 months (0-month period preintervention, 24-month period postintervention)
	Source of Data	Self-Report
	Type of Costing	Cost Comparison Analysis
	Perspective	Physical Healthcare & Mental Healthcare Systems
	Costs Assessed	Inpatient Medical/dental treatment; Outpatient medical/dental treatment; Inpatient mental healthcare; Outpatient mental healthcare; Inpatient substance abuse services, Outpatient substance abuse services
	Statistically Significant Differences between Intervention and Comparison Group (Nonsignificant results not reported)	Total quarterly healthcare costs were significantly higher for intervention group participants due to increased use of outpatient mental health and substance abuse services

Other Types of Housing		
Dickey et al. (1997)	Location	Boston, Massachusetts
	Study Design	Experimental (Randomized Controlled Trial), Prospective
	Sample Size	Overall N = 112, Intervention Group A: n = 61, Intervention Group B: n = 51
	Selection Criteria	Inclusion Criteria: Homeless (in shelter); Mental illness
		Exclusion criteria: Imminently dangerous to self or others, prior convictions for violence
	Intervention Received by Comparison Group	N/A
	Intervention Received by Intervention Group (s)	A) Evolving Consumer Household: subsidized, single-site, permanent, shared housing without requirement of treatment compliance, with on-site housing support staff, on-call clinician, and ICM support (15 to 1 ratio)
		or B) Independent Living Apartment: subsidized, single-occupancy, scattered-site, furnished apartment in public housing, with on-call clinician, and ICM support (15 to 1 ratio)
	Length of Study	18 Months (0-month period preintervention, 18-month period postintervention)
	Source of Data	Administrative Records, Client Self-Report, Case Manager Self-Report
	Type of Costing	Cost Comparison Analysis
	Perspective	Governmental
	Costs Assessed	Outpatient hospital services; Hospitalization; Emergency room visits; Community medical services; Psychiatric hospitalization; Substance abuse treatment; Detox; Incarceration; Housing (including housing assigned during intervention, and other housing used during the study period, including shelters, group homes, jail and substance abuse treatment centres); Case management; Community support services

	Statistically Significant Differences between Intervention and Comparison Group (Nonsignificant results not reported)	Total housing costs, and total annual expenditures, were both significantly lower for those assigned to Independent Living Apartments compared with Evolving Consumer Households
Galster, Champney, & Williams (1994)	Location	Newark, Ohio, and Mount Vernon, Ohio
	Study Design	Quasi-Experimental, Prospective
	Sample Size	Overall $N = 82$, Intervention Group A: $n = 16$, Intervention Group B: $n = 24$, Intervention Group C: $n = 11$, Intervention Group D: $n = 11$, Intervention Group E: $n = 20$
	Selection Criteria	Inclusion criteria: State-certified severely mentally disabled; Bearing some form of financial responsibility for a rental dwelling unit; Receiving gov't income assistance; Receiving mental health services from a local, publicly funded, mental health service agency
		Exclusion criteria: Property owner; In a nursing home
	Intervention Received by Intervention Groups	(Clients were intentionally selected for particular intervention programs by mental healthcare professionals, based on their perceptions of what program was most appropriate for each client)
		A) Public, single-site housing or subsidized, private, scattered-site housing with ICM support (average of 1–3 hours weekly of support)
		B) Public, single-site housing or subsidized, private, scattered-site housing with nonintensive case management support (average of 1–3 hours monthly of support)
		C) Nonsubsidized private housing with ICM support
		D) Nonsubsidized private housing and nonintensive case management support

	or E) Public, single-site housing or subsidized, private, scattered-site housing with extraordinarily intensive Community Services Team (CST) support (average of 3.5–5 hours weekly of support)
Length of Study	29 months (0-month period preintervention, 29-month period postintervention)
Source of Data	Administrative Records, Client Self-Report
Type of Costing	Cost Comparison Analysis
Perspective	Physical Healthcare & Mental Healthcare Systems
Costs Assessed	Operating cost components including: Mental, dental, and mental health services; Clients' out-of-pocket expenses for these services; Hospitalization; Housing expenses (fair-market rent, assumed to be the opportunity cost of a dwelling); Personal consumption expenditure costs (personal income, employment, volunteer work, and general community services and food banks)
Statistically Significant Differences between Intervention and Comparison Group (Nonsignificant results not reported)	Housing services: Intervention groups A and B cost significantly more. Intervention group E cost a significantly different, intermediate level of cost. Intervention groups C and D cost significantly less
	Mental health services: Intervention group E cost significantly more than intervention groups A and B, who in turn were significantly more costly than groups C and D
	Personal consumption: Intervention group C cost significantly less than all other intervention groups

		Total operating costs: Intervention group D cost significantly less than all other intervention groups, with the exception of group C. Intervention group E cost significantly more than all other intervention groups
Jarbrink, Hallam, & Knapp (2001)	Location	London, England
	Study Design	Quasi-Experimental, Retrospective
	Sample Size	Overall $N = 238$, Intervention Group A: $n = 25$, Intervention Group B: $n = 132$, Intervention Group C: $n = 76$
	Selection Criteria	Inclusion criteria: Living in some form of accommodation received from a housing provider for a minimum of 9 months (Included people with histories of homelessness, mental illness, substance abuse, and criminal justice system involvement); Designated by housing provider as "vulnerable."
	Intervention Received by Comparison Group	N/A
	Intervention Received by Intervention Group (s)	Some form of assisted accommodation received from a housing provider A) Scattered-site housing with no formal support B) Supportive housing (single site or scattered site) with regular visits from housing officers or community care workers C) Group/residential/hostel homes plus on-site staff support with a ratio of one staff member to 5 clients or less
	Length of Study	Single time point for data collection
	Source of Data	Administrative Records, Client Self-Report
	Type of Costing	Cost Comparison Analysis
	Perspective	Program

	Costs Assessed	Accommodation services (mortgage, maintenance and staffing; living expenses)
		Nonaccommodation services (day centers; other visited services; domiciliary services; hospital inpatient care; aid and adaptations; informal care)
	Statistically Significant Differences between Intervention and Comparison Group (Nonsignificant results not reported)	The costs of mortgage, maintenance and staffing, total cost of accommodation, weekly costs for visits to day centers, and total combined accommodation and nonaccommodation services is higher in group/residential homes than in other housing categories
		Costs for aids and adaptations and informal care are higher in general housing than in other housing categories
		The total cost of nonaccommodation service use was lower in supported housing than in other housing categories
Tsai, Mares, & Rosenheck (2010)	Location	National, 11 sites: Chattanooga, TN; Chicago, IL; Columbus, OH; Denver, CO, Fort Lauderdale, FL; Los Angeles, CA; Martinez, CA; New York, NY; Philadelphia, PA; Portland, OR; and San Francisco, CA
	Study Design	Quasi-Experimental, Retrospective
	Sample Size	Overall $N = 709$, Comparison Group $n = 131$, Intervention Group $n = 578$
	Selection Criteria	Inclusion criteria: Chronically homeless (continuously homeless for 1 year or more or has had at least four episodes of homelessness in the past 3 years); Unaccompanied, Disabling condition
	Intervention Received by Comparison Group	Received residential treatment or transitional housing before being placed into permanent independent housing with supportive primary healthcare and mental health services. (Specific housing intervention varied across sites)

Intervention Received by Intervention Group (s)	Immediately placed into permanent independent housing with supportive primary healthcare and mental health services. (Specific housing intervention varied across sites)
Length of Study	24 Months (0-month period preintervention, 24-month period postintervention)
Source of Data	Client Self-Report
Type of Costing	Cost Comparison Analysis
Perspective	Physical Healthcare & Mental Healthcare Systems
Costs Assessed	Inpatient Medical/dental treatment; Outpatient medical/dental treatment; Inpatient mental healthcare; Outpatient mental healthcare, Inpatient substance abuse services, Outpatient substance abuse services
Statistically Significant Differences between Intervention and Comparison Group (Nonsignificant results not reported)	The comparison group incurred significantly more total healthcare, mental health service, and substance abuse service costs than the intervention group

HOUSING THEORY
AND RESEARCH METHODS

5

Theory and Research on Housing Programs for People with Serious Mental Illness

GEOFFREY NELSON AND TIMOTHY MACLEOD

In this chapter, we examine theory and research on supportive housing programs, both scattered-site and single-site, for people with serious mental illness. While the type of housing that consumers choose depends on their preferences, scattered-site supportive housing is typically private market apartments that can be located anywhere in the community. Moreover, such programs strive not to concentrate consumers in one apartment building. The number of clients in one building should not exceed 20% of building occupants. In contrast, supportive single-site housing is congregate in nature, with 100% of the available units in a building being reserved for people with mental illness. As well, some single-site programs may have staff that work on-site in offices.

Program theory is important for understanding how programs are intended to have beneficial impacts on program participants. Theory provides guidance in terms of how program principles, components, and outcomes are linked and thus informs program evaluation studies. In the first section of the chapter, we focus on housing program theory, while in the second section we focus on housing program research. Theory and research on the larger social context of housing are covered in the next chapter.

Housing Program Theory

In this section, we introduce the concept of housing program theory and then apply it to scattered-site and single-site programs.

Theory of Change

Scattered-site and single-site supportive housing are interventions. Like any intervention, supportive housing is based on an implicit or explicit theory of how the intervention produces outcomes. In this section on theory, we use concepts from the theory of change literature to highlight the implicit or explicit theories underlying independent and single-site supportive housing.

Theory of change is a concept from the field of program evaluation. Chen and Rossi (1992) developed a "theory-driven approach" in which a program's theory of change is clearly specified and is used as the basis for implementation and outcome evaluation research. Bickman (1987) framed program theory as "a plausible and sensible model of how a program is supposed to work" (p. 5). The hallmark of theory of change evaluation is connecting inputs and program activities with outcomes through specified theoretical pathways. With a clear theory of change and an evaluation of both process and outcome, evaluation researchers should be able to determine, when a program does not produce its intended effects, whether this resulted from poor implementation or an inadequate theoretical framework. Often, a visual representation, or logic model, is used to depict a program's theory of change (Rush & Ogborne, 1991).

Chen (2005) distinguished between action and change components of theory of change. The change component specifies the casual linkages of the theory of change, while the action component specifies a systematic plan for implementation and program delivery. Using the example of an antismoking campaign, Chen describes how the program staff collaborates with schools and teachers and communicates with parents and obtains their support as elements of the action component. In contrast, he argues that the change component includes the program curriculum and class discussions that form the core program activities and are designed to change students' beliefs, attitudes, and behaviors regarding smoking.

Theory of Change for Scattered-Site Supportive Housing

Housing First Theory of Change

Dunn, van der Meulen, O'Campo, and Muntaner (2013) have noted the importance of theory-informed evaluation for Housing First. Moreover, researchers have described resident and service-provider perspectives on the critical ingredients of Housing First (Kirsh, Gewurtz, & Bakewell, 2011; Watson, Wagner, & Rivers, 2013), and Tsemberis and Asmussen (1999) presented an early logic model of Housing First. More recently, Nelson, Goering, and Tsemberis (2012) laid out a comprehensive framework of the Pathways Housing First model. The four key theoretical principles of the Pathways Housing First model are (1) delivery of consumer-driven services; (2) separation of housing and clinical services; (3) adoption of a recovery orientation; and (4) focus of services on facilitating community integration.

Consumer-driven services occur when services are provided by assertive community treatment (ACT) teams or intensive case management (ICM) teams with peer support workers, and are underpinned by values of consumer choice and social justice. Housing and clinical services are considered separate when housing is rented from commercial landlords, there are no service requirements for tenancy, and services are portable. A recovery orientation refers to an intervention that foregrounds the values of choice and self-direction, person-centered care, empowerment, a strengths orientation, personal responsibility, and hope for the future. Finally, community integration is marked by the dispersal of housing geographically in conjunction with the limiting of apartment buildings to a 20% composition of program tenants so that they will live next to and have contact with other community residents. The program model presented below forms a complete sketch of the elements of the Housing First logic model (see Table 5.1). The theoretical principles, noted above, are directly linked with program activities that can be assessed with a measure of program fidelity that we discuss later in the chapter.

This program logic model shows that a care plan is prepared at intake by an ACT team member or ICM case manager. There are several critical immediate interventions central to the recovery of participants who have a mental illness and experiencing chronic homelessness upon entering the program: (1) immediate assessment of consumer preferences for housing and rapid housing; (2) immediate assistance in organizing finances of participants including support applying for public assistance to ensure income eligibility for a lease; (3) participants and service coordinators forming a working alliance to facilitate participant-guided treatment goals; and (4) staff members identifying and assisting in accessing community health services for the treatment of critical and chronic health issues.

These activities should lead to the immediate outcomes of rapid housing, reduced contact with nonsupportive peers, new relationships with landlords and neighbors, the development of a working alliance with support workers, reduced use of emergency services, hospitalization, and involvement in the criminal justice system, increased participation in treatment, and increased access to public benefits. Once the participant is stably housed, assistance is provided in establishing client-guided social, family, vocational, educational, and spiritual goals. This assistance should lead to increased community integration, community functioning, social support, and quality of life, and improved clinical outcomes over the longer term.

Housing First Theory of Change and Community Psychology Theory

Like Brown and Lucksted's (2010) explication of community psychology and mental health self-help, we believe that it is useful to distinguish between the outcomes and processes of the Housing First theory of change described above. Nelson, Lord, and Ochocka (2001) described three key outcomes of a new paradigm approach to community mental health that apply to Housing First: (1) personal

Table 5.1 Pathways Housing First Logic Model

Domain/ Inputs	Theoretical Principles	Program Activities	Outcomes		
			Immediate (0–6 months)	Medium-term (6–24 months)	Long-term (> 2 years)
Housing/ Housing vouchers	Housing choice and community integration	• Assess consumer housing preferences • Rapid housing procurement • Permanent housing • Obtain rent supplement • Assistance with furnishing housing • Typically scattered-site housing, but depends on consumer choice • Lease with private landlord	• Rapidly housed in place of choice • Reduced contact with nonsupportive contacts • Development of new relationships with landlords and neighbors	• Increased housing stability • Reduced homelessness • Increased housing choice • Increased quality of housing • Increased housing satisfaction • Positive relationships with landlords, neighbors, and other community members	• Increased housing stability • Reduced homelessness • Maintenance of housing choice, quality, and satisfaction even if housing changes • Maintenance of relationships with landlords, neighbors, and other community members
Services/ ACT or ICM services	Separation of housing and services	• Mobile ACT or ICM outreach	• Development of working alliance with ACT or ICM staff	• Maintenance of working alliance with staff	• Maintenance of working alliance with staff • Increased community integration

Service choice and recovery-oriented services				
	Service philosophy • Staff values of choice and recovery • Assertive engagement • Assess consumer interests (e.g., work, education, social, family) • Assist consumer in accessing public benefits and health services • Harm reduction • Individualized consumer-centered planning • Broad range of goals Service array • Housing • Psychiatric services • Primary care • Social integration services Program structure • Weekly visits • Team meetings • Low consumer:staff ratio • Peer specialist	• Increased participation in mental health treatment • Increased participation in substance use treatment • Increased access to public benefits and health services • Reduced use of hospital and emergency services • Reduced involvement in criminal justice system	• Maintenance of reduced use of hospital and emergency services and involvement in criminal justice system • Improved community functioning • Increased subjective quality of life • More positive consumer narratives • Development of future-focused orientation • Improved clinical outcomes (i.e, reduced psychiatric symptoms and substance use)	• Maintenance of reduced use of hospital and emergency services and involvement in criminal justice system • Maintenance of community functioning, subjective quality of life, and consumer narratives • Increased involvement in work or education

Source: Reprinted from Aubry, T., Nelson, G., & Tsemberis, S. (2015). Pathways Housing First for people with severe mental illness who are homeless: A review of the research. *Canadian Journal of Psychiatry, 60,* 467–474.

empowerment and recovery, (2) community integration, and (3) acquisition of valued resources. While recovery has become a popular concept in mental health, it is closely aligned with the concept of personal/psychological empowerment (Nelson et al., 2001) and the strengths orientation of community psychology (Rappaport, 1977). The concept of community integration emerged in the context of individuals with developmental disabilities, but it includes the component of psychological integration or sense of community that has its roots in community psychology (Brown & Lucksted, 2010). Finally, resource acquisition, which includes stable and affordable housing, is a key component of community psychology's theory of transformative change in mental health (Nelson et al., 2001; Nelson, Kloos, & Ornelas, 2014).

Empowerment theory in community psychology provides a good fit to explain how Housing First produces these outcomes. Zimmerman (1995) contends that "domain specific perceived control" (p. 588) is one aspect of psychological empowerment. The specific domains of perceived control in Housing First are choice/control over one's housing (i.e., choice over where and with whom one lives and control over decisions regarding daily life in one's residence, such as having guests over) and control over the support that one receives (i.e., how often, when, and where the individual meets with her/his case manager). Moreover, this sense of control is hypothesized to be directly associated with other components of psychological empowerment, such as the behavioral component of adaptation to community living (Zimmerman, 1995), and other outcomes, such as quality of life (Nelson et al., 2001). As we show later in this chapter, there is empirical support for this hypothesis. In sum, empowerment theory suggests that choice and control over one's housing and services, which are foundational concepts in Housing First, can enhance feelings of self-efficacy and quality of life.

Theory of Change for Single-Site Supportive Housing

With few exceptions, single-site supportive housing programs have not formulated program logic models (Conrad et al., 1998) or theories of change (Fairweather et al., 1969; Haertl, 2007; Schutt, 2011) that can guide the development of fidelity measures. Both the Fairweather Lodge (Fairweather, Sanders, Maynard, & Cressler, 1969) and the Evolving consumer households (Schutt, 2011) models emphasized social networks, reciprocal relationships, social cohesion, and mutual peer support as the critical ingredients of single-site housing programs. Moreover, both programs strived to have residents eventually take over all of the functions initially performed by staff. While this occurred in the Fairweather Lodge, residents with lengthy histories of homelessness, cumulative adversity, and substance use continued to require staff support in the evolving consumer households project. It is incumbent on the developers of different forms of single-site housing to develop theories of change to guide research and practice.

Research on Housing Programs

There are several different types of research that have examined the adaptive functioning and well-being of people with serious mental illness in the context of their housing, including outcome evaluations, studies of fidelity and implementation, qualitative studies of consumer and staff experiences, and correlational studies.

Outcome Evaluations

Outcome evaluations focus on the outcome goals of a theory of change and are aimed at determining the impacts of a housing program on consumers' well-being and adaptive functioning. There are different types of experimental designs that can be used to evaluate the causal impacts of programs on consumer outcomes, including pre-test post-test designs, quasi-experimental designs (e.g., nonequivalent comparison group designs), and true experimental designs, or randomized controlled trials (RCTs), in which participants are randomly assigned to the housing program that is evaluated or to some other program or to treatment as usual (TAU). In this section, we review outcome evaluations of independent supportive housing and single-site supportive housing, a distinction that we made in chapter 2 (Nelson & Caplan, this volume). We focus primarily on evaluations that used an RCT design or quasi-experimental design, as they provide the strongest evidence of causal impacts of programs.

There are two specific challenges to reviewing and evaluating this research. First, there is the issue of specifying the type of housing program that is being evaluated. While some investigators clearly specify the type of housing program and its key components, in other cases the nature of the program is not well described. A second and similar problem concerns the comparison or control group. To determine the effectiveness of a housing program, it is best if the program can be compared to TAU. However, it is important to define the nature of TAU, as some settings may offer more or better housing programs than others. Another important goal of evaluative studies is to compare two different types of programs to determine which approach yields the best outcomes. In the following review, we attempt to clarify not only the program that is being evaluated, but also the comparison program(s).

Scattered-Site Supportive Housing

Reviews

There are two recent reviews of scattered-site supportive housing (Aubry, Ecker, & Jetté, 2014; Rog et al., 2014). Aubry et al. (2014) located six RCT studies and three quasi-experimental evaluations of scattered-site supportive housing. Of these nine studies, three RCTs compared scattered-site supportive housing to TAU (Cheng,

Lin, Kasprow, & Rosenheck, 2007; Hurlburt, Wood, & Hough, 1996; Stefancic & Tsemberis, 2007). All of the three studies found superior outcomes on measures of housing stability and homelessness compared with TAU. As well, Cheng et al. (2007) found significantly better outcomes on days of institutionalization, measures of alcohol use, and community adaptation. Rog et al. (2014) located seven RCT studies and five quasi-experimental evaluations of permanent supportive housing, but they did not clearly describe the conditions to which scattered-site supportive housing programs were compared. They concluded that scattered-site supportive housing led to significant improvement on the following outcomes: reduced homelessness, increased housing tenure, reduced emergency room use and hospitalizations, and increased consumer satisfaction.

Two earlier reviews examined the magnitude of impacts of scattered-site supportive housing (Leff et al., 2009; Nelson, Aubry, & Lafrance, 2007). Nelson, Aubry, et al. (2007) found that compared with TAU, permanent, independent supportive housing had an average effect size (ES) of .67 on measures of housing stability. In contrast, ACT alone or ICM alone had lower ESs of .47 and .28, respectively, on housing stability. Similarly, Leff et al. (2009) reported an average ES of .63 for permanent, independent supportive housing on housing stability. Moreover, the impact on housing stability was significantly greater for independent supportive housing than for TAU, which they termed "non-model" housing. The Leff et al. (2009) review is limited in that it reported pre-post ESs and included studies without a control or comparison group. In support of Rog et al.'s (2014) conclusions, Leff et al. (2009) reported positive effects for permanent, independent supportive housing on reductions in hospitalization (ES = .72), alcohol use (ES = .21), and drug abuse (ES = .51), and increased employment (ES = .27) and consumer satisfaction (ES = .73). None of the reviews have found significant reductions in consumers' experience of psychiatric symptoms in the primary research.

Recent Studies

There are several new studies of scattered-site supportive housing that were not covered in the aforementioned reviews. The At Home/Chez Soi program in Canada evaluated the impacts of the Pathways Housing First model for more than 2,000 homeless people with mental illness in five Canadian cities (Goering et al., 2011). Two groups were studied—one with high needs who were served by ACT and one with moderate needs who were served by ICM. All Housing First participants received rent supplements. Using an RCT design in which participants were randomly assigned to Housing First or TAU, the researchers found significantly better housing stability, community functioning, and quality of life, and significant reductions in hospital and emergency room use for the Housing First group at 1- and 2-year follow-ups compared with a TAU group.

These positive results were reported for both the high-needs ACT participants (Aubry, Tsemberis, et al., 2015; Aubry et al., 2016) and the moderate-needs ICM participants (Stergiopoulos et al., 2015).

Three recent studies using a quasi-experimental design have been conducted. Tsai, Kasprow, and Rosenheck (2011) compared homeless veterans with mental illness who lived independently with a rent subsidy with those who lived independently without a rent subsidy over a 3-month period. Those with the rent subsidy were significantly more likely to have a lease, to be living on their own, to report fewer negative problems with their housing, and to have greater satisfaction with their living situation. Burt (2012) compared the impacts of scattered-site supportive housing with an employment program with TAU on chronically homeless people with mental illness. After 1 year, those in the scattered-site supportive housing program had significantly higher rates of housing stability and paid employment than those in the comparison group. Srebnik, Connor, and Sylla (2013) studied the impacts of Housing First for a group of homeless individuals with medical needs and substance use problems, relative to a comparison group. Over 1 year, the Housing First group showed a significantly greater reduction in use of emergency rooms and a sobering center than those in the comparison group.

Summary

There is clear evidence that the Pathways Housing First model, relative to TAU, residential treatment, and the residential continuum, has shown better outcomes in terms of reduced homelessness and increased housing stability, reduced use of hospitalization and emergency rooms, and improved quality of life or consumer satisfaction. Compared with single-site group living or integrated service models, most studies have shown slightly better outcomes for scattered-site supportive housing, but these impacts appear small and are not always statistically significant.

Single-Site Supportive Housing

In this section we review research on the different types of single-site housing that we described in chapter 2 (Nelson & Caplan, this volume). We aim to determine whether single-site supportive housing models show positive outcomes compared with TAU, as well as examining studies that directly compare single-site models with scattered-site supportive housing.

Residential Treatment

Research on residential treatment programs dates back to the 1970s (e.g., Mosher & Menn, 1978; Samuels & Henderson, 1971) and continues to the present time. These programs are typically short-term in nature and provide some form of psychiatric and/or psychosocial treatment for people with mental illness and substance use.

It is important to note, however, that the nature of the treatment programs varies considerably. Residential treatment is in many ways the polar opposite of Housing First (Tsai, Mares, & Rosenheck, 2012b). It operates from a "treatment first" perspective, where treatment is mandatory. This contrasts with Housing First, where treatment is optional and depends on consumer preferences. Housing is short-term in residential treatment, but permanent in Housing First. Some residential treatment programs require mandatory abstinence from alcohol and drugs, whereas Housing First operates from a harm reduction approach. Finally, clinical services are provided on-site in residential treatment, whereas Housing First separates housing from clinical services.

Based on their review of residential treatment programs, Leff et al. (2009) reported positive impacts of residential treatment programs on post-program housing stability (ES = .48), psychiatric symptoms (ES = .65), hospitalization (ES = .34), alcohol abuse (ES = .87), drug abuse (ES = .41), and employment (ES = .27). We located four RCT evaluations (Burnam et al., 1996; Conrad et al., 1998; Dickey, Cannon, McGuire, & Gudeman, 1986; Samuels & Henderson, 1971; Velasquez & McCubbin, 1980) and three quasi-experimental evaluations (Blankertz & Cnaan, 1994; Mosher & Menn, 1978; Tsai, Mares, & Rosenheck, 2012a) of residential treatment programs.

Three early studies compared residential treatment with hospitalization. Samuels and Henderson (1971) randomly assigned men with mental illness to a residential token economy program, a state psychiatric hospital, or the psychiatric ward of a general hospital. Token economy participants were less likely to be rehospitalized and more likely to be employed than participants in the other two conditions. In a quasi-experimental study of people with mental illness, Mosher and Menn (1978) compared participants in a nonmedically oriented program, Soteria House, with a comparison group of participants admitted to the psychiatric ward of a general hospital. At a 2-year follow-up, the groups did not differ on rates of rehospitalization or symptoms, but the Soteria House participants were more likely to be living independently in the community. In an RCT, Dickey et al. (1986) randomly assigned people with mental illness to a residential treatment program or an inpatient psychiatric program. At a 2-year follow-up, participants in the residential program had spent significantly fewer days in hospital, but the two groups did not differ on a measure of symptoms.

Four studies have compared residential treatment with TAU. In a RCT, Velasquez and McCubbin (1980) randomly assigned young adults with mental illness, who were not homeless, to a residential program based on therapeutic milieu principles or TAU. At a 6-month follow-up, those in the residential program had significantly higher scores on measures of social participation, self-responsibility, rehospitalization, self-concept, social functioning, and problem-solving. Four more recent studies have focused on homeless adults with mental illness and substance use problems. The results of these studies show a mixed picture of outcomes post residential treatment. Burnam et al. (1996) and Conrad et al. (1998) found few differences over time in measures of housing stability, drug or alcohol use, and psychiatric symptoms between participants in residential treatment and control groups. Blankertz and Cnaan (1994) found a trend that those who had participated in residential treatment lived more independently following discharge from the program, but they did not test this statistically because of the small sample size. As well, the follow-up period was only 3 months. There was a significant difference on a measure of alcohol and drug use 3 months post-program, with participants in the residential program having lower rates of use.

Tsai et al. (2012a) studied chronically homeless adults with mental illness and/or substance use problems who entered residential treatment or transitional housing programs versus those who directly entered scattered-site supportive housing at baseline and follow-up intervals of 3, 6, 9, 12, 15, 18, 21, and 24 months. Over time, those in scattered-site supportive housing lived significantly more in their own places, spent fewer days incarcerated, and reported having more choice over their treatment than those who participated in residential treatment first. The two groups did not differ in terms of measures of alcohol or drug use, psychiatric symptoms, or community adjustment.

Transitional Housing

Like residential treatment programs, transitional housing programs are short-term in nature. Halfway houses were originally designed to ease the transition from hospital to the community and to support people in becoming involved in the community. These programs had more of a focus on providing support for community integration, and less of a focus on professionally trained staff providing the types of clinical services that are part and parcel of residential treatment. While halfway houses were very popular during the early days of deinstitutionalization, the mental health field has moved toward permanent housing. Today, transitional housing programs are aimed at homeless people and are part of the residential continuum in many communities (Barrow & Zimmer, 1998; Tsai, Rosenheck, & McGuire, 2012). Unfortunately, there has been little outcome research on transitional housing for homeless people with mental illness.

Gumrukcu (1968) conducted an evaluation of Conard House, which included both formerly hospitalized participants with mental illness and nonpatient-residents who did not have a history of mental illness. Programs included social activities and a cooking cooperative, and the length of residence was limited to 1 year. Compared with a matched comparison group, participants who left Conard House after 1 year were significantly more likely to be employed. In the only RCT of halfway houses, Lamb and Goertzel (1972) randomly assigned participants to a "high expectations" halfway house or a "low expectations" board-and-care home upon discharge from psychiatric hospital. The halfway house members also participated in a day treatment program. At follow-up intervals of 6, 12, 18, and 24 months, the halfway house participants were significantly less likely to be rehospitalized and significantly more likely to be employed in the community. Schinka, Francis, Hughes, LaLone, and Flynn (1998) compared a 3-week inpatient treatment program for substance use with transitional housing and treatment for substance use without housing. Both substance use programs were abstinence-based and used Alcoholics Anonymous or Narcotics Anonymous. At a 2-month follow-up, there were no differences between the groups in terms of abstinence. In a study in Australia, participants could stay in the program for up to 6 months and support was provided by an off-site team (Siskind et al., 2014). Using a matched comparison group design, the researchers compared the two groups on measures collected 1 year prior to and 1 year after transitional housing. Those in the transitional program showed a significant reduction in in-patient bed days and significantly more problems with housing relative to the comparison group.

Residential Continuum

The residential continuum characterizes housing for people with mental illness in many cities and consists of a range of different types of housing (i.e., large facilities, small group homes, apartments, shelters, residential treatment, transitional housing) that vary in terms of the intensity of support services available and whether those services are provided on-site or are separate from housing (Lipton, Siegel, Hannigan, Samuels, & Baker, 2000; Wherley & Bisgaard, 1987). It is important to note that the residential continuum is not one type of housing, but rather a heterogeneous mix of different types of housing that are variable in terms of their defining features and quality. Leff et al. (2009) reported positive pre-post impacts of the residential continuum on housing stability (ES = .80), psychiatric symptoms (ES = .68), and satisfaction (ES = .55). However, these ESs are based on only one to three studies and do not include comparisons with other housing approaches.

There are three RCTs (Tsemberis, Gulcur, & Nakae, 2004; Stefancic & Tsemberis, 2007; Goering et al., 2011) and two quasi-experiments (O'Connell, Kasprow, & Rosenheck, 2009; Tsemberis & Eisenberg, 2000) that have compared the Pathways Housing First approach with the residential continuum. While there is increased housing stability for people living in a residential continuum setting over time, as Leff et al. (2009) reported, four of the studies found that participants in the Pathways Housing First programs achieved significantly better outcomes than participants in the residential continuum in terms of housing stability and less time spent in hospital and emergency services, as well as improved community functioning and quality of life in the At Home/Chez Soi study.

The one exception to these findings comes from a quasi-experimental evaluation that compared scattered-site supportive housing with "multistage" residential continuum housing in which participants were placed in residential settings to get them "ready" for independent supportive housing (O'Connell et al., 2009). While the multistage housing participants had a significantly poorer profile on outcome measures at baseline, they improved significantly more over time than the independent supportive housing group, so that at follow-up the two groups no longer differed on the outcome measures. While the findings of this study challenge the Housing First model, the design of the study was less rigorous than the four studies reporting more favorable outcomes for Housing First.

Group Living

Another single-site model consists of small group homes or group living arrangements in which staff provides on-site support. Fairweather et al. (1969) evaluated the "Lodge" program for men who were recently discharged from a psychiatric ward in a VA hospital using an RCT design. Participants were randomly assigned to the Lodge or to standard discharge. While the Lodge participants spent significantly more time in the community and in paid employment than the control group at follow-up intervals of 6, 12, 18, 24, 30, 34, and 40 months, there were no significant differences between the groups in terms of symptomatology or a measure of community adjustment. Using a quasi-experimental design, Okin, Dolnick, and Pearsall (1983) compared hospitalized patients discharged to small community residences with a group of patients that was ready for discharge. The two groups were compared before discharge and then 2 and 8 months after discharge. Participants in the community residences improved significantly more than those in the comparison group on measures of social networks, capacity to meet basic needs, and perceptions of autonomy.

Two studies have directly compared group living with scattered-site supportive housing. In an RCT, Goldfinger et al. (1999) randomly assigned homeless people with mental illness to independent supportive housing or a group living condition that they termed "Evolving Consumer Households." They did not find any differences between the two groups in terms of the percentage of people housed after 18 months or in hospitalizations or use of other services. In a nonequivalent comparison group study, Nelson, Hall, and Walsh-Bowers (1997) compared 1-year follow-up outcomes of participants in supportive apartments, group homes, and board-and-care homes. The residents of both supportive apartments and group homes achieved significantly better outcomes than those in board-and-care homes in terms of increased personal growth, community involvement, and independent functioning, but the supportive apartment and group living participants did not differ significantly from one another.

Integrated Housing and Services

As we noted in chapter 2 (Nelson & Caplan, this volume), the defining feature of integrated or comprehensive housing is that it strives to coordinate housing and support services, with services often offered on-site. As well, an integrated housing and services program often consists of multiple units within one large building with on-site services. This approach is quite heterogeneous in terms of the services offered and the nature of the housing. However, unlike residential treatment or transitional housing, integrated housing is typically permanent. We located three RCT studies (Lipton, Nutt, & Sabatini, 1988; McHugo et al., 2004; Patterson et al., 2013) and seven quasi-experiments of this program model (Brown, Jason, Malone, Srebnik, & Sylla, 2016; Clark & Rich, 2003; Drake et al., 1997; Hodgins, Cyr, & Gaston, 1990; Mares & Rosenheck, 2011; Pearson, Montgomery, & Locke, 2009; Siegel et al., 2006).

An early study compared people with mental illness living in apartments in one congregate setting with a matched comparison group (Hodgins et al., 1990). One staff member was available on-site to provide support services for the 20 residents, and participants could also attend a drop-in center. The two groups were compared at follow-up intervals of 6, 12, 18, and 24 months, and there were no significant differences between the groups on measures of hospitalization, use of health and social services, and adaptive functioning. The supervised apartment group showed significantly higher levels of thought disorder at 24 months relative to the comparison group. The authors stated that the apartment blocks were stressful environments for the residents.

Two studies have compared housing and support services with support services only for homeless adults with mental illness. In a quasi-experiment, Clark and Rich (2003) compared comprehensive housing, which combined housing, housing support services, and case management, with a case management only program for homeless adults with mental illness at 6- and 12-month follow-up intervals. Significant differences between the groups were found in terms of the proportion of time spent in stable housing, but only for the group of participants with high levels of mental health and substance use impairment. Those in comprehensive housing had higher rates of stable housing (88%) than those in case management only (56%). The two groups also did not differ at follow-up on measures of psychiatric symptomatology or substance use.

McHugo et al. (2004) randomly assigned homeless people with mental illness to "integrated" housing or "parallel" housing. In the integrated housing model, housing and case management services were closely linked and provided by the same agency, whereas in the parallel housing, a mobile ACT team was delinked from housing. However, unlike the Pathways Housing First model, participants in parallel housing did not receive rent supplements. At an 18-month follow-up, the integrated housing participants were significantly more likely to be stably housed and reported significantly higher levels of life satisfaction and lower levels of psychiatric symptoms. The results of these two studies show the benefits of providing both housing and support over providing case management or ACT only.

Five studies have examined integrated housing and support services for homeless adults with mental illness in comparison with TAU. Lipton et al. (1988) compared homeless adults with mental illness randomly assigned to integrated housing or TAU. The residential program consisted of individual units in a single room occupancy (SRO) hotel that provide a comprehensive array of on-site services, including psychiatric treatment and case management. Participants were studied at baseline and at 4-, 8-, and 12-month follow-up intervals. Relative to control participants, program participants were significantly more likely to be stably housed during the course of the study and to report a significantly higher level of satisfaction with their housing.

In a five-site study, Mares and Rosenheck (2011) compared housing and support services developed through a Collaborative Initiative on Chronic Homelessness (CICH) with TAU for homeless adults with mental illness. The types of housing and support services provided by CICH varied greatly from site to site, with some sites providing the scattered-site Housing First model, while others provided support on-site, sometimes in SRO hotels. The two groups were compared at 3-month intervals over a period of 24 months. The CICH participants showed significant reductions in number of days homeless over time relative to the TAU group, but the two groups did not differ significantly on measures of substance use, health status, or community functioning.

A similar approach, called Full Service Partnerships, combined ACT with a variety of residential settings (board-and-care homes, SRO hotels, private apartments), and used some principles of the Housing First approach (Gilmer, Stefancic, Ettner, Manning, & Tsemberis, 2010). There was a significant reduction in homelessness for those in this program from 1 year before the program to 1 year after the program. Also, relative to a matched TAU comparison group that did not participate in the program, those participating in this program showed a significant decline in hospitalization, emergency room use, and involvement in the criminal justice system and significantly higher scores on a measure of quality of life.

Drake et al. (1997) provided evidence of the positive impacts of integrated treatment for people with mental illness with substance use problems. One agency provided mental health and substance use treatment and housing services for those in the integrated treatment program, while those in the comparison group received services from multiple agencies. At an 18-month follow-up, participants in the integrated program had significantly better outcomes than comparison group participants on measures of housing stability, reduced hospitalization, and reduced drug and alcohol use.

Brown et al. (2016) examined two groups of participants in single-site housing, those who were chronically homeless and those who were non-chronically homeless but who were high users of psychiatric services. These participants were compared with matched controls in TAU after one year and they showed significant reductions in homelessness and use of psychiatric services relative to the TAU group.

Three studies have compared a single-site model of integrated housing and services with the Pathways Housing First model (Patterson et al., 2013; Pearson et al., 2009; Siegel et al., 2006). Siegel et al. (2006) compared Pathways Housing First in New York City with a single-site model in which participants lived in individual units in a former hotel. The single-site model provided on-site case management and crisis supports, required sobriety, and could evict residents because of problem behaviors. The two groups were compared at baseline and at 6, 12, and 18 months and did not differ significantly in terms of housing outcomes. However, those in Pathways reported significantly higher levels of housing satisfaction in terms of autonomy and economic situation.

Pearson et al. (2009) compared the Pathways Housing First model in New York City with the single-site Downtown Emergency Service Center (DESC) model in Seattle that provides on-site services for homeless people with substance use problems (see the description of this program in chapter 2), and the Reaching Out and Engaging to Achieve Consumer Health (REACH) program in San Diego that uses multiple types of housing with delinked case management. There were no significant differences between these three treatment conditions on housing outcomes. However, Pathways' participants reported significantly fewer housing problems than those participants in the other two programs.

Finally, the Vancouver site of At Home/Chez Soi compared a single-site model with on-site services with Housing First, as well as a TAU control group in an RCT study. Participants in both the single-site program and the Pathways Housing First model reported significantly higher subjective quality of life than those in TAU (Patterson et al., 2013), but the Housing First group had significantly reduced levels of criminal offending (Somers, Rezansoff, Moniruzzaman, Palepu, & Patterson, 2013) and emergency department use (Russolillo, Patterson, McCandless, Moniruzzaman, & Somers, 2014) than those in TAU, while those in the single-site program did not.

Summary of Research on Single-Site Programs

First, there is evidence that residential treatment programs reduce rates of hospitalization, but little evidence that they reduce homelessness or the drug and alcohol use and psychiatric symptoms that they aim to treat. Second, transitional housing has been shown to reduce rates of rehospitalization and increase employment. Third, group living has also been shown to reduce rehospitalization and increase employment. Fourth, permanent single-site housing, which is integrated with a comprehensive array of services, has been shown to achieve better housing outcomes than case management alone or TAU.

Future Directions for Evaluation of Scattered-Site and Single-Site Supportive Housing

First, more research is needed that compares scattered-site and single-site supportive housing models, such as the study that is currently underway in Australia

(Whittaker et al., 2015). Second, since most studies follow participants for 1 or 2 years at most, longer-term follow-up studies are needed of different housing approaches. Third, greater attention should be devoted to the examination of peer-run supportive housing, as an alternative to existing models that emphasize professional staff and teams (see Wireman, chapter 13, this volume). Fourth, since many people become stably housed in scattered-site and single-site supportive housing, participants then face the issue of what to do with their lives. The addition of other evidence-based practices, like work supports, should be studied, since they show promise in improving other aspects of participants' lives (Burt, 2012). Finally, more research is needed on the impacts of different housing models on various subgroups (e.g., gender, age, history of trauma).

Fidelity and Implementation Evaluation

While it is important to examine program outcomes, it is also important study program fidelity and implementation, as the way a program is implemented can have marked impacts on the outcomes that are achieved.

Fidelity Evaluation

There has been a growing emphasis on evaluating the fidelity of evidence-based mental health programs. Fidelity evaluation focuses on the program activities of a program's theory of change and is concerned with the adherence of a program to the key components of a program model.

Fidelity assessments are a mechanism to assess program drift over time and location to specify if an intervention retains its core components in different implementation contexts (Pleace & Bretherton, chapter 11, this volume). For example, in a study of the implementation of Housing First in six European countries, Greenwood, Stefancic, Tsemberis, and Busch-Geertsma (2013) found evidence of fidelity to some components of Housing First, but not to others. It is not uncommon to hear staff from single-site supportive housing programs describe these programs as Housing First, even though they do not offer consumers much choice in their housing, do not provide rent supplements, do not offer scattered-site housing, and provide services on-site. Considerable variation in the fidelity of the Full Service Partnerships program in California to the Housing First model has been reported (Gilmer, Katz, Stefancic, & Palinkas, 2013). Additionally, O'Connell, Kasprow, and Rosenheck (2010) found substantial drift away from the key elements of Housing First when this program was scaled up for use with US veterans.

The core components of scattered-site housing and measures to assess these components have been identified (Rog & Randolph, 2002; Tabol, Drebing, & Rosenheck, 2010; Wong, Filoromo, & Tennille, 2007). More recently, Pathways to Housing First has developed a fidelity scale that requires an in-depth site visit

(Stefancic, Tsemberis, Messeri, Drake, & Goering, 2013) and a survey measure of fidelity that program staff and consumers can complete on their own (Gilmer, Stefancic, Sklar, & Tsemberis, 2013). The key components that are assessed in both of these measures include housing choice and structure (including scattered-site housing), separation of housing and services (including no on-site services), service philosophy (e.g., individualized, recovery orientation), service array, and team structure. In a study using the in-depth scale, Nelson et al. (2014) reported that 10 of the At Home/Chez Soi Housing First programs scored significantly higher than programs described earlier in the Full Service Partnerships in California (Gilmer et al., 2010).

One might ask why fidelity to the model is important. In the Full Service Partnerships study, Gilmer et al. (2014) found that fidelity was positively correlated with housing outcomes—the higher the fidelity, the greater the reduction in days homeless for consumers. Similarly, Davidson et al. (2014) found that Housing First fidelity was related to greater housing retention and reduced use of stimulants or opiates. In the At Home/Chez Soi project, Goering et al. (2016) also found that fidelity was directly related to the outcomes of housing stability, community functioning, and quality of life.

One might also ask whether the Pathways Housing First model can be adapted. In the At Home/Chez Soi project, the Pathways model was adapted to race, culture, community size, and existing services, while maintaining fidelity to the key components of the Pathways model (Keller et al., 2013; Stergiopoulos et al., 2012). Pathways Housing First has also been adapted to a rural context (Henwood, Melekis, & Stefancic, 2014; Stefancic, Henwood, et al., 2013). Thus, it is possible to have both fidelity to and adaptation of the model, both of which are important for program success and community relevance.

Implementation Evaluation

There is a growing body of research that is referred to as implementation science. Implementation science includes fidelity evaluation but is also concerned with the context in which implementation occurs and the resources that are provided, or not provided, for implementation (Damschroder et al., 2009; Fixsen, Naoon, Blase, Friedman, & Wallace, 2005; Raghavan, Bright, & Shadoin, 2008; Watson et al., 2014). Conceptual frameworks for implementation suggest two broad sets of factors that influence implementation: service delivery system factors and support system factors. Service delivery factors include policy, organizational, and community capacities, the capacities of individuals, and qualities of the program, while support system factors include training and technical assistance.

Studies of the implementation of At Home/Chez Soi, reported that organizational, community, and individual capacity factors and training and technical assistance facilitated both early (Nelson et al., 2014) and later program implementation

(Macnaughton et al., 2015) and led to improvements in fidelity ratings over time. Steadman et al. (2002) have conducted a study of the sustainability of housing programs for homeless people with mental illness. They describe what happened to the Access to Community Care and Effective Services and Supports (ACCESS) programs after federal funding for this 5-year demonstration project in the United States ended. While the programs continued, the integrity of the original programs was compromised by reduced staffing, higher client-staff ratios, changes in eligibility criteria, fewer clients served, and considerably fewer systems integration activities.

Summary of Fidelity and Implementation Evaluation

There is considerable risk of supportive housing programs drifting away from the original program model, as has been seen in the scaling up of Housing First. The development of fidelity scales has been a major advance. More research is needed to determine the fidelity of new programs to the original program models, since fidelity has been shown to be critically important for outcomes. As well, research needs to examine the key elements of single-site models and develop fidelity scales for these models (Sylvestre, Ollenberg, & Trainor, 2007). Finally, implementation research is needed to pinpoint factors that are important for achieving fidelity, such as adequate training and technical assistance.

Qualitative Research

Qualitative research provides an important window into the lived experiences of consumers and staff with housing and support.

Studies of Consumers' Experiences with Housing

Qualitative research has been used to provide a more in-depth picture of the experiences of mental health consumers with housing than can be obtained from standardized outcome measures. Nelson, Clarke, Febbraro, and Hatzipantelis (2005) found that after obtaining permanent housing with support, mental health consumers who had been homeless reported positive personal changes (e.g., greater independence), social changes (e.g., improved relationships), and the acquisition of resources (e.g., work). Similarly, Kirkpatrick and Byrne (2009) conducted qualitative interviews with formerly homeless people with mental illness three times after they obtained permanent supportive housing and found that participants reported positive life changes.

Padgett, Stanhope, Henwood, and Stefancic (2011) compared Housing First participants with "treatment first" participants at baseline and 6 and 12 months after program entry. They found that the Housing First participants were less likely to use substances and more likely to participate in substance use treatment compared with the "treatment first" group. In the At Home/Chez Soi study, Nelson,

Patterson, et al. (2015) selected a representative subsample of the larger study for qualitative interviews at baseline and 18 months. In this RCT, Housing First participants were significantly more likely to report positive life changes compared with TAU participants. In the same study, Macnaughton et al. (2016) found that the positive life changes reported primarily by the Housing First participants included the transition from the street to a home, the transition from home to community, and the transition from the present to the future. Henwood, Hsu, et al. (2013) found that the transition from homelessness to Housing First was characterized by participants as a "fresh start."

In the only long-term follow-up of scattered-site supportive housing, Tsai, Klee, Remmele, and Harkness (2013) conducted three case studies of formerly homeless veterans with mental illness 20 years after their participation in the HUD-VASH program. The three individuals showed different trajectories that can be characterized as "sustained participation in subsidized housing," "successful discharge followed by re-engagement," and "case management was more important than the rent subsidy."

In another study of engagement and retention in services, Padgett, Henwood, Abrams, and Davis (2008) interviewed 21 formerly homeless persons with mental illness and substance abuse in Housing First and 18 participants in treatment first programs. They found that staff acts of kindness, pleasant surroundings (e.g., housing quality and privacy), and the promise or achievement of scattered-site supportive housing promoted engagement, while the lack of one-to-one staff support and program rules and restrictions impeded engagement. An example of consumer disempowerment in a traditional housing setting is found in the following quote.

> It was like a totem pole, you know, and clients are at the bottom and the staff they've got the top and they have their laws or this rule or that rule ... And they're very, very controlling these people. (Padgett et al., 2008, p. 230)

Studies of Staff Experiences with Housing

A number of studies have examined frontline Housing First staff in the original Pathways program in New York. Housing First staff members were more concerned with clinical issues, since participants had already obtained housing, whereas the staff of "treatment first" programs were more preoccupied with finding housing for participants (Henwood & Tiderington, chapter 15, this volume; Henwood, Shinn, Tsemberis, & Padgett, 2013; Henwood, Stanhope, & Padgett, 2011). As well, Housing First staff placed a higher priority on consumer values and showed a greater tolerance for participants' "deviant" behaviors than staff from "treatment first" programs. Finally, Housing First staff viewed housing as a right, whereas staff of "treatment first" programs saw housing as something that participants needed to earn by demonstrating "readiness."

Qualitative research has been used to examine some of the quandaries that case managers face in relating to consumers with mental illness and substance use issues in Housing First programs. Stanhope, Henwood, and Padgett (2009) interviewed 18 case managers about service disengagement. These staff attributed disengagement, which led to homelessness, to substance use and poor decision-making. In Finland, Juhila, Hall, and Raitakari (2010) observed 23 meetings of professionals in a supported housing unit with a focus on how staff accounted for what they perceived to be "troublesome behavior" on the part of their clients. While the nature of the program is not clearly described, they found that blaming clients, excusing clients, or blaming others and excusing clients were the common ways that staff explained these behaviors.

Studies That Examined Both Consumer and Staff Perspectives

Stanhope (2012) interviewed 14 case manager and 10 consumers and observed consumer-staff interactions regarding service engagement. She found that paying attention, communicating, and making a connection were important aspects of consumer-staff relationships that promoted service engagement. Tiderington, Stanhope, and Henwood (2013) used the same sample to examine staff use of harm reduction strategies. They found that strong consumer-staff relationships enabled open discussions about drug use and greater use of a harm reduction approach to substance use.

Juhila, Hall, Günther, Raitakari, and Saario (2015) observed 30 consumer-staff meetings in three supported housing programs in Finland based largely on the Housing First model to examine consumer choice in interactions with staff. They found that in the vast majority of instances, staff members accept consumer choices. However, there were some instances in which staff questioned consumers' choices and negotiated with them.

In the Toronto At Home/Chez Soi site, Zerger et al. (2016) examined housing delays and transfers through interviews with housing 23 case managers or housing specialists and 25 consumers. They found that housing delays and transfers were influenced by consumer-staff collaboration, consumer preferences, and staff prioritization of consumer choice over immediate housing access. Enhancing consumer-staff communication and involving consumers in housing searches were suggested as ways to avoid housing delays and transfers. This same study was used to examine the need for and meaning of interim housing within the Housing First model (Zerger et al., 2014). They found that safe, flexible housing options are needed when consumers' choices cannot be immediately satisfied within normal market conditions.

Summary

Qualitative research has added to the understanding of consumer and staff experiences in supportive housing. This research has been particularly valuable in unpacking the moral dilemmas of translating abstract principles like choice and harm reduction into everyday practice and interactions between consumers and the staff that support them. However, with a few exceptions, outcome evaluations and qualitative studies are done separately rather than integrated. Thus, there is a need for more use of mixed methods approaches that integrate qualitative and quantitative methods (Lewin, Glenton, & Oxman, 2009; Macnaughton, Goering, & Nelson, 2012; Nelson, Macnaughton, et al., 2015; Sylvestre et al., chapter 8, this volume).

Correlational Research

In contrast to the outcomes studies reviewed earlier that use experimental or quasi-experimental designs, correlational research has been used to determine the relationship between housing characteristics and consumers' well-being and adaptive functioning. Two particularly important housing characteristics that have been examined are (1) housing quality and (2) housing preferences, choice, and control.

Housing Quality

Housing quality refers to the physical condition of the housing, including its appearance, maintenance, safety, presence of pests, and so forth. Several reviews of the literature have reported findings that demonstrate that housing quality is positively related to consumers' satisfaction with their housing and inversely related to negative affect and symptom distress (Kloos & Shah, 2009; Nelson & Saegert, 2009; Parkinson, Nelson, & Horgan, 1999). While it stands to reason that poor quality housing would be stressful for participants, there are nevertheless some cautions about this research. One problem is that the findings are typically based on self-report measures of housing quality, which are subjective in nature, rather than more objective observer ratings. In support of this concern, Wright and Kloos (2007) found that a self-report measure of housing quality, but not an observer-rated measure, was related to psychiatric symptoms, recovery, housing satisfaction, and adaptive functioning. Another problem is that correlation does not mean causation. However, two longitudinal studies have found that after controlling for earlier levels of subjective quality of life, mastery, and negative affect that housing quality was a significant predictor of later assessments of these outcomes (Nelson, Hall, & Walsh-Bowers, 1998; Nelson, Sylvestre, Aubry, George, & Trainor, 2007). This type of longitudinal research suggests that poor housing quality may lead to negative outcomes. Finally, Adair et al. (2014) found that observer-rated housing quality was significantly higher for Housing First participants than for those in TAU, and that there was more variability in housing quality for those in TAU.

Housing Preferences, Choice, and Control

Housing First is based on the premise of consumer preference, choice, and control over housing and support (Tsemberis et al., 2004). A number of surveys (Nelson, Hall, & Forchuk, 2003; Piat et al., 2008; Tanzman, 1993) and qualitative studies (Forchuk, Nelson, & Hall, 2006; Tsai, Bond, Salyers, Godfrey, & Davis, 2010) of consumer preferences for housing have consistently found that the vast majority of mental health consumers prefer to live in scattered-site housing with no live-in staff, but rather off-site support workers who can visit or be available by phone. Moreover, in comparing the preferred and actual housing of people with mental health issues, Nelson et al. (2003) found that participants who were living in the type of housing that they preferred reported significantly greater satisfaction with their living situation than participants who were living in housing that was not what they preferred. O'Connell, Rosenheck, Kasprow, and Frisman (2006) similarly reported that the greater the number of desired features obtained in housing, the greater was participants' overall quality of life and satisfaction with living situation 3 months and 1 year later.

Some studies have measured consumers' perceptions of choice and control over their housing and have found that choice and control measures are related to positive outcomes, including mastery and reduced psychiatric symptoms (Greenwood, Schaefer-McDonald, Winkel, & Tsemberis, 2005), independent functioning (Nelson et al., 1998), subjective quality of life and community functioning (Nelson, Sylvestre, et al., 2007), a positive reaction to obtaining housing (Yanos, Barrow, & Tsemberis, 2004), housing satisfaction and residential stability (Srebnik, Livingston, Gordon, & King, 1995), and the psychological dimension of community integration (Gulcur, Tsemberis, Stefancic, & Greenwood, 2007). Also, Nelson, Sylvestre, et al. (2007) found that the greater the control participants felt they had over case management support, the better was their functioning in the community. In a study of homeless persons with mental illness living in independent supportive housing, Tsai and Rosenheck (2012) found that choice over one's living environment was significantly inversely related to symptoms at 6 months and 1 year and significantly directly related to subjective quality of life at 6 months and 1 year. Choice over mental health treatment and case management were not related to outcomes. Finally, studies have shown that residents of scattered-site supportive housing show significantly higher levels of housing choice and control than residents of other types of housing (Nelson, Hall, et al., 1997; Nelson, Sylvestre, et al., 2007; Tsemberis et al., 2004; Tsemberis, Rogers, Rodis, Dushuttle, & Skryha, 2003).

Summary of Correlational Research

Correlational research has identified the importance of housing quality and housing choice for consumers' well-being and adaptive functioning. In view of their importance, measures of these characteristics need to be incorporated into outcome evaluations, as was done in the At Home/Chez Soi study.

Conclusions

Research on housing and mental health has grown steadily since the first literature reviews appeared in the 1970s. Recently, housing programs for people with mental illness have shifted toward scattered-site housing. In particular, research on Housing First, including outcome studies, studies of fidelity and implementation, and qualitative studies, has dominated the field. Moreover, Housing First has developed a clear theory of change and measures of fidelity to determine whether the model is implemented as specified by Housing First theory. Single-site models also need to develop their unique theories of change and measures of fidelity, just as Housing First developers have done. Moreover, there is a need to examine further the comparative effectiveness of Housing First and other single-site supportive housing models.

Acknowledgment

The authors thank Ben Henwood for his suggestions of research to include in this chapter.

References

Adair, C.E., Kopp, B., Lavoie, J., Distasio, J., Hwang, S.W., Watson, A., ... Goering, P. (2014). Development and initial validation of the Observer-rated Housing Quality Scale (ORHQS) in a multisite trial of Housing First. *Journal of Urban Health: Bulletin of the New York Academy of Medicine, 91,* 242–255.

Aubry, T., Ecker, J., & Jetté, J. (2014). Supported housing as a promising Housing First approach for people with severe and persistent mental illness. In M. Guirguis-Younger, R. McNeil, & S.W. Hwang (Eds.), *Homelessness and health* (pp. 155–188). Ottawa: University of Ottawa Press.

Aubry, T., Goering, P., Veldhuizen, S., Adair, C.E., Bourque, J., Distasio, J., ... Tsemberis, S. (2016). A multiple-city RCT of Housing First with Assertive Community Treatment for homeless Canadians with serious mental illness. *Psychiatric Services, 67,* 275–281.

Aubry, T., Nelson, G., & Tsemberis, S. (2015). Pathways Housing First for people with severe mental illness who are homeless: A review of the research. *Canadian Journal of Psychiatry, 60,* 467–474.

Aubry, T., Tsemberis, S., Adair, C.E., Veldhuizen, S., Streiner, D., Latimer, E., ... Goering, P. (2015). One-year outcomes of a randomized controlled trial of Housing First with ACT in five Canadian cities. *Psychiatric Services, 66,* 463–469.

Barrow, S., & Zimmer, R. (1999). Transitional housing and services: A synthesis. In L.B. Fosburg & D.L. Dennis (Eds.), *Practical lessons: The National Symposium on Homelessness Research*

(Chapter 10). Washington, DC: Department of Housing and Urban Development and Department of Health and Human Services.

Bickman, L. (1987). The functions of program theory. In L. Bickman (Ed.), *Using program theory in evaluation* (pp. 5–18). San Francisco: Jossey-Bass.

Brown, L.D., & Lucksted, A. (2010). Theoretical foundations of mental health self-help. In L.D. Brown & S. Wituk (Eds.), *Mental health self-help: Consumer and family initiatives* (pp. 19–38). New York: Springer.

Brown, M.M., Jason, L.A., Malone, D.K., Srebnik, D., & Sylla, L. (2016). Housing First as an effective model for community stabilization among vulnerable individuals with chronic and non-chronic homelessness histories. *Journal of Community Psychology, 44*, 384–390.

Burnam, M.A., Morton, S.C., McGlynn, E.A., Petersen, L.P., Stecher, B.M., Hayes, C., & Vaccaro, J.V. (1996). An experimental evaluation of residential and nonresidential treatment for dually diagnosed homeless adults. *Journal of Addictive Diseases, 14*, 111–134.

Chen, H.-T. (2005). *Practical program evaluation: Assessing and improving planning, implementation and effectiveness.* Thousand Oaks, CA: Sage.

Chen, H.-T., & Rossi, P.H. (1992). *Using theory to improve program and policy evaluations.* Westwood, CT: Greenwood.

Cheng, A., Lin, H., Kasprow, W., & Rosenheck, R.A. (2007). Impact of supported housing on clinical outcomes: Analysis of a randomized trial using multiple imputation technique. *Journal of Nervous and Mental Disease, 195*, 83–88.

Clark, C., & Rich, A.R. (2003). Outcomes of homeless adults with mental illness in a housing program and in case management only. *Psychiatric Services, 54*, 78–83.

Conrad, K.J., Hultman, C.I., Pope, A.R., Lyons, J.S., Baxter, W.C., Daghestani, A.N., . . . Manheim, L.M. (1998). Case managed residential care for homeless addicted veterans: Results of a true experiment. *Medical Care, 36*, 40–53.

Davidson, D., Neighbors, C., Hall, G., Hogue, A., Cho, R., Kutner, B., & Morgenstern, J. (2014). Association of Housing First implementation and key outcomes among homeless persons with problematic substance use. *Psychiatric Services, 65*, 1318–1324.

Damschroder, L.J., Aron, D.C., Keith, R.E., Kirsh, S.R., Alexander, J.A., & Lowery, J.C. (2009). Fostering implementation of health services research findings into practice: A consolidated framework for advancing implementation science. *Implementation Science, 4*, 50. doi:10.1186/1748-5908-4-50

Dickey, B., Cannon, N.L., McGuire, T.G., & Gudeman, J.E. (1986). The quarterway house: A two-year cost study of an experimental residential program. *Hospital and Community Psychiatry, 37*, 1136–1143.

Drake, R.E., Yovetich, N.A., Bebout, R.R., Harris, M., & McHugo, G.J. (1997). Integrated treatment for dually diagnosed homeless adults. *Journal of Nervous and Mental Disease, 185*, 298–305.

Dunn, J.R., van der Meulen, E., O'Campo, P., & Muntaner, C. (2013). Improving health equity through theory-informed evaluations: A look at housing first strategies, cross-sectoral health programs, and prostitution policy. *Evaluation and Program Planning, 36*, 184–190.

Fairweather, G.W., Sanders, D.H., Maynard, H., & Cressler, D.L. (1969). *Community life for the mentally ill.* Chicago: Aldine.

Fixsen, D.L., Naoom, S.F., Blase, K.A., Friedman, R.M., & Wallace, F. (2005). *Implementation research: A synthesis of the literature.* Tampa: University of South Florida National Implementation Research Network.

Forchuk, C., Nelson, G., & Hall, G.B. (2006). "It's important to be proud of the place you live in": Housing problems and preferences of psychiatric survivors. *Perspectives in Psychiatric Care, 42*, 49–59.

Gilmer, T.P., Katz, M.L., Stefancic, A., & Palinkas, L.A. (2013). Variation in the implementation of California's full service partnerships for persons with serious mental illness. *Health Services Research, 48*, 2245–2267.

Gilmer, T.P., Stefancic, A., Ettner, S.L., Manning, W.G., & Tsemberis, S. (2010). Effect of full-service partnerships on homelessness, use and costs of mental health services, and quality of life among adults with serious mental illness. *Archives of General Psychiatry, 67,* 645–652.

Gilmer, T.P., Stefancic, A., Katz, M.L., Sklar, M., Tsemberis, S., & Palinkas, L.A. (2014). Fidelity to the Housing First model and effectiveness of supported housing. *Psychiatric Services, 65,* 1311–1317.

Gilmer, T.P., Stefancic, A., Sklar, M., & Tsemberis, S. (2013). Development and evaluation of a Housing First fidelity survey. *Psychiatric Services, 64,* 911–914.

Goering, P.N., Streiner, D.L., Adair, C., Aubry, T., Barker, J., Distasio, J., ... Zabkiewicz, D.M. (2011). The At Home/Chez Soi trial protocol: A pragmatic, multi-site, randomized controlled trial of Housing First in five Canadian cities. *BMJ Open,* 1–18. Retrieved from http://bmjo-pen.bmj.com/content/1/2/e000323.full

Goering, P., Veldhuizen, S., Nelson, G., Stefancic, A., Tsemberis, S., Adair, C., ... Streiner, D. (2016). Further validation of the Pathways Housing First fidelity scale. *Psychiatric Services, 67,* 111–114.

Goldfinger, S.M., Schutt, R.K., Tolomiczenko, G.S., Seidman, L., Penk, W.E., Turner, W., . . . Caplan, B. (1999). Housing placement and subsequent days homeless among formerly homeless adults with mental illness. *Psychiatric Services, 50,* 674–679.

Greenwood, R. M., Schaefer-McDonald, N. J., Winkel, G., & Tsemberis, S. (2005). Decreasing psychiatric symptoms by increasing choice in services for adults with histories of homelessness. *American Journal of Community Psychology, 36,* 223–238.

Greenwood, R.M., Stefancic, A., Tsemberis, S., & Busch-Geertsma, V. (2013). Implementations of Housing First in Europe: Challenges in maintaining model fidelity. *American Journal of Psychiatric Rehabilitation, 16,* 290–312.

Gulcur, L., Tsemberis, S., Stefancic, A., & Greenwood, R.M. (2007). Community integration of adults with psychiatric disabilities and histories of homelessness. *Community Mental Health Journal, 43,* 211–228.

Gumrukcu, P. (1968). The efficacy of a psychiatric halfway house: A three-year study of a therapeutic residence. *Sociological Quarterly, 9,* 374–386.

Haertl, K.L. (2007). The Fairweather mental health housing model—A peer supportive environment: Implications for psychiatric rehabilitation. *American Journal of Psychiatry, 10,* 149–162.

Henwood, B.F., Hsu, H.-T., Dent, D., Winetrobe, H., Carranza, A., & Wenzel, S. (2013). Transitioning from homelessness: A "fresh-start" event. *Journal of the Society for Social Work and Research, 4,* 47–57.

Henwood, B.F., Melekis, K., & Stefancic, A. (2014). Introducing Housing First in a rural service system: A multistakeholder perspective. *Global Journal of Community Psychology Practice, 5*(1), 1–13.

Henwood, B.F., Shinn, M., Tsemberis, S., & Padgett, D.K. (2013). Examining provider perspectives within Housing First and traditional programs. *American Journal of Psychiatric Rehabilitation, 16,* 262–274.

Henwood, B.F., Stanhope, V., & Padgett, D.K. (2011). The role of housing: A comparison of frontline provider views in Housing First and traditional programs. *Administration and Policy in Mental Health, 38,* 77–85.

Hodgins, S., Cyr, M., & Gaston, L. (1990). Impact of supervised apartments on the functioning of mentally disordered adults. *Community Mental Health Journal, 26,* 507–516.

Hurlburt, M.S., Wood, P.A., & Hough, R.L. (1996). Providing independent housing for the homeless mentally ill: A novel approach to evaluating long-term longitudinal housing patterns. *Journal of Community Psychology, 24,* 291–310.

Juhila, K., Hall, C., Günther, K., Raitakari, S., & Saario, S. (2015). Accepting and negotiating service users' choices in mental health transition meetings. *Social Policy and Administration, 49,* 612–630.

Juhila, K., Hall, C., & Raitakari, S. (2010). Accounting for the clients' troublesome behaviour in a supported housing unit: Blames, excuses and responsibility in professionals' talk. *Social Work, 10*, 59–79.

Keller, C., Goering, P., Hume, C., Macnaughton, E., O'Campo, P., Sarang, A., ... Tsemberis, S. (2013). Initial implementation of Housing First in five Canadian cities: How do you make the shoe fit, when one size does not fit all? *American Journal of Psychiatric Rehabilitation, 16*, 275–289.

Kirkpatrick, H., & Byrne, C. (2009). A narrative inquiry: Moving on from homelessness for individuals with a major mental illness. *Journal of Psychiatric and Mental Health Nursing, 16*, 68–75.

Kirsh, B., Gewurtz, R., & Bakewell, R.A. (2011). Critical characteristics of supported housing: Resident and service provider perspectives. *Canadian Journal of Community Mental Health, 30*(1), 15–30.

Kloos, B., & Shah, S. (2009). A social-ecological approach to investigating relationships between housing and adaptive functioning for people with serious mental illness. *American Journal of Community Psychology, 44*, 316–326.

Lamb, H.R., & Goertzel, V. (1972). High expectations of long-term ex-state hospital patients. *American Journal of Psychiatry, 24*, 29–34.

Leff, H.S., Chow, C.M., Pepin, R., Conley, J., Allen, I.E., & Seaman, C.A. (2009). Does one size fit all? What we can and can't learn from a meta-analysis of housing models for persons with mental illness. *Psychiatric Services, 60*, 473–482.

Lewin, S., Glenton, C., & Oxman, A.D. (2009). Use of qualitative methods alongside randomised controlled trials of complex healthcare interventions: Methodological study. *British Medical Journal, 339*, 732–734.

Lipton, F.R., Nutt, S., & Sabatini, A. (1988). Housing the homeless mentally ill: A longitudinal study of a treatment approach. *Hospital and Community Psychiatry, 39*, 40–45.

Lipton, F.R., Siegel, C., Hannigan, A., Samuels, J., & Baker, S. (2000). Tenure in supportive housing for homeless persons with severe mental illness. *Psychiatric Services, 51*, 479–486.

Macnaughton, E., Goering, P., & Nelson, G. (2012). Exploring the value of mixed methods within the At Home/Chez Soi Housing First project: A strategy to evaluate the implementation of a complex population health intervention for people with mental illness who have been homeless. *Canadian Journal of Public Health, 103*(Suppl. 1), S57–S62.

Macnaughton, E., Stefancic, A., Nelson, G., Caplan, R., Townley, G., Aubry, T., ... Goering, P. (2015). Implementing Housing First across sites and over time: Later fidelity and implementation evaluation of a pan-Canadian multi-site Housing First program for homeless people with mental illness. *American Journal of Community Psychology, 55*, 279–291.

Macnaughton, E., Townley, G., Nelson, G., Caplan, R., MacLeod, T., Polvere, L., ... Goering, P. (2016). How does housing catalyze recovery in Housing First participants? Qualitative findings from the At Home/Chez Soi Project. *American Journal of Psychiatric Rehabilitation, 19*(2), 1–24.

Mares, A.S., & Rosenheck, R.A. (2011). A comparison of treatment outcomes among chronically homeless adults receiving comprehensive housing and health services versus usual local care. *Administration and Policy in Mental Health, 38*, 459–475.

McHugo, G.J., Bebout, R.R., Harris, M., Cleghorn, S., Herring, G., Xie, H., ... Drake, R.E. (2004). A randomized controlled trial of integrated versus parallel housing services for homeless adults with severe mental illness. *Schizophrenia Bulletin, 30*, 969–982.

Nelson, G., Aubry, T., & Lafrance, A. (2007). A review of the literature on the effectiveness of housing and support, assertive community treatment, and intensive case management for persons with mental illness who have been homeless. *American Journal of Orthopsychiatry, 77*, 350–361.

Nelson, G., Clarke, J., Febbraro, A., & Hatzipantelis, M. (2005). A narrative approach to the evaluation of supportive housing: Stories of homeless people who have experienced mental illness. *Psychiatric Rehabilitation Journal, 29*, 98–104.

Nelson, G., Goering, P., & Tsemberis, S. (2012). Housing for people with lived experience of mental health issues: Housing First as a strategy to improve quality of life. In C.J. Walker, K. Johnson, & E. Cunningham (Eds.), *Community psychology and the socio-economics of mental distress: International perspectives* (pp. 191–205). Basingstoke, UK: Palgrave Macmillan.

Nelson, G., Hall, G.B., & Forchuk, C. (2003). Current and preferred housing of psychiatric consumer/survivors. *Canadian Journal of Community Mental Health, 22*(1), 5–19.

Nelson, G., Hall, G.B., & Walsh-Bowers, R. (1997). A comparative evaluation of supportive apartments, group homes, and board-and-care homes for psychiatric consumer/survivors. *Journal of Community Psychology, 25,* 167–188.

Nelson, G., Hall, G.B., & Walsh-Bowers, R. (1998). The relationship between housing characteristics, emotional well-being and the personal empowerment of psychiatric consumer/survivors. *Community Mental Health Journal, 34,* 57–69.

Nelson, G., Kloos, B., & Ornelas, J. (2014). Transformative change in community mental health: A community psychology framework. In G. Nelson, B. Kloos, & J. Ornelas (Eds.), *Community psychology and community mental health: Towards transformative change* (pp. 3–20). Oxford: Oxford University Press.

Nelson, G., Lord, J., & Ochocka, J. (2001). *Shifting the paradigm in community mental health: Towards empowerment and community.* Toronto: University of Toronto Press.

Nelson, G., Macnaughton, E., & Goering, P. (2015). What qualitative research can contribute to a randomized controlled trial of a complex community intervention: Lessons learned from the At Home/Chez Soi Project for homeless persons with mental illness. *Contemporary Clinical Trials, 45,* 377–384.

Nelson, G., Patterson, M., Kirst, M., Macnaughton, E., Isaak, C.A., Nolin, D., . . . Goering, P. (2015). Life changes among persons with mental illness: A longitudinal study of Housing First and usual treatment. *Psychiatric Services, 66,* 592–597.

Nelson, G., & Saegert, S. (2009). Housing and quality of life: An ecological perspective. In V.R. Preedy & R.R. Watson (Eds.), *Handbook of disease burdens and quality of life measures* (pp. 3363–3382). Heidelberg, Germany: Springer-Verlag.

Nelson, G., Sylvestre, J., Aubry, T., George, L., & Trainor, J. (2007). Housing choice and control, housing quality, and control over professional support as contributors to the subjective quality of life and community adaptation of people with severe mental illness. *Administration and Policy in Mental Health Services and Mental Health Services Research, 34,* 89–100.

O'Connell, M.J., Kasprow, W., & Rosenheck, R. (2009). Direct placement versus multistage models of supported housing in a population of veterans who are homeless. *Psychological Services, 6,* 190–201.

O'Connell, M.J., Kasprow, W., Rosenheck, R. (2010). National dissemination of supported housing in the VA: Model adherence versus model modification. *Psychiatric Rehabilitation Journal, 33,* 308–319.

O'Connell, M.J., Rosenheck, R., Kasprow, W., & Frisman, L. (2006). An examination of fulfilled housing preferences and quality of life among homeless persons with mental illness and/or substance use disorders. *Journal of Behavioral Health Services and Research, 33,* 354–365.

Okin, R.L., Dolnick, J.A., & Pearsall, D.T. (1983). Patients' perspectives on community alternatives to hospitalization: A follow-up study. *American Journal of Psychiatry, 140,* 1460–1464.

Padgett, D.K., Henwood, B.F., Abrams, C., & Davis, A. (2008). Engagement and retention in services among formerly homeless adults with co-occurring mental illness and substance abuse: Voices from the margins. *Psychiatric Rehabilitation Journal, 31,* 226–233.

Padgett, D.K., Stanhope, V., Henwood, B.F., & Stefancic, A. (2011). Substance use outcomes among homeless clients with serious mental illness: Comparing Housing First with Treatment First programs. *Community Mental Health Journal, 47,* 227–232.

Parkinson, S., Nelson, G., & Horgan, S. (1999). From housing to homes: A review of the literature on housing approaches for psychiatric consumer/survivors. *Canadian Journal of Community Mental Health, 18,* 145–163.

Patterson, M., Moniruzzaman, A., Palepu, A., Zabkiewicz, D., Frankish, C.J., Krausz, M., & Somers, J.M. (2013). Housing First improves subjective quality of life among homeless adults with mental illness: 12-month findings from a randomized controlled trial in Vancouver, British Columbia. *Social Psychiatry and Psychiatric Epidemiology, 48,* 1245–1259.

Pearson, C., Montgomery, A.E., & Locke, G. (2009). Housing stability among homeless individuals with serious mental illness participating in Housing First programs. *Journal of Community Psychology, 37,* 404–417.

Piat, M., Lesage, A., Boyer, R., Dorvil, H., Courure, A., Grenier, G., & Bloom, D. (2008). Housing for persons with serious mental illness: Consumer and service provider preferences. *Psychiatric Services, 59,* 1011–1017.

Raghavan, R., Bright, C.L., & Shadoin, A.L. (2008). Towards a policy ecology of implementation of evidence-based practices in mental health settings. *Implementation Science, 3,* 26. doi. org/ 10.1186/1748-5908-3-26

Rappaport, J. (1977). *Community psychology: Values, research, and action.* New York: Holt-Rinehart-Winston.

Rog, D.J., Marshall, T., Dougherty, R.H., George, P., Daniels, A.S., Ghose, S.S., & Delphin-Rittmon, M.E. (2014). Permanent supportive housing: Assessing the evidence. *Psychiatric Services, 65,* 287–294.

Rog, D.J., & Randolph, F.L. (2002). A multisite evaluation of supported housing: Lessons learned from cross-site collaboration. *New Directions for Evaluation, 94,* 61–72.

Rush, B., & Ogborne, A. (1991). Program logic models: Expanding their role and structure for program planning and evaluation. *Canadian Journal of Program Evaluation, 6,* 95–106.

Russolillo, A., Patterson, M., McCandless, A., Moniruzzoman, A., & Somers, J. (2014). Emergency department utilization among formerly homeless adults with mental disorders after one year of Housing First interventions: A randomised controlled trial. *International Journal of Housing Policy, 14,* 79–97.

Samuels, J.S., & Henderson, J.D. (1971). A community-based operant learning environment: III. Some outcome data. In R.D. Rubin, H. Fersterheim, A.A. Lazarus, & C.H. Franks (Eds.), *Advances in behavior therapy* (pp. 263–271). New York: Academic Press.

Schinka, J.A., Francis, E., Hughes, P., LaLone, L., & Flynn, C. (1998). Comparative outcomes of inpatient care and supportive housing for substance-dependent veterans. *Psychiatric Services, 49,* 946–950.

Schutt, R.K., with Goldfinger, S.M. (2011). *Homelessness, housing, and mental illness.* Cambridge, MA: Harvard University Press.

Siegel, C.E., Samuels, J., Tang, D.-I., Berg, I., Jones, K., & Hopper, K. (2006). Tenant outcomes in supported housing and community residences in New York City. *Psychiatric Services, 57,* 982–991.

Siskind, D., Harris, M., Kisely, S., Siskind, V., Brogan, J., Pirkis, J., . . . Whiteford, H. (2014). A retrospective quasi-experimental study of a transitional housing program for patients with severe and persistent mental illness. *Community Mental Health Journal, 50,* 538–547.

Somers, J.M., Rezansoff, S.N., Moniruzzaman, A., Palepu, A., & Patterson, M. (2013). Housing First reduces re-offending among formerly homeless adults with mental disorders: Results of a randomized controlled trial. *PLoS ONE, 8*(9), e72946.

Srebnik, D., Connor, T., & Sylla, L. (2013). A pilot study of the impact of Housing First—Supported housing for intensive users of medical hospitalization and sobering services. *American Journal of Public Health, 103,* 316–321.

Srebnik, D., Livingston, J., Gordon, L., & King, D. (1995). Housing choice and community success for individuals with serious and persistent mental illness. *Community Mental Health Journal, 31,* 139–152.

Stanhope, V. (2012). The ties that bind: Using ethnographic methods to understand service engagement. *Qualitative Social Work, 11,* 412–430.

Stanhope, V., Henwood, B.F., & Padgett, D.K. (2009). Understanding disengagement from the perspective of case managers. *Psychiatric Services, 60*, 459–464.

Steadman, H.J., Cocozzo, J.J., Dennis, D.L., Lassiter, M.G., Randolph, F.L., Goldman, H., & Blaskinsky, M. (2002). Successful program maintenance when federal demonstration dollars stop: The Access program for homeless mentally ill persons. *Administration and Policy in Mental Health, 29*, 481–493.

Stefancic, A., Henwood, B.F., Melton, H., Shin, S.-M., Lawrence-Gomez, R., & Tsemberis, S. (2013). Implementing Housing First in rural areas: Pathways Vermont. *American Journal of Public Health, 103*(S2), S206–S209.

Stefancic, A., & Tsemberis, S. (2007). Housing First for long-term shelter dwellers with psychiatric disabilities in a suburban county: A four-year study of housing access and retention. *Journal of Primary Prevention, 28*, 265–279.

Stefancic, A., Tsemberis, S., Messeri, P., Drake, R., & Goering, P. (2013). The Pathways Housing First Fidelity Scale for individuals with psychiatric disabilities. *American Journal of Psychiatric Rehabilitation, 16*, 240–261.

Stergiopoulos, V., Hwang, S.W., Gozdzik, A., Nisenbaum, R., Latimer, E., Rabouin, D., . . . Goering, P.N. (2015). Effect of scattered-site housing using rent supplements and intensive case management on housing stability among homeless adults with mental illness: A randomized controlled trial. *Journal of the American Medical Association, 313*, 905–915.

Stergiopoulos, V., O'Campo, P., Godzik, A., Jeyaratnam, J., Corneau, S., Sarang, A., & Hwang, S.W. (2012). Moving from rhetoric to reality: Adapting Housing First for homeless individuals with mental illness from ethno-racial groups. *BMC Health Services Research, 12*, 345. http://www.biomedcentral.com/1472-6963/12/345

Sylvestre, J., Ollenberg, M., & Trainor, J. (2007). A participatory benchmarking strategy for describing and improving supportive housing. *Psychiatric Rehabilitation Journal, 31*, 115–124.

Tabol, C., Drebing, C., & Rosenheck, R.A. (2010). Studies of "supported" and "supportive" housing: A comprehensive review of model descriptions and measurement. *Evaluation and Program Planning, 33*, 446–456.

Tanzman, B. (1993). An overview of surveys of mental health consumers' preferences for housing and support services. *Hospital and Community Psychiatry, 44*, 450–455.

Tiderington, E., Stanhope, V., & Henwood, B.K. (2013). A qualitative analysis of case managers' use of harm reduction in practice. *Journal of Substance Abuse Treatment, 44*, 71–77.

Tsai, J., Bond, G.R., Salyers, M.P., Godrey, J.L., & Davis, K.E. (2010). Housing preferences and choices among adults with mental illness and substance use disorders: A qualitative study. *Community Mental Health Journal, 46*, 381–388.

Tsai, J., Kasprow, W., & Rosenheck, R.A. (2011). Exiting homelessness without a voucher: A comparison of independently housed and other homeless veterans. *Psychological Services, 8*, 114–122.

Tsai, J., Klee, A., Remmele, J., & Harkness, L. (2013). Life after supported housing: A case series of formerly homeless clients in the Department of Veterans Affairs-Supportive Housing (HUD-VASH) Program 20 years later. *Journal of Community Psychology, 41*, 1039–1046.

Tsai, J., Mares, A.S., & Rosenheck, R.A. (2012a). A multisite comparison of supported housing for chronically homeless adults: "Housing First" versus "Residential Treatment First." *Psychological Services, 7*, 219–232.

Tsai, J., Mares, A.S., & Rosenheck, R.A. (2012b). Does housing chronically homeless adults lead to social integration? *Psychiatric Services, 63*, 427–434.

Tsai, J., & Rosenheck, R.A. (2012). Consumer choice over living environment, case management, and mental health treatment in supported housing and its relation to outcomes. *Journal of Health Care for the Poor and Underserved, 23*, 1671–1677.

Tsai, J., Rosenheck, R.A., & McGuire, J.F. (2012). Comparison of outcomes of homeless female and male veterans in transitional housing. *Community Mental Health Journal, 48*, 705–710.

Tsemberis, S., & Asmussen, S. (1999). From streets to homes: The Pathways to Housing consumer preference supported housing model. *Alcoholism Treatment Quarterly, 17*, 113–131.

Tsemberis, S., & Eisenberg, R.F. (2000). Pathways to Housing: Supported housing for street-dwelling homeless individuals. *Psychiatric Services, 51*, 487–493.

Tsemberis, S., Gulcur, L., & Nakae, M. (2004). Housing First, consumer choice, and harm reduction for homeless individuals with a dual diagnosis. *American Journal of Public Health, 94*, 651–656.

Tsemberis, S., Rogers, E.S., Rodis, E., Dushuttle, P., & Skryha, A. (2003). Housing satisfaction for persons with psychiatric disabilities. *Journal of Community Psychology, 31*, 581–590.

Velasquez, J.S., & McCubbin, H.I. (1980). Towards establishing the effectiveness of community-based residential treatment: Program evaluation by experimental research. *Journal of Social Service Research, 3*, 337–359.

Watson, D.P., Wagner, D.A., & Rivers, M. (2013). Understanding the critical ingredients for facilitating consumer change in Housing First programming: A case study approach. *Journal of Behavioral Health Services and Research, 40*, 169–179.

Watson, D.P., Young, J., Ahonen, E., Xu, H., Henderson, M., Shuman, V., & Tolliver, R. (2014). Development and testing of an implementation strategy for a complex housing intervention: Protocol for a mixed methods study. *Implementation Science, 9*, 138. http://www.implementationscience.com/content/9/1/138

Wherley, M., & Bisgaard, S. (1987). Beyond model programs: Evaluation of a countywide system of residential treatment programs. *Hospital and Community Psychiatry, 38*, 852–857.

Whittaker, E., Swift, W., Flatau, P., Dobbins, T., Schollar-Root, O., & Burns, L. (2015). A place to call home: Study protocol for a longitudinal, mixed methods evaluation of two housing first adaptations in Sydney, Australia. *BMC Public Health, 15*, 342, open access

Wong, Y.-L.I., Filoromo, M., & Tennille, J. (2007). From principles to practice: A study of implementation of supported housing for psychiatric consumers. *Administration and Policy in Mental Health and Mental Health Services Research, 34*, 13–28.

Wright, P.A., & Kloos (2007). Housing environment and mental health outcomes: A levels of analysis perspective. *Journal of Environmental Psychology, 27*, 79–89.

Yanos, P.T., Barrow, S.M., & Tsemberis, S. (2004). Community integration in the early phase of housing among homeless persons with severe mental illness: Successes and challenges. *Community Mental Health Journal, 40*, 133–150.

Zerger, S., Pridham, K.F., Jeyaratnam, J., Connelly, J., Hwang, S.W., O'Campo, P., & Stergiopoulos, V. (2014). The role and meaning of interim housing in Housing First programs for people experiencing homelessness and mental illness. *American Journal of Orthopsychiatry, 84*, 431–437.

Zerger, S., Pridham, K.F., Jeyaratnam, J., Hwang, S.W., O'Campo, P., Kohli, J., & Stergiopoulos, V. (2016). Understanding housing delays and relocations within the Housing First model. *Journal of Behavioral Health Services and Research, 43*, 38–53.

Zimmerman, M.A. (1995). Psychological empowerment: Issues and illustrations. *American Journal of Community Psychology, 23*, 581–600.

6

Theory and Research on the Social Context of Housing

Policy and Planning, Informal Systems, and the Geosocial Environment

GEOFFREY NELSON AND TIMOTHY MACLEOD

We begin this chapter by presenting a social-ecological framework of the larger social context of housing for people with mental illness (Hall, Nelson, & Smith Fowler, 1987; Kloos & Shah, 2009; Nelson & Saegert, 2009; Winkel, Saegert, & Evans, 2009). Next, we review theory and research that is pertinent to the three dimensions of this framework that are relevant to housing: (1) policy and planning systems, (2) informal systems, and (3) the geosocial environment. It is important to understand these larger social systems because the relationships between housing programs and individuals with mental illness, reviewed in chapter 5, are influenced by these dimensions of the social context.

A Social-Ecological Framework for Housing and Mental Health

The social-ecological framework draws attention to the multilayered nature of the social context and considers the impact of intervention beyond the level of the individual (Bronfenbrenner, 1977). In the previous chapter (chapter 5), we reviewed theory and research related to individuals with mental illness in the context of the micro-environments of housing settings. In this chapter, we review theory and research related to the proximal neighborhood and community contexts in which housing is embedded, and the more distal macro-social structures that impact on neighborhoods and communities. Understanding the experiences of any one person in her or his housing requires seeing how life in the housing, and interactions with others in one's neighborhood and community, are influenced by a variety of factors that are often far removed from the housing itself.

In their social-ecological analysis of housing, Hall et al. (1987) identified three dimensions that cut across the different proximal and distal environments. One dimension consists of formal systems, which include programs, planning, and policy. Formal systems involve public sector professionals who play different roles in housing for people with mental illness from direct service to policy formulation. Whereas planning often occurs at a community level, policymaking is often constructed at the macro-level. A second dimension is informal systems, which includes other residents, neighbors, landlords, and peers in one's proximal environment, and the general public, which is more distal. This dimension is important because it involves roles and relationships that focus more on citizenship and community membership than clienthood. The resident with a mental illness plays the roles of neighbor, tenant, peer, and community member in their relationships with others in their informal social networks and citizen in the larger community and society. The final dimension is the geosocial environment, which includes the geographic location and spatial concentration of housing in the proximal neighborhood environment and the more distal community environment.

The social-ecological framework is not a theory with specific, testable hypotheses. Rather, it is a broad framework with several orienting principles that aims to contextualize mental illness within social and geographic structures (Kloos & Shah, 2009). This framework draws attention to both the physical and social aspects of housing environments, a focus on human growth and adaptive functioning, how different qualities of the environment promote or impede human growth and adaptation. Moreover, the social-ecological framework has an explicit value orientation, including values of empowerment, social justice, and social change.

Drawing on this social-ecological framework, we now turn to a review of theory and research that is pertinent to the three dimensions of this framework: (1) policy and planning systems, (2) informal systems, and (3) the geosocial environment.

Policy and Planning Systems

How do different types of housing programs and their underlying values and assumptions arise and how are they sustained? To answer these questions, one must investigate the policy and planning context of housing programs. Theory and research on the policy and planning context of housing for people with mental illness have focused on (1) policy formulation, (2) advocacy, (3) planning, and (4) knowledge transfer.

Policy Formulation

In the United States, Stanhope and Dunn (2011) provided an example of policy formulation with what they called the "curious case" of Housing First. They argued that Housing First has taken root in US policy because it is compatible in some ways with the tenets of neoliberalism. Housing First relies on the private rental market and is concerned with cost savings that can be achieved by targeting chronically homeless persons who use costly health services. Kuhn and Culhane (1998) found that chronically or episodically homeless persons constitute only about 15% of the homeless population, but that they account for over 50% of shelter use, as well as other costly services, such as hospitalization and emergency rooms. So it may be less expensive to provide chronically and episodically homeless persons with Housing First. A similar situation in Canada led to the conception of the At Home/ Chez Soi project (Aubry, Farrell, Hwang, & Calhoun, 2013; Macnaughton, Nelson, & Goering, 2013).

Theory

Nelson (2013) has described two theoretical approaches to policy formulation that are pertinent to housing and mental health policy. The first approach, evidence-based policy, emphasizes the role of empirical research in policymaking. Oliver, Lorenc, and Innvaer (2014) note that the evidence-based policy approach has been guided by the "two communities" theory of policymaking. According to this perspective, researchers and policy makers function in different communities and have different worldviews (Caplan, 1979), and the goal of researchers is to "bridge the gap" between policy and research so that evidence is brought to bear on policy. A second approach to policy formulation, discursive policy analysis (Fischer, 2003), emphasizes the importance of policy "windows," "streams" (problems, politics, and policies), "arenas," and "entrepreneurs" (Kingdon, 2005; Mintrom & Norman, 2009; Weiss, 1999). Policy windows are opportunities for change when different policy streams converge toward a particular policy solution. Policy entrepreneurs are strategically located individuals who recognize these opportunities for policy change and are able to advance a policy solution that cuts across different policy arenas and constituencies.

While the evidence-based approach was relevant to the uptake of Housing First in the United States in terms of research that identified chronically homeless people as a costly problem and Housing First as a cost-effective solution, Stanhope and Dunn (2011) argued that evidence was only part of the story. They emphasized the key role that policy entrepreneurs, such as Philip Mangano (chapter 9, this volume), played in framing the problem and the solution in a way that was palatable to the conservative George W. Bush administration. Similarly, in the case of At Home/ Chez Soi in Canada, Macnaughton et al. (2013) found that federal approval of this initiative had little to do with evidence, but was motivated more by an initial concern about dealing with the chronically homeless population in the downtown east end of Vancouver in the lead up to the 2010 Vancouver Winter Olympics. These different theoretical perspectives on policy formulation can inform research on housing and mental health policy.

Research

A qualitative study of the conception of the At Home/Chez Soi project in Canada found support for the discursive approach to policy analysis (Macnaughton et al., 2013). These researchers found that in the lead-up to the 2010 Winter Olympics in Vancouver, the federal conservative government was concerned that Canada's image would be tarnished because the world would see the homelessness and open drug use in the city's downtown east end. The government consulted with former Senator Michael Kirby, newly appointed chair of the Mental Health Commission of Canada, who was able to parlay their concerns into a pan-Canadian homelessness and mental illness research demonstration project, At Home/Chez Soi, to test the effectiveness of the Housing First approach. The researchers underscored the importance of "policy entrepreneurs," like Kirby, in taking advantage of windows of opportunity to create policy change. These policy entrepreneurs are strategically located close to government, know how to frame problems and solutions in such a way that bridges different stakeholder groups, and can take advantage of timing and opportunities to make change.

Advocacy Coalitions

Closely related to policy formulation are advocacy coalitions, which strive to create social change, including policy changes.

Theory

Whereas the theoretical approaches to policy formulation discussed in the previous section focus on policy elites, including researchers, policy makers, and policy entrepreneurs, the theories discussed in this section focus on the role of coalitions in policy change. Both Nelson (1994) and Trainor, Lurie, Ballantyne, and Long (1987) used resource mobilization theory (Edwards & Gillham, 2013; Jenkins, 1983) to understand advocacy coalitions in housing and mental health. Resource mobilization theory holds that claims-making or grievances are insufficient to create social change. Additionally, there must be organizational bases of support for coalition activities and changes in the political climate (i.e., windows of opportunity for change).

Another theoretical framework that can be used to study advocacy coalitions in housing and mental health is advocacy coalition theory (Sabatier & Weible, 2007). Similar to resource mobilization theory, advocacy coalition theory hypothesizes that some change in external conditions is necessary for policy change. However, this theory places much more emphasis on the belief systems of policy actors. They differentiate between types of beliefs, asserting that there are some deep core beliefs (i.e., assumptions about human nature) and policy core beliefs (e.g., beliefs about individual responsibility) that are resistant to change, while secondary beliefs are narrower in focus (e.g., the value of a particular program) and are more amenable to change. Moreover, these beliefs are embedded in social networks that they call advocacy coalitions. Sabatier and Weible (2007) also argue that there are two or more advocacy coalitions on any policy issue. Policy change occurs, they hypothesize, when there are changes in external conditions and policy-oriented learning in which the beliefs of coalition members are modified.

Research

While advocacy for housing for persons with mental illness and/or homelessness is common (Hopper, 2003), there have been few empirical studies of advocacy coalitions. Trainor, Lurie, Ballantyne, and Long (1987) and Nelson (1994) both used resource mobilization theory to understand the development of housing programs for people with mental illness in the 1980s in Ontario.

Trainor et al. described the emergence of the Toronto Supportive Housing Coalition (SHC), as well as providing longitudinal data on the growth of housing before and after the coalition. The Toronto SHC was formed in response to deinstitutionalization of psychiatric hospitals in the city of Toronto that led to a psychiatric ghetto nearby one of the psychiatric hospitals. Discharged patients lived in poor quality board-and-care homes and were quite visible in this community, which resulted in considerable media attention. Through concerted advocacy efforts, the SHC was able to make a partnership with the Minister of Health that led to the rapid development of supportive housing programs for this population that were dispersed across the city rather than concentrated in one area.

On the heels of the success of the Toronto SHC, the Region of Waterloo, Ontario formed a similar coalition and advocated with provincial politicians and the Ministry of Health, engaging in letter-writing campaigns, meetings, and public education (Nelson, 1994). As was the case in Toronto, the number of supportive housing programs grew in Waterloo Region, as did funding for community mental health services. Moreover, Nelson (1994) showed that this growth in housing and support occurred at a higher rate for Waterloo Region compared with the province of Ontario as a whole.

Fleury, Grenier, Vallée, Hurtubise, and Levésque (2014) used advocacy coalition theory to understand the planning of the At Home/Chez Soi project at the Montreal site. They identified several different coalitions with different belief systems and underscored the importance of policy brokers who were able to move project planning forward in a way that was acceptable to different coalitions.

Planning

Planning is complementary to policy in the policy and planning systems. Planning typically involves how a policy will be implemented in a community or how communities strive to create their own plans.

Theory

Sylvestre (2014) has described two theoretical approaches to understanding systems change in mental health: planned versus emergent. Whereas planned change is top-down, highly controlled, designed to be predictable, and focused on whole systems, emergent change is bottom-up, lacking in control, unpredictable by nature, and focused on parts of the system. In the field of housing and mental health, a planned change effort to reform housing would focus on a systematic change strategy led by professionals that is based on a review of best practices and involves extensive stakeholder consultation, resulting in a final report with recommendations for change (e.g., Sylvestre, George, Aubry, Durbin, Nelson, & Trainor, 2007). In contrast, an emergent change approach would entail consumers speaking out about their housing and mental health services without professional guidance (e.g., Capponi, 1992; Howell & Voronka, 2012).

Research

Nelson et al. (2013) conducted a qualitative study of the relationships between the national team and the five local sites in Canada's At Home/Chez Soi project. Their study demonstrated that both planned and emergent change characterizes the development of complex community interventions like Housing First. They found that a key to the successful launching of this project was the collaborative relationship and power sharing that occurred between the national team and five local sites. While the sites pushed for and achieved adaptation of the Housing First approach to local contexts, culture, and services, the core principles of Housing First provided the moral and empirical foundations for the project that led to a common vision and common values across sites. Collaboration among partners at the local level and the involvement of persons with lived experiences were also important for successful planning (Nelson et al., 2016).

Henwood, Melekis, and Stefancic (2014) conducted a qualitative case study of planned change for Housing First in rural communities in Vermont. While the Housing First program brought new resources and expertise, planning was complicated by limited input and consultation of local service providers during the planning of the grant. The planning processes pushed for shifting the paradigm from a medical-institutional approach to a community-based approach. Eventually, there were changes in state-level policy toward the adoption of the Housing First approach.

Sylvestre et al. (2007) reported on another planned change approach to housing for people with mental illness in Toronto. Their multimethod study included literature reviews, policy document reviews, and round-table discussions aimed at describing and improving Ontario's system of housing for people with mental illness. The focus of their community-based participatory action research was consultation with the provincial government. They found that most people with mental illness were in housing in which they were "overserved" and could live in independent housing if they had the financial and clinical supports to do so (Sylvestre, Nelson, Durbin, George, Aubry, & Ollenberg, 2006).

Knowledge Transfer

Knowledge transfer refers to strategies that researchers undertake to "scale-up" research demonstration projects. In the field of housing and mental health, examples of knowledge transfer efforts include the Fairweather Lodge (Fairweather, Sanders, & Tornatzky, 1974) and Housing First (Tsemberis, 2010).

Theory

There is increasing recognition that program dissemination does not move in a linear fashion from research to practice (Oliver et al., 2014), but rather in a more iterative way in which there is a dialogue between researchers and community-based practitioners. In response to this recognition, Wandersman et al. (2008) have developed an interactive systems framework to understand and guide the dissemination of evidence-based programs (Flaspohler, Lesesne, Puddy, Smith, & Wandersman, 2012). This framework identifies three interconnected systems that are important for knowledge transfer and program dissemination. First, there is the knowledge translation and synthesis system in which research evidence is presented in user-friendly formats, including toolkits, research summaries, videos, and so forth, that are relevant and accessible to community practitioners. Second, the support system consists of general and innovation-specific resources that are available to support communities in translating research into practice in different community contexts. Importantly, this system includes training and technical assistance as important sources of support. Third, the delivery system focuses on community capacity for using the materials and supports provided by the first two systems, including a community's readiness for change. Wandersman et al. (2008) emphasize the interactive nature of these systems, as well as larger macro-systemic influences on adoption and implementation, including policy, funding, climate, and existing research. The interactive systems framework can be used to inform research on the knowledge transfer of different housing models for people with mental illness.

Research

Dissemination of knowledge has become a major initiative in healthcare. Austin et al. (2014) described the expansion of Housing First programs in the US Department of Veterans Affairs (VA). In their study, the authors reported a number of challenges in "scaling-up" Housing First, including difficulties in rapidly housing participants, staff challenges in balancing their time between housing and case management issues, and midlevel leadership issues. In another study of the dissemination of Housing First in the VA, O'Connell et al. (2010) found that service delivery became less intensive over time and 75% of the veterans ended their involvement with the program within 5 years. The authors concluded that the new programs that were created did not adhere closely to the original Housing First model. Aside from the implementation challenges, it is important to note that the Housing First model and research described earlier led to a change in policy in the VA toward a Housing First approach to ending homelessness. Tsai (2014) noted the importance of timing and readiness in creating this policy change. The limited research on scaling-up Housing First has been atheoretical and could benefit from the guidance of theoretical perspectives such as Wandersman et al.'s (2008) framework.

Summary of Policy and Planning Theory and Research

Very little research has examined the contexts in and the processes by which housing programs for people with mental illness arise, are sustained, or are disseminated. Thus, there is a need for more research on policy formulation, advocacy, planning, and knowledge transfer in this area. Moreover, the roles that people with mental illness play in policy and planning need to be further examined (Nelson et al., 2016). Several theories were reviewed that can help to inform future research on policy and planning in mental health housing.

Informal Systems

Informal systems stand apart from formal policy and planning systems in which people with mental illness have traditionally played the role of "client." Informal systems have more potential to recognize the citizenship of people with mental illness through the roles of neighbor, tenant, friend, coworker, and fellow student as well as participation in the larger civil society. A substantive dimension of life for people with mental illness involves social relationships and community life. Historically people with mental illness have been excluded from social life, and a critical challenge for community psychology is to theorize and research the processes of social inclusion for these individuals. Theory and research on informal systems related to housing have focused on (1) the social network relationships of people with mental illness with neighbors, landlords, and peers; (2) community integration; and (3) social integration with the larger society.

Relationships with Social Network Members

Theory

Social network and social support theory holds that being embedded in a social network can result in either positive or negative social support (Nelson, Hall, Squire, & Walsh-Bowers, 1992). Positive support can include emotional, socializing, tangible, and problem-solving support, while negative support includes emotional abuse, social exclusion, refusal to provide practical help, and encouragement to avoid or deny problems. As well, the principles of self-help suggest that peer-provided support can increase social networks and social support for consumer/survivors (Mead, Hilton, & Curtis, 2001).

Research

Neighbors
Research on community housing for people with mental illness and relationships with neighbors began in the 1970s and 1980s with a focus on neighborhood opposition to single-site facilities for discharged patients (Hall et al., 1987). Much of this research focused on NIMBY (not in my backyard) responses from community members who were opposed to the placement of these facilities in their neighborhoods (Dear, 1992). Opposition to such programs is typically rooted in community members' perceived threats to their safety and concerns about negative impacts on their property values. While opposition to community housing occurs in up to 50% of cases, research has suggested that opposition diminishes over time when neighbors realize that they will not experience adverse effects from such housing (Zippay & Lee, 2008). As well, opposition typically subsides as long as people with mental illness do not display bizarre or disruptive behavior (Hall et al., 1987). Moreover, a survey conducted by Tefft, Segall, and Trute (1987) found that roughly 65% of community members rated mental health facilities, including housing programs, as either desirable or neutral, even when they were located on their block.

Zippay (2007) conducted a survey of mental health administrators and on-site staff of community residences for people with mental illness regarding relations with neighbors. She found that programs that notified neighbors encountered significantly more opposition initially than those that did not. Moreover, those sites that notified neighbors were more likely to hold open houses and other events to build positive relations with neighbors. While the majority of neighbors were described as "very accepting" or "accepting" of the housing, few neighbors had developed relationships with anyone from the psychiatric residences. In a survey of neighbors, Zippay and Lee (2008) found that only 27% of those surveyed said they were aware of a psychiatric residence in their neighborhood. Among those who were aware of the residence, only 9% believed that the facility had an adverse effect on neighborhood quality of life; most believed that the site had a positive impact or no impact on the quality of life of the neighborhood.

Kloos and Townley (2011) found that psychiatric distress for people with mental illness was mediated by the quality of their relationships with neighbors. The better the relationships with neighbors, the less distress. In a qualitative study of consumer experiences with neighbors, Wong, Metzendorg, and Min (2006) found that consumers identified respect and courtesy as the qualities of "good neighbors," while noise and hostility characterized "bad neighbors." The participants also described experiences of stigma and social rejection from neighbors.

With the recent growth of scattered-site housing, which is less likely to engender opposition, research on NIMBY in community residences for people with mental illness has waned (DeVerteuil, 2013). However, continued research on relationships with neighbors is important for both single-site and scattered-site housing approaches to understand the positive and negative roles that neighbors can play vis-à-vis residents with mental illness (Yanos, 2007).

Landlords

We do not review research on landlord relationships with tenants with mental illness in this chapter since we will review this material in chapter 16 (MacLeod et al., this volume). Suffice it to say here that the little research that has been done on landlords has shown that they can act in the same discriminatory way as neighbors (e.g., Page, 1996), but that they can also be significant sources of support to tenants with mental illness (Bengtsson & Hansson, 2014).

Peers

In the mental health field, the term "peer" refers to other people with lived experience of mental illness. While there is now ample evidence that peers are important sources of support, through self-help groups, consumer-run organizations, and as paid peer specialists (Miyamoto & Sono, 2012; Pitt et al., 2013), as noted in chapter 4 (Aubry, Rae, & Jetté, this volume), there have been few program models and little research on peer support in the context of supportive housing (Tsai, Rosenheck, Sullivan, & Harkness, 2011).

Bean, Shafer, and Glennon (2013) conducted an evaluation of a peer support model for independent supportive housing for homeless people who were medically vulnerable. Over the course of 1 year, 98% of participants maintained their housing, and they showed significant increases in planned healthcare use and quality of life, and significantly reduced involvement with the criminal justice system and abuse of drugs and alcohol. Yamin et al. (2015) described the findings of an evaluation of single-site peer supportive housing for homeless mentally ill people with multiple evictions from independent housing. A "peer support couple" provided on-site support to 5 residents, each with their own apartment within a six-unit apartment complex. This model led to improved housing and psychological stability among residents.

Community Integration

Theory

Wolfensberger (1999) proposed social role valorization theory as a way to understand and promote the inclusion of people with developmental disabilities. Social role valorization expanded on his earlier concept of "normalization," which he defined as "the utilization of means which are as culturally normative as possible in order to establish and/or maintain personal behaviours and characteristics which are as culturally normative as possible" (Wolfensberger, 1972, p. 28). Social role valorization draws on the importance of valued social roles for individuals who have been historically excluded from social life (e.g., those with psychiatric and developmental disabilities). In this sense, social role valorization signals a paradigm shift from the active social exclusion of individuals with psychiatric disabilities, through institutionalized segregation, to the active social inclusion of these individuals. Social role valorization suggests that it is important to provide opportunities for individuals with mental illness to develop and take on new social identities within the norms of the community beyond that of "client" (McKnight, 1996).

Drawing on social role valorization theory, Wong and Solomon (2002) presented an important theory of community integration in the context of supportive independent housing programs. They define community integration as "the extent to which an individual spends time, participates in activities, and uses goods and services in the community outside his/her home in a self-initiated manner" (Wong & Solomon, 2002, p. 9). Expanding on the work of Aubry and Myner (1996), Wong and Solomon described three dimensions of social integration: (1) physical integration, (2) psychological integration, and (3) social integration. Physical integration signifies the accessibility of services and the degree of participation in community life. Social integration indicates the degree of social interaction with nondisabled individuals in the community including the quantity and quality of social connections. Psychological integration refers to the degree to which individuals feel a part of their community and have an emotional connection to their neighborhood. Wong and Solomon specify four components of service design that are essential to facilitating community integration: (1) the housing environment, (2) the behavioral environment, (3) the support environment, and (4) personal factors.

Research

Aubry, Flynn, Virley, and Neri (2013) applied social role valorization theory and community integration theory to people with psychiatric disabilities. They found that the degree to which housing programs value consumer participation in social roles in the community was significantly related to consumers' physical, psychological, and social integration. Moreover, psychological integration was associated with life satisfaction.

One question that research on housing and community integration has addressed is whether people with mental illness differ from other community members in community integration. Aubry and Myner (1996) found that people with mental illness scored significantly lower on a measure of social integration, but not physical or psychological integration, than a sample of residents from the same neighborhoods. Yanos, Stefancic, and Tsemberis (2011, 2012) found that their consumer sample scored significantly lower than their community sample on measures of physical integration, social integration, and citizenship, but not psychological sense of community.

Given that people with mental illness show lower levels on some dimensions of community integration than other community members, another question is whether supportive housing can improve community integration. Yanos, Barrow, and Tsemberis (2004) found that formerly homeless people with mental illness reported few problems with fitting in the community after they obtained supportive independent or single-site housing. In another study of formerly homeless people with mental illness, Tsai et al. (2012) found that over time (from baseline to 6 months to 1 year after obtaining supportive housing), participants showed a mixed picture of change regarding community integration. Participants' work and volunteering significantly declined over time; there was no change in social support; but there were significant increases in physical integration and citizenship activities. In a qualitative study, Wong et al. (2006) found that housing staff believe that community integration is a process for people with mental illness that requires the development of social and independent living skills, having a supportive consumer network, and overcoming stigma and an identity as a homeless person.

Research has also examined the correlates of community integration. Gulcur, Tsemberis, Sefancic, and Greenwood (2007) found that housing choice and independent, scattered-site housing were positively related to psychological and social integration. Research by Townley and colleagues has found that distal social support (i.e., contact with community members rather than one's immediate social network) (Townley, Miller, & Kloos, 2013) and individual perceptions of the quality of one's neighborhood are positively related to psychological integration (Townley & Kloos, 2014).

Social Integration

Theory

Ware, Hopper, Tugenberg, Dickey, and Fisher (2007, 2008) have presented a theory of social integration that challenges existing concepts of community integration.

Ware et al. (2007) define social integration "as a process, unfolding over time, through which individuals who have been psychiatrically disabled increasingly develop and exercise their capacities for connectedness and citizenship" (p. 469). Three key components of their theory are (1) connectedness, (2) citizenship, and (3) capacities or capabilities.

Connectedness

Ware et al.'s (2007) focus on connectedness is somewhat akin to Wong and Solomon's (2002) social and psychological integration components of community integration. Connectedness refers to reciprocal interpersonal relationship and also to the identification with a larger group. Moreover, Ware et al. note that social (e.g., communication skills), moral (e.g., trust), and emotional (e.g., empathy) competencies are needed to sustain interpersonal connectedness.

Citizenship

In the literature on housing and mental health, citizenship is an important concept that is related to community integration. Davidson has argued that recovery should begin with restoring the citizenship rights and responsibilities of individuals who have psychiatric disabilities (Davidson, 2006; Davidson, Ridgway, Wieland, & O'Connell, 2009). Individuals with psychiatric disabilities have been systematically excluded from community life, and restoring citizenship rights is important in fostering inclusion for these individuals. According to Rowe et al. (2012), citizenship for people with mental illness includes personal responsibilities, government and infrastructure, caring for self and others, civil rights, legal right, choices, and world stewardship.

A content analysis of the literature on mental health and housing identified therapeutic and citizenship values as overarching categories of this literature (Sylvestre, Nelson, Sabloff, & Peddle, 2007). The authors associate access and affordability, accountability, housing rights, and security of tenure with citizenship values, and choice, quality, and community integration with therapeutic values. Sylvestre et al. suggest that therapeutic values dominate the housing literature and advocate for more attention to citizenship. Similarly, Davidson et al. (2009) and Ware et al. (2007, 2008) suggest that citizenship values should be more prevalent in research that seeks to document the process of community integration and argue that Sen's (1999) capabilities framework is well positioned to foreground these rights. Citizenship is an important concept insofar as it pushes research to engage with the broader social and political contexts in which individuals with disabilities are embedded (see chapter 7 this volume, Sylvestre). An important contribution of the citizenship literature is in documenting social processes important in understanding social, political, and economic inclusion and exclusion (Pancer, 2014).

Capabilities

The approach to social integration proffered by Ware et al. (2008) draws on Sen's (1999) capabilities approach—an approach to the conceptualization and measurement of the standards of living for people living in countries of the global south. Sen's (1999) capabilities approach is a promising framework for balancing both therapeutic and citizenship values with regard to research on mental health and housing (Davidson et al. 2009; Hopper, 2007; MacLeod, 2014; Ware et al., 2008). At its core, the capabilities approach balances the importance of rights and social process with therapeutic outcomes.

Sen (1999) developed the capabilities approach as a novel framework of measurement for programs and policies targeting poverty in the global South. For Sen, mainstream econometric data, guided by a utilitarian/consequentialist philosophy tend to be overly focused on social consequences (income, commodity consumption, etc.). The utilitarian/consequentialist approach focuses on how successful individuals are in obtaining tangible resources. Sen has contended that this consequentialist framing negates the salience of rights and ignores social and political context. In contrast, the philosophy of deontology emphasizes the importance of rights and freedoms. Sen also critiqued deontology, which he charged was insensitive to consequences and tended to favor rights to resources and personal property. He cited the example of famine in Ethiopia and India, where the nonviolation of property rights (i.e., exporting food) led to widespread suffering and death.

Sen's capabilities approach can be translated into research on housing and mental health. The framework highlights rights and allows for the measurement of therapeutic outcomes (e.g., symptom severity, social functioning, community integration), while allowing room for social context, including citizenship rights. The capabilities approach is interested in specifying "functionings"—the ability of individuals to do and to be, including the ability to choose between functionings. Capabilities refer to all the combinations of functionings available to an individual (i.e., the capabilities set). A crucial part of the capabilities approach is the idea of conversion. For Sen, an input (like money) is converted into a functioning (the ability to find and maintain permanent housing) through a socially mediated process. For example, two individuals possessing the same amount of money might convert this into housing very differently. An individual with mental illness who has experienced homelessness may not be able to convert money into housing in the same way as a nondisabled individual because of factors like social stigma and the lack of rental and employment records. In Figure 6.1, we present an overview of the capabilities approach.

In Figure 6.1, we can observe that the goal of the capabilities approach is to assess well-being, a goal that is congruent with therapeutic values. It is also clear that specifying conversion implies a serious consideration of social and political context and can adequately incorporate considerations of citizenship rights. The specification

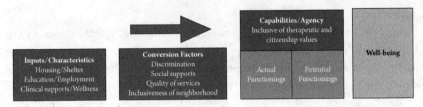

Figure 6.1 A model of the capabilities approach.

of conversion addresses socially disabling circumstances, while the capabilities set captures the choices, values, and social roles valuable to individuals. What is apparent from Figure 6.1 is that inputs (rights and resources) and characteristics of individuals do not directly affect well-being. Rather it is how the inputs and characteristics of individuals can be converted into capabilities that enable people to choose and do what they want that is important for well-being.

The capabilities approach has also been elaborated by the philosopher Martha Nussbaum (2000). Her list of central human capabilities includes life, bodily health, bodily integrity, sense, imagination, thought, emotions, practical reason, affiliation, other species, play, and control over one's environment. Shinn (2014) has noted how these capabilities are often denied people with mental illness, and she suggests ways that community psychology interventions in mental health can promote such capacities.

Connectedness, Citizenship, and Capabilities

Ware et al. (2008) have put the components of connectedness, citizenship, and capabilities together into a model of social integration. The outcomes of connectedness and citizenship are they key dimensions of social integration, with connectedness denoting reciprocal interpersonal relationships and citizenship as the ability to exercise rights and responsibilities. An example of a positive social integration outcome for an individual with a mental illness according to this framework would include both positive relationships with one's landlord and neighbors and learning to become a responsible tenant who can exercise his or her rights. According to Ware et al. (2008), capacities and opportunities (one's capabilities set) influence social integration via individual agency, the freedom to do and to be.

Research

While Ware et al. (2008) have put together a broad, innovative, and potentially useful theory of social integration, this theory has yet to generate research on housing for people with mental illness. In order to enable research on this theory, measurement development is needed to operationalize key concepts of citizenship, capabilities, and conversion factors (Shinn, 2015).

Summary of Theory and Research on Informal Systems

Theory and research on informal systems is multilayered and ecological, spanning from social network relationships, including those with neighbors, landlords, and peers, to community integration and broader social integration and citizenship roles. Informal systems go beyond the person in the context of a housing program to broader social processes of inclusion and citizenship. Ware et al.'s (2008) theory of social integration provides an elaborate and interesting direction for future research on informal systems, but the core constructs of this approach have yet to be operationally defined and measured.

The Geosocial Environment

The geosocial environment is another important system in which housing programs for people with mental illness are embedded. The term "geosocial" refers to the geographic qualities that are related to housing programs and the social qualities of that geographic space. Theory and research on the geosocial environment of housing programs has focused on (1) location and spatial concentration and (2) neighborhood characteristics.

Location and Spatial Concentration

Mental health geography has been historically concerned with the location and spatial concentration of housing for people with mental illness and with community opposition to the siting of housing for people with mental illness (DeVerteuil, 2000; Wolch & Philo, 2000).

Theory

While people with mental illness often live in low-income, inner-city neighborhoods that come to be known as "psychiatric ghettos" (Hall et al., 1987), there is debate about whether location and spatial concentration variables reflect compositional or contextual effects. Compositional effects are those that can be attributed to characteristics of the people who live in close proximity to one another, while contextual effects are attributed to unique qualities of the social and physical environment in which one lives (Curtis & Jones, 1998). DeVerteuil (2000) has argued that initial work on location and spatial concentration was largely quantitative with a focus on hypothesis-testing and lacked a critical, historical, and political analysis. Moreover, he observed that more recently conflict-oriented theories that focus on larger political and structural determinants of housing location and concentration have gained more prominence (DeVerteuil, 2000), and that the focus on NIMBYism has been replaced with a broader emphasis on social justice (DeVerteuil, 2013).

Similar to DeVerteuil (2000), Wolch and Philo (2000) have argued that the emphasis of mental health geography beginning in the 1970s constituted a "first wave" of analysis that focused on the location and spatial concentration of mental health consumers and their housing and support services. More recently, they have noted the emergence of a "second wave" that focuses more on different views of what constitutes mental illness, in particular, and disability, more generally (Dear, Wilton, Gaber, & Takahishi, 1997). This second wave challenges the medicalized construct of "mental illness," which focuses on disease and deficits, and offers a competing view about difference, and how people who are different by virtue of disability, including psychiatric disability, become socially excluded. For example, Dear et al. (1997) have noted a "hierarchy of acceptance," or social exclusion, with people with mental illness and shelters for homeless people as the most likely to be stigmatized and socially excluded.

With this focus on the politics of difference and structural determinants in second wave mental health geography, Housing First for homeless mentally ill people has emerged as a counter-force in its emphasis on person-centered treatment, self-determination and choice, recovery, and community integration (Tsemberis, 2010). Of particular importance for mental health geography is Housing First's emphasis on scattered-site housing (Yanos, 2007). The scattered-site approach of Housing First has given rise to different theoretical perspectives in mental health geography. Townley, Kloos, and Wright (2009) have introduced the idea of "activity spaces" in their research using participatory mapping of the space in which people with mental illness operate in a community. Wider activity spaces may give rise to new potential for community integration (e.g., contact with neighbors and community members who do not share a history of mental illness), as well as posing their own unique challenges (e.g., social isolation).

More structural analyses have invoked Giddens's (1984) structuration theory (see Moos & Dear, 1986) to understand the interface between individual agency and social structure. Giddens argues that both social structures and individual agency operate in how society is structured, which coincides with the view that both contextual (social structure) and agency (composition) operate simultaneously. Moreover, Giddens argues that structures are the properties of social systems. Therefore, different structural properties, such as signification (communication of meaning), domination (use of power), and legitimation (social norms), are the mechanisms that interface between social systems, including social institutions, and individuals. Individuals, in turn, exercise agency, through reflexive action, which shapes social structures. Moreover, transactions between systems and individuals also have time and space dimensions. Finally, structures can either constrain or enable individual agency.

Research

Early work by mental health geographers found that housing for people with mental illness in the early days of deinstitutionalization was concentrated in low-income, inner-city neighborhoods, leading to the development of "psychiatric ghettos" (see Hall et al., 1987 for a review). While there was a lull in research in this area after the 1980s, there has recently been renewed interest and a rediscovery of the importance of neighborhoods. This has come about in part with research by community psychologists (e.g., Townley & Kloos, 2014) and the development of new research methods to study neighborhoods (see Sylvestre, Bassi, & Bendell, chapter 8, this volume).

In an early study, Trainor et al. (1987) found that prior to the development of the Toronto Supportive Housing Coalition in 1980, all but one of the residences for people with mental illness were located in the inner city. However, by 1987, the Supportive Housing Coalition had created new housing that was dispersed across the six boroughs of the city. In another early study, Dear and Moos (1986) provided a concrete example of structuration theory in their analysis of housing for people with mental illness in Hamilton, Ontario. Their analysis shows the role of provincial, regional, and municipal governments, board-and-care home operators, and deinstitutionalized mental health consumers in the ghettoization of consumers in board-and-care homes in the inner city.

More recent research has revealed a mixed picture with regard to the location and spatial concentration of housing for people with mental illness. In a three-city study, Newman (1994) found that compared with the general population, people with mental illness live in neighborhoods that have more problems with crime and poor upkeep. In a study in Philadelphia, Wong and Stanhope (2009) found that compared with housing for people with developmental disabilities, housing for people with mental illness was located in neighborhoods with a higher concentration of people with mental illness and with higher levels of distress and lower levels of stability and safety. Another study in Philadelphia found that neighborhoods with higher levels of crime, physical and structural inadequacy (e.g., vacant buildings), drug-related activity, social instability (e.g., transience), and social isolation were associated with higher concentrations of persons with serious mental illness (Byrne et al., 2013). At the same time, people with serious mental illness in Philadelphia lived in neighborhoods where they were significantly closer to a number of amenities (e.g., supermarkets, public transportation), and where there was a significantly greater concentration of amenities within a half a mile of the individual's residence (Metraux, Brusilovskiy, Prvu-Bettger, Wong, & Salzer, 2012). All this research suggests that people with mental illness reside in less desirable neighborhoods than people who do not have mental illness.

In a multistate study, Tsai, Mares, and Rosenheck (2011) compared the location of housing for people with mental illness before and one year after obtaining independent supportive housing. They found that both before and after obtaining housing, participants were significantly more likely to be living in neighborhoods with higher population density, lower levels of education and income, and higher levels of crime. In a multistate study of psychiatric residences, Zippay and Thompson

(2007) also found that the blocks on which the residences were located were significantly more likely to have higher levels of population density and lower levels of education than the municipal averages, but they did not differ in terms of income levels. In fact, the residences were spread throughout neighborhoods that varied in terms of poverty levels.

Townley, Kloos, and Wright (2009) used geographic information systems (GIS) to geocode the areas that encompassed all of the places in which people with mental illness were engaged in activity in the community. They found that the larger the activity space area, the greater the life satisfaction of the participants, but the lower the neighborhood sense of community. However, a more recent study of formerly homeless people found that activity space was unrelated to social and psychological integration, and quality of life, but inversely related to physical integration (Chan, Helfrich, Hursh, Rogers, & Gopal, 2014).

Neighborhoods

Theory

While some researchers have developed analytic models to test relationships between neighborhood characteristics, housing, mediating or moderating factors, and health inequalities (e.g., Dunn & Hayes, 2000; Winkel et al., 2009), these models have not been based on specific theories that provide a rationale for inclusion of key factors in the model. Bernard et al. (2007) have put forward a theory of how neighborhoods produce health inequalities that is relevant to research on neighborhoods, housing, and mental health. This theory also borrows from Giddens (1984), whose ideas were described in the previous section, and Godbout (2003). As we have noted, Giddens's structuration theory emphasizes the dialectical relationships between structures and agency. Moreover, social structures, according to Giddens, consist of both resources and rules about how resources are produced and distributed. Godbout adds to this theory by highlighting that resources are exchanged through market rules, state rules, and rules of informal social reciprocity.

Using this theoretical backdrop, Bernard et al. (2007) propose that access to resources determines health inequalities. They further argue that access to resources is determined by several interacting rules, including proximity, prices, rights, and informal reciprocity. Moreover, these rules give rise to five neighborhood domains, with specific rules applying primarily to different domains: (1) physical, guided by the rule of proximity; (2) economic, guided by the rule of price; (3) institutional, guided by the rule of rights; (4) local sociability; and (5) community organization, both guided by the rule of informal reciprocity. What this theory can add to research on neighborhoods and housing for people with mental illness is some direction in the examination of the mechanisms, resource availability and rules, of how housing and neighborhoods promote mental health, social inclusion, and citizenship.

Research

The social component of the geosocial environment has focused on neighborhood characteristics, such as social climate, safety, and poverty. These characteristics have been assessed through census or other archival data sources or though surveys of people with mental illness. Research conducted in the 1970s and 1980s found that while low-income, high-crime neighborhoods provide an inhospitable environment for people with mental illness, so too do high-income, cohesive neighborhoods in which residents may unite in opposition to a residence for people with mental illness (Hall et al., 1987).

More recent research has shown mixed evidence regarding the importance of neighborhood social characteristics for the well-being and adaptation of people with mental illness. Tsai et al. (2011) found that neighborhood social class indices (i.e., education and income) were positively related to participants' satisfaction with the neighborhood, while population density was positively related to social support and inversely related to symptom distress.

A study in South Carolina found that neighborhood quality and social climate were significantly related to the recovery and residential satisfaction of people with mental illness (Wright & Kloos, 2007), while neighborhood quality and safety were significantly inversely related to psychiatric distress and loneliness/isolation (Kloos & Townley, 2011; Townley & Kloos, 2014). However, this study found that these effects were strongest for individual perceptions of the environment, as opposed to aggregated measures of perception of the environment. Similarly, a study conducted in Philadelphia found that community-level predictors (e.g., crime rates, social capital) were much more weakly related to psychiatric symptoms, quality of life, empowerment, and recovery for people with mental illness than individual-level predictors (e.g., homelessness history, being married or in a relationship) (Brusilovskiy & Salzer, 2012).

Summary of Theory and Research on Geosocial Systems

There has been considerable research on the location, concentration, and social dimensions of the neighborhoods in which people with mental illness live. This research suggests that the neighborhoods with higher concentrations of people with mental illness are less desirable than the neighborhoods with lower concentrations of people with mental illness, and that less desirable neighborhoods are associated with higher levels of distress for people with mental illness.

Much of the research on locational concentration and neighborhoods has been atheoretical. Bernard et al.'s (2007) theory of neighborhoods and health can help to inform and guide future research, as it has clearly identified its key constructs and how they can be measured. Moreover, recent research on neighborhoods has used new methods of GIS and participatory mapping. Also, with the introduction of scattered-site housing models, like Housing First, more research is needed on the locational concentration and neighborhood characteristics of such programs.

Conclusions

In this chapter, we have reviewed theory and research on the larger social context of housing for people with mental illness, including (1) policy and planning, (2) informal systems, and (3) the geosocial environment. Much of the existing research on these three systems is atheoretical and can benefit from a better use of theory. There are a number of theories that can be applied to research on policy and planning, depending on the specific focus. Moreover, Ware et al.'s (2008) social integration theory shows particular promise in guiding future research on informal systems, with its attention to concepts of citizenship and capabilities. As well, Bernard et al.'s (2007) theory of neighborhoods and health provides a useful framework for understanding the geosocial environment and its impacts on individuals with mental illness and the housing programs that serve them.

In conducting this review, we have observed that there is much more research on housing programs (see chapter 5) than on the larger context of policy and planning, informal systems, and the geosocial environment. Similarly, Sylvestre et al. (2007) noted that there has been much more research devoted to the therapeutic dimensions of housing and mental health than to the citizenship dimension of housing and mental health. Since most people with mental illness live in housing with no evidence base, including many different types of custodial housing, there needs to be more research attention on systems transformation to promote the adoption of evidence-based housing. This requires paying greater attention to policy and planning, informal systems, and the geosocial environment. Community psychology has much to offer theory and research on the larger social context of housing, as is clear from the field's recent contributions to the ecological perspective on housing and mental health (Kloos & Shah, 2009), the capabilities approach in mental health (Shinn, 2014, 2015), planning and systems-level interventions (Sylvestre, 2014; Sylvestre et al., 2007), policy formulation (Nelson, 2013), and neighborhoods and community integration (Townley & Kloos, 2014).

Acknowledgment

We thank Greg Townley for his suggestions of material to include in this chapter.

References

Aubry, T., Farrell, S., Hwang, S., & Calhoun, M. (2013). Identifying the patterns of emergency shelter stays of single individuals in Canadian cities of different sizes. *Housing Studies, 28,* 910–927.

Aubry, T., Flynn, R.J., Virley, B., & Neri, J. (2013). Social role valorization in community mental health housing: Does it contribute to the community integration and life satisfaction of people with psychiatric disabilities? *Journal of Community Psychology, 41,* 218–235.

Aubry, T., & Myner, J. (1996). Community integration and quality of life: A comparison of persons with psychiatric disabilities in housing programs and community residents who are neighbours. *Canadian Journal of Community Mental, 15,* 5–20.

Austin, E.L., Pollio, D.E., Holmes, S., Schumacher, J., White, B., Lukas, C.V., & Kertesz, S. (2014). VA's expansion of supportive housing: Successes and challenges on the path toward Housing First. *Psychiatric Services, 65,* 641–647.

Bean, K.F., Shafer, M.S., & Glennon, M. (2013). The impact of Housing First and peer support on people who are medically vulnerable and homeless. *Psychiatric Rehabilitation Journal, 36,* 48–50.

Bengtsson-Tops, A., & Hansson, L. (2014). Landlords' experiences of housing tenants suffering from severe mental illness: A Swedish empirical study. *Community Mental Health Journal, 50,* 111–119.

Bernard, P., Charafeddine, R., Frolich, K.L., Daniel, M., Kestens, Y., & Potvin, L. (2007). Health inequalities and place: A theoretical conception of neighbourhood. *Social Science and Medicine, 65,* 1839–1852.

Bronfenbrenner, U. (1977). Toward an experimental ecology of human development. *American Psychologist, 32,* 513–531.

Brusilovskiy, E., & Salzer, M.S. (2012). A study on the environmental influences on the well-being of individuals with psychiatric disabilities in Philadelphia, PA. *Social Science and Medicine, 74,* 1591–1601.

Byrne, T., Prvu-Bettger, J.A., Brusilovskiy, E., Wong, Y.-L.I., Metraux, S., & Salzer, M.S. (2013). Comparing neighborhoods of adults with serious mental illness and of the general population: Research implications. *Psychiatric Services, 64,* 782–788.

Caplan, N. (1979). The two-communities theory and knowledge utilization. *American Behavioral Scientist, 22,* 459–470.

Capponi, P. (1992). *Upstairs in the crazy house: The life of a psychiatric survivor.* Toronto: Viking.

Chan, D.V., Helfrich, C.A., Hursh, N.C., Rogers, E.S., & Gopal, S. (2014). Measuring community integration using geographic information systems (GIS) and participatory mapping for people who were once homeless. *Health and Place, 27,* 92–101.

Curtis, S., & Jones, I.R. (1998). Is there a place for geography in the analysis of health inequality? *Sociology of Health and Illness, 20,* 645–672.

Davidson, L. (2006). What happened to civil rights? *Psychiatric Rehabilitation Journal, 30,* 11–14.

Davidson, L., Ridgway, P., Wieland, M. & O'Connell, M. (2009). A capabilities approach to mental health transformation: A conceptual framework for the recovery era. *Canadian Journal of Community Mental Health, 28*(2), 35–46.

Dear, M. (1992). Understanding and overcoming the NIMBY syndrome. *Journal of the American Planning Association, 58,* 288–300.

Dear, M.J., & Moos, A. (1986). Structuration theory in urban analysis: 2. Empirical application. *Environment and Planning A, 18,* 351–373.

Dear, M., Wilton, R., Gaber, L., & Takahashi, L. (1997). Seeing people differently: The sociospatial construction of disability. *Environment and Planning, 15,* 455–480.

DeVerteuil, G. (2000). Reconsidering legacy of urban public facility location theory in human geography. *Progress in Human Geography, 24*, 47–69.

DeVerteuil, G. (2013). Where has NIMBY gone in urban social geography? *Social and Cultural Geography, 14*, 599–603.

Dunn, J.R., & Hayes, M.V. (2000). Social inequality, population health, and housing: A study of two Vancouver neighborhoods. *Social Science and Medicine, 51*, 563–587.

Edwards, B., & Gillham, P.F. (2013). Resource mobilization theory. *The Wiley-Blackwell encyclopedia of social and political movements.* Toronto: Canada.

Fairweather, G.W., Sanders, D.H., & Tornatzky, L.G. (1974). *Creating change in mental health organizations.* New York: Pergamon Press.

Fischer, F. (2003). *Reframing public policy: Discursive politics and deliberative practices.* Oxford: Oxford University Press.

Flaspohler, P., Lesesne, C.A., Puddy, R., Smith, E., & Wandersman, A. (2012). Advances in bridging research and practice: Introduction to the section special issue on the Interactive Systems Framework for dissemination and implementation. *American Journal of Community Psychology, 50*, 271–281.

Fleury, M.-J., Grenier, G., Vallée, C., Hurtubise, R., & Levésque, P.-A. (2014). The role of advocacy coalitions in a project implementation process: The example of the planning phase of the At Home/Chez Soi project dealing with homelessness in Montreal. *Evaluation and Program Planning, 45*, 42–49.

Giddens, A. (1984). *The constitution of society.* Berkeley: University of California Press.

Godbout, J.T. (2003). *The world of the gift.* Montreal: McGill-Queen's University Press.

Gulcur, L., Tsemberis, S., Stefancic, A., & Greenwood, R.M. (2007). Community integration of adults with psychiatric disabilities and histories of homelessness. *Community Mental Health Journal, 43*, 211–228.

Hall, G.B., Nelson, G., & Smith Fowler, H. (1987). Housing for the chronically mentally disabled: Part I. Conceptual framework and social context. *Canadian Journal of Community Mental Health, 6*(2), 65–78.

Henwood, B.F., Melekis, K., & Stefancic, A. (2014). Introducing Housing First in a rural service system: A multistakeholder perspective. *Global Journal of Community Psychology Practice, 5*(1), 1–13.

Hopper, K. (2003). *Reckoning with homelessness.* Ithaca, NY: Cornell University Press.

Hopper, K. (2007). Rethinking social recovery in schizophrenia: A capabilities approach. *Social Science and Medicine, 65*, 868–879.

Howell, A., & Voronka, J. (2012). Introduction: The politics of resilience and recovery in mental health care. *Studies in Social Justice, 6*, 1–7.

Jenkins, J.C. (1983). Resource mobilization theory and the study of social movements. *Annual Review of Sociology, 9*, 527–553.

Kingdon, J.W. (2005). *Agendas, alternatives, and public policies* (2nd ed.). Boston: Addison-Wesley.

Kloos, B., & Shah, S. (2009). A social-ecological approach to investigating relationships between housing and adaptive functioning for people with serious mental illness. *American Journal of Community Psychology, 44*, 316–326.

Kloos, B., & Townley, G. (2011). Investigating the relationship between neighborhood experiences and psychiatric distress for individuals with serious mental illness. *Administration Policy and Mental Health, 38*, 105–116.

Kuhn, R., & Culhane, D.P. (1998). Applying cluster analysis to test a typology of homelessness by pattern of shelter utilization: Results from the analysis of administrative data. *American Journal of Community Psychology, 26*, 207–232.

MacLeod, T. (2014). The capabilities approach, transformative measurement, and Housing First. *Global Journal of Community Psychology Practice, 5*(1), 1–10. Retrieved from http://www.gjcpp.org/

Macnaughton, E., Nelson, G., & Goering, P. (2013). Bringing politics and evidence together: Policy entrepreneurship and the conception of the At Home/Chez Soi Housing First initiative for addressing homelessness and mental illness in Canada. *Social Science and Medicine, 82,* 100–107.

McKnight, J. (1996). *The careless society: Community and its counterfeits.* New York: Basic Books.

Mead, S., Hilton, D., & Curtis, L. (2001). Peer support: A theoretical perspective. *Psychiatric Rehabilitation Journal, 25,* 134–141.

Metraux, S., Brusilovskiy, E., Prvu-Bettger, J.A., Wong, Y.-L.I., & Salzer, M.S. (2012). Geographic access to and availability of community resources for persons diagnosed with severe mental illness in Philadelphia, USA. *Health and Place, 18,* 621–629.

Miyamoto, Y., & Sono, T. (2012). Lessons from peer support among individuals with mental health difficulties: A review of the literature. *Clinical Practice and Epidemiology in Mental Health, 8,* 22–29.

Mintrom, M., & Norman, P. (2009). Policy entrepreneurship and policy change. *Policy Studies Journal, 37,* 649–667.

Moos, A., & Dear, M.J. (1986). Structuration theory in urban analysis: 1. Theoretical exegesis. *Environment and Planning A, 18,* 231–252.

Nelson, G. (1994). The development of a mental health coalition: A case study. *American Journal of Community Psychology, 22,* 229–255.

Nelson, G. (2013). Community psychology and transformative policy change in the neo-liberal era. *American Journal of Community Psychology, 52,* 211–223.

Nelson, G., Hall, G.B., Squire, D., & Walsh-Bowers, R.T. (1992). Social network transactions of psychiatric patients. *Social Science and Medicine, 34,* 433–445.

Nelson, G., Macnaughton, E., Curwood, S.E., Egalité, N., Voronka, J., Fleury, M.-J., . . . Goering, P. (2016). Community collaboration and involvement of persons with lived experience in planning Canada's At Home/Chez Soi project: A multi-site Housing First initiative for homeless people with mental illness. *Health and Social Care in the Community, 24,* 184–193.

Nelson, G., Macnaughton, E., Goering, P. Dudley, M., O'Campo, P., Patterson, M., . . . Vallée, C. (2013). Planning a multi-site complex intervention for homeless people with mental illness: The relationships between the national team and local sites in Canada's At Home/Chez Soi project. *American Journal of Community Psychology, 51,* 347–358.

Nelson, G., & Saegert, S. (2009). Housing and quality of life: An ecological perspective. In V.R. Preedy & R.R. Watson (Eds.), *Handbook of disease burdens and quality of life measures* (pp. 3363–3382). Heidelberg, Germany: Springer-Verlag.

Newman, S.J. (1994). The housing and neighborhood conditions of persons with severe mental illness. *Psychiatric Services, 45,* 338–343.

Nussbaum, M.C. (2000). *Women and human development: The capabilities approach.* Cambridge: Cambridge University Press.

O'Connell, M.J., Kasprow, W., & Rosenheck, R. (2010). National dissemination of supported housing in the VA: Model adherence versus model modification. *Psychiatric Rehabilitation Journal, 33,* 308–319.

Oliver, K., Lorenc, T., & Innvaer, S. (2014). New directions in evidence-based policy research: A critical analysis of the literature. *Health Research and Policy Systems, 12,* 34. Open access.

Pancer, S.M. (2014). *The psychology of citizenship and civic engagement.* Oxford: Oxford University Press.

Pitt, V.J., Ryan, R., Lowe, D., Berends, L., Hetrick, S., & Hill, S. (2013). A systematic review of consumer-providers' effects on client outcomes in statutory mental health services: The evidence and the path beyond. *Journal of the Society for Social Work and Research, 4,* 333–356.

Rowe, M., Clayton, A., Benedict, P., Bellamy, C., Antunes, K., Miller, R., . . . O'Connell, M.J. (2012). Going to the source: Creating a citizenship outcome measure by community-based participatory research methods. *Psychiatric Services, 63,* 445–450.

Sabatier, P.A., & Weible, C.M. (2007). The advocacy coalition framework: Innovations and clarifications. In P.A. Sabatier (Ed.), *Theories of the policy process* (2nd ed., pp. 189–220). Boulder, CO: Westview Press.

Sen, A. (1999). *Development as freedom*. New York: Anchor Books.

Shinn, M. (2014). The capabilities approach to transformative change in mental health. In G. Nelson, B. Kloos, & J. Ornelas (Eds.), *Community psychology and community mental health: Towards transformative change* (pp. 75–86). New York: Oxford University Press.

Shinn, M. (2015). Community psychology and the capabilities approach. *American Journal of Community Psychology, 55*, 243–252.

Stanhope, V., & Dunn, K. (2011). The curious case of Housing First: The limits of evidence based policy. *International Journal of Law and Psychiatry, 34*, 275–282.

Sylvestre, J. (2014). Perspectives on transformative change in community mental health. In G. Nelson, B. Kloos, & J. Ornelas (Eds.), *Community psychology and community mental health: Towards transformative change* (pp. 51–74). New York: Oxford University Press.

Sylvestre, J., George, L., Aubry, T., Durbin, J., Nelson, G., & Trainor, J. (2007). Strengthening Ontario's system of housing for people with serious mental illness. *Canadian Journal of Community Mental Health, 26*(1), 79–95.

Sylvestre, J., Nelson, G., Durbin, J., George, L., Aubry, T., & Ollenberg, M. (2006). Housing for people with serious mental illness: Challenges for system-level community development. *Community Development, 37*, 35–45.

Sylvestre, J., Nelson, G., Sabloff, A., & Peddle, S. (2007). Housing for people with serious mental illness: A comparison of values and research. *American Journal of Community Psychology, 40*, 125–137.

Tefft, B., Segall, A., & Trute, B. (1987). Neighbourhood response to community mental health facilities for the chronically mentally disabled. *Canadian Journal of Community Mental Health, 6*(2), 37–49.

Townley, G., & Kloos, B. (2011). Examining the psychological sense of community for individuals with serious mental illness residing in supported housing environments. *Community Mental Health Journal, 47*, 436–446.

Townley, G., & Kloos, B. (2014). Mind over matter: The role of individual perceptions in understanding the social ecology of housing environments for individuals with psychiatric disabilities. *American Journal of Community Psychology, 54*, 205–218.

Townley, G., Kloos, B., & Wright, P.A. (2009). Understanding the experience of place: Expanding methods to conceptualize and measure community integration of persons with serious mental illness. *Health and Place, 15*, 520–531.

Townley, G., Miller, H., & Kloos, B. (2013). A little goes a long way: The impact of distal social support on community integration and recovery of individuals with psychiatric disabilities. *American Journal of Community Psychology, 52*, 84–96.

Trainor, J., Lurie, S., Ballantyne, R., & Long, D. (1987). The Supportive Housing Coalition: A model for advocacy and program development. *Canadian Journal of Community Mental Health, 6*(2), 93–106.

Tsai, J. (2014). Timing and momentum in VA's path toward Housing First. *Psychiatric Services, 65*, 836.

Tsai, J., Mares, A.S., & Rosenheck, R.A. (2011). A geographic analysis of chronically homeless adults before and after enrollment in a multi-site supported housing initiative: Community characteristics and migration. *American Journal of Community Psychology, 48*, 341–351.

Tsai, J., Mares, A. S., & Rosenheck, R. A. (2012). Does housing chronically homeless adults lead to social integration? *Psychiatric Services, 63*, 427–434.

Tsai, J., Rosenheck, R.A., Sullivan, J., & Harkness, L. (2011). A group-intensive peer support model of case management for supported housing. *Psychological Services, 8*, 251–259.

Tsemberis, S. (2010). *Housing First: The Pathways model to end homelessness for people with mental illness and addiction*. Center City, MN: Hazelden Press.

Wandersman, A., Duffy, J., Flaspohler, P., Noonan, R., Lubell, K., Stillman, L., . . . Saul, J. (2008). Bridging the gap between prevention research and practice: The interactive systems framework for dissemination and implementation. *American Journal of Community Psychology, 41*, 171–181.

Ware, N.C., Hopper, K., Tugenberg, T., Dickey, B., & Fisher, D. (2007). Connectedness and citizenship: Redefining social integration. *Psychiatric Services, 58*, 469–474.

Ware, N.C., Hopper, K., Tugenberg, T., Dickey, B., & Fisher, D. (2008). A theory of social integration as quality of life. *Psychiatric Services, 59*, 27–33.

Weiss, C.H. (1999). The interface between evaluation and public policy. *Evaluation, 5*, 468–486.

Winkel, G., Saegert, S., & Evans, G.W. (2009). An ecological perspective on theory, methods, and analysis in environmental psychology: Advances and challenges. *Journal of Environmental Psychology, 29*, 318–328.

Wolch, J., & Philo, C. (2000). From distributions of deviance to definitions of difference: Past and future mental health geographies. *Health and Place, 6*, 137–157.

Wolfensberger, W. (1972). *The principle of normalization in human service.* Toronto: National Institute of Mental Retardation.

Wolfensberger, W. (1999). Concluding reflections and a look ahead to the future for normalization and social role valorization. In R.J. Flynn & R.A. Lemay (Eds.), *A quarter-century of normalization and social role valorization: Evolution and impact* (pp. 489–506). Ottawa: University of Ottawa Press.

Wong, Y.-L.I., Metzendorf, D., & Min, S.-Y. (2006). Neighborhood experiences and community integration: Perspectives from mental health consumers and providers. *Social Work in Mental Health, 4*, 45–59.

Wong, Y.L.I., & Solomon, P. L. (2002). Community integration of persons with psychiatric disabilities in supportive independent housing: A conceptual model and methodological considerations. *Mental Health Services Research, 4*, 13–28.

Wong, Y.L.I., & Stanhope, V. (2009). Conceptualizing community: A comparison of neighborhood characteristics of supportive housing for persons with psychiatric and developmental disabilities. *Social Science and Medicine, 68*, 1376–1387.

Wright, P.A., & Kloos, B. (2007). Housing environment and mental health outcomes: A levels of analysis perspective. *Journal of Environmental Psychology, 27*, 79–89.

Yamin, S., Aubry, T., Volk, J., Jette, J., Bourque, J., & Crouse, S. (2015). Peer supportive housing for consumers of Housing First who experience ongoing housing instability. *Canadian Journal of Community Mental Health.*

Yanos, P.T. (2007). Beyond "Landscapes of Despair": The need for new research on the urban environment, sprawl, and the community integration of persons with serious mental illness. *Health and Place, 13*, 672–676.

Yanos, P.T., Barrow, S.M., & Tsemberis, S. (2004). Community integration in the early phase of housing among homeless persons diagnosed with serious mental illness: Successes and challenges. *Community Mental Health Journal, 40*, 133–150.

Yanos, P.T., Stefancic, A., & Tsemberis, S. (2011). Psychological community integration among people with psychiatric disabilities and nondisabled community members. *Journal of Community Psychology, 39*, 390–401.

Yanos, P.T., Stefancic, A., Tsemberis, S. (2012). Objective community integration of mental health consumers living in supported housing and of others in the community. *Psychiatric Services, 63*, 438–444.

Zippay, A. (2007). Psychiatric residences: Notification, NIMBY, and neighborhood relations. *Psychiatric Services, 58*, 109–113.

Zippay, A., & Lee, S.-K. (2008). Neighbors' perceptions of community-based psychiatric housing. *Social Service Review, 82*, 395–417.

Zippay, A., & Thompson, A. (2007). Psychiatric housing: Locational patterns and choices. *American Journal of Orthopsychiatry, 77*, 392–401.

7

The Contributions of the Concept of Citizenship to Housing Practice, Policy, and Research

JOHN SYLVESTRE

In this chapter I discuss the contributions that the concept of citizenship can make to practice, policy, and research on housing for people with serious mental illness. The chapter is not only concerned with whether people can access housing, their relationships to the housing, or how the housing and its characteristics affects them. It is also concerned with how housing can enable people to take control over their lives, to influence their surroundings and the communities in which they live. The chapter considers three conceptions of citizenship: (1) legal citizenship, (2) normative citizenship, and (3) lived citizenship. It proposes a citizenship framework for practice, policy, and research. Then, the chapter uses the citizenship concept to examine the strengths and weaknesses of single-site, scatter-site, and Housing First approaches. The chapter concludes by comparing the citizenship concept to other concepts that have been associated with housing, evaluating its relative merits and weaknesses.

The chapter builds from the historical overview of housing provided in chapter 1, which described a gradual shift in the values underlying the conception and delivery of community housing programs since deinstitutionalization in North America. The earliest approaches emphasized custodial care and management, reflecting an extension of perspectives and practices from the institution to the community. Whereas later approaches emphasized rehabilitation and the building of skills to increase independence, even more recent approaches have emphasized community integration, a recovery orientation, greater self-determination, and citizenship (Nelson, 2010; Parkinson, Nelson, & Horgan, 1999; Sylvestre, Nelson, Sabloff, & Peddle, 2007a). This increased emphasis on choice, control, self-determination, and increased access to resources, all indicative of citizenship, has led to the identification of scatter-site supportive housing and Housing First approaches as *transformational* changes in the provision of community-based housing (Nelson, 2010).

To ensure that these forms of housing achieve real transformative change we must ensure that practice, policy, and research also evolve to reflect, support, and promote the values that underlie this shift. In part, this will require a shift from the valuing of community housing largely in terms of its therapeutic benefits toward valuing community housing in terms of its role in advancing the citizenship of tenants. In a comprehensive review, Sylvestre et al. (2007a) identified from the writings of consumers, policy makers, and academics two categories of values for community housing programs. First, the review identified *therapeutic values* (choice and control, quality, community integration), which emphasized how the characteristics of housing improved the well-being or quality of life of tenants. In contrast, *citizenship values* (access and affordability, accountability, housing rights and security of tenure) referenced participation, influence, and access to resources in housing as well as at broader programmatic, organizational, and systemic levels. In a second review, Sylvestre et al. (2007a) examined research findings associated with these two categories of values. They found that whereas housing was frequently studied in terms of therapeutic benefits of housing, it was rarely studied from a citizenship perspective.

Thus, the risk is that despite a shift in values or approaches to housing, our overall interest, understanding, and practice may not undergo a corresponding change. A continued emphasis on the therapeutic benefits of housing that ignores the citizenship dimension may risk limiting the transformative potential of newer housing approaches. In order to bring citizenship to the fore, we must first understand its multiple facets.

The Citizenship Concept

The meaning of citizenship has been vigorously debated, and a number of different definitions have been proposed. Hall and Williamson (1999) distinguished between three approaches to the concept: (1) legal citizenship, (2) normative citizenship, and (3) lived citizenship. In the following paragraphs I examine each of these perspectives and their implications for community-based housing for people with serious mental illness.

Legal Citizenship

Legal citizenship refers to an individual's legal status as a member of a political community, such as a nation-state (Hall & Williamson, 1999). It is typically concerned with denoting the kinds of rights and responsibilities that citizens have within particular states. Although citizenship rights tend to be well defined, citizenship responsibilities are often discussed more abstractly. The importance of rights from a legal citizenship perspective is that they ensure equal status and treatment of all citizens and equal opportunities to participate in political activities and civic life. These rights promote individual autonomy and protect the ability of individuals to live how they wish (Oldenfield, 1990).

Marshall (1950) is credited with having launched the modern study of citizenship and for having identified three categories of citizen rights in democratic societies: civil, political, and social rights (Lister, 2010; Marsh, 1998; Turner, 1990). *Civil rights* are necessary for individual freedom, such as liberty of the person; freedom of speech, thought, and faith; the right to own property and to valid and private contracts; and the right to justice and a fair trial (Lister, 2010; Marsh, 1998; Turner, 1990). *Political rights* concern the ability to exercise political power. They include the right to participate in political structures or organizations invested with political authority along with the right to vote and stand for political office (Lister, 2010; Marsh 1998).

Social rights, a concept introduced by Marshall (1950), refer to what a state should provide to ensure that all citizens can live according to the prevailing standards in a society (Lister, 2010). These rights identify welfare services such as education, income security, housing, and social services as essential for citizenship, as they support autonomous individuals to meet their own needs and participate in the public realm (Marsh, 1998). This type of rights is distinctly different from the other two as it requires the development, distribution, or redistribution of resources within a state (Turner, 1990) rather than defining relationships among citizens and between citizens and the state. These services and resources are citizenship rights because without them individuals could not express agency and participate effectively as autonomous citizens (Lister, 2003, 2010).

Lister (2003) proposes understanding rights as "a mutually supportive web of the formal (civil and political) and the substantive (social and economic)" that is "a prerequisite for the realisation of human agency" (p. 35). From this perspective, the failure to ensure decent housing, as well as a sufficient income, education, training, or social and health services, is significant beyond implications for health and well-being. The failure to protect these rights is a subversion of citizenship through the denial of the foundations for effective individual agency.

Although the legal citizenship perspective emphasizes the necessary conditions for citizenship, these rights are insufficient for citizenship. The status of citizen does not ensure that an individual can act on his or her civil or political rights or will receive the opportunities, resources, and supports to live according to the prevailing standards of a society. In almost every society there are rampant inequalities in how rights are distributed or can be acted on. These inequalities accumulate among people according to gender, socioeconomic status, ethnoracial background, or disability. These disparities subvert the ability of individuals or groups to express, obtain, or act on their rights and hence to be fully enfranchised citizens. These disparities result in what Rappaport (1981, p. 13) characterized as a "cruel joke" where people have rights but no resources or services to enable them or support them to act on their rights.

Among people with serious mental illness there are certainly limits to their civil and political rights, such as in police harassment and risk of incarceration, or restrictive or invasive treatment. However, the great range of social disadvantages and marginalization among people with serious mental illness, including high risk for homelessness or prevalence of substandard housing, poor rates of completion of high school and higher levels of education, poverty level income, and higher rates of unemployment, speaks in particular to the neglect of social citizenship rights. The neglect of these social citizenship rights further excludes people from acting on their civil and political rights by undermining their autonomy and their agency.

Unfortunately, the legal citizenship perspective is silent on the mechanisms underlying these disparities and the means of addressing them. To the extent to which these mechanisms are known, they may be intractable. In addition, rights-based appeals for social justice and equity are not particularly effective, in and of themselves, for ensuring that people have adequate housing and the supports they want or need to thrive in the community. Moreover, the endorsement of abstract rights, such as the right to adequate shelter, does not typically include the prescription for how, and the assurance that, all will be adequately housed. Although most democratic societies may agree that housing is a basic social right, there may be little agreement on what constitutes sufficient shelter, within or between countries. Finally, the legal citizenship perspective presents a passive view of citizenship (Lister, 1997; Turner, 1990). Whereas it describes a status that people have within a state, it does not characterize the agency that these rights are intended to support or how people are able or not able to act on their rights in their everyday lives.

Normative Citizenship

Whereas legal citizenship emphasizes a status or a relationship between citizens and a state, normative citizenship is concerned with how citizens are active within civic, political, or social organizations or processes (Hall & Williamson, 1990). The perspective, rooted in civic republicanism, emphasizes citizenship as a set of practices rather than a legal status (Oldenfield, 1990). It refers to what are presumed to be the normative ways in which individuals can, and should, participate in political structures or activities such as voting or standing for office, contributing to political debates, joining community organizations, or serving on citizen committees or boards of directors. It is similar to the concept of citizen participation, popular in community psychology, which has emphasized the importance of people taking part in the programs, settings, or institutions that affect them (Heller, Price, Reinharz, Riger, & Wandersman, 1984, cited in Wandersman & Florin, 2000). Citizen participation is associated with a variety of benefits including improved and more relevant programs and institutions, improved neighborhoods and relationships among community members, and improved perceptions of control, helpfulness, responsibility, and inclusion (Wandersman & Florin, 2000).

One possibility for expanding normative citizenship participation of people with serious mental illness is through mediating structures or alternative settings. Mediating structures include families, neighborhoods, religious settings, and voluntary organizations that provide a niche within which people can participate effectively and have more control (Rappaport, 1981). Alternative settings are organizations that are developed when current opportunities do not provide people with meaningful ways of participating. Alternative settings provide opportunities, resources, and support for people to work collectively to meet their needs and achieve their goals (Kloos et al., 2012).

Consumer-run organizations are examples of alternative settings that can benefit people living in community housing. Consumer-run organizations are operated by and for people who have used mental health systems. They can emphasize a variety of activities and goals such as empowerment, recovery, peer support, advocacy and social justice, and employment (Nelson, Janzen, Trainor, & Ochocka, 2008). They typically have inclusive and participatory management, and provide meaningful roles and a voice to people who are interested in participating. A longitudinal study by Nelson, Ochocka, Janzen, and Trainor (2006) has shown that those who participate in these organizations experience a number of positive outcomes such as improved social support and quality of life and participation in employment and education.

Normative citizenship calls to mind the notion of duties (Lister, 1997) and what it means to be a "good citizen" (Hall & Williamson, 1990): one who is engaged and contributing to political processes or to public groups or institutions. This emphasis on individual action and engagement in public affairs introduces an element missing from the legal citizenship perspective. However, normative citizenship can also channel and regulate social action toward formal and explicitly political arenas and de-emphasize social action that takes place elsewhere, in other parts of daily life (Lister, 1997, 2003). These normative modes of participation are also those of more privileged and resourced groups who have the power, time, skills, and opportunities to participate effectively in formal civic, political, and social organizations and processes (Beckett, 2005; Lister, 1997).

The implications are that those who do not meet the normative obligations of citizenship are not fully citizens (Lister, 1997) and that what occurs in private, domestic, or commercial spheres does not count as citizenship or citizen participation (Ellison, 2000; Lister, 1997, 2003). The normative citizenship perspective may discount the great variety of ways that people express their citizenship and contribute to the betterment of their settings, organizations, neighborhoods, or communities.

Normative citizenship assumptions may also create pressure on people to participate in overtly political processes, or in the governance of social service and welfare system on advisory committees or boards of directors. Though these forms of participation are important, the risk may come from valuing participation in a restricted set of activities and forums that people may not want to or feel comfortable contributing to. Feelings of guilt, frustration, or embarrassment may arise from not being included, opting not to participate, or by participating ineffectively in these ways.

Notably, the normative modes of citizenship do not reflect how people are increasingly turning away from traditional political processes or formal community groups (Putnam, 2000). Ellison (2000) has pointed to an increased involvement in what he characterizes as *temporary solidarities*, rather than longer-term commitments. He points to the more fractured nature of citizenship due to the increasing complexity and diversity of our identities. People increasingly identify with particular, specific, issues or movements for more limited amounts of time, rather than their membership in larger collectivities or with long-term investments in causes or organizations (Ellison, 2000). These identifications with particular issues or movements may be more rapidly shifting, evolving, and emerging as new issues or movements come to the fore or appear more salient, or as new opportunities for participating appear or recede. These forms of participation might occur in physical settings or they might be assisted by technology, or might involve both together. To participate in these ways might be as demanding and excluding as more normative ways, in that they might require a high degree of mobility, access to and knowledge about technology, and particular personal and social skills resources. Thus, these new modes of participation are also reflective of privileged and resourced groups who have the power, time, skills, and opportunity to participate effectively in these newer ways.

Beckett (2005) also argues that many people with disabilities do not identify with social movements for people with disabilities. They prefer to identify and to participate in mainstream society even though they are being marginalized. The consequence is that their individual and collective voices might continue to be largely unheard and their opportunities to advance the discussion concerning their needs or rights or to prevent the infringement on their rights might be limited (Beckett, 2005).

Lived Citizenship

The third perspective, lived citizenship, refers to the meaning and experience of citizenship in daily life (Hall & Williamson, 1990; Lister, 1997). In common with normative citizenship, lived citizenship emphasizes agency. However, lived citizenship includes a broader range of settings. Normative citizenship is concerned with formal political, organizational, and community structures and processes. In contrast, lived citizenship shifts the focus to citizenship in everyday settings and interactions (Lister, 1997). According to Lister (1997), a focus on lived citizenship provides an opportunity to recast participatory political citizenship in terms of rights and opportunities to participate rather than obligations or expectations to participate. It draws attention to how people perceive or experience discrimination, exclusion, and barriers to places or resources they want access to in their everyday lives.

The lived citizenship perspective questions the line drawn between public and private spheres. It expands what is considered political (Lister, 2003), focusing on whether people, individually and collectively, can exert choice and control in work, family, home, and community settings. Although lived citizenship may involve formal settings such as organizations and programs, and more overtly political settings, it may also involve participation in settings that are more informal, less structured, and less clearly political. As Ellison (2000) notes, citizenship is increasingly enacted in a variety of public, private, corporate spaces rather than in explicitly political contexts. Among these different contexts, Lister (1997) has identified women's negotiation with welfare institutions and participation in informal neighborhood politics through which social capital is developed and individuals can develop increased confidence as political actors.

Expanding citizenship to include nonovertly political realms is particularly important for people with serious mental illness. Because many live lives of exclusion and poverty, they may find their agency and rights frequently threatened or infringed on in everyday activities and settings. Corrigan et al. (2003) reported that about 38% of people with serious mental illness reported discrimination in areas such as employment, education, housing, law enforcement, access to commercial settings such as hotels or restaurants, traditional mental health services, or consumer-operated services. Wahl (1999) reported that as many as 70% of individuals he surveyed avoided disclosing their mental illnesses to avoid discrimination when applying for jobs, housing, or licenses, and about a third of respondents reporting having been turned down from a job because of their mental health history.

This expansion is also significant because many parts of the daily lives of people with serious mental health issues occur where the lines between the public and private are blurred. For most people, housing, leisure, work, or the receipt of support are clearly private and personal or commercial domains of life. For many people with serious mental illness, however, they occur within the context of social or health programs or services. Thus, the expression of agency in these contexts, particularly in the form of choice and control over these programs and services is an important act of citizenship. The pertinence of this agency for citizenship is even clearer because these programs and services are, or should be, offered as social rights in support of citizenship.

Complementarity of the Three Perspectives on Citizenship

Though they emerged at different times and from different schools of thought, the three perspectives on citizenship are complementary. Together, they provide an ecological perspective on the citizenship challenges of people with serious mental illness and also point to opportunities for action.

Legal citizenship draws attention to the broadest or macro levels (be they at national, province or state, or municipal levels) where it is determined what are the rights of citizens, how they will be protected, and how they will be distributed. These are the levels at which advocacy can be directed to expand rights or arguments can be made to prevent the erosion or encroachment on existing rights. An analysis at this level also provides for an examination of disparities in the ability of individuals to act on or avail themselves of these rights.

The lived citizenship perspective invites a complementary micro level consideration of the experience and meaning of these rights and the ability to act on them in a variety of settings. It invites an examination of the extent to which people are able or not to act as citizens on a daily basis, their actual experiences of discrimination and infringement of their rights and the identification of those settings and actors where they find their rights and their citizenship affirmed or denied. It also invites a consideration of the ways in which people do actively participate and contribute to their relationships and settings, in both formal and public ways as well as more informally and privately.

Lived citizenship also complements a normative citizenship perspective that is concerned with participation in more formal groups, settings, or organizations. An analysis that combines these perspectives might look at rates and effectiveness of participation in the traditional normative and newer normative modes of participation among people with serious mental illness, as well as in alternative settings identified earlier. Such an analysis might also examine their exclusion, by themselves or others, from opportunities to participate in ways that a have bearing on their daily lives, or the settings, programs, and services that affect them.

Implications of the Citizenship Concept for Housing for People with Serious Mental Illness

In this section I sketch the major implications from this tripartite perspective on citizenship. First I identify the general implications for practice, policy and research on housing. Then, I examine the specific implications for understanding the strengths and potential limitations of single-site and scatter-site housing and Housing First.

Implications for Practice, Policy, and Research

Table 7.1 describes the implications for housing practice, policy, and research stemming from the citizenship concept. In the following paragraphs I examine these implications in greater detail. The discussion is not exhaustive, but instead suggests

Table 7.1 **Implications of Citizenship Concepts for Practice, Policy, and Research**

Conception of Citizenship	Practice	Policy	Research
Legal Citizenship	• Document discrimination and denial of access to housing, settings, resources, and services • Advocacy for equitable access for clients to housing, settings, resources, and services free from discrimination • Advocacy and support regarding civil and political rights, particularly with respect to housing rights • Advocacy and support regarding accessing and maintaining access to programs and services in support of social rights	• Advocacy and development of protections of rights of people with serious mental illness for ability to act on civil and political rights and to satisfaction of social rights • Advocacy for and development of sanctions for discrimination on the basis of mental health • Development of legal support for people to secure and act on their rights	• Studies of indicators of citizenship among people with serious mental illness: social security, employment, housing, health, education and community services; democratic process, legislation regarding access to services (Huxley & Thornicroft, 2003) • Studies of indicators of experience of discrimination and denial of rights
Normative Citizenship	• Developing, securing, and supporting diverse means and opportunities for participation based on interests; including Formal opportunities (boards or directors, committees, tenants' associations, neighborhood watch); informal community opportunities; emergent opportunities; and alternative settings (e.g., consumer/survivor organizations)	• Creating and funding opportunities and support for diverse forms of participation	• Studies of indicators of extent, outcomes, and effectiveness of participation in diverse forms of participation

Table 7.1 **Continued**

Conception of Citizenship	Practice	Policy	Research
Lived Citizenship	• Locating housing in diverse neighborhoods with many opportunities for participation • Creating and supporting diverse opportunities for tenant voice in housing • Supporting and respecting tenant voice, choice, and control in housing • Working with tenants to gain access and reduce barriers to settings and resources	• Encouraging location of housing in diverse, resource- and opportunity-rich neighborhoods • Protection of tenant rights among marginalized people • Requiring and supporting diverse opportunities for tenant participation in housing	• Study effects of neighborhoods (e.g., resources, opportunities) on tenant participation • Study experiences of discrimination, abuses of tenancy rights, and exclusion from community settings • Study citizen participation outcomes for different forms of housing

some of the more important implications. Though some of these implications are already a part of current practice, policy, and research, it is also apparent that many of these implications have not been the focus of action in these areas.

Implications of Legal Citizenship for Practice, Policy, and Research

The implications of legal citizenship are to ensure that a diverse array of civil, political, and social rights exist to enable people to access good housing and adequate community-based support so that tenants have the foundations to participate in community life. In terms of practice, an emphasis must be placed on understanding how tenants are able or unable to act on their civil, political, and social rights and to advocate with them to address issues or barriers. Housing and support workers should see issues of discrimination and exclusion as of equal importance with therapeutic concerns such as the acquisition of skills and achievement of treatment goals. A citizenship approach shifts focus from primarily individual-level goals to include plans for change in those settings that routinely discriminate against or exclude tenants. From a legal citizenship standpoint, access to housing and the right to sign a lease and enjoy the rights associated with being a tenant are fundamental.

Equally fundamental is access to community support that promotes normative and lived citizenship. This community support extends beyond the formal aspects of the mental health system to include self-help and consumer-run organizations, generic community services and groups, and family and friends (Trainor, Pomeroy, & Pape, 2004).

In terms of policy, the advancement and protection of the civil, political, and social rights of people with serious mental illness must be a primary concern. Of particular relevance to housing must be a focus on access to high-quality community housing and support that meets the needs and preferences of citizens. This access requires an adequate supply, along with the financial means of acquiring housing (such as rent supplements) and laws that prevent discrimination against people with disabilities. Equally important is a focus on ensuring that tenants are aware of and can act on their rights as tenants regardless of the type of housing in which they live.

Finally, consistent with Huxley and Thornicroft's (2003) conception of *demos*, research should focus on a broad range of indicators of citizenship among people with serious mental illness living in community housing in order to determine the nature, the extent, and the susceptibility of various subgroups to infringement of their rights in areas such as social security, employment, housing, health, education and community services, and participation in community settings and groups and democratic processes.

Implications of Normative Citizenship for Practice, Policy, and Research

The implications of the concept of normative citizenship involve creating opportunities for participation in a diverse range of housing-based or community-based roles and settings. At the level of practice, addressing normative participation requires diverse opportunities for citizen participation as well as working to ensure that people can effectively participate to the extent that they wish. This can occur either by modifying current formal ways of participating (e.g., committees, boards of directors) to make them more accommodating or to provide training and support so that people can participate more effectively. Promoting normative citizenship means enabling people to participate in neighborhood groups and associations and supporting the development of alternative consumer-run organizations including tenants' associations in co-ops or single-site supportive housing settings. Finally, supporting normative citizenship requires providing the technological requirements and the support for participating in more rapidly evolving emergent citizenship opportunities.

At the level of policy, supporting normative citizenship requires opportunities to participate in more diverse ways. It may include policies for formal organizational decision-making bodies to be more inclusive. It would require recognizing that access to new technologies is critical for citizenship. A lack of access creates a significant divide in terms of people's abilities to participate as citizens. Supporting normative citizenship also involves creating and funding more consumer-run organizations that provide opportunities for people to test and develop their skills for participating in more formal organizations.

Research could support advances in the practice and policy domains by studying the extent, nature, outcomes, and effectiveness of people's participation in these diverse ways and opportunities for participating. Here, attention would be paid to participation in formal decision-making or policy-setting groups, in community groups, in political processes, and in more issue-oriented and emergent opportunities.

Implications of Lived Citizenship for Practice, Policy, and Research

In terms of lived citizenship, practice can focus on the relationship between tenants and the people, settings, and communities with whom they interact. In addition to documenting therapeutic or life skill goals, support workers can work with tenants to identify those settings from which they are excluded or where they are being discriminated against. They then can formulate plans to advocate for successful participation or to identify alternative community settings or resources. Working toward change requires change strategies that are beyond the individual level. It entails a focus on the features and actors of these settings to determine whether a resolution is possible. The goal is to ensure that the tenant has a measure of voice, choice, and control in the full range of his or her daily interactions. This voice, choice, and control includes their housing, be it in their in own apartment or through participation on decision-making bodies such as tenants' associations or co-op boards. It is also essential that tenants understand and can act on their rights as tenants.

At the level of policy, there must be the encouragement to locate housing in a diverse range of resource- and opportunity-rich neighborhoods, as well as enabling tenants to choose the form of housing and neighborhood in which they wish to live. Also, at the policy level the protection of tenancy rights must be a priority. This means requiring that tenants have the support to act when their rights are infringed on. Independent, consumer-run housing resource centers with access to legal counsel are one means of achieving this goal. Finally, in single-site supportive housing arrangements, direction and support are required to find effective means of incorporating tenant decision-making in the day-to-day affairs of the housing. In part, this requires ensuring that housing provider agencies are accountable not only to funders and boards of directors but also to their tenants.

Research informed by a lived citizenship perspective would consider the location of housing and the effects of neighborhood characteristics on tenant participation. Research would study more closely the everyday experiences of discrimination, abuses of tenancy rights, and exclusion from community settings to understand how common these experiences are and how and where they occur. Studies may also examine citizen participation outcomes associated with different forms of housing to determine how different approaches support or hinder the expression of citizenship within the housing and in the community.

Citizenship and Single-Site, Scatter-Site, and Housing First Housing

Though citizenship has been more closely tied to scatter-site and Housing First approaches (Nelson, 2010), in this section I consider how all housing approaches present risks and opportunities for the citizenship of tenants. This section does not address custodial housing beyond acknowledging in its design and underlying values a lack of concern with the citizenship of its tenants. A summary of risks is presented in Table 7.2.

With respect to single-site supportive housing it is useful to note that this term refers to a range of forms of housing (Parkinson et al., 1999; also, see chapter 2). It includes earliest transitional models in which residents transitioned from settings with higher levels of structure and support to ones with lower levels as they gained more skills and capacity for independence. The term includes group homes as well independent apartments that are colocated in a single building or one or more floors of an apartment building. All single-site housing provides support that is linked, in whole or in part, to residency in the housing, such that should tenants move some of the support they have received does not follow with them (Parkinson et al., 1999). Newer approaches to single-site housing have, however increasingly integrated some of the practices and values of scatter-site and Housing First housing, including the delinking of some forms of housing from residency in the housing and the full tenancy of residents who sign their own leases (Sylvestre, Ollenberg, & Trainor, 2007b; see also chapter 14 of this book). Unfortunately, it is has not been documented what are the common practices in single-site supportive housing and the extent to which these progressive shifts have occurred (Sylvestre et al., 2007b).

For single-site housing, there are certain risks for citizenship that may come from the stigmatization of tenants who live in housing that is identifiably different from other housing. It may lead to them being treated differently than others in the community. There may also be a risk that comes from the development of supports and resources internal to the housing that may replace or discourage seeking these supports and resources in the community. There may be a risk of a dependency that arises with a support provider who is also a housing provider, leading to an encroachment on the individual's agency and their tenancy.

Despite these risks, a substantial and minority of people (20% or more) identify single-site housing as a preferred housing option (Aubry, Ecker, & Jetté, 2014). Single-site programs that offer independent apartments and that reflect progressive values expressed in independent and Housing First approaches also provide

Table 7.2 **Risks and Opportunities for Promoting Citizenship in Supportive Housing**

Type of Housing	Risks	Opportunities
Single-Site Housing	• Stigmatization of tenants living in housing that is identifiable as different from other housing in the neighborhood • Provision of supports and resources internal to the housing that may replace or discourage seeking supports and resources in the community. • Risk of dependency	• Peer support • Opportunities to develop agency within supportive housing • Opportunities for participation of tenants in democratic housing decision-making • Housing provider may advocate for tenant involvement in local neighborhood organizations
Scatter-site Housing and Housing First	• Social isolation • A focus on autonomy over interdependence	• Recognition of housing as a social right • Control over own housing

for opportunities to develop agency and citizenship. This is in addition to the peer support that may come from clustered apartments. Through a reorientation of single-site housing there are opportunities for it to take on participatory management processes to support individual and collective internal tenant agency, choice, and control. Through formal decision-making bodies, democratic processes, and more emergent or issue-based participatory opportunities (e.g., small time-limited projects), formally passive tenants can find ways of exercising their agency in the context of a mutually supportive environment. What is required is a shift in the perspective of the agency and staff from provider to partner or collaborator, and possibly even to playing an increasingly supportive role in the decision-making of tenants in the housing.

It is also possible to see the association of the tenant to the identifiable housing and housing agency as not strictly stigmatizing. Housing agencies and their tenants can also strive to be active contributors to their neighborhoods by working with other residents around issues of safety, cleanliness, and resources (see chapter 14 of this book). The positive and proactive role of the agency in the community can create space for interested tenants to play roles in neighborhood functions and groups, such as neighborhood watch programs or local organizing committees. Acting as representatives of their fellow tenants, people can gain access to local activities or decision-making groups they may have had difficulties accessing on their own.

Risks for citizenship in independent supportive housing may come from the isolation of living in apartments (Siegel et al., 2006; Yanos, Barrow, & Tsemberis, 2004). This risk may be increased when people who are already socially isolated are living in poverty, and when apartments are located in poorer, disorganized neighborhoods. It may be that there has been too strong an emphasis on individual autonomy and control without a counterbalancing appreciation for the importance of interdependence (see Lister, 1997). Interdependence is critical not only for well-being but also as a means for agency to improve one's standing and that of others. Links to alternative settings, such as consumer-run organizations, can provide those opportunities for agency and social capital to be developed.

For both scatter-site housing and Housing First approaches, the opportunities are the direct access to housing that are provided and the direct inclusion in normal community housing. However, the risk is assuming that it is access itself to normal housing that is the key outcome, and the transformative element. Instead, a longer-term focus is required: one that appreciates that access to housing is reflective of one's legal citizenship status but is no guarantee of effective normative or lived citizenship experiences. Key to both approaches is a long-term support oriented to increasing agency in daily life.

Comparison of Citizenship to Other Housing Values and Approaches

The citizenship concept is far from new, and it is clear from the foregoing discussion that the concept may overlap with other concepts that have influenced practice, policy, and research on housing for people with serious mental illness. In this section, I discuss areas of overlap and identify the unique contributions of citizenship.

Earlier in this chapter I contrasted therapeutic values with citizenship values. Here I return to this theme by more broadly considering the relationship between citizenship and health. Comprehensive and progressive definitions of health, such as the World Health Organization's Ottawa Charter for Health Promotion (WHO, 2009), define health not as an end, in and of itself, but as a resource for living. It emphasizes social, personal, and physical capacities of individuals and groups to achieve their aspirations, satisfy their needs, and cope with their environments (WHO, 2009). The fundamental conditions and resources for health include peace, food, a stable ecosystem, social justice, and equity along with what have been previously identified as social rights, including shelter, income, and education (WHO, 2009). A key area of overlap in the health and citizenship concepts is agency. Whereas health is seen as a resource to support the agency of individuals and groups to achieve their goals, citizenship refers to the rights, processes, and daily interactions through which agency is expressed to improve one's own life and the lives of others. In this regard, the unique contribution of the citizenship concept is in the identification of the individual and group's relationship to the state, the rights of the individual to express this agency, and the obligation of the state to provide the means and opportunities for this agency to be expressed. The citizenship concept contributes an ecological appreciation for how agency is supported or thwarted and identifies some of the means through which infringement of agency can be addressed. It reinforces that health is a foundation, but is not sufficient, for effective community and civic participation.

The therapeutic perspective that has dominated the study of housing for people with serious mental illness has tended to emphasize a narrower range of outcomes than a broad definition of health has suggested, emphasizing community adaptation, functioning, symptoms, or quality of life (Aubry et al., 2014; Sylvestre et al., 2007b). Moreover, the strong focus on therapeutic outcomes has tended to see these outcomes as the focus of housing, at the expense of an appreciation for how these are the foundations for full community life. The risk lies in establishing a view of people with disabilities as people who are dependent, and who require therapy, socialization, and training rather than as citizens who should be supported in acting on their rights and provided with control and choices (Rappaport, 1981). In contrast, citizenship speaks to what may be accomplished based on a foundation of good housing and therapeutic outcomes.

Citizenship also extends our understanding of the commonly investigated community integration outcome. Much of the research on community integration among people with serious mental illness has focused on presence in the community in terms of frequency of participation in community events or use of community resources (Townley, Kloos, & Wright, 2009). Though more recent approaches have adopted a multidimensional perspective examining physical, social, and psychological dimensions, little research has considered neighborhood acceptance or the nature of this integration in terms of the effectiveness of participation (Townley et al., 2009). Beyond an assessment of the type and extent of neighborhood participation, citizenship invites a consideration of the nature and quality of this participation, barriers to participation, and to the ability of citizens to exert influence and power in these interactions.

Ware et al. (2007) have proposed redefining social integration to include citizenship. However, their definition of citizenship emphasizes legal aspects (i.e., rights, privileges, and responsibilities of members of a democratic society), overlooking the normative and lived citizenship aspects. Yanos, Stefancic, and Tsemberis (2012) also integrated citizenship within the study of community integration by examining normative aspects of citizenship such as voting and volunteerism. They found that tenants living in scatter-site housing tended to report lower levels of involvement in these activities than people in a community sample. These differences were small, however, and both the tenants and community sample reported low levels of citizenship and community integration more generally.

Citizenship also provides a complement and extension of the recovery concept. Recovery has emphasized a unique and personal process of acquiring meaningful roles in the community (Anthony, 1993). The emphasis on securing meaningful roles, agency, and increased personal control, self-determination, and empowerment (Anthony, 1993; Jacobson & Greenley, 2001; Ochocka, Nelson, & Janzen, 2005; Onken, Craig, Ridgway, Ralph, & Cook, 2007; Piat et al., 2009) overlaps with a citizenship perspective that emphasizes effective participation in a diverse set of groups, settings, and organizations. Although there has been a recognition of the importance of external conditions for supporting or creating barriers to recovery (Jacobson & Greenley, 2001; Ochocka et al., 2005; Onken et al., 2007), the citizenship concept provides an extension to the recovery concept with a recognition that access to meaningful roles or the struggles for greater personal empowerment are not only personal struggles. That these struggles are common among many people with mental illness speaks to infringements on citizenship that occur on multiple levels, from micro-systems such as community settings and organizations, to macro-level policy and funding decisions. In short, citizenship provides collective, ecological, and legal dimensions that seem to be lacking in the recovery concept.

More broadly, the contributions that the citizenship concept can make over therapeutic or recovery concepts are a focus on what people are, have, and are due. Inherent in therapeutic and recovery concepts are notions of becoming and improving; an emphasis on goals that people are, or should be, working toward but might never achieve. Therapeutic and recovery concepts invite discourses of goal-setting and achievement as the focus of service provision. Certainly some of these elements would be present in a citizenship-focused agenda. However, the starting point would be the recognition of the person as citizen with rights, who requires opportunities and support to express their agency. The focus is on addressing the relationship between person and setting in which this agency is being suppressed. This work can focus on support for the person, advocacy in the setting, or working with both together. It also links these individual-level struggles to broader actions that seek to create opportunities and resources to support the individual and collective agency of people with serious mental illness.

Despite these strengths of the citizenship concept, there are also limitations. One key limitation lies in the exclusion of the social and emotional dimensions of living in housing and in communities. Huxley and Thornicroft (2003) have provided a distinction between *demos* and *ethnos*. Whereas *demos* refers to citizenship and citizenship rights, *ethnos* "refers to a shared cultural community rather than a national community, and to the shared values, identification and sense of cohesion that are engendered by membership of particular social groups and communities" (p. 289). This concept of *ethnos* is a necessary complement to the citizenship concept. Moreover, it is equally clear that it is not only along the *demos* dimension that people with serious mental illness have been excluded but also along this critical *ethnos* dimension. Thus, attending to both dimensions would provide an important and complete understanding of citizenship participation and agency.

Conclusion

An inherent risk in a continued emphasis on a therapeutic perspective on housing is that the causes and solutions to problems of isolation and social exclusion will only be found within individuals. It leads to a continuous focus on new goals to be achieved in the ongoing quest for an active and satisfying life. It takes attention away from the fact that exclusion is the product of others, of groups, of systems that exclude, and that passivity and isolation are the product of hopelessness and fear that come from poverty, lack of opportunities, or experiences of rejection. The inclusion of a citizenship agenda within and complementary to our current efforts in housing practice, policy, and research provides a complementary focus that draws attention to both the means and opportunities for supporting the agency of people who wish to obtain or who live in community housing as well as those features of practice, organizations, neighborhoods, and social and health systems as well as civil and political structures and processes that subvert that agency.

References

Anthony, W.A. (1993). Recovery from mental illness: The guiding vision of the mental health service system in the 1990's. *Psychosocial Rehabilitation Journal, 16*, 11–23.

Aubry, T., Ecker, J., & Jetté, J. (2014). Supported housing as a promising Housing First approach for people with severe and persistent mental illness. In M. Guirguis-Younger, R. McNeil, & S.W. Hwang (Eds.), *Homelessness and health* (pp. 155–188). Ottawa: University of Ottawa Press.

Beckett, A.E. (2005). Reconsidering citizenship in light of the concerns of the UK disability movement. *Citizenship Studies, 9*, 405–420. doi: 10.1080/13621020500211412

Corrigan, P., Thompson, V., Lambert, D., Sangster, Y., Noel, J.G., & Campbell, J. (2003). Perceptions of discrimination among persons with serious mental illness. *Psychiatric Services, 54*, 1105–1110.

Ellison, N. (2000). Proactive and defensive engagement: Social citizenship in a changing public sphere. *Sociological Research Online, 5.* http://www.socresonline.org.uk/5/3/ellison.html

Hall, T., & Williamson, H. (1999). *Citizenship and community.* Leicester, UK: Youth Work Press.

Heller, K., Price, R., Reinharz, S., Riger, S., & Wandersman, A. (1984). *Psychology and community change: Challenges of the future.* Homewood, IL: Dorsey.

Huxley, P., & Thornicroft, G. (2003). Social inclusion, social quality and mental illness. *British Journal of Psychiatry, 182*, 289–290. doi: 10.1192/bjp.00.675

Jacobson, N., & Greenley, D. (2001). What is recovery? A conceptual model and explication. *Psychiatric Services, 52*, 482–485.

Kloos, B., Hill, J., Thomas, E., Wandersman, A., Elias, M.J., & Dalton, J.H. (2012). *Community psychology: Linking individuals and communities* (3rd ed.). Belmont, CA: Wadsworth.

Lister, R. (1997). Dialectics of citizenship. *Hypatia, 12*, 6–26.

Lister, R. (2003). *Citizenship: Feminist perspectives* (2nd ed.). Washington Square: New York University Press.

Lister, R. (2010). *Understanding theories and concepts in social policy.* Bristol, UK: Policy Press.

Marsh, A. (1998). Processes of change in housing and public policy. In A. Marsh & D. Mullens (Eds.), *Housing and public policy: Citizenship, choice and control* (pp. 1–29). Maidenhead, UK: Open University Press.

Marshall, T. (1950). *Citizenship and social class.* Cambridge: Cambridge University Press.

Nelson, G. (2010). Housing for people with serious mental illness: Approaches, evidence, and transformative change. *Journal of Sociology and Social Welfare, 37,* 123–146.

Nelson, G., Janzen, R., Trainor, J., & Ochocka, J. (2008). Putting values into practice: Public policy and the future of mental health consumer-run organizations. *American Journal of Community Mental Health, 42,* 192–201. doi: 10.1007/s10464-008-9191-y

Nelson, G., Ochocka, J., Janzen, R., & Trainor, J. (2006). A longitudinal study of mental health consumer/survivor initiatives: Part 2 – A quantitative study of impacts of participation on new members. *Journal of Community Psychology, 34(3),* 261–272. doi:10.1002/jcop.20098

Ochocka, J., Nelson, G., & Janzen, R. (2005). Moving forward: Negotiating self and external circumstances in recovery. *Psychiatric Rehabilitation Journal, 28,* 315–322.

Oldenfield, A. (1990). *Citizenship and community: Civic republicanism and the modern world.* London: Routledge.

Onken, S.J., Craig, C.M., Ridgway, P., Ralph, R.O., & Cook, J.A. (2007). An analysis of the definitions and elements of recovery: A review of the literature. *Psychiatric Rehabilitation Journal, 31,* 9–22.

Parkinson, S., Nelson, G., & Horgan, S. (1999). From housing to homes: A review of the literature on housing approaches for psychiatric consumer/survivors. *Canadian Journal of Community Mental Health, 18,* 145–163.

Piat, M., Sabetti, J., Couture, A., Sylvestre, J., Provencher, H., Botschner, J., & Stayner, D. (2009). What does recovery mean to me? Perspectives of mental health consumers. *Psychiatric Rehabilitation Journal, 32,* 585–593.

Putnam, R.D. (2000). *Bowling alone: The collapse and revival of American community.* New York: Simon & Schuster.

Rappaport, J. (1981). In praise of paradox: A social policy of empowerment over prevention. *American Journal of Community Psychology, 9(1),* 1–25.

Siegel, C.E., Samuels, J., Tang, D., Berg, I., Jones, K., & Hopper, K. (2006). Tenant outcomes in supported housing and community residences in New York City. *Psychiatric Services, 57,* 982–991.

Sylvestre, J., Nelson, G., Sabloff, A., & Peddle, S. (2007a). Housing for people with serious mental illness: A comparison of values and research. *American Journal of Community Psychology, 40,* 125–137.

Sylvestre, J., Ollenberg, M., & Trainor, J. (2007b). A participatory process benchmarking strategy for describing and improving supportive housing. *Psychiatric Rehabilitation Journal, 31,* 115–124.

Townley, G., Kloos, B., & Wright, P.A. (2009). Understanding the experience of place: Expanding methods to conceptualize and measure community integration of persons with serious mental illness. *Health and Place, 15,* 520–531.

Trainor, J., Pomeroy, E., & Pape, B. (2004). *A framework for support* (3rd ed.). Toronto, ON: Canadian Mental Health Association, National Office.

Turner, B.S. (1990). Outline of a theory of citizenship. *Sociology, 24,* 189–217.

Wandersman, A., & Florin, P. (2000). Citizen participation and community organizations. In J. Rappaport & E. Seidman (eds.), *Handbook of community psychology* (pp. 247–271). New York: Kluwer Academic/Plenum.

Ware, N.C., Hopper, K., Tugenberg, T., Dickey, B., & Fisher, D. (2007). Connectedness and citizenship: Redefining social integration. *Psychiatric Services, 58,* 469–474.

Whal, O. (1999). Mental health consumers' experience of stigma. *Schizophrenia Bulletin, 25,* 467–478.

World Health Organization. (2009). *Milestones in health promotion: Statements from global conferences*. Geneva: WHO Press. Retrieved from http://www.who.int/healthpromotion/Milestones_Health_Promotion_05022010.pdf

Yanos, P.T., Barrow, S.M., & Tsemberis, S. (2004). Community integration in the early phases of housing among homeless persons diagnosed with severe mental illness: Successes and challenges. *Community Mental Health Journal, 40,* 133–150.

Yanos, P.T., Stefancic, A., & Tsemberis, S. (2012). Objective community integration of mental health consumers living in supported housing and of others in the community. *Psychiatric Services, 63,* 438–444. doi: 10.1176/appi.ps.201100397

8

Expanding Methodological Options for Housing Research

JOHN SYLVESTRE, AMANDEEP BASSI, AND KATHERINE BENDELL

In this chapter we describe and discuss a variety of methods for studying the lives of people who have experienced serious mental illness and who are living in community-based housing. There have been a number of notable reviews of housing research to date, testifying to a robust, maturing field of research (Nelson, Aubry, & Lafrance, 2007; Rog, 2004; Rogers, Farkas, Anthony, Kash, Harding, & Olschewski, 2008; Rog et al., 2014). One example of progress in research is the At Home/Chez Soi study in Canada, which involves a randomized controlled trial examining the effectiveness of Housing First approaches in four Canadian cities (Goering et al., 2011; Goering et al., 2014). To date, much of the research that has captured attention has been quantitative and nomothetic in nature—research that is concerned with general relationships among variables associated with characteristics of people, characteristics of housing, and characteristics of the support available to them. Much of this research relies on the completion of measures or scales, whether self-reports completed by tenant participants or those completed by service providers or others. Though the significance of this research is clear, it has left us with only a limited understanding of the everyday lives of people living with mental illness in the community.

This chapter considers the merits of other methods. Of particular interest are those that advance our concern with citizenship, as outlined in chapter 7 of this book. There are two issues we consider with respect to these methods. First, we consider the roles participants play in research. Whereas in more conventional research participants are limited to being sources of data, we are also interested in considering the potential for the increased voice, agency, accountability, and control associated with a citizenship agenda extended to housing research. Second, our interest in investigating these methods lies in their capacity to contribute a greater understanding of how people navigate the particular social ecologies in which they live. In essence, our interest is the extent to which these methods enable us to learn about the particular landscapes, neighborhoods, settings, and people with whom they interact, the kinds of interactions they have, the meaning they ascribe to these interactions, and the consequences of these interactions. A related concern is how different approaches to research can represent people's experiences. The chapter considers what different research approaches can say or communicate about these experiences.

In the following sections we explore these issues in greater detail. First, we examine roles that participants may play in the production of data in research. Then we consider how we may appraise the contributions of research from a citizenship perspective. Finally we selectively present and discuss research approaches and methods that may contribute to a citizenship-informed research agenda. Some, though not all, of these methods are qualitative or interested in idiographic representations of people's experiences. The list is not exclusive. It is also not meant to imply that conventional quantitative approaches cannot contribute to a citizenship agenda. Instead, the discussion is offered in the hope of expanding the methodological options available to researchers.

The Production of Research Data

The term "data collection" is used everywhere in research, but masks an important fact about data. Data are not *collected*. Data are *produced* by researchers through interactions with the people or the phenomena they are studying. In most research, the researcher plays a powerful role in the production of data. The researcher decides what constructs should be measured, the questions that should be asked of participants, how participants will answer those questions, the conditions under which the answers will be provided, and who will be the participants who will provide the answers. The researcher constrains the ways in which people may account for themselves, their health, or their lives. The data are therefore reflective of the researcher's preoccupations, values, and assumptions about what or who is being studied, and what is important to know about them. As we will see, the power of the researcher may be diluted through the introduction of more participatory elements, particularly in community-based research, where various stakeholders may contribute to the development of research questions and methods. However, the relative differences in power, experience, and expertise of the researcher can mean that the research is still suffused with his or her interests and concerns.

Though participants may be constrained in various ways, they also play roles in the production of data. Participants can differ considerably in how they interpret the questions that are asked of them, and how they interpret the response options that are provided to them (see for example research on the measurement of coping by Stone, Greenberg, Kennedy-Moore, & Newman, 1991). These interpretations are distinct from the decisions they may make about how much they wish to reveal to researchers, or self-presentation concerns that may influence how they answer. Their responses, then, are interpretive and creative and are products of their interactions with researchers, the study, and the instruments. Their responses are unique social products of uncertain relationship to any particular object, thought, or experience researchers assume them to represent. Thus, both researchers and participants, in different ways and to different degrees, are active in the process of creating data, although the greater power over these productive activities typically rests with the researcher.

The interactions that produce quantitative data are as odd as they are constrained. Though these interactions may produce useful data, it is certainly not controversial to suggest that these data provide only a limited view of the experiences and lives of participants, as they are only suitable for statistical analyses that count occurrences of phenomena or estimates co-occurrences or interrelationships of variables (Curry, Nembhard, & Bradley, 2009). Qualitative research methods have for some time now provided alternative research approaches, and the increasing popularity of these methods has been accompanied by an increased attention to the quality and rigor in their application (e.g., Angen, 2000; Cho & Trent, 2006; Whittemore, Chase, & Mandle, 2001). Though they allow for more space for participants to express their views, and more opportunity to gain a more complex and holistic understanding of their experiences, to some extent the most common applications of these methods can replicate some of the same power imbalances of more conventional quantitative approaches. The use of face-to-face interviews in which participants are expected to speak to a predetermined set of themes, risks perpetuating a power dynamic in which the researcher constrains the opportunities for participants to describe their experiences. Again, though data from such studies are useful, we can also consider the implications that may follow from research approaches that alter the roles that researchers and participants play in the production and analysis of data.

The concept of citizenship focuses attention on the capacity of individuals and groups to take control of their lives, to act in their own interests, and to advocate for themselves. At its root, citizenship is about power—the power of people to speak and act on their own behalf—and how this power may be usurped or denied (see chapter 7, this volume). More traditional research focuses power in the hands of the researcher. It is the researcher who sets the research agenda, who controls the means of data production, and who controls the analysis, interpretation, and dissemination of research findings. This imbalance of power in the research relationship is predicated on the scientific need for rigor. The risk, however, is that ultimately the research embodies and replicates the assumptions and priorities of the researcher, however well intentioned. These assumptions and priorities can certainly overlap with those of the people who are studied, but they may also not represent the full scope of their experiences and concerns.

Moreover, researcher-driven and -controlled research risks perpetuating a set of relationships that are increasingly discredited in other areas, notably in the provision of housing and community-based supports. Services and supports are moving away from a professionally dominated, expert-based, approach toward increasingly consumer-focused and consumer-directed models. Can research in this area remain immune to these developments? Despite risks, we should consider the benefits that may come from research approaches and methods that offer opportunities for enhanced power and control among people or groups being studied. In program evaluations, these opportunities may also be extended to other stakeholders such as service providers, funders, and family members. These enhanced roles may be found in a variety of stages of the research, from conception to dissemination. The hope is that enhanced roles have benefits in terms of research findings that explore a broader range of issues and concerns in the daily lives of people living in community-based housing, but also that promote more collaborative relationships between researchers and participants.

Valuing Housing Research

A focus on citizenship can also invite questions about what we should strive to learn from research and how to value the products of research. Both scientific and nonscientific criteria can be used to value research. Traditionally, quantitative research is assessed in terms of criteria for reliability and validity. A range of criteria has also been proposed for evaluating the rigor of nonquantitative research (e.g., Lincoln & Guba, 1985). These methodological criteria are principally concerned with actions and interactions undertaken within the context of the research itself. They do not take into account the broader social context of the research. Nonmethodological criteria are, however, routinely and uncontroversially used to evaluate research. When sitting on review boards for granting agencies, when acting as peer reviewers of submissions to academic journals, when considering new hires for academic positions, methodological rigor is only one consideration. Originality, impact, relevance, import, ethical conduct, and other factors are routinely factored in evaluations. Well-conducted but banal and inconsequential research is less likely to be funded and likely to be ignored if published.

Considerations of the merit of the research can be extended beyond methodological concerns and also made explicit. In particular, we propose a valuing of research that holds the greatest emancipatory promise for people with serious mental illness. Prior work has established that housing research has been primarily concerned with therapeutic outcomes from housing interventions (Sylvestre, Nelson, Sabloff, & Peddle, 2007a). In other words, we principally study housing in terms of benefits for mental health, community functioning, and integration. Much less frequently do we consider other benefits, such as citizenship outcomes. This is due not only to a mismatch between the concerns of the researcher with those who live in the housing but also likely to a failure to conceive of what other outcomes should be assessed. Beyond the suggestions made in chapter 7 of this book, we offer two other considerations for priorities for housing research. The suggestion is that we should be prioritizing and valuing research that probes these issues, in addition to more common therapeutic concerns.

One criterion for assessing the value of research lies in a consideration of the social and political context of the research. Prilleltensky (2003, 2008) has proposed psychopolitical validity as one basis for evaluating research. According to Prilleltensky, psychopolitical validity concerns the extent to which research or interventions consider how the dynamics of power, in both psychological and political domains, affect health, well-being, and freedom from oppression. Following Prilleltensky (2003, 2008), psychopolitical validity requires the production of knowledge of how power dynamics at multiple levels affect people living with mental illness in community-based housing. These levels include personal ones where studies may be focused on processes by which people gain and express power in their lives, overcome helplessness or hopelessness, or find strength, resilience, and solidarity. At relational levels, studies may be focused on power to forge egalitarian, supportive, and cohesive relationships and understanding social exclusion and discrimination. At collective levels, studies may be focused on broader political and economic forces in creating injustice, exploitation, and suffering. These levels coincide with the levels and dimensions proposed by Hall, Nelson, and Smith Fowler (1987) in their ecological conceptual framework (discussed in chapters 5 and 6, this volume).

Another of concept that may guide research comes from the work of Sen (1999, 2000). Sen's concern with "capabilities" reflected an interest in the kinds of lives that people can actually lead (see also chapter 6). For Sen, disability, poverty, social exclusion, racism, or gender discrimination are significant because they limit the potential of individuals to choose to lead the lives they wish to live (Kuklys, 2005). In particular, Sen (2000) was interested with how deprivations such as social exclusion lead to other deprivations such as being excluded from employment, to being unable to gain credit, or to living in poverty. According to Kuklys (2005), there are two levels of considerations in the capabilities approach: the potential and realized welfare. Whereas the former refers to the opportunities or affordances in the environment (or capabilities) that provide opportunity for the individual to act in his or her own interest, the latter refers to the choices and actions that people undertake and their consequences (or functionings).

It is easy to see how increasing capabilities can improve functioning. Imagine the prospects for a fulfilling life that people with spinal cord injury would have had 100 years ago, in contrast to their prospects today. Note that the increased ability to live independently, to be socially integrated, to work, or to pursue an education has been achieved despite our continuing inability to repair damaged spinal cords. Gains in these areas (or functionings) have been achieved through increases in capabilities; through change in policy, legislation, urban design, architecture, and changes in a host of other areas.[1] Increases in capabilities are not always sufficient, however, to improve functionings. Supportive programs, training, and rehabilitation may also play a role in enabling people to take advantage of the increased capabilities afforded them (Hopper, 2007).

Psychopolitical validity and the capabilities perspective offer additional principles for us to assign value to the products of research. At their core is a concern with agency—the ability of people individually and collectively to act in their own interest. Each is concerned with how the expression of agency is facilitated or hindered by the environments in which people live. The implication for housing research, then, is greater attention to the capacity of individuals to express agency and act on their own behalf in their homes, communities, and programs and the various ways, various actors, and various environments that inhibit the expression of this agency. In addition, the implication is that the outcomes of research that are studied must extend beyond therapeutic or clinical outcomes, to include an understanding of the improved ability of people to meet their own needs and achieve their own goals in life (Sylvestre, Nelson, et al., 2007).

Research Approaches and Methods

In this section, we consider different research approaches and methods that hold the promise for furthering a citizenship-focused research agenda. The review is not intended to be exhaustive. The goal is to introduce options, not commonly found in the field of housing research, and to assess how they help us enhance the role of people with lived experience in the research process and to understand their experiences of citizenship, living in housing in the community.

Participatory Action Research

Participatory action research (PAR) is far from new. There is a rich history of use of as well as critical discussion of PAR. Nelson, Ochocka, Griffin, and Lord (1998) defined PAR as "a research approach that consists of the maximum participation of stakeholders, those whose lives are affected by the problem under study, in the systematic collection and analysis of information for the purpose of taking action and making change" (p. 885). This participation extends from developing research questions and research instruments, to data collection, analysis, interpretation, and dissemination. Thus, PAR is built on an explicit concern with a rebalancing of power between the researcher and the participants. It is based on values of democratic participation and collaborative inquiry with the goal of producing knowledge that is practically useful and that promotes growth and empowerment among participants as was well as broader social change (Nelson et al., 1998; Schneider, 2010).

Nelson, Janzen, Ochocka, and Trainor (2010) have argued that the values of the research approach one uses should be congruent with the values of the program that is being studied. Their discussion identified the values of PAR as congruent with those of the mental health self-help initiatives they studied. These values included (1) empowerment and power-sharing, (2) social inclusion, (3) social change and social justice, and (3) continuous, mutual learning (Nelson et al., 2010). The values of PAR also appear to be congruent with citizenship-focused housing values, particularly with respect to increased individual and collective power, collaboration, increased agency, social inclusion, and social justice. Continuous, mutual learning currently seems less directly relevant, largely because there is little discussion in the single-site supportive housing literature on collaborations between tenants and housing providers (for exceptions see Sylvestre, Cousins, Sundar, Aubry, & Hinsperger, 2008; Sylvestre et al., 2006; Sylvestre, Ollenberg, & Trainor, 2007) and a focus in independent scattered-site supportive housing or housing first approaches on individual-level intervention (for an example of collective action for scattered-site housing, see Kloos et al., 2012).

Nelson and colleagues (Janzen et al., 2006; Nelson, Ochocka, Janzen, & Trainor, 2006a, 2006b; Nelson et al., 2007; Nelson, Ochocka, Janzen, Trainor, & Lauzon, 2004; Ochocka, Nelson, Janzen, & Trainor, 2006) have reported extensively on their PAR study of mental health self-help initiatives, which included quantitative and qualitative findings at multiple ecological levels. The use of PAR in this study, which included common techniques such as a project steering committee and consumer-researchers and interviews, provided increased access and credibility to the findings.

In housing, the use of PAR has produced useful and novel findings as well. Sylvestre, Ollenberg, et al. (2007) collaborated with providers and tenants of supportive housing programs in Toronto to describe optimal delivery of supportive housing programs. Both Sylvestre, Ollenberg, and Trainor (2009) and Schneider (2010) have described participatory research to provide unique perspectives on the concept of housing stability that go beyond the common definitions in research that emphasize the number of days in housing or the number of housing moves. Sylvestre et al. (2009) collaborated with tenants, advocates, family members, and housing providers to characterize housing stability as built on a dynamic relationship between person characteristics, housing characteristics, and support characteristics. As the person, housing, and support are potentially each changing over time (due to forces at various ecological levels), instability could be threatened by changes in one without compensatory changes in the others. Communication and collaboration among tenants, housing providers, and support providers was seen as a key for promoting stable housing on an ongoing basis.

Schneider (2010) reported on a PAR study that focused on housing stability. This study also produced a dynamic view of the concept, with participants reporting a tension between the care and support they received and their perceptions of control over their own lives. Feelings of instability while living in community-based housing were related to the ambivalence people felt about the support they received.

They said that, on the one hand, they were told they were responsible for their own recovery, but on the other hand, they believed that their options were restricted to those actions approved by their support providers. Participants also described the tension in wanting to lead normal lives though their access to services and supports were based on having been labeled as different. Schneider (2010) reported that participants were ambivalent about feeling required to express gratitude for support that they did not necessarily want and feared inviting more control over their lives should they ask for more help.

Elements of PAR have also been incorporated into larger evaluative research. Nelson, Macnaughton, et al. (2015) reported on the use of collaboration among the various stakeholders at five project sites across Canada in the planning of the At Home/Chez Soi project, including researchers, service-providers, and persons with lived experience (PWLE). Nelson et al. reported that factors that facilitated collaborations were preexisting relationships and partnerships, opportunities to develop locally relevant variants of the Housing First approach, as well as a common value base that recognized the credibility of the contributions of PWLE. Despite these facilitators, challenges also included tensions among various collaborators, particularly where there were past experiences of competition, differing priorities, or unfamiliarity. In particular, service providers and researchers sometimes found themselves at odds due to perceptions that researchers dominated the early planning efforts and the wariness of some of the Housing First approach. One of the most significant challenges involved engaging PWLE, particularly in those sites without a history of PWLE involvement.

Challenges with PAR include practical and professional challenges facing communities and research professionals such as the lengthy process of conducting PAR that does not fit within the limited time requirements for completing funded research projects (see for example Nelson, Macnaughton, et al., 2015), or the uncertainty of publishable research projects required to further academic careers.

Other obstacles relate to the core values that inform PAR approaches. For example the notion of equal power-sharing and collaboration requires parties that can operate with equal levels of organization, confidence, and effectiveness. As PAR is essentially a research activity, it is the community members who are invited onto the terrain where the professional researcher is well established, has the most expertise, and is most comfortable. Ultimately, as the products of these activities are research products, these products may be valued solely using research-based criteria (e.g., reliability, validity). Moreover, egalitarian power-sharing and collaboration would require community participants to be equally organized and ready to participate (Sundar & Todd, 2007). Often, though, researchers may encounter communities that are relatively disorganized or unready to participate. In fact, community organization or development itself may sometimes be seen as the end goal of PAR process.

Issues can also arise with respect to the representativeness of the community members who become involved in a PAR project. Those who participate may be more articulate or confident, more advanced in their personal recovery, or more successful in their housing, than those who are not selected to participate or who choose not to participate (Sundar & Todd, 2007). Alternatively, nonparticipation may be discounted as apathy or a lack of concern, rather than an act of passive resistance or "a healthy self-affirming choice" to not become involved in what is assumed to be an inclusive, nonthreatening process (Sundar & Todd, 2007, p. 7). The knowledge that is produced, then, may not be useful or relevant to all people the participants are thought to represent.

In addition, the knowledge that is produced may also be assigned an unwarranted significance of truth or realness by virtue of the means through which it is produced (Sundar & Todd, 2007). The knowledge from PAR projects is produced, much like the production of knowledge from traditional research, through constrained and peculiar interactions among people with varying levels of participation and power within the project. The knowledge may be as much attributable to these interactions as to any phenomena we might presume them to represent that lie outside of the study.

Beyond the knowledge that is produced, issues may also arise when promises held out for PAR do not transpire. Though PAR may be positioned as being able to produce useful knowledge, and positive, if not emancipatory, consequences for participants and their communities, it is likely that many projects fall short in this regard. The outcomes of research, particularly applied research, are never certain, and the additional complexity of PAR may sometimes lead to experiences and outcomes that are inconsequential or disappointing.

These critiques do not invalidate PAR, nor imply that it cannot or should not be pursued. Rather they point to the need for care, humility, patience, and resolve in such projects. The values of PAR suggest an ideal that may often, in practice, not be met. However, the pursuit of these values in the context of our work with community members, particularly those who have had no prior opportunity to participate in the creation of knowledge about themselves may be worthy in its own right, despite risks.

Methods for Understanding Neighborhoods, Neighborhood Use, and Social Integration

In the previous section we examined PAR as a research approach that embraces many of the values underlying a citizenship-driven agenda for housing. Notably, there is a range of research methods that also exemplify many of these values although they may not fully embrace PAR principles. These methods use nonquantitative means of representing and communicating about social experience and phenomena. Numbers inadequately represent our experiences, our lives. It is sometimes uncertain how the numbers we use map onto the concepts, characteristics, and experiences we seek to measure. The value of the methods we examine here lies in the extent to which they are meaningful to participants and produce novel understandings of housing-related phenomena. These methods can, though they do not necessarily, provide an enhanced role for tenants in representing their own lives rather than only being the subjects of representation and interpretation. In the following sections we examine these methodological options for researchers. For each method we discuss the ways in which research participants may extend greater control over the research process and how their experiences are represented. Where available we also provide examples of uses of these methods in housing research.

Narrative Approaches

Qualitative research is now commonplace—within and outside of the housing research field. There is not sufficient space here to describe and review this large and growing body of literature. Instead, we focus on a particular approach that may hold some promise for providing more voice and control to participants in how their perspectives are represented in qualitative research. In this section we explore one particular approach that builds on assumptions of how people characteristically speak about themselves and their experiences—narrative inquiry. A key assumption of narrative inquiry is that humans are essentially storytellers. Narratives are a uniquely human means of organizing our interpretations and making meaning of our experiences (Murray, 2000). By telling a coherent story, narratives help us to organize and give meaning to ceaseless change and the flow of events of our lives (Murray, 2000).

Most commonly, we think about a narrative as the product of an individual act—as a means of creating personal understanding and communication. At a personal level, narratives can help us to control and bring order to our otherwise chaotic experiences (Murray, 2000). Telling stories helps us to make sense of ourselves and our experiences. Narratives are also constructed at collective levels. Collective narratives can reflect shared histories, assumptions, myths, and beliefs. Narratives can be created by marginalized groups as a means of resisting or providing an alternative to dominant narratives (Murray, 2012; Schneider, 2010). Narratives can point to possible futures that "can also become an organizing framework to facilitate social change" (Murray, 2012, p. 254). Murray (2000) reminds us that narratives are created in an interpersonal or social context. They are oriented to and co-constructed with actual or potential listeners. The nature of the relationship, interactions, and context shape both the content and form of a narrative. In particular, the relative positions of the teller and listener (e.g., differences in power or health status) can shape a narrative.

Murray (2000) claims that narratives may be useful for examining disruptions in people's lives, such as those caused by illness. Researchers have used the process of gaining housing as a critical time period in the lives of homeless people with mental illness that may disrupt negative life trajectories and direct them in more desirable directions. Nelson, Clarke, Febbraro, and Hatzipantelis (2005) used a narrative approach in an evaluation of a supportive housing initiative in Ontario, Canada. They examined how the move from homelessness or unstable housing to stable supportive housing affected the quality of life of 15 people with serious mental illness. Findings showed that the lives of the participants, prior to obtaining housing were characterized by poor health, an absence of supportive relationships, cycles of victimization, and a lack of resources. In contrast, after becoming housed, participants reported improvements across a number of areas including well-being, personal relationships and personal safety, control over their lives, and access to resources. Participants also reported some concerns with the quality of housing that they had obtained, as well as a desire for greater independence and privacy in their housing.

Patterson, Rezansoff, Currie, and Somers (2014) and Nelson, Patterson, et al. (2015) reported longitudinal narrative research on the trajectories of recovery among participants in the At Home/Chez Soi Housing First study. The study involved a comparison between those who received housing through a Housing First program and those who were assigned to a "treatment as usual" group. In this study, participants worked with interviewers at baseline to develop a personal narrative that included "(1) their pathway into homelessness; (2) experiences of being homeless or inadequately housed; (3) experiences around first learning that they had a mental illness and obtaining help for their illness; and (4) key life events" (Patterson et al., 2014, p. 3). Eighteen months later, interviews focused on changes since the first interview. In general, participants assigned to the Housing First intervention described more positive narrative trajectories in comparison with those of participants in the treatment as usual condition. Treatment as usual participants described trajectories characterized by disappointment, failure, and loss of health and social relationships (Patterson et al., 2014) as well as challenges related to housing, health, substance use, and community functioning (Nelson, Patterson, et al., 2015). Participants in the Housing First condition provided narratives characterized by more hope and confidence, increased social contacts, and having opportunities to take on valued social roles (Nelson, Patterson et al., 2015). Housing First provided participants with a foundation for slowly shifting their identities from ones linked to homelessness to new roles and activities, though participants still maintained connections with their older identities, neighborhoods, and routines (Patterson et al., 2014).

In these examples, the narratives were produced in the context of a formal research study, with interviews conducted by members of research teams. In contrast, Schneider (2010) described a study that combined PAR and narrative approaches. In this work, the interviews were conducted by interviewers who themselves had experienced mental health issues. Previously we have described findings from this work on the topic of housing stability. Schneider (2010) also described a separate study of communication between people diagnosed with schizophrenia and medical professionals. Among the findings reported by Schneider (2010) was the uncertainty of diagnoses and physicians avoiding discussing, being unclear about, or revising diagnoses. Schneider reported limited communication from physicians related to medication, either not providing information on the medications, the treatment options available, or being relatively unconcerned with the impact of side effects. Participants described frustrating experiences with physicians who appeared unsympathetic or unresponsive to them. For Schneider (2010) these findings echo concerns previously identified in her study of housing stability, in terms of the experience of control in the receipt of professional treatment and support. In subtle ways, people come to believe that, though they are told that they have a voice in their treatment, their support, and their housing, they also feel that their perspectives are discounted, that they should follow the prescriptions of professionals, and that they are perceived as ungrateful when they voice dissatisfaction.

Taken together, these examples suggest the complexity of the lives of people living with mental illness. They touch on themes of power, of the challenges in expressing agency, and of the substantial personal gains that may be made through housing. They also speak to the challenges that may remain despite gaining housing, such as concerns of the quality of the housing, conflicted feelings about treatment and support, and the challenges of forging a new identity. They provide unique details and resonance that may be lacking in quantitative research.

It is important to remember, though, that these narratives were constructed in the context of research. These particular narratives may be quite different from the narratives that people may choose or be able to tell in other settings, for other purposes, and with other listeners. People are invited to participate in these studies because they are labeled as someone with a mental illness. The invitation to participate based on this label invites narratives focused on wellness, or unwellness, or struggling to get better (Murray, 2002). It is possible that if people were invited to participate as tenants, as citizens, or as concerned community members, that their mental illness label, and struggles to get better may be absent or peripheral to their stories. Also missing from these examples are collective narratives. The narratives are taken from and essentially about individuals. Equally informative may be collective attempts to construct a narrative about people who have experienced shared challenges but who also can imagine a positive shared future. This will be a consideration in some of the methods we explore in a following section.

Visual Methods

One way to increase participation and to expand the roles that participants play in research is through how they can express or represent their experiences. Typically in quantitative research participants are limited to expressing themselves in terms of fixed responses to items on scales in surveys or structured interviews. Qualitative interviews provide a more flexible and open opportunity for participants to express themselves. Qualitative research approaches, however, can also be limited by imbalances in power, the nature or quality of the data that are generated, and the understanding that the researcher may gain about the experiences of the participant. First, they feature a data collection approach that involves one person in a position of greater power who interrogates another who is required to provide answers and to account for themselves. A second issue is that the research approach may appeal to those participants who have better language skills and who are more comfortable expressing themselves verbally. Researchers may favor talk that is more complex or reflective over statements from participants that are more direct or descriptive. A third issue concerns the ability of the researcher to ensure that she fully understands what the participant is referencing in her interview. Qualitative interviews that rely only on a single face-to-face encounter may not enable the interviewer to more fully understand the housing situation or the neighborhood that the participant is describing.

An alternative involves the use of images. Recent years have seen an explosion in the use of images in research, though it has a long history in other fields such as anthropology (Blinn & Harrist, 1991). There are many potential uses of images in research, though a useful distinction can be made between images that are produced or supplied by the researcher and images that are produced by the participants themselves (Clark-Ibáñez, 2004). Photo-elicitation is a technique in which photographs are used as stimuli in the context of a semistructured interview (Banks, 2007). The photographs can be chosen by the researcher, or created and selected by study participants themselves (Banks, 2007). The use of photographs or other stimuli can have a number of benefits, including facilitating a less interrogative interview style. The use of photographs in interviews can help to shift the focus of the interview from the participant to the photographs, creating a less demanding and intimidating experience for participants (Klitzing, 2004). Radley, Hodgetts, and Cullen (2005) concluded that the use of photographs in interviews foster a greater sense of agency in participants and more open interaction with the interviewer.

In other approaches, participants themselves can generate images on topics or issues that are most important to them. One increasingly popular example of the use of images produced by participants is photovoice. Photovoice combines the use of photography with a PAR approach (Wang & Burris, 1994). The major elements of a photovoice project involve participants working with facilitators to determine the goal of the project, participants receiving some training on how to take photos, a period of time during which participants take photos on the agreed theme of the project, developing captions for photos that participants wish to display, and a public showing of the photos to community members and decision-makers. Photovoice projects can also involve individual interviews or group discussions of the meaning of photos or the issues that they depict. Photovoice has been credited with a range of outcomes such as increased self-esteem and sense of empowerment (Strack, Magill, & McDonagh, 2004) and the generation of rich data (Hodgetts, Chamberlain, & Radley, 2007; Wang, Cash, & Powers, 2000).

The most notable challenge that photovoice presents to traditional research approaches is that it places a key data generating tool under the control of the participants themselves (Bolton, Pole, & Mizen, 2001; Didkowsky, Ungar, & Liebenberg, 2010). Though the themes or goals of the project may be set collaboratively with the researcher, the participants choose what to photograph, what the photograph should show, and participate in determining what the photograph means. This represents a potential for a substantial increase in power relative to other approaches. The photography, or data collection, occurs in settings themselves that are important to participants and therefore give the viewers of the photographs visual access to the people, places, and things that most concern the participants. The photos ground the study and the viewers in the contexts that are most significant to the participants. Finally, the dissemination of findings is an integral part of the project. The public display of photos presents opportunities for participants to directly share their views with other community members as well as policy makers.

Schneider (2010) reported on a housing-focused photovoice study on the subject of "What Home Means to Me." The process of taking and discussing the photos led to the identification of various themes related to the elements of housing that were associated with a sense of home, including sanctuary, privacy, safety and security, spirituality, community, and thankfulness. In this project, a poster was produced that included over 200 photos and quotes from participants. The poster was shown at a number of conferences and community events, and distributed within Calgary, Alberta, to various housing and mental health agencies.

Despite its strengths, there are also a number of limitations to photovoice. One of the assumptions of photovoice is that photography is a familiar activity that provides an alternative means for self-expression for people who may not be as comfortable with verbal expression. Harrison (2002) has noted that photography is informed by everyday norms and conventions. Taking photographs for a photovoice project, however, is not a familiar context for taking photos. Klitzing (2004) has noted that photography may be challenging for some participants wishing to represent abstract concepts. In dissertation research conducted by one of the authors of this chapter, we observed that the possibility of participating in a photovoice project on the topic of single-site supportive housing could be intimidating for prospective participants (Bendell & Sylvestre, 2016). When hearing of the project, some fretted about their ability to take good pictures, particularly when they learned that the project was affiliated with a university and that there would be a public display of the photos.

Bendell and Sylvestre (2016) also found that once participants began to participate some continued to experience anxiety. Over the course of this photovoice project, Bendell interviewed participants about their experiences with the project as well as how they went about taking photos. She found that participants had diverse strategies for taking pictures that were associated with the extent to which they experienced anxiety. Some participants were characterized as planful and deliberate in their approaches, with clear ideas about what they wanted to photograph and what they wanted the photos to depict and say. These participants were the most confident with their participation in the project. Other participants adopted a more spontaneous approach, taking pictures of people, places, or things they happened upon that they thought were interesting or relevant to the project. A third group of participants adopted a more literal, task-focused approach, photographing what they believed to fit with the goals of the project and the facilitator's expectations. These last two groups appeared to have the least sense of ownership of the project, were sometimes confused about the goals of the project, and had the most concerns about their ability to take pictures and how these pictures would be evaluated by others (Bendell & Sylvestre, 2016).

Notably, similar to those themes identified by Schneider (2010), this project also included a number of themes about communication and relationships beyond the places where participants lived. Many participants pointed to their aims through the project to speak to and to counteract the stigma they believed was associated with people who lived in single-site supportive housing (Bendell & Sylvestre, 2016). Photovoice is a unique opportunity for participants to individually and collectively represent their experiences and communicate them to diverse audiences. The approach has the value of placing increased power and control in their hands and a means of reaching audiences with their images and their messages. The approach ensures that the findings from the project are grounded in the interests and experiences of the participants. At the same time, the approach may also be demanding on participants who may be uncomfortable with photography or having their photos viewed by others.

Walking Tours, Mapping, and Geographic Information Systems

The final approaches that we discuss involve ways not only of representing individual experiences but also of representing the communities in which they live, and their relationships and participation in these communities. The limitation of the previously discussed approaches is that the research produces little understanding of where people live and what are the resources and limitations of these communities. One option for researchers is to accompany participants to visit their neighborhoods to generate both quantitative and qualitative data on neighborhoods (Carpiano, 2009; Fink, 2011; Emmel & Clark, 2009) Evans & Jones, 2011; Kloos & Shah, 2009). Variously known as "go-alongs," "walking tours," "walk alongs," "walking interviews," or "guided tours," these methods can produce quantitative data from the routes taken by the participant and qualitative data by discussing with the participants their relationships to their neighborhoods (Jones & Evans, 2011).

Carpiano (2009) described a "go-along" qualitative interview method for understanding how people relate to the places in which they conduct their daily activities. In this method, researchers accompany participants (on foot or while driving) and conduct in-depth interviews about the participants' experiences, activities, and interpretations of their neighborhoods, while also making their own observations (Carpiano, 2009). Walking tours help to reduce power imbalances by having the participant act as a tour guide who leads the researcher through significant places in a community (Carpiano, 2009). Participants act as experts in their communities and can lead researchers not only to identify the negative aspects of communities but also to learn about their strengths.

In ongoing dissertation research, one author of this chapter (Bassi) has used a walking tour method to learn how women participating in a Housing First program have experienced their communities. In addition to qualitative interviews conducted during the walking tour, the participants and researcher created neighborhood maps and photographed significant locations in the neighborhood. These maps and photographs were then used as stimuli for in-depth interviews conducted one week after the tour. During the walking tours, participants provided insight into their neighborhoods that would have been inaccessible through other data collection tools, as well as creating unique and dynamic relationships between the interviewer and the participants. For example, participants have been able to show their strength and act as protectors of the interviewer by alerting the interviewer to risky or dangerous places that the participant is able to navigate but that the interview should steer clear of.

Along with a number of strengths, the walk-along method also has a number of challenges. One of these, suggested in the foregoing example is safety, particularly when the tours are conducted in locales with higher levels of criminal or drug-related activity (Carpiano, 2009). In particular, interviewers may be perceived as outsiders or associated with authorities such as the police (Carpiano, 2009). Since walking tours occur outside, weather and time of day can affect data collection, either by limiting how long the tour lasts or where it goes, or by influencing activity levels of others in the community (Carpiano, 2009). The effects of weather may be substantial in those geographical regions that can experience great seasonal variability in weather conditions. The walking tour method can present technical challenges as well. Movement and street noise can make recordings difficult to hear and a failure to take note of locations or state what is being observed may make it difficult to know what is being referred to on a recording (Carpiano, 2009).

One of the strategies that Carpiano (2009) suggests to address this latter challenge is to create or annotate maps as the tour moves through a neighborhood. Moreover, the maps themselves may serve as a unique source of data. Participatory mapping refers to the process of having participants create their own maps of the places where they live and participate (Cornwall & Jewkes, 1995; Townley, Kloos, & Wright, 2009). The process involves participants drawing a map of where they live or participate by identifying the boundaries of their communities and the important locations or resources in their communities (Townley et al., 2009). Maps may reveal features of environments that are most important to people in contrast to an objective documentation of what is present (Townley et al., 2009). Thus, participating in mapping puts local people in positions of expertise on their community (Cornwall & Jewkes, 1995). The resulting maps can be analyzed on their own or can be used as stimuli for subsequent interviews or to generate directions for future research (Knigge & Cope, 2006).

A different mapping approach relies on geographic information systems (GIS), which "is a set of database, mapping, and statistical tools that allow visual and quantitative assessment of geographic information" (Luke, 2005, p. 191). Although primarily thought of as a quantitative research tool, there is also a diversity of qualitative application of GIS (Kwan & Knigge, 2006). Also, GIS has many potential applications for understanding the experiences of people with mental illness living in community housing.

Tsai, Mares, and Rosenheck (2010) used GIS to study the movement and community characteristics of 394 people participating in a national housing initiative in the United States. The goal of the study was to learn whether the characteristics of the neighborhoods of chronically homeless adults change as they become housed, and if so, what these changes are. This study found hat there was not a notable change in the neighborhood characteristics of participants after moving into housing. These characteristics included the education, income, rent, quality of life, and crime levels of the communities. Most of the communities into which the participants moved continued to be characterized by lower levels of education and income, and higher levels of crime, than the state averages.

Townley et al. (2009) described a unique study of community integration of people with serious mental illness that relied on both participatory mapping and GIS to define *activity spaces* of participants. Activity spaces were the areas within which people moved as they complete their daily activities. In this study, 40 participants (21 living in single-site supportive housing and 19 living in scattered-site supportive housing) met with researchers on three occasions. At a first meeting, participants were interviewed about their housing and their experiences in their communities and were asked to draw maps of their communities. In the mapping exercise, participants identified locations where they (1) spent time, (2) felt a sense of belonging, and (3) that were important to them. At a second meeting, participants led researchers on a walking tour of their neighborhood and described important places in their neighborhoods. At a third meeting, participants completed a quantitative survey of their perceptions of their neighborhood, life satisfaction, and their recovery from mental illness. Information from the participatory mapping and walking tour exercises were used to calculate activity spaces for the participants, using GIS.

The study found no differences in the size of the activity spaces of participants who lived in single-site and scattered-site housing. Whereas participants who had larger activity spaces reported greater life satisfaction, those who had smaller activity spaces reported a greater sense of community for their neighborhood. An analysis of qualitative data revealed that although participants may participate in a variety of settings (e.g., social/leisure, volunteer, activities of daily living), home remained their most important activity location and the place where they spent most of their time.

Similar to other methods discussed in this chapter, walking tours and participatory mapping provide alternative tools for learning about the contexts in which people live. They provide for a greater measure of agency on the part of the participants and, like the findings of other studies that have been reviewed, suggest that there are lingering challenges for community participation that face people who have moved from homelessness to housing. There is great promise in these methods that has not yet been realized. For example, as Townley et al. (2009) suggest, the methods can be used to gain a greater understanding of not only where people go in their communities but also the nature of their experiences and interactions in these settings and the meaning of these experiences and interactions to the individuals.

Uses of These Methods

The discussion of these methods has focused on use in research. They also have the potential for applied application in program evaluations. For example, photovoice has been used in public health research and evaluation. The use of photography enables an assessment of public health concerns and programs where participants can focus attention on issues or program elements that researchers or evaluators may not be aware of, or not aware of their significance. In evaluation photography may be focused on capturing how program components are implemented, program experiences, areas of satisfaction and dissatisfaction, and representations of program outcomes. Walking tours may also have applications for program evaluation. Walking tours may be adapted to provide guided tours of housing environments, where participants can show positive and negative aspects of their housing, in addition to tours of surrounding environments to investigate program outcomes in areas such as community integration.

In terms of uses of these approaches, it is also important to note their value in mixed-methods research. Although qualitative and quantitative methods are associated with different epistemological traditions, they are increasingly used in complementary ways. Rather than being seen as incommensurable, increasingly more pragmatic perspectives emphasize the value of linking these methods in the service of better understanding social phenomena, participant experiences, or the implementation and outcomes of social interventions. According to Greene (2007), "most fundamentally, to mix methods in social inquiry is to set a large table, to invite diverse ways of thinking and valuing to have a seat at the table, and to dialogue across such differences respectfully and generatively toward deeper and enhanced understanding" (p. 14). The At Home/Chez Soi study (mentioned earlier in this chapter) is one example of research that has extensively used quantitative and qualitative methods to examine participant outcomes.

Our view is that the methods presented in this chapter can both challenge and complement the methods that are more commonly used in housing research. In many ways these methods challenge the inherent power of the researcher associated with the use of quantitative measures. This disruption of power allows for different perspectives and, consequently, a more complex view of community housing to emerge. As some of the studies cited above have shown, a sharing of power in research can shed light on concerns that are not typically found in housing research. At the same time, these methods can provide a deeper and richer understanding of the experiences of people living in community housing. They provide detail, context, and associations that may be missed in quantitative research that emphasizes relationships among a limited number of variables.

Conclusion

At the outset of this chapter, a number of criteria were proposed to assess these methodological options for housing research. They included providing more agency, control, and voice for participants in research and providing a better understanding of the social ecologies and contexts in which people participate. The various methods that are described certainly provide for a variety of ways of enhancing the roles that participants may play in research. In addition, they suggest the ability to more fully understand how people participate in their neighborhoods. Taken together, the findings from the selected studies reviewed here provide a more complex and nuanced view of the lives of people living in community housing than has commonly been provided by more quantitatively oriented housing research. The picture that emerges is that although becoming housed is an important turning point in people's lives, there are still significant gains to be made. People may still be living in more dangerous communities, be primarily attached to their homes, be somewhat dissatisfied with their housing, and be conflicted about the support they receive. The research points to new areas for support, resources, and action to ensure that people can live fulfilling lives in the community.

Other criteria introduced in this chapter related to Prilleltensky's (2003, 2008) concept of the psychopolitical, and Sen's (1999, 2000) concept of capabilities. Here, the picture is less complete. These methods each hold the promise for exploring issues of power. Participatory action research, and photovoice in particular, appear best poised to examine issues of power at more distal ecological levels that affect the health and well-being of people living in community housing. The other methods (e.g., narrative, walking tours) are better suited for examining how power is expressed in everyday interactions, in everyday settings, that limit or promote the agency of individuals and groups. Similarly, these methods appear to be best suited for understanding capabilities and functionings in terms of everyday settings and interactions, rather than broader forces that shape these capabilities. Though they hold this promise, this promise is yet to be realized.

Fulfilling this promise requires research to be driven by new questions and priorities. These questions and priorities must be focused on the experiences and concerns of those who live in community housing. To accomplish this, as researchers we must be willing to adopt a more collaborative stance to ensure that our primary concerns are aligned with those lives we wish to help to improve.

Note

1. This example is borrowed and adapted from John Trainor.

References

Angen, M.J. (2000). Evaluating interpretive inquiry: Reviewing the validity debate and opening the dialogue. *Qualitative Health Research, 10*, 378–395.

Banks, M. (2007). *Using visual data in qualitative research.* Thousand Oaks, CA: Sage.

Bendell, K., & Sylvestre, J. (2016). How different approaches to taking pictures influences participation in a photovoice project. *Action Research.* Advance online publication. doi: 10.1177/1476750316653812

Blinn, L., & Harrist, A. W. (1991). Combining native instant photography and photo-elicitation. *Visual Anthropology, 4*, 175–192.

Bolton, A., Pole, C., & Mizen, P. (2001). Picture this: Researching child workers. *Sociology, 35*, 501–518.

Carpiano, R.M. (2009). Come take a walk with me: The "Go-Along" interview as a novel method for studying the implications of place for health and well-being. *Health and Place, 15*, 263–272.

Cho, J., & Trent, A. (2006). Validity in qualitative research revisited. *Qualitative Research, 6*, 319–340.

Clark-Ibáñez, M. (2004). Framing the social world with photo-elicitation interviews. *American Behavioral Scientist, 47*, 1507–1527.

Cornwall, A., & Jewkes, R. (1995). What is participatory research? *Social Sciences and Medicine, 41*, 1167–1676.

Curry, L.A., Nembhard, I.M., & Bradley, E.H. (2009). Qualitative and mixed methods provide unique contributions to outcomes research. *Circulation, 119*, 1442–1452.

Didkowsky, N., Ungar, M., & Liebenberg, L. (2010). Using visual methods to capture embedded processes of resilience for youth across cultures and contexts. *Journal of the Canadian Academy of Child and Adolescent Psychiatry, 19*, 12–18.

Emmel, N., & Clark, A. (2009). *The methods used in connected lives: Investigating networks, neighbourhoods, and communities.* Southhampton, UK: National Centre for Research Methods.

Evans, J., & Jones, P. (2011). The walking interview: Methodology, mobility and place. *Applied Geography, 31*, 849–858.

Fink, J. (2011). Walking the neighbourhood, seeing the small details of community life: Reflections from a photography walking tour. *Critical Social Policy, 32*, 31–50.

Goering, P.N., Streiner, D.L., Adair, C., Aubry, T., Barker, J., Distasio, J., . . . Zabkiewicz, D.M. (2011). The At Home/Chez Soi trial protocol: A pragmatic, multi-site, randomised controlled trial of a Housing First intervention for homeless individuals with mental illness in five Canadian cities. *BMJ Open, 1*, e000323. doi:10.1136/bmjopen-2011-000323

Goering, P., Veldhuizen, S., Watson, A., Adair, C., Kopp, B., Latimer, E., . . . Aubry, T. (2014). *National At Home/Chez Soi final report*. Calgary, AB: Mental Health Commission of Canada. Retrieved from: http://www.mentalhealthcommission.ca

Greene, J.C. (2007). *Mixed methods in social inquiry*. San Francisco, CA: Wiley.

Hall, G.B., Nelson, G., & Smith Fowler, H. (1987). Housing for the chronically mentally disabled: Part I. Conceptual framework and social context. *Canadian Journal of Community Mental Health, 6*, 65–78.

Harrison, B. (2002). Photographic visions and narrative inquiry. *Narrative Inquiry, 12*, 87–111.

Hodgetts, D., Chamberlain, K., & Radley, A. (2007). Considering photographs never taken during photo-production projects. *Qualitative Research in Psychology, 4*, 263–280.

Hopper, K. (2007). Rethinking social recovery in schizophrenia: What a capabilities approach might offer. *Social Sciences and Medicine, 65*, 868–879.

Janzen, R., Nelson, G., Trainor, J. & Ochocka, J. (2006). A longitudinal study of mental health consumer/survivor initiatives: Part IV. Benefits beyond the self? A quantitative and qualitative study of system-level activities and impacts. *Journal of Community Psychology, 34*, 285–303.

Klitzing, S.W. (2004). Women living in a homeless shelter: Stress, coping and leisure. *Journal of Leisure Research, 36*, 483–512.

Kloos, B., Scrimenti, K., Masson, N., Zimmerman, S.O., Davis, B.A., & Snow, D.L. (2012). Developing a tenant organization as a resource for supported housing. In C. Walker, K. Johnson, & L. Cunningham (Eds.), *Community psychology and the economics of mental health: Global perspectives* (pp. 206–221). London: Palgrave Macmillan.

Kloos, B., & Shah, S. (2009). A social ecological approach to investigating relationships between housing and adaptive functioning for persons with serious mental illness. *American Journal of Community Psychology, 44*, 316–326.

Knigge, L., & Cope, M. (2006). Grounded visualization: Integrating the analysis of qualitative and quantitative data through grounded theory and visualization. *Environment and Planning A, 38*, 2021–2037.

Kuklys, W. (2005). *Amartya Sen's capabilities approach: Theoretical insights and empirical applications*. Berlin: Springer.

Kwan, M.-P., & Knigge, L. (2006). Doing qualitative research using GIS: An oxymoronic endeavor? *Environment and Planning A, 38*, 1999–2002.

Lincoln, Y.S., & Guba, E.G. (1985). *Naturalistic inquiry*. Newbury Park, CA: Sage.

Luke, D.A. (2005). Getting the big picture in community science: Methods that capture context. *American Journal of Community Psychology, 35*, 185–200.

Murray, M. (2000). Levels of narrative analysis in health psychology. *Journal of Health Psychology, 5*, 337–347.

Murray, M. (2002). Connecting narrative and social representation theory in health research. *Social Science Information, 41*, 653–673.

Murray, M. (2012). Art, social action and social change. In C. Walker, K. Johnson, & L. Cunningham (Eds.), *Community psychology and the economics of mental health: Global perspectives* (pp. 253–265). London: Palgrave Macmillan.

Nelson, G., Aubry, T., & Lafrance, A. (2007). A review of the literature on the effectiveness of housing and support, assertive community treatment, and intensive care management interventions for persons with mental illness who have been homeless. *American Journal of Orthopsychiatry, 77*, 350–361.

Nelson, G., Clarke, J., Febbraro, A., & Hatzipantelis, M. (2005). A narrative approach to the evaluation of supportive housing: Stories of homeless people who have experienced serious mental illness. *Psychiatric Rehabilitation Journal, 29*, 98–104.

Nelson, G., Janzen, R., Ochocka, J., & Trainor, J. (2010). Participatory action research and evaluation with mental health self-help initiative: A theoretical framework. In L. Brown & S. Wituk (Eds.), *Mental health self-help: Consumer and family initiatives* (pp. 39–58). New York: Springer.

Nelson, G., Macnaughton, E., Curwood, S. E., Egalité, N., Voronka, J., Fleury, M.-J., . . . Goering, P. (2015). Collaboration and involvement of persons with lived experience in planning Canada's At Home/Chez Soi project. *Health and Social Care in the Community, 24,* 184–193. doi: 10.1111/hsc.12197

Nelson, G., Ochocka, J., Griffin, K., & Lord, J. (1998). "Nothing about me without me": Participatory action research with self-help/mutual aid organizations for psychiatric consumer/survivors. *American Journal of Community Psychology, 26,* 881–912.

Nelson, G., Ochocka, J., Janzen, R., & Trainor, J. (2006a). A longitudinal study of mental health consumer/survivor initiatives: Part I. Literature review and overview of the study. *Journal of Community Psychology, 34,* 247–260.

Nelson, G., Ochocka, J., Janzen, R., & Trainor, J. (2006b). A longitudinal study of mental health consumer/survivor initiatives: Part II. A quantitative study of impacts of participation on new members. *Journal of Community Psychology, 34,* 261–272.

Nelson, G., Ochocka, J., Janzen, R., Trainor, J., Goering, P., & Lomotey, J. (2007). A longitudinal study of mental health consumer/survivor initiatives: Part V—Outcomes at three-year follow-up. *Journal of Community Psychology, 35,* 655–665.

Nelson, G., Ochocka, J., Janzen, R., Trainor, J., & Lauzon, S. (2004). A comprehensive evaluation approach for mental health consumer-run organizations: Values, conceptualization, design, and action. *Canadian Journal of Program Evaluation, 19,* 29–53.

Nelson, G., Patterson, M., Kirst, M., Macnaughton, E., Isaak, C.A., Nolin, D., . . . Goering, P.N. (2015, February 16). Life changes among homeless persons with mental illness: A longitudinal study of housing first and usual treatment. *Psychiatric Services in Advance. 66,* 592–597. http://dx.doi.org/10.1176/appi.ps.201400201

Ochocka, J., Nelson, G., Janzen, R., & Trainor, J. (2006). A longitudinal study of mental health consumer/survivor initiatives: Part III. A qualitative study of impacts of participation on new members. *Journal of Community Psychology, 34,* 273–283.

Patterson, M.L., Rezansoff, S., Currie, L., & Somers, J.M. (2014). Trajectories of recovery among homeless adults with mental illness who participated in a randomised controlled trial of Housing First: A longitudinal, narrative analysis. *BMJ Open, 3,* e003442. doi:10.1136/bmjopen-2013-003442

Prilleltensky, I. (2003). Understanding, resisting, and overcoming oppression: Toward psychopolitical validity. *American Journal of Community Psychology, 31,* 195–201.

Prilleltensky, I. (2008). The role of power in wellness, oppression, and liberation: The promise of psychopolitical validity. *Journal of Community Psychology, 36,* 116–136.

Radley, A., Hodgetts, D., & Cullen, A. (2005). Visualizing homelessness: A study in photography and estrangement. *Journal of Community and Applied Social Psychology, 15,* 273–295.

Rog, D.J. (2004). The evidence on supported housing. *Psychiatric Rehabilitation Journal, 27,* 334–344.

Rog, D.J., Marshall, T., Dougherty, R.H., George, P., Daniels, A.S., Ghose, S.S., & Delphin-Rittmon, M.E. (2014). Permanent supportive housing: Assessing the evidence. *Psychiatric Services, 65,* 287–294.

Rogers, E.S., Farkas, M., Anthony, A., Kash, M., Harding, C., & Olschewski, A. (2008). *Systematic review of supported housing literature, 1993–2008.* Boston: Center for Psychiatric Rehabilitation.

Schneider, B. (2010). *Hearing (our) voices: Participatory research in mental health.* Toronto, ON: University of Toronto Press.

Sen, A. (1999). *Development as freedom.* New York: Oxford University Press.

Sen, A. (2000). *Social exclusion: Concept, application and scrutiny.* Manila, PH: Asian Development Bank.

Stone, A.A., Greenberg, M.A., Kennedy-Moore, E., & Newman, M.G. (1991). Self-report, situation-specific coping questionnaires: What are they measuring? *Journal of Personality and Social Psychology, 61,* 648–658.

Strack, R.W., Magill, C., & McDonagh, K. (2004). Engaging youth through photovoice. *Health Promotion Practice, 5*, 49–58.

Sundar, P., & Todd, S. (2008). Opening the space between innocent and oppressive ways of knowing: Challenges and opportunities in doing research with diverse communities. *Currents: New Scholarship in the Human Services, 7*, 1–19.

Sylvestre, J., Cousins, J.B., Sundar, P., Aubry, T., & Hinsperger, V. (2008). Engaging stakeholders in the planning of a collaborative multi-agency evaluation: The HousingPlus Collaborative Communities Project. *Studies in Educational Evaluation, 34*, 212–217.

Sylvestre, J., Nelson, G., Durbin, J., George, L., Aubry, T., & Ollenberg, M. (2006). Housing for people with serious mental illness: Challenges for system level development. *Community Development: Journal of the Community Development Society, 37*, 35–45.

Sylvestre, J., Nelson, G., Sabloff, A., & Peddle, S. (2007). Housing for people with serious mental illness: A comparison of values and research. *American Journal of Community Psychology, 40*, 125–137.

Sylvestre, J., Ollenberg, M., & Trainor, J. (2007). A participatory process benchmarking strategy for describing and improving supportive housing. *Psychiatric Rehabilitation Journal, 31*, 115–124.

Sylvestre, J., Ollenberg, M., & Trainor, J. (2009). A model of housing stability for people with serious mental illness. *Canadian Journal of Community Mental Health, 28*, 195–207.

Townley, G., Kloos, B., & Wright, P.A. (2009). Understanding the experience of place: Expanding methods to conceptualize and measure community integration of persons with serious mental illness. *Health and Place, 15*, 520–531.

Tsai, J., Mares, A.S., & Rosenheck, R.A. (2010). A geographic analysis of chronically homeless adults before and after enrollment in a multi-site supported housing initiative: Community characteristics and migration. *American Journal of Community Psychology, 48*, 341–351.

Wang, C., & Burris, M.A. (1994). Empowerment through photo novella: Portraits of participation. *Health Education Quarterly, 21*, 171–186.

Wang, C.C., Cash, J.L., & Powers, L.S. (2000). Who knows the streets as well as the homeless? Promoting personal and community action through photovoice. *Health Promotion Practice, 1*, 81–89.

Whittemore, R., Chase, S.K., & Mandle, C.L. (2001). Validity in qualitative research. *Qualitative Health Research, 11*, 522–537.

SECTION III

INTERNATIONAL PERSPECTIVES ON HOUSING POLICY FOR PEOPLE WITH SERIOUS MENTAL ILLNESS

9

The Primacy of Research

Getting to Housing First in the United States—
A Policymaker's Perspective

PHILIP MANGANO

For more than a quarter century, good intentions masked a misapprehension of what homeless people actually wanted for themselves. Uninformed by research evidence and lacking a customer-centric approach, vested interests maintained a status quo that was blind to ending the moral, spiritual, and economic wrong that is homelessness. The common sense approach of what worked and what did not was left out of the equation. If the intent was détente with the long misery of homelessness, well-meaning programs would suffice to hide partially the problem. The anointing of these programs as "God's work" and their practitioners as "saints" every holiday season assured that this status quo of inputs and occasional "miracles" was institutionalized as the "best we can do" in communities throughout America.

In the approach we fashioned during my years as executive director of the Massachusetts Housing and Shelter Alliance (MHSA), we adopted the mindset that our moral forebears had taken regarding another social wrong. Abolitionists led by William Lloyd Garrison and Frederick Douglass, abetted by the success of William Wilberforce in England, complemented their moral agitation with strategic approaches and political opportunism. Their intent was clear and unambiguous—end the moral disgrace and wrong of slavery.

When I was appointed by the president to lead the then dormant United States Interagency Council on Homelessness, we took that abolitionist approach to Washington and the country. But unlike previous moral and ideological approaches, the underlying foundational principles of this reframing of homelessness policy would be clear:

1. Data- and research-driven strategies
2. Performance in reducing and ending homelessness
3. Prioritization of what worked

4. Rapid dissemination of innovation
5. Business principles and practices serving the poorest

The outcome of this reframing was the first documented reduction in street and chronic homelessness in the lifetime of the issue. Between 2005 and 2009, homelessness decreased across the country and most especially for those who were seemingly the most intractably caught in the misery. The data indicate that in that period nearly 40% of street and chronic homeless people who were living on streets and sidewalks and languishing in shelters moved into housing (US Department of Housing and Urban Development, 2008, 2010).

In this chapter I look at that reframing of policy, resources, and expectations in achieving our abolitionist intent. Principles and assumptions that guided the work are as central as are the factors that had inhibited such results in the past. I begin with the rethinking of policy made possible by the research of Dr. Dennis Culhane and the innovation of Dr. Sam Tsemberis. Dr. Culhane's research taught us that the old approach that homogenized homelessness left us funding an uninformed singular approach to the issue that was absent strategic focuses for each subpopulation. His research demonstrated that 80% of all homeless people came in and left homelessness needing little intervention. He allowed us to understand the necessity of focusing on the remaining 20% whose disabilities and vulnerabilities required governmental intervention, without which they would continue to populate our streets and shelters with little hope of ending their homelessness (Kuhn & Culhane, 1998). Dr. Tsemberis's (2010) Housing First intervention, supported by longitudinal data, offered us the remedy for that 20% (Tsemberis, 1999; Tsemberis & Eisenberg, 2000; Tsemberis et al., 2004). Controversial in its challenges to a well-intentioned status quo, Housing First made it possible to apply the verbs "end" and "abolish" to chronic homelessness. That combination led to jurisdictionally owned plans across the United States and Canada. I then describe the implementation of this research and innovation during my more than 7 years leading the federal US Interagency Council on Homelessness and the resulting local and national strategies that evolved to "disturb the stationary" status quo, as Joseph Schumpeter (2011) would say. And, more importantly, to offer a strategic vision that was shaped by new approaches that traded inputs for outcomes, process for performance, and a social service frame for a business and economic lens.

Understanding the Customer

One of the most significant barriers to progress in housing for people with serious mental illness was that government policy makers and funders, as well as philanthropic organizations, mistook the providers of homeless services as the key stakeholders of programs. As Clay Christensen described in his best-selling management book, *The Innovator's Dilemma* (1997), businesses mistake their sales force for their customers when they ask their salespeople what new products should be created. Businesses that make this mistake risk losing market share and going out of business. Conversely when businesses recognize that their customers must identify the next products to be created, not surprisingly when those products are created and marketed, they find ready consumers.

For decades, the providers of services for people who are homeless were thus misidentified by the government. This was especially evident in the US Department of Housing and Urban Development's Continuum of Care, a non-evidence-based service and funding model to coordinate a local process to meet the needs of people who are homeless and in which people were expected to move from higher to lower support housing settings as their ability to function independently improved. Just as Christensen discovered with sales forces, more focused on their own interests rather than that of their customers, providers were more focused on their own capacities and standards, rather than what their consumers preferred.

That provider-centric approach was exemplified in "soft services" that they could offer such as meals, shelter beds, and so-called case management, which covered a multitude of "services." There was no consideration of quantifiable outcomes or results, and the unfortunate thing was that most homeless agencies fell into this cat-egory. Unlike the private businesses studied by Christensen, however, the consum-ers of these services could not take their business elsewhere. They were required to consume these services or receive nothing.

The rise of these services was linked to the policy failure of deinstitutionalization that led to the first wave of visible homelessness in the late 1970s and early 1980s. Deinstitutionalization promised the three legs of the stool—accommodation in the community, new psychotropic medications that relieved symptoms, and commu-nity. When only the first two were made readily available (a place to live and the new meds), the stool fell over. Without supports, especially in taking meds that had a host of side effects, people decompensated in place, lost their tenancies, and for lack of the institutions that had been closed under deinstitutionalization, fell all the way to the streets.

I witnessed much of this in my time as a first responder in Los Angeles and Boston. My colleagues and I saw that many people on the streets had recently been in housing but had not been successful in sustaining it. From our nonclinical per-spective, the conclusion was that these folk could not sustain housing. After all, they had just been in and now they were out. We were unaware of the broader policy failures. The notion of housing as the remedy for their homelessness seemed naïve to most. Instead we committed ourselves to everything but housing: food, clothing, a place to sleep, amicable relationships, spare change, benefits. We were servicing our homeless friends endlessly, but never ending their homelessness.

Now, of course, some "graduated" to a single room occupancy (SRO) or a room at the "Y." Chance would tell us that, even in those heavily serviced environments, some would make their way out. But the programs claimed credit and raised new funds to do business as usual. The individual miracles were fundraising gifts; that part of the population became the poster-people of the ads to raise more money to do what was being done. Meanwhile, the miracles never became commonplace. For many, permanent housing of their own was unattainable.

The numbers being served in shelters grew, and the numbers coming in far exceeded those leaving. The programs dutifully reported that the problem was worse and that they needed more money to service those coming in the front door while there was little movement out the back door. When these service-based programs reported to government and philanthropy, government and philanthropy accommodated with more funding, leading to the institutionalization of a response that ensured that the numbers would daily grow and the problem only worsen. They, of course, never read Clay Christensen (1997) or Jim Collins (2001), or for that matter Malcolm Gladwell (2006). Or, if they did, they had no idea of the relevancy of business insight and change to the issue of homelessness.

The media also became an accomplice, turning to the service providers who were invested in the system, rather than looking to new or dissident voices when questions were raised about how dollars were being spent and resources were being used. What was painful was that the intent of reducing and ending homelessness was not even seriously considered. Sure, there were governmental rhetorical flourishes, advocacy agencies put it in their titles, but neither had a clue on how to get there. If government challenged any of the complex, cub reporters immediately set off to interview the nearest "radical" Birkenstock-wearing, flannel-shirted director who would provide the pithy quote, the self-righteous rebuff of any government interference.

One reason is that they lacked the insight that would come later from business writers like Clay Christensen or Jim Collins. Nor had they heard the lessons that would come later from Malcolm Gladwell's (2006) story of "Million Dollar Murray". Later also came the move toward evidence-based policymaking and evidence-based practice (Pawson, 2006; SAMSHA NREPP, 2015). At the time in the 1980s to 1990s, wandering in the wilderness, government policy makers and service providers contented themselves with collecting data that only represented outputs—how many meals served, how many shelter beds filled—and not on the important outcomes. Though there was rhetoric of ending homelessness, absent was the systematic collection of data that would point to which efforts, if any, were making progress toward this goal. Instead, attention was riveted on emergencies at the front door, not solutions at the back end.

There were, at the time, some dissenting voices, though they were not much heard or heeded. In a *New York Times* op-ed piece University of Pennsylvania researcher Dr. Dennis Culhane (1993) bravely predicted that the federal continuum of care would only increase the numbers of programs and numbers of homeless people.

Willie Brown, mayor of San Francisco from 1996 to 2004, had the audacity to propose that information on the number of homeless people in San Francisco be collected so that the magnitude of the problem could be quantified. Up until that suggestion, the conjectures of so-called advocates for the homeless were the only measure. And there is a long track record of advocate estimates, beginning with the activist Mitch Snyder's off-the-cuff guess of 3 million before a congressional sub-committee, being wildly inflated.

Judging by the response you would think that Mayor Brown, elected by the people to remedy problems, had suggested reopening Alcatraz and relocating every homeless person in the city to that island fortress. But, in fact, Brown had cam-paigned on the issue in a compassionate and caring way. Assessing the size of the problem was to be the first step in the larger response. However, the attacks were unrelenting by a small coterie of ideologues who wanted none of that reasonable approach. Their comments were well reported by the enabling press, and Brown eventually backed away from the idea and from the issue. As he would recount, a mayor has hundreds of issues pressing for attention and resources. If the advocates had only the status quo to preserve and were strategically myopic, there were other causes less stagnated. The several pages he devotes in his autobiography (Brown, 2008) to his term of office has some of its most pointed criticism for that group who betrayed his trust, the issue, and homeless people with their self-righteous and wrong-headed approach.

Fortunately, his successor as mayor of San Francisco, drawn from the business world and now lieutenant governor of California, Gavin Newsom fended off the ideologues and implemented an innovative business strategy that reduced seemingly intractable street homelessness in San Francisco by more than 50%. Similarly, John Hickenlooper, a businessman then mayor of Denver, now governor of Colorado, pursued a business strategy and saw a significant reduction in street and chronic homelessness, as did many other mayors across the United States.

Housing First: Listening to the Customer and to the Evidence

What could rescue the issue and the people? What could turn the page on decades of misdirection? What could take on a status quo that was not working for commu-nities, homeless people, or the taxpayer? Who could ride to the rescue?

In the late 1990s Dr. Dennis Culhane began publishing research on home-lessness that was filled with counterintuitive insights. Contrary to a prevail-ing notion that most homeless adults stayed a long time in homelessness, his research in the 1990s taught us that 80% were short-stay and exited with little, if any, assistance from government (Kuhn & Culhane, 1998). Contrary to the notion that the vast majority of homeless people were mentally ill, substance using, or both, Culhane's research demonstrated that a much smaller percentage had these disabilities, just 20%. Contrary to the notion that all homeless people needed clinical and substantial interventions in their lives to leave homelessness, this long-stay cohort with disabilities needed the interventions. To a sector that had long been enabled by controlling the numbers and resisting research, Culhane's work was nothing if not threatening. Suddenly, data were "disturbing the stationary" and challenging the basis of the approach that had been taken over several decades.

Enter a number of years later a new administration in Washington. The Bush administration, taking office in 2001, had a new perspective on federal responsibility and resources. Reflecting that perspective was the President's Management Agenda (PMA, Executive Office of the President/Office of Management and Budget, 2002). Although a long and measured document, the PMA could be distilled to a few regnant principles. First, government resources were no longer considered funding, but were instead evaluated as investments. As investments, government programs needed to correspond to the basic premise of any investment: a return on investment (or ROI) needed to be derived. Second, every investment needed to be research and data based and performance oriented. Third, and finally, all investment was to be results-driven. Opposites were to be rejected—conjecture, anecdote, process, and funding. They were old school. Every federal agency and department was to develop this approach.

While no one ever required this approach from the newly revitalized US Interagency Council on Homelessness, I adopted it knowing that we would not only reframe the issue in a business approach but also ensure that activities undertaken by the Council conformed to the highest authoritative principles of the new administration, the PMA. In the coming years that context would serve the work of the Council well, most often with career federal employees who were content with the old approaches or at odds with the new administration. I contended successfully that the Council's work was in line with the PMA and that was our direction, period. In the work I had done in Massachusetts, we had learned the hard way that data and research were new school, and anecdote and conjecture the past.

Our secretary of human services, and subsequently the Massachusetts governor's budget person (now governor), Charlie Baker, taught us that the old snowy day sob stories had no traction. Numbers were the new vehicle of advocacy; especially if those numbers resulted in other numbers that had a dollar sign affixed in the "savings" column of the budget. That wakeup call, combined with the first reliable research on homelessness delivered by Dennis Culhane, was the perfect preface to the PMA, years before such an approach would have seemed inappropriate. What do those parameters have to do with the suffering of homeless people? We came to understand that relief for that suffering, and those numbers and that approach, were inexorably connected. With that background in Massachusetts combined with the PMA, one thing was clear in moving forward to reduce and to end homelessness: the primacy of research. Culhane's research told us that 20% of the homeless population needed significant interventions to leave homelessness. The other 80% would leave on their own or with a shallow investment of resources (Culhane & Metraux, 2008). So rather than the old amorphous approach that had one set of resources and interventions for all, a marketing strategy had to be focused on the most vulnerable, most disabled, longest stayers, who we later discovered, again through formative research, were the most expensive, not only in homelessness, but to the community purse.

We were decidedly old fashioned. To approach any issue, especially a social problem, (1) begin with data and research, (2) set policy based on the research, (3) implement and invest in innovative interventions that are field tested and evidence based (researched), (4) aggregate results, (5) evaluate outcomes, (6) recalibrate policy and investment to maximize results, (7) reinvest knowing efficacy of various approaches and agencies, and (8) identify new innovations and upgrade old ones. All of that, every step, every investment, every recalibration, every evaluation, every stage is based on one thing—the primacy of research. In giving research the ascendant position and crafting strategies around its findings, we oversaw the first documented decrease in street and long-term homelessness in more than 50 years. From 2005 to 2009, we saw a 37% decrease in chronic homeless, with an overall net reduction of almost 65,000 people (US Department of Housing and Urban Development, 2008, 2010).

That decrease of almost 65,000 Americans leaving homelessness—nearly 4 in 10 individuals moved from the streets to housing—is the most important number, but there were other numbers that were driven and influenced by the research. As a result of locating the chronic homelessness initiative within the context of the PMA, and demonstrating unprecedented results, total federal investment in homelessness increased from slightly more than $2 billion in 2003 to more than $5 billion in the 2007 president's budget.

Another number that research influenced was in local planning. Eventually more than 1,000 mayors and county executives partnered in over 350 local 10-Year Plans to End Homelessness shaped around business principles and practices. Those business principles included quantifying the magnitude of the problem, identifying evidence-based innovative initiatives to implement, establishing benchmarks, and quantifying results. All were dependent on research. Cost studies and cost-benefit analyses have created sustained political will and leadership to drive the implementation of innovation resulting in outcomes of decreased homelessness (Culhane, Gross, Parker, Poppe, & Sykes, 2008). Without research and data, cost-benefit analysis is not possible. Without cost-benefit analysis, initiating and sustaining political and civic will is not possible. Without sustaining political and civic will, our poorest neighbors will continue to suffer the long misery of their homelessness.

Conclusion

Old school approaches that are not refined by research from beginning to end are a betrayal of our moral responsibility to our poorest neighbors. For 30 years I have campaigned to abolish homelessness: to change the verb, the vocabulary, and the equation. The primacy of research in that abolitionist quest has never been more apparent to me, or more impactful. When combined with the innovations we now have—Housing First being preeminent—and cost studies, that trifecta is a winning ticket—a ticket to housing and stability. Most importantly, it is a trajectory out of the long misery and human tragedy of homelessness for our poorest neighbors.

References

Brown, W.L. (2008). *Basic Brown: My life and our times.* New York: Simon & Schuster.

Collins, J. (2001). *Good to great: Why some companies make the leap . . . And others don't.* New York: Harper Collins.

Culhane, D.P. (1993, December 19). Shelters lead nowhere. *New York Times.*

Culhane, D.P. (2008). The costs of homelessness: A perspective from the United States. *European Journal of Homelessness, 2,* 97–114.

Culhane, D.P., Gross, K.S., Parker, W.D., Poppe, B., & Sykes, E. (2008). *Accountability, cost-effectiveness, and program performance: Progress since 1998.* National Symposium on Homelessness Research. Available from http://repository.upenn.edu/spp_papers/114

Executive Office of the President/Office of Management and Budget. (2002). *The President's management agenda.* Washington, DC: US Government Printing Office. https://www.whitehouse.gov/sites/default/files/omb/assets/omb/budget/fy2002/mgmt.pdf

Kuhn, R., & Culhane, D.P. (1998). Applying cluster analysis to test a typology of homelessness by pattern of shelter utilization: Results from the analysis of administrative data. *American Journal of Community Psychology, 26,* 207–232.

Malcolm Gladwell. (2006). *Million-Dollar Murray: Why problems like homelessness may be easier to solve than to manage* (p. 96). Department of Social Services: The New Yorker. Available at: http://www.newyorker.com/magazine/2006/02/13/million-dollar-murray

Pawson, R. (2006). *Evidence-based policy: A realist perspective.* Los Angeles: Sage.

SAMHSA's National Registry of Evidence-Based Programs and Practices. (2015). *Pathways' Housing First Program.* http://www.nrepp.samhsa.gov/ViewIntervention.aspx?id=

Schumpeter, J.A. (2011). The entrepreneur. In M. Becker, T. Knudsen, & R. Swedberg (Eds.), *The entrepreneur: Classic texts by J. Schumpeter* (pp. 227–260). Stanford, CA: Stanford University Press.

Tsemberis, S. (1999). From streets to homes: An innovative approach to supported housing for homeless adults with psychiatric disabilities. *Journal of Community Psychology, 27,* 225–241. doi: 10.1002/(SICI)1520-6629(199903)27:2<225::AID-JCOP9>3.0.CO;2-Y

Tsemberis, S. (2010). *Housing First: The Pathways model to end homelessness for people with mental illness and addictions.* Center City, MN: Hazelden.

Tsemberis, S., & Eisenberg, R.F. (2000). Pathways to housing: Supported housing for street-dwelling homeless individuals with psychiatric disabilities. *Psychiatric Services, 51,* 487–493. doi: 10.1176/appi.ps.51.4.487

Tsemberis, S., Gulcur, L., & Nakae, M. (2004). Housing First, consumer choice, and harm reduction for homeless individuals with a dual diagnosis. *American Journal of Public Health, 94,* 651–656. doi: 10.2105/AJPH.94.4.651

U.S. Department of Housing and Urban Development (2008). *The second annual homeless assessment report to Congress.* Washington: Author.

U.S. Department of Housing and Urban Development (2010). *The 2010 annual homeless assessment report to Congress.* Washington: Author.

Mental Health Housing Policy in Canada

JOHN TRAINOR, SUSAN ECKERLE CURWOOD, REENA SIROHI,

AND NICK KERMAN

Housing policy in Canada has, historically, been framed as economic policy rather than social policy (Harris, 1999). Of the three core objectives toward which Canadian housing policy has been directed—(1) housing development and revitalization, (2) facilitating home ownership, and (3) providing assistance to people whose housing needs cannot be met through the private market—the focus has largely been on the first two, to the detriment of the third (Pomeroy, 2004). There has in fact been relatively little policy in Canada that takes mental health housing as its particular focus.

Despite this, a number of forces have shaped where people with mental illness live. In this chapter we recognize this reality by using a very broad notion of the term "policy," defined as a course of action adopted and pursued by groups of social actors who may be organized as governments, professional bodies, consumer groups, private entrepreneurs, or community agencies. The policies and in particular the actual practices of these groups are critical, regardless of whether they are enshrined in formal documents, laws, or regulations. This approach emphasizes that policy is best defined by its actual impact on people with mental illness. Following this approach, we not only look at written policy documents but also trace the evolution of ideas about where people with serious mental illness should be located from a historical perspective, examining the broader political and cultural shifts that have situated people with mental illness in Canadian society. We have chosen the historical perspective to keep our focus as concrete as possible and to look at what happened in the actual lives of the people affected. As an example, formal policy documents in Ontario did not state as a goal that patients being deinstitutionalized in the 1960s and 1970s would be transferred to custodial mini-institutions that were often in isolated settings and were operated for profit. Yet this is what happened, and placing people in what the psychiatrist H.B.M. Murphy called the "new back wards"[1] is one of the most significant outcomes of deinstitutionalization (Murphy, Pennee, & Luchins, 1972).

There are two dimensions to consider when we look at where people with mental illness are situated in society. The first is an individual's physical location. This aspect could include, for example, whether or not a person is in a hospital or other institution, and if not, the type of community dwelling and its location. Problems with location are still common, with an example being people situated in non-recovery-oriented boarding homes located in isolated rural areas. The second dimension is a broader societal perception of an individual through the current set of cultural lenses. This aspect could refer to, for example, what society deems their capacity or rights to be. It is the group of perceptions and categories that are used to define a person as a social being.

Racism, prejudice against people with disabilities, and sexism are examples of societal perceptions that reduce and dehumanize people. Other lenses, such as ones that see certain groups as having superior capabilities, are also examples. A fundamental reality in Canadian policy and practice in housing has been to ignore or limit the consideration of societal perceptions. It is critical to note that ideas about what capabilities people have (Sen, 1995, pp. 39–55), what rights they should have as citizens (see chapter 7, this volume), and how they fit into broader society have profound implications for how housing is conceived and implemented. The importance of this cannot be overstated. All of the major developments in how and where people with mental illness live are based on it. As we will see, the failure to develop an accurate societal perception of people with mental illness has repeatedly led to failures in policies and programs that affect them.

The societal perception of people with mental illness is conditioned by two levels. The first is determined by views of the illness and disability itself. The assumption that having a mental illness makes you helpless, unreliable, or dangerous has historically been a common view. Another has been that having a mental illness means you need constant care and supervision, or that rights such as the vote should be denied to you. These considerations stem from ideas about the impact of illness and disability, and these change over time. A good comparison can be found in the example of people with paraplegic injuries. In the 1950s the idea that people in wheelchairs could work or have families was often seen as farfetched. We now understand that we overestimated the impact of this condition, and that the actual barriers to social inclusion were often external to the person, coming in the form of prejudice or physical barriers. The disability itself has not changed; it still cannot be successfully treated. The positive changes that have occurred were driven by revisions in our societal perception.

The second level of societal perception is based on broader social attitudes. These attitudes affect people with disabilities, but also have implications for all members of society. An example is social expectations of self-reliance. After World War II a marked change took place that altered our sense of who is responsible for certain key aspects of well-being. These new ideas took the form of the welfare state and were based on a more collective idea of society. Medicare is the most prominent

Canadian example, and it exemplified the idea that by working together the well-being of all citizens could improve. Government welfare and disability pension programs are other examples.

The notions that led to the welfare state embodied a new way of seeing members of society and affected all Canadians, including people with mental illness. But by the 1980s a new wave of ideas was spreading that changed this climate significantly. Grouped under the term "neoliberalism," the new ideas emphasized individual, not collective, responsibility. As we will see, these ideas have had significant impact on people with mental illness.

Institutionalization

The first large-scale example of government intervention in housing the mentally ill was what might actually be called the great dehousing movement represented by institutionalization. It began in the 1800s and was established in the Maritime provinces, Quebec, and Ontario by the middle of the century. By 1950, the asylum population had reached 66,000 (Moran, 2009). Across Canada people with mental illness were removed from the community and put in what was then considered state of the art in treatment—the asylum. Although asylums came to have a negative reputation by the 1950s, they in fact started out as optimistic forms of treatment. They were based on an approach to mental illness called moral treatment that called for supportive care in a protected setting. Moral treatment replaced earlier forms of care that focused on the body and used practices like bleeding, cupping, and strong purgatives as well as incarceration in jails. Moral treatment often used social explanations to understand the causes of mental illness, with examples from early asylum records being such things as "loss at love," or "political excitement." People needed to be removed from these risks—hence the asylum. Brown (1980) writes:

> Then, ironically, it was the mental hospital, or lunatic asylum as it was first called, that was itself heralded as the long-sought panacea for the problem of madness. The asylum, it was confidently believed through the use of a new system called "moral treatment," would soon be curing ninety per cent or more of the insane, and in the not-too-distant future would virtually eliminate insanity as a pressing social problem. (p. 100)

The asylum regime was based on moral discipline and instruction and was seen as the answer to the problem of mental illness. It was seen as more humane and more effective.

Despite this portrayal, moral treatment was complex and was not simply a new and more humane approach. It represented a new expression of social power and authority. Victorian society was afraid of the spread of mental illness and wanted it stopped. While in the past a mentally ill person was more likely to be left alone, moral treatment called for forced confinement in asylums. Although it did not target the body with barbaric treatments, it targeted the mind with moral instruction and a regime of close supervision. The sense of a new understanding of mental illness, and having therapeutic power over it, coupled with the fear of what might occur if illness were allowed to go untreated, resulted in a mass societal commitment to asylum construction.

From a housing point of view, the asylum concept meant relocation, and its application removed people with serious mental illness from the community. Additionally, early asylums had a particular approach to building design. Many asylums used classical revival architecture to symbolize reason and were physically situated overlooking water, which was felt to be calming. Where staff members worked and lived was also carefully designed. The asylum superintendent, for example, was seen as the father of the moral family of the asylum and as central to its operation. In one example, the Lunatic Asylum of Upper Canada in Toronto, the superintendent worked and actually lived in the center of the central block of the building (Brown, 1980).

Moral treatment was also based on a particular version of societal perception. Because it saw social conditions as critical to causing illness, and because these conditions could be modified, illness was seen as curable. This was a positive shift, and given some more recent ideas about mental illness that emphasize fundamental defects such as genetic makeup, it may seem surprising. But in light of what we now know about mental illness, the idea of this cure was misplaced in many cases. Even today mental illness is not well understood, but it is known that there are many causes and that a variety of treatments are needed. Asylums represented a new and humane technology, but were not the answer that moral treatment proponents had hoped for.

The asylums had not been intended for long-term care, but for many patients they did not offer a complete cure and instead highlighted the reality of ongoing symptoms and disability. In these cases, long-term asylum care was in fact isolating and destructive. Moral treatment practitioners misread this; they wanted cures, and if this failed, they saw the only option as ongoing confinement. They were not able to see people as both having mental illness and having capacities and aptitudes. Instead, the fact of ongoing illness overwhelmed any positive understanding of the people affected. Moral treatment could not envision a life in the community for people with ongoing levels of disability, and as a result the asylums began to fill up with what was thought of as the "incurable."

The second level of societal perception, the level of broader social attitudes, also had a significant impact on the evolution of moral treatment and asylums. The Victorian fear of the spread of mental illness had resulted in forced confinement in asylums, even if there was optimism about cures. But by the early 20th century it was widely understood that the asylum model was a failure as a treatment approach and was also very costly. One reason they were not dismantled is the social attitudes that were becoming dominant at the time in Canadian society. The Victorian belief in the asylum was replaced by new thinking that had a profound effect on where many people with serious mental illness lived. The new thinking coalesced in two social movements that emerged in the late 19th and early 20th century and proved to be pivotal: the social hygiene movement and eugenics. In both cases they began within professional circles but grew in scope to influence the attitudes of the public, and their ideas shaped a new approach to the societal perception of people with mental illness.

Social hygiene was a broad social movement with a public health focus that addressed topics ranging from communicable diseases to what was referred to as immoral conduct. Mental hygiene was a part of social hygiene that initially focused on conditions in institutions and then moved on to the overall mental health of the population (Bridges, 1928). It was also concerned with what physicians at the time referred to as feeble mindedness. The term "feeble mindedness" covered what we would now call mental illness and intellectual disability (MacLennan, 1987). Mental hygiene called for healthy social and personal practices to promote mental health but also called for the removal of "defective" people from communities. Like moral treatment, it had a strong environmental focus and argued that conditions in families and schools could promote or hinder good mental health. The desired outcome was a mentally healthy population.

Eugenics was related to mental hygiene, but was centered on heredity. Commenting on this close association, in 1928, J. W. Bridges, a psychiatrist at McGill University wrote, "Mental hygiene thus has fundamentally the same object as eugenics" (p. 8). The objective was a healthy population that limited the production of so called defectives, or when this failed, segregated them in institutions. Bridges (1928) supported this segregation and called for more and better institutions. Segregation was seen as necessary in part to prevent defective populations from reproducing. It led to forced sterilization laws being passed in some Canadian provinces and the actual practice of sterilization taking place in many more. The last such law in Canada was in Alberta and was not abolished until the 1970s. In its most extreme form eugenics was used by the Nazis and led to the murder of people with mental illness and intellectual disability. This can be seen as a societal perception that saw no place of any kind for people with serious mental illness. During the years of World War II, it is estimated that between 200,000 and 250,000 people with mental illness and intellectual disability were murdered (Jaroszewski, 1987).

The net result of mental hygiene and eugenics was a set of attitudes that shunned people with more serious cases of mental illness or intellectual disability and that called for their removal from normal social life, either through segregation or murder. This resulted in the widespread use of institutions long after their efficacy was in doubt, and was the foundation of the policies that led to the location of so many people outside of regular communities. This represented the status quo until the 1950s.

Deinstitutionalization

The period after World War II brought profound changes to the lives of people with mental illness. These changes are referred to as deinstitutionalization and led to a massive rehousing movement that was characterized by a series of largely unplanned experiments with housing models and reforms. In brief, the period of deinstitutionalization, which began in Canada in the mid-1950s in Saskatchewan, has been a long process to rethink both the physical location and societal perception of people with mental illness. The steps in the process have included the closure of asylums, the physical move to community settings, and a recalibration of the societal perception. At the first level of societal perception—our conceptions about people with mental illness—this has taken the form of a long battle to define capacities, rights, and social position.

By 1976, the bed capacity of provincial mental hospitals had decreased by 68.5% as a result of deinstitutionalization (Sealy & Whitehead, 2004). While the stated goal of deinstitutionalization was to integrate former hospital patients back into society by creating or expanding community-based facilities as the asylums wound down (Aubry, 2003; Bachrach, 1978), the outcomes that occurred in practice were not always so positive. Provincial governments moved slowly in reallocating resources from institutions to the community sector, meaning that deinstitutionalization was well underway before crucial and sufficient community services had been developed, particularly in the areas of employment and housing (Aubry, 2003).

Chapter 1 of this volume describes the evolution of housing models that reflect these trends in detail. From the point of view of the actual forces driving the new housing models, the societal perception of the time was again the primary factor. The most important of these, and what were in fact contradictory factors, led to the policies and practices we see today within mental health housing programs. Nelson and Macleod describe the values that lay behind the three main housing models that emerged: custodial housing, single-site supportive housing, and independent, scattered-site housing (Nelson & Macleod, chapter 1, this volume). On one side a person with a mental illness was seen as a disabled object of care and on the other side they were seen as a full citizen with rights and capacities.

The early period of deinstitutionalization reveals these two perspectives simultaneously in action. The first was an extension of the institutional thinking that characterized the asylum era. People with mental illness were viewed as incapable of self-care and self-determination. Their disabilities were all encompassing, and the need was for an institutional kind of care in the community. The result was the custodial boarding home or foster home. These models provide shared, routinized settings in which basic services like meals and laundry are provided. They are typically operated for profit by untrained owners and staff, and the philosophy of care is custodial rather than rehabilitative. Surprisingly these models are still with us today and many still reflect a surviving layer of the societal perception of the institutional era. This kind of thinking is, de facto, part of the policies that govern mental health housing.

After deinstitutionalization, many former patients found themselves living in what Nelson (2010) has described as "psychiatric ghettos" (including board-and-care homes, semi-institutional facilities, or poor-quality rental housing). A study conducted in the early 1980s highlights the lack of housing options that were available to people with mental illness, showing that, 6 months after discharge, 20 per cent of people were living in inadequate housing and one-third had been readmitted to hospital (Goering et al., 1984). Many patients had transitioned from the custodial care of psychiatric hospitals to the custodial care of community facilities that did no more to enable their recovery than did that of the institutional approach (Nelson, 2010). The continued idea that people with mental illness were a population that required caretaking was seen in the proliferation of housing models that sought to solve "the problem of the intractable psychiatric patient with no home to go to" (Sylph, Eastwood, & Kedward, 1976, p. 233), characterized by, among other things, the "cessation of active treatment" (pp. 233–234).

The second, and more positive stream of the societal perception of individuals with mental illness that emerged during deinstitutionalization led to very different outcomes than the custodial boarding home, or mini-institution. This perspective emphasized the capacities of people with mental illness. Its early expression is found in a landmark document issued in 1963 by the Canadian Mental Health Association; *More for the Mind* (Tyhurst et al., 1963) became a rallying point for proponents of deinstitutionalization. It called for mental illness to be "dealt with in the same organizational, administrative, and professional framework as physical illness" (p. 38). The new thinking was that people could be treated in general hospitals and live in the community with other citizens, with the only planning needed being for treatment capacity in the community. This approach was strikingly optimistic, and in some ways similar to the early optimism of moral treatment.

In the absence of well-developed community services and supports, this optimism was often misplaced. Bachrach (1976, 1978) points out that the many functions of the old asylums, which included housing and feeding people, medical care, and some activities, were not planned for in the community. The implicit assumption was that most people with mental illness could or should take care of themselves, and the result was poorly prepared communities and inadequate support services. The lack of planning led to serious consequences including homelessness, poor physical health, and social isolation.

The positive perspective that emphasized the capacities of people with mental illness was not simply the product of professionally dominated groups like the Canadian Mental Health Association. It was also during the 1960s that the concept of recovery began to gain traction, put forth by the consumer/survivor movement as a rebuttal of the medical model of mental illness (Carpenter, 2002). The voices of people with mental illness and their lived experience were increasingly brought forward as being equal to professional expertise, and the idea that they could lead meaningful lives in the community became increasingly accepted in some circles.

This second and more positive perspective on the societal perception of people with mental illness led to housing models that were far removed from the non-recovery-oriented custodial boarding home. These models emphasized the capabilities of mental health consumers and grew from an initial emphasis on rehabilitation in specialized community housing facilities to the idea of people as full citizens with rights and the ability to live in the community without the use of specialized facilities. Halfway houses, cooperative group homes, and satellite housing programs were considered the "alternative housing" options in the early days of deinstitutionalization (see chapter 2, this volume). They were based on the assumption that people could learn new skills and in time move on to greater independence. They were typically operated by nonprofit agencies and in many cases had on-site staff. Many models of this type are still operating. Over time, however, this thinking evolved to a consensus on what is called supported housing models (referred to in this volume as independent scattered-site housing). This housing is characterized by scattered-site apartments or houses lived in by people with mental illness in the same way as other members of society, typically as individuals or families. There are no special physical characteristics to the housing units, and people are tenants or owners like anyone else. Support, if needed, comes from outside staff who are not tied to the housing itself.

In the early phases of deinstitutionalization the two lines of thinking (the person as disabled and dependent, or the person as a citizen with rights, responsibilities, and capacities) were both themes in the first level of societal perception—our way of thinking about people with mental illness and their rights and capacities. We can now turn to the second level of societal perception—broader public conceptions of individual and collective responsibility—and can situate the changes in this area within the historical context of the development of the Canadian welfare state, and subsequently in the increasing influence of neoliberal ideas on Canadian society. This second level of perception of people with mental illness has significantly affected the housing picture we see today.

A critical foundation of deinstitutionalization was in fact the emergence of the welfare state. Its provisions, which we will discuss below, allowed for the basics of community life such as income, housing, and medical care, and shaped our ideas about where people with mental illness fit in. In general, the welfare state was about collective responsibility and inclusion. But as the predominant political ideology in Canada has moved away from one in which social welfare is recognized as the responsibility of the state, to one in which it is increasingly viewed as the responsibility of the individual, the picture has changed. People with mental illness find themselves in a situation where basic social services are being reduced and they are increasingly expected to fend for themselves.

Generally speaking, societies, and consequently, the public policies of those societies, have viewed the components of human welfare—housing, education, health care, and so forth—in one of two ways—as rights or as privileges. When these things are viewed as rights, conferred by one's humanity, governments are seen as having a responsibility to ensure that all residents have equal access to those goods and services that ensure their well-being (see the discussion of social rights in chapter 7, this volume). On the other hand, when the components of social welfare are viewed as privileges, it is understood that one must attain them either through barter (market participation) or through gifting (charity). Social services attain the status of commodities, or things to be bought and sold.

Esping-Andersen (1990) describes a system of decommodified social services as the central feature of the welfare state. Decommodification refers to the degree to which social services are considered to be public goods, accessible to all, and not subject to market processes. In a decommodified society, people are not reliant on their incomes, and therefore on their ability to participate in the labor market, to attain those services that are necessary to health and well-being. On the other hand, when social welfare is commodified, so, too, is the ability of the individual to participate in the labor market, whether formally or informally. A person must work to produce goods or services that can then (usually through the intermediary of a legally recognized currency) be traded for the things they need and want.

Canada's welfare state began developing in the 1940s, peaked in the 1960s and 1970s, and in the 1970s, began a decline that has continued to the present day. This rise and fall is apparent in many areas of Canadian public policy, including housing policy, as the role that government has played in promoting the well-being of its citizens has waxed and waned. With regard to mental health housing, we can trace the development of a policy system that saw its primary responsibility as caring for members of the most vulnerable sectors of society to one that views self-care as a responsibility of the citizenry, rather than of the government.

Housing and the Canadian Welfare State

Canada's federal government first began to take an active role in housing during the Great Depression. The first national housing legislation, the Dominion Housing Act, was passed in 1935. The development of Canada's conventional welfare state began shortly afterward, in the early 1940s. At this time, people with mental illness were still largely housed in isolated psychiatric institutions. A number of policies were enacted during this time period that would greatly affect the lives of people with mental illness during deinstitutionalization. Although the federal government had implemented social welfare policies as early as the turn of the 20th century, World War II would prove to be the catalyst for the rise of the welfare state in Canada. The 1943 *Report on Social Security for Canada* (known as the Marsh Report) articulated the vision of a postwar social order in which government played an essential role in the provision of social security, and established the social rights of citizenship as equally as important as political or civil rights (Maioni, 2004). It was at this time that the federal government made significant investments in social security that would cultivate the development of a welfare state, including the introduction of two income maintenance programs and initiation of planning for a comprehensive social security system for Canada (Guest, 1997).

Early reviews and planning on social security, including the Marsh Report, focused on implementing measures to protect employment, income, and health insurance. It was not until 1944 and the release of the Curtis Report on Housing and Community Planning that housing entered the postwar social security discourse. The Curtis Report highlighted the serious deficiencies in the housing stock available to low-income Canadians and recommended large-scale government intervention into the housing market, particularly in the provision of low-rent housing (Guest, 1997). Despite the Curtis Report's focus on housing as a social good, the federal legislation introduced in response to the report, the National Housing Act[2] (1944), had a focus that was fundamentally economic (prevention of another national depression) rather than social (Guest, 1997). The Canada Mortgage and Housing Corporation (CMHC) was established as a crown corporation in 1945 to administer the federal role in housing as described by the National Housing Act. The main role of the CMHC was to promote home ownership by middle-income Canadians, with the needs of lower-income Canadians continuing to be largely neglected.

The first public housing project in the country in 1948, Toronto's Regent Park, was actually created by a local government initiative (Harris, 1999). At the federal level, some token nods toward providing housing for low-income families, the elderly, and the disabled were made in 1954 amendments to the National Housing Act (Guest, 1997), but not until 1964, when the Act was further amended, did the growth of public housing in Canada begin in earnest. The 1964 amendments announced the objective of producing 1,000,000 social housing units over a 5-year period (Hulchanski, 2002). During the same time period, provincial government initiatives in British Columbia, Ontario, and Quebec were beginning to develop home ownership and social housing initiatives to meet local needs (Leone & Carroll, 2010).

We have seen that housing for people with mental illness was transformed in the 1950s and 1960s with the beginning of deinstitutionalization, which caused tens of thousands of people to be discharged from psychiatric institutions to the community. Many factors played a role in bringing about the change, including a greater understanding of mental illness and new advancements in treatment, the high cost of institutional psychiatric care, and growing concern about human rights violations within hospitals (Nelson, 2012; Trainor, Ballantyne, & Groskind, 1984).

As deinstitutionalization gathered momentum in the 1960s, changes that furthered the decommodification of social welfare that had begun in the postwar period were put in place. These changes included the introduction of the Canada Pension Plan in 1965 and, in 1966, nationally mandated universal health insurance, the Guaranteed Income Supplement for senior citizens, and the Canada Assistance Plan, which established welfare as a universal right. The development of a public welfare state meant that the government would be able to provide a minimal support system to people with mental illness living in the community (Nelson, 2012). Although we see now that the quantity of housing and support system resources was insufficient, the development of the welfare state paved the way for the discontinuation of formal institutionalized care.

The growing belief that housing was a right and that its production and distribution should not be left to the market culminated in increased government involvement in Canadian housing policy during the early 1970s (Colderley, 1999; Smith, 1977). This period of transformation led to the development of new federal and provincial housing policies, such as the construction and subsidization of new dwellings for low-income households; the introduction of rent control; and revisions to acts covering tenants' rights.

We can see this period as the zenith of the broader societal perception embodied in the welfare state. Advocates at the time foresaw a future where people with mental illness would live in a highly supportive social environment that offered most basic social and health services. This future did not, however, come to pass.

The Rise of Neoliberalism and Decline of the Welfare State

"Neoliberalism"[3] is a term used to describe an ideology that promotes adherence to the free market principles of classical economics while opposing state interventionist theories (Coburn, 2000; Harvey, 2005; Peters, 2001). When put into practice, neoliberalism produces a system characterized by deregulation, privatization, commodification, and withdrawal of the state from social service provision. The world oil crisis of 1973 and other stimuli created a time of global stagflation in the 1970s, with industrialized nations uniformly experiencing high unemployment, high inflation, and low economic growth. In Canada and other countries, the policy responses to this crisis were essentially neoliberal in character, including efforts to stimulate the economy by deregulating industry, reducing corporate taxes, and reducing government spending on social programs. At the federal level, key policy changes have included changing the old age pension from a universal program to a means-tested program and the creation of the Canada Health and Social Transfer, demonstrating the withdrawal of a federal presence from welfare, social service, and health programs. The responsibility for social housing also began to be downloaded to the provinces in the 1970s (Carter & Polevychok, 2004). In 1977, the Established Programs Financing Act reduced the federal government's portion of the cost-sharing for health and postsecondary education, representing the beginning of the federal government's withdrawal from what had previously been considered public goods. From this time, and continuing to the present day, the Canadian welfare state has been steadily eroding, and Canadian social policy has become increasingly neoliberalized.

Under neoliberalism, with its shift of focus from societal responsibility to individual responsibility, we see an increase in the role of the market in the provision of human services. A number of government services have been privatized, contracting work, which had previously been considered public services, to the private sector. This has included many services to marginalized populations—for example, the National Homelessness Initiative, which ran from 1999 to 2007, and subsequently the Homelessness Partnering Strategy (HPS), downloaded homelessness programming to private and voluntary-sector organizations in local communities.

Alongside the privatization of services formerly provided by the government, systems working under a neoliberal paradigm also engage in what Ilcan (2009) refers to as "privatizing responsibility." This phenomenon "emphasizes individual competition and self-reliance and consumer choice rather than dependence on public resources" (p. 212). The idea of citizenship is closely tied to self-sufficiency and individual responsibility, and these values are further tied to morality, with a "good" or "moral" citizen being one who is self-reliant, accountable, exhibits a strong work ethic, and is a productive participant in the market economy (Dean, 1999; Harvey, 2005).

The neoliberal focus on individual responsibility is an aspect of the broader level of societal perception. But it has also had an effect on how we see individuals with mental illness. Neoliberal ideas make it difficult to support a psychiatric model that assumes that people with mental illness do not need to, or lack the ability to, take responsibility for their actions (Rose, 1996). As society has become more neoliberal, so, too, has the view of the psychiatric patient as someone who is responsible for symptom self-management—and self-care has increasingly been viewed as an important component of mental health recovery.

In the moral treatment era we saw that more humane conditions and protection in asylums were actually the flip side of incarceration and harsh regimens of moral education. In our era, empowerment and self-care are in part the flip side of abandonment by the neoliberal state. Higgs (1998) describes a system in which "disease concerns have become privatized," with the responsibility for the health and illness of the body and mind increasingly viewed as being among those things for which individuals must bear responsibility. People are expected to self-manage their own health, and those who do not are considered to be, in fact, *morally* culpable[4] (Brandt, 1997; Galvin, 2002). People with mental illness have become divided into "good patients," "who are 'medicine compliant', keep appointments, are able to assess their coping performance in a way that aligns with the assessment of professionals" (Rose, 1996, p. 14) and "bad patients," who do not do these things. The notion of empowerment has also grown to incorporate the idea of self-responsibility. Rose (1996) notes that while "empowerment" was originally a concept used by consumers and advocates in challenging professional authority, it is now something that professionals do to clients, by "according them the capacity for managing their own lives by way of acceptable logics of life-strategy" (p. 15). *Changing Directions, Changing Lives: The Mental Health Strategy for Canada* (Mental Health Commission of Canada, 2012) sums this up: "To the greatest extent possible, they [people with mental illness] control and maintain responsibility for their mental health and well-being" (p. 12).

Recovery is a multifaceted concept, which originated in the consumer/survivor movement of the 1960s and 1970s as a challenge to the medical model approach to healthcare, particularly the idea that mental illnesses should be treated as chronic, defining ailments requiring symptom-focused treatment (Carpenter, 2002). Recovery, from a consumer/survivor perspective, is primarily a matter of individual empowerment. It is a process, rather than an outcome (Davidson et al., 2009), related to overcoming the effects of being a mental health service user (including recovery from poverty, isolation, unemployment, and inadequate housing) and having a meaningful life in the community, which may or may not include symptom amelioration (Davidson et al., 2005). Various models of recovery have been proposed, which commonly include elements of hope, empowerment, self-determination, healing, and community.

However, within this broad description of recovery as an empowering paradigm, focusing on people's strengths and capabilities rather than their symptoms, diagnoses, and deficits, different elements of recovery can be emphasized. Constructions of "recovery" are deeply related to cultural contexts (Adeponle, Whitley, & Kirmayer, 2012; Barker & Buchanan-Barker, 2011). A society's concept of recovery both influences and is influenced by its ideas about the societal perception of people with mental illness. While neoliberal definitions of recovery emphasize choice, individual control, and self-determination, other cultural traditions emphasize notions of connectedness to family, spirituality, and community as central to recovery (Adenpole et al., 2012).

The adoption of an individualistic notion of "recovery" within neoliberal policy frameworks has met with some criticisms (e.g., Braslow, 2013; Harper & Speed, 2012; Teghtsoonian, 2009). It has been argued that recovery has been co-opted by professionals, and that it has been used as a justification for service cutbacks, reductions in social welfare benefits, and forcing people back to work. The individualistic concept of recovery is also reflected in recent mental health housing policy, which increasingly espouses the value of self-sufficiency and locates the recovering individual in the physical location of scattered-site apartments without on-site mental health supports.

Recent Developments in Mental Health Housing Policy

In 2006, the first national report on the state of Canada's mental health system—*Out of the Shadows at Last* (Kirby & Keon, 2006)—was released, which would greatly shape the direction of mental health housing policy across the country. The report by senators Michael Kirby and Wilbert Keon led to the increasing prominence of mental health in the public eye, as well as its increasing importance in public policy. One of the first, and perhaps the most important, outcomes of *Out of the Shadows at Last* was the establishment of the Mental Health Commission of Canada (MHCC), created in 2007 with the endorsement of all federal parties, as well as all provincial and territorial governments except for Quebec. The MHCC operates as an independent, nonprofit organization, operating at arm's length from government. With its 10-year mandate from Health Canada, the MHCC embarked on the creation of a national knowledge exchange center, implementation of a national antistigma initiative, and development of a national mental health strategy, which was published in 2012 as *Changing Directions, Changing Lives: The Mental Health Strategy for Canada.*

Both *Out of the Shadows at Last* and *Changing Directions, Changing Lives* identify housing as an integral part of a recovery-oriented mental health system. The former recognized, "for people living with serious mental illness, there is strong evidence that with the proper supports in place they can not only live in the community but also lead fulfilling and productive lives" (Kirby & Keon, 2006, p. 49) and called on the federal government for a 10-year investment in the development of new affordable housing stock. A less-specific version of this call was echoed in the mental health strategy as a priority area moving forward: "increase the availability of safe, secure, and affordable housing with supports for people living with mental health problems and illness" (MHCC, 2012, p. 75). Together, the two reports contend that recovery for many people with mental illness can and does happen in the physical geography of the community but that without sufficient affordable housing stock with available support, recovery is compromised. In essence, recovery hinges on housing.

In 2008, the MHCC also undertook a 5-year research demonstration project, *At Home/Chez Soi*, on mental health and homelessness that has profoundly affected how we view best practices in housing for people with mental illness. The project, the largest of its size in the world, evaluated the effectiveness of the "Housing First" approach in five Canadian cities. While there are different Housing First models, the fundamental premise of the approach is the provision of housing to people in need as the first step with no strings attached. It was developed in response to traditional "treatment first" approaches in which people had to be clean, sober, and compliant with their medication prior to receiving housing. In combination with support services, the Housing First approach addresses people's most pressing need *first*. For more on Housing First, see chapters 1, 2, and 15 of this volume.

The *At Home/Chez Soi* project involved the participation of over 2,000 people, of whom about half received the Housing First intervention. Results of housing outcomes have been impressive; those that received Housing First had more stable housing, improved quality of life and community functioning, and reduced use of hospital services as compared with a treatment-as-usual group of roughly the same size (Goering et al., 2014). These findings are consistent with past research and have added to a rapidly growing body of evidence on the model. The project's final report asserts, "there are few interventions or strategies designed to address homelessness that can truly be described as best practices; Housing First is one of them" (Goering et al., 2014, p. 32).

In large part due to the promising early findings from At Home/Chez Soi and the influence of the MHCC, Housing First has been formally adopted as the best practice housing model by the federal government. Although Canada does not have a national housing strategy, the federal government introduced the National Homelessness Initiative in 1999 to help communities address homelessness. Its successor, the HPS was launched in 2007 and "encouraged" a Housing First approach (Homeless Partnering Strategy, n.d.). When the HPS was renewed in 2013, the endorsement of Housing First was more absolute, with the objective to "work with communities, provinces, and territories and the private and not-for-profit sectors to implement a Housing First approach to homelessness" (Homelessness Partnering Strategy, 2014, para. 1). With $600 million earmarked for the HPS until early 2019, the federal government has put all its eggs in the Housing First basket, meaning that Housing First *is* mental health housing policy in Canada for the time being.

A handful of concerns have been expressed about the HPS, including the restrictiveness of program funding; the learning curve associated with the Housing First approach, for both governments and communities; the capacities of communities to meet the requirements of Housing First; the 5-year length of the commitment being insufficient to produce results that the federal government expects; and the unknown level of support of provincial and territorial governments related to the implementation of Housing First programs (Gaetz et al., 2014). The At Home/Chez Soi project demonstrates just how essential it is for provincial and territorial governments to be onboard with the HPS and the consequences if they are not. When the 4-year $110 million project began nearing its end in 2013, funding became the major topic of discussion. With the research ending, no ongoing funding was in place at that time. In Ontario and New Brunswick, the provincial governments agreed to provide the funding needed to continue providing housing and support for participants at the Toronto and Moncton sites, respectively. The aftermath was not as positive in Quebec. Following cessation of federal funding, services were extended to transition those in the program to other services. Ongoing rent subsidies have been provided from the Montreal Office Municipal de l'Habitation, but some of the clinical teams have been defunded. While the situation in Montreal best highlights the breakdowns that can occur with short-term funded initiatives that lack consensus between federal and provincial governments, many of the other four At Home/Chez Soi sites went through difficult processes of securing funding to continue the provision of services. Given the 5-year mandate of HPS, we will no doubt see programs scrambling if the HPS is not again renewed after 2019.

At the provincial and territorial levels, many governments are following suit. In Alberta, its 10-year plan to end homelessness, which began in 2008, noted a Housing First philosophy as "the heart of the plan for Alberta" (Alberta Secretariat for Action on Homelessness, 2008, p. 16). Similarly, the government of Ontario recently released a policy statement that states its "housing and homelessness plans are based on a Housing First philosophy" (Government of Ontario, 2013, p. 4). In eastern Canada, Housing First is central to the housing strategies of both New Brunswick and Nova Scotia, with the former asserting that it is the "foundation" of its strategy (New Brunswick Housing Corporation & Department of Social Development, 2010, p. 47) and the latter identifying Housing First as the approach that will be adopted to help house people with mental illness and addiction (Government of Nova Scotia, 2013). More information about each province and territory's housing policies as they relate to people with mental illness can be found in the appendices of the MHCC's *Turning the Key: Assessing Housing and Related Supports for Persons Living with Mental Health Problems and Illness* report (Trainor et al., 2012).

The endorsement of Housing First within the HPS, and provincial housing strategies and mandates has great implications for the mental health housing system. First, as previously mentioned, Housing First takes many different shapes and forms that range from a specific model of housing to a general approach to reducing homelessness. At one end is the Pathways to Housing model that defines Housing First as "a type of 'supported housing' that separates treatment from housing, considering the former voluntary and the latter a fundamental need and human right" (Padgett et al., 2006, p. 75). The model provides housing via scattered-site apartments without on-site support (the physical location of tenants is autonomous living in the community). At the other end is a much broader notion of Housing First that asserts housing is provided up front and that individuals do not have to be abstinent or receiving treatment before obtaining housing. Using this definition, a range of housing models, including custodial housing, could implement this tenet and be considered Housing First (Aubry, Ecker, & Jetté, 2014). This raises the question: What form of Housing First is being adopted by the HPS, and provincial and territorial housing strategies?

The Housing First approach of the HPS has six mandatory principles: (1) rapid housing with supports (housing readiness is not a requirement); (2) housing choice; (3) separation of housing and supports (tenants must consent to weekly visits, though); (4) tenancy rights; (5) integration of housing in the community (prioritization of scattered-site housing); and (6) promotion of self-sufficiency (Employment and Social Development Canada, 2014). The principles provide some flexibility, and consideration is given to communities where scattered-site housing is not a feasible option but, overall, the definition of Housing First is more closely aligned to the Pathways to Housing model. As for the provincial and territorial strategies in which Housing First is a component or philosophy, all identify Housing First much more generally, primarily in terms of rapid rehousing that is permanent and offers the necessary supports.

Second, while there has been a rapid growth in the study of Housing First programs, research is only emerging from its infancy stage. In a review of the evidence on Housing First, Waegemakers Schiff and Rook (2012) assert that, given the paucity of rigorous research studies, the labeling of Housing First as a best practice appears to have been a political decision rather than a scientific one. Despite this, they acknowledge that the approach has shown to be effective for stably housing many people with mental illness in certain contexts. Findings from At Home/Chez Soi provide further support to this but also show, as other studies have found, that, for some people, the approach does not work. Given the Housing First mandate of the HPS and other provincial and territorial strategies, there are serious implications for people who were not successful in Housing First or who did not find it to be the right fit, as well as providers of non–Housing First housing. As more and more Canadian housing policies shift toward making Housing First their foundation, housing prospects for people with mental illness appear very promising so long as they *choose* Housing First.

Conclusion

In this chapter, we discussed how housing policy in Canada has historically been devised as economic policy as opposed to social policy. This stance has meant that policy has seldom focused specifically on mental health housing. Because of this, to understand where people with mental illness live, it is necessary to use a very broad notion of the term "policy" that not only reflects formal written policy documents but also incorporates the various actions taken to locate people with mental illness within the physical and social worlds. In doing this, we propose the use of two dimensions: physical location (i.e., the physical location of an individual; e.g., an institution or in the community) and a broader societal perception (i.e., how we view someone as a person through the current cultural lens). The latter dimension is conditioned by two levels: (1) perceptions of mental illness and disability itself, and (2) broader social attitudes.

The great dehousing movement in the 1800s represented by institutionalization was the first large-scale example of government intervention in housing the mentally ill in Canada. From a housing point of view, this meant a change in physical location for people with serious mental illness from community to asylum. The asylum, in the early stages of the dehousing movement, was seen as a state of the art in treatment based on an underlying approach to mental illness called moral treatment, which called for supportive care in a protected setting. While it was becoming understood during the early 20th century that the institutionalization approach was costly and an ineffective form of treatment, broader social attitudes related to the social hygiene movement and eugenics delayed the cessation of asylum treatment.

In Canada, the period of deinstitutionalization began in the mid-1950s in Saskatchewan and represented a long process to rethink the physical location and societal perception of people with mental illness. The goal was to integrate former hospital patients back into society by housing them in community-based facilities. However, provincial governments were slow to act in the reallocation of resources from institutions to the community sector, resulting in serious consequences including homelessness, poor physical health, and social isolation. As the deinstitutionalization movement was reaching its zenith in the 1970s, attitudes about housing generally within Canadian society were changing simultaneously. The shift toward housing being viewed as a right and no longer as something that should be left to the market culminated in increased government involvement in Canadian housing policy during this period. The results saw the development of new federal and provincial housing policies, such as the construction and subsidization of new dwellings for low-income households, the introduction of rent control, and revisions to acts covering tenants' rights.

Canadian housing policy for people with mental illness in the 21st century has been influenced by a rise in neoliberalized social policy and the recovery movement. The latter, which espouses the value of self-sufficiency and locates recovering individuals in the physical location of scattered-site apartments without on-site mental health supports, is exemplified by the Pathways to Housing Housing First model. The approach's core tenet of addressing homeless people's most pressing need by providing housing *first* has seen great traction in Canada in recent years. Stemming from the positive results of the MHCC's At Home/Chez Soi project, the federal government has adopted Housing First as the best practice housing model, and provincial governments are beginning to follow suit. While the language around Housing First within many of the housing policies and strategies is vague, it is clear that there has been a major shift, at least in name, toward making Housing First the foundation of housing policy for people with mental illness in Canada.

Notes

1. The term "back wards" was used to refer to the worst long-term wards of the old mental hospitals.
2. The National Housing Act of 1944 represents the third version of the Act, the first being the Dominion Housing Act of 1938 and the second being National Housing Act of 1938.
3. Note that the term "liberal" and "neoliberal" use "liberal" in the same way as classical political economy, not in the way it is used in Canadian politics today. Liberalism in political economy means a free market focus in which things like healthcare and social welfare are treated as commodities, as discussed above. Government intervention is discouraged.
4. It is notable to see this reintroduction of the concept of morality, which echoes its use in the mid 19th-century notion of moral treatment. In both periods the dominant political approach is based on the liberal principles of classical political economy.

References

Alberta Secretariat for Action on Homelessness. (2008). *A plan for Alberta: Ending home-lessness in 10 years.* Retrieved from http://alberta.ca/albertacode/images/Alberta PlantoEndHomelessness.pdf

Adeponle, A., Whitley, R., & Kirmayer, L. (2012). Cultural contexts and constructions of recovery. In A. Rudnick (Ed.), *Recovery of people with mental illness: Philosophical and related perspectives* (pp. 109–132). doi:10.1093/med/9780199691319.003.0008

Aubry, T. (2003). *Mental health and mental illness: Phase one. Roundtable eleven: Deinstitutionalization and rehabilitation.* Brief presented to the Standing Senate Committee on Social Affairs, Science, and Technology. Ottawa, Ontario, Canada: University of Ottawa, Centre for Research on Community Services.

Aubry, T., Ecker, J., & Jetté, J. (2014). Supported housing as a promising Housing First approach for people with serious mental illness. In M. Guirguis-Younger, R. McNeil, & S.W. Hwang (Eds.), *Homelessness and health in Canada* (pp. 155–188). Ottawa, ON: University of Ottawa Press.

Bachrach, L.L. (1976). *Deinstitutionalization: An analytical review and sociological perspective.* DHEW Publication No. [ADM] 76–351. Washington, DC: US Government Printing Office.

Bachrach, L.L. (1978). A conceptual approach to deinstitutionalization. *Hospital and Community Psychiatry, 29,* 573–578.

Barker, P.J., & Buchanan-Barker, P. (2011). Mental health nursing and the politics of recovery: A global reflection. *Archives of Psychiatric Nursing, 25,* 350–358. doi:10.16/j.apnu.2011.03.009

Brandt, A.M. (1997). Behavior, disease, and health in the twentieth-century United States. In A.M. Brandt & P. Rozin (Eds.), *Morality and health* (pp. 53–78). New York: Routledge.

Braslow, J.T. (2013). The manufacture of recovery. *Annual Review of Clinical Psychology, 9,* 781–809. doi:10.1146/annurev-clinpsy-050212-185642

Bridges, J.W. (1928). The mental hygiene movement. *Public Health Journal, 19*(1), 1–8.

Brown, T. (1980). Architecture as therapy. *Archivaria, 10,* 99–124.

Carpenter, J. (2002). Mental health recovery paradigm: Implications for social work. *Health and Social Work, 27,* 86–94. doi:10.1093/hsw/27.2.86

Carter, T., & Polevychok, C. (2004). *Housing is good social policy (Research report F|50 family network).* Ottawa, Ontario, Canada: Canadian Policy Research Networks Inc.

Coburn, D. (2000). Income inequality, social cohesion and the health status of populations: The role of neo-liberalism. *Social Science and Medicine, 51,* 135–146.

Colderly, C. (1999). Welfare state retrenchment and the nonprofit sector: The problems, policies, and politics of Canadian housing. *Journal of Policy History, 11,* 283–312. doi:http://dx.doi.org/10.1353/jph.1999.0003

Davidson, L., O'Connell, M. J., Tondora, J., Lawless, M., & Evans, A. C. (2005). Recovery in serious mental illness: A new wine or just a new bottle? *Professional Psychology: Research and Practice, 36,* 480–487.

Davidson, L., Tondora, J., Lawless, M. S., O'Connell, M. J., & Rowe, M. (2009). *A practical guide to recovery-oriented practice: Tools for transforming mental health care.* New York: Oxford.

Dean, M. (1999) *Governmentality: Power and rule in modern society.* Los Angeles: Sage.

Employment and Social Development Canada. (2014). *Housing first approach.* Retrieved from http://www.esdc.gc.ca/eng/communities/homelessness/housing_first/service_delivery/case_studies.shtml

Esping-Andersen, G. (1990). *The three worlds of welfare capitalism.* London: Polity.

Gaetz, S., Gulliver, T., & Richter, T. (2014). *The state of homelessness in Canada 2014.* Toronto, ON: Homeless Hub Press.

Galvin, R. (2002). Disturbing notions of chronic illness and individual responsibility: Towards a genealogy of morals. *Health, 6,* 107–137.

Goering, P., Veldhuizen, S., Watson, A., Adair, C., Kopp, B., Latimer, E., . . . Aubry, T. (2014). *National At Home/Chez Soi final report*. Calgary, AB: Mental Health Commission of Canada.

Goering, P., Wasylenki, D., Farkas, M., Lancee, W., & Freeman, S. J. (1984). From hospital to community: Six-month and two-year outcomes for 505 patients. *Journal of Nervous and Mental Disease, 172,* 667–673.

Government of Nova Scotia. (2013). *Building community and affordability for Nova Scotia families: A housing strategy for Nova Scotia*. Retrieved from https://www.novascotia.ca/coms/hs/Housing_Strategy.pdf

Government of Ontario. (2013). *Ontario housing policy statement*. Retrieved from http://www.ontario.ca/housing

Guest, D. T. (1997). *The emergency of social security in Canada* (3rd ed.). Vancouver, British Columbia, CA: UBC Press.

Harper, D., & Speed, E. (2012). Uncovering recovery: The resistible rise of recovery and resilience. *Studies in Social Justice, 6*(1), 9–25.

Harris, R. (1999). Housing and social policy: An historical perspective on Canadian-American differences—A comment. *Urban Studies, 36,* 1169–1175.

Harvey, D. (2005). *A brief history of neoliberalism*. New York: Oxford.

Higgs, P. (1998). Risk, governmentality and the reconceptualization of citizenship. In G. Scambler & P. Higgs (Eds.), *Modernity, medicine and health* (pp. 176–197). London: Routledge.

Homelessness Partnering Strategy. (2014). Retrieved from http://actionplan.gc.ca/en/initiative/homelessness-partnering-strategy

Homelessness Partnering Strategy. (n.d.). Retrieved from http://actionplan.gc.ca/en/backgrounder/homelessness-partnering-strategy

Hulchanski, D. (2002). *Housing policy for tomorrow's cities*. Ottawa, Ontario: Canadian Policy Research Network.

Ilcan, S. (2009). Privatizing responsibility: Public sector reform under neoliberal government. *Canadian Review of Sociology, 46,* 207–234. doi:10.1111/j.1755-618X.2009.01212.x

Jaroszewski, Z. (1987). *German extermination of psychiatric patients in occupied Poland 1939–1945.* Paper presented at the Regional Symposium of the World Psychiatric Association in Warsaw. Retrieved from http://www.projectinposterum.org/docs/Jaroszewski1.htm

Kirby, M. J. L., & Keon, W. J. (2006). *Out of the shadows at last: Transforming mental health, mental illness and addiction services in Canada—Final report of the Standing Senate Committee on Social Affairs, Science and Technology*. Retrieved from www.parl.gc.ca

Leone, R., & Carroll, B. W. (2010). Decentralisation and devolution in Canadian social housing policy. *Environment and Planning C: Government and Policy, 28,* 389–404.

MacLennan, D. (1987). Beyond the asylum: Professionalization and the mental hygiene movement in Canada, 1914–1928. *Canadian Bulletin of Medical History, 4,* 7–23. Retrieved from www.cbmh.ca/index.php/cbmh/article/viewFile/176/175

Maioni, A. (2004). New century, new risks: The Marsh report and the post-war welfare state in Canada. *Policy Options,* 20–23. Retrieved from http://policyoptions.irpp.org/magazines/social-policy-in-the-21st-century/new-century-new-risks-the-marsh-report-and-the-post-war-welfare-state-in-canada/

Mental Health Commission of Canada. (2012). *Changing directions, changing lives: The mental health strategy for Canada*. Calgary, AB: Author.

Moran, J. E. (2009). *History of madness and mental illness: A short history of care and treatment in Canada*. Retrieved from http://www.historyofmadness.ca/index.php?option=com_content&view=article&id=80&Itemid=109&lang=en

Murphy, H.B.M., Pennee, B., & Luchins, D. (1972). Foster homes: The new back wards? *Canada's Mental Health, 71,* 1–17.

Nelson, G. (2010). Housing for people with serious mental illness: Approaches, evidence, and transformative change. *Journal of Sociology and Social Welfare, 37,* 123–146.

Nelson, G. (2012). Mental health policy in Canada. In A. Westhues & B. Wharf (Eds.), *Canadian social policy: Issues and perspectives* (5th ed., pp. 229–252). Waterloo, ON: Wilfred Laurier University Press.

New Brunswick Housing Corporation, & Department of Social Development. (2010). *Hope is a home: New Brunswick's housing strategy.* Retrieved from http://www2.gnb.ca/content/dam/gnb/Departments/sd-ds/pdf/Housing/housingstrategy-e.pdf

Padgett, D.K., Gulcur, L., & Tsemberis, S. (2006). Housing First services for people who are homeless with co-occurring serious mental illness and substance abuse. *Research on Social Work Practice, 16*(1), 74–83. doi:10.1177/1049731505282593

Peters, M.A. (2001). *Poststructuralism, Marxism, and neoliberalism: Between theory and politics.* Lanham, MD: Rowman & Littlefield.

Pomeroy & Focus Consulting, Inc. (2004). *Leaks in the roof, cracks in the floor: Identifying gaps in Canada's housing system.* Paper prepared for the Canadian Housing and Renewal Association's *Building Housing: Building the Nation* national symposium.

Rose, N. (1996). Psychiatry as a political science: Advanced liberalism and the administration of risk. *History of the Human Sciences, 9*(2), 1–23.

Sealy, P., & Whitehead, P.C. (2004). Forty years of deinstitutionalization of psychiatric services in Canada: An empirical assessment. *Canadian Journal of Psychiatry, 49,* 249–257.

Sen, A. (1995). *Inequality reexamined.* Cambridge, MA: Harvard University Press.

Smith, L.B. (1977). *Anatomy of a crisis: Canadian housing policy in the seventies.* Vancouver, British Columbia: Fraser Institute.

Sylph, J.A., Eastwood, M.R., & Kedward, H.B. (1976). Long-term psychiatric care in Ontario: The homes for special care program. *Canadian Medical Association Journal, 114,* 233–237.

Teghtsoonian, K. (2009). Depression and mental health in neoliberal times: A critical analysis of policy and discourse. *Social Science and Medicine, 69,* 28–35. doi:10.1016/j.socscimed.2009.03.037

Trainor, J., Ballantyne, R., & Groskind, V. (1984). *Handbook of alternative community housing for psychiatric patients in Canada.* Toronto, Ontario: Canadian Mental Health Association.

Trainor, J., Taillon, P., & Pandalangat, N. (2012). *Turning the key: Assessing housing and related supports for persons living with mental health problems and illness.* Calgary, AB: Mental Health Commission of Canada.

Tyhurst, J.S., Chalke, F.C.R., Lawson, F.S., McNeel, B.H., Roberts, C.A., Taylor, G.C., ... Griffin, J.D. (1963). *More for the mind: A study of psychiatric services in Canada.* Toronto, Ontario: Canadian Mental Health Association.

Waegemakers Schiff, J., & Rook, J. (2012). *Housing first—Where is the evidence?* Toronto, ON: Homeless Hub.

11

What Do We Mean by Housing First?

Considering the Significance of Variations in Housing First Services in the European Union

NICHOLAS PLEACE AND JOANNE BRETHERTON

This chapter explores the introduction of Housing First services for homeless people with severe mental illness in Europe. Housing First, already becoming characterized by paradigm drift as it spreads across the United States, might appear to have become ever more mutable as it crossed the Atlantic to Europe. Yet while the differences in operational detail are numerous, the core philosophy followed by Housing First services, being piloted and rolled out across the European Union, is actually very close to the pioneer model. This chapter argues that what may be termed a philosophical consistency with the core principles of Housing First, rather than very high fidelity with the operational detail of the pioneer model, has led to a practical and effective use of Housing First in the European context.

The Rise of Housing First

While the origins of Housing First are sometimes contested, the pioneering Housing First service model operated in New York between 1992 and 2014 (Tsemberis, 2010a, 2010b; Tsemberis, Kent, & Respress, 2012). The pioneer model drew heavily on supported housing models originally developed for the resettlement of former patients of psychiatric hospitals (Ridgway & Zipple, 1990) being designed specifically for homeless people with severe mental illness and addiction (Tsemberis, 2010a; 2010b). Housing First had an assertive community treatment (ACT) team and an intensive case management (ICM) team. The model offered a nurse practitioner, psychiatrist, peer specialists (formerly homeless people with a supportive mentoring role), drug and alcohol specialists, and a specialist in securing private rental housing (Tsemberis, 2010b).

Unlike step-based service models,[1] Housing First began by offering a service user an ordinary apartment in an ordinary neighborhood, their own home, over which they could exercise a high degree of control. Housing First service users were therefore supported in the home they were going to live in; they did not start their journey in communal or congregate setting and then have to pass a series of tests to show they were ready to live independently in their own home. Housing First had no housing readiness tests, no requirement for treatment compliance, or even abstinence from drugs and alcohol; housing was offered as a first step, rather than as the last (Tsemberis, 2010a, 2010b).

The goals of Housing First center on housing stability, engagement with treatment, and positive social integration for service users–objectives that are essentially the same as those of step-based models (Hansen Löfstrand & Juhila, 2012). However, the way in which these goals are pursued is quite different from step-based services. Consumer choice, person-centered planning, and the formal separation of housing from support are emphasized by Housing First services that place an equal effort into active engagement, harm reduction, and following a recovery orientation. Housing First constantly encourages engagement with support and treatment, while simultaneously emphasizing that housing is a human right and stressing consumer choice and person-centered planning (Tsemberis, 2010b).

Housing First immediately offers homeless people with severe mental illness their own home and also enables them to have a high degree of choice and control over their lives. However, is it clear that Housing First is not passive; the model actively seeks what is termed recovery, from severe mental illness, from the effects of problematic use of drugs and alcohol (within a harm reduction framework), from poor physical health, and from the consequences of homelessness itself. Housing First does not require, coerce, or push homeless people into actions that will enhance their health and well-being, but it does, always and constantly, seek to persuade and support service users toward choices that are intended to enhance their health and well-being and to make their exit from homelessness permanent.

As Housing First came to international prominence, the importance of the recovery orientation and active engagement within the model was sometimes less visible than the seemingly more revolutionary aspects. The immediate access to housing, the lack of requirement to stop drinking or using drugs, and the high degree of service user choice attracted more attention—mainly because they were often seen as new ideas—than the *equal* emphasis on actively seeking to promote positive changes in the lives of homeless people. Difference, rather than continuity with the service models that had come before, became the defining narrative of Housing First. Yet in reality, like the step-based models that preceded it, Housing First sought behavioral change as the means to end homelessness among people with severe mental illness.

The key differences lay in *how* that behavioral change was sought and in the nonjudgmental attitudes toward the people using Housing First services (Hansen Löfstrand & Juhila, 2012).

The rate of housing sustainment, usually at least 80 per cent of service users for at least 1 year, compared with community housing services achieving between 40 per cent and 60 per cent, was a major attraction of Housing First from a European perspective (Padgett et al., 2006; Pleace, 2008; Tsemberis, 2010a; Tsemberis & Asmussen, 1999; Tsemberis et al., 2012). The step-based, "staircase" service models for homeless people with complex needs, forms of community housing used in Europe that paralleled North American models, were also encountering high rates of attrition and many service users were becoming "stuck" between the steps they were supposed to take toward independent housing (Busch-Geertsema & Sahlin, 2007; Sahlin, 2005).

Europe also saw what it perceived as the potential for Housing First to significantly enhance the cost effectiveness of existing public expenditure by reducing complex forms of homelessness more effectively than existing services (Culhane, 2008; Tsemberis, 2010a). Housing First becoming integral to US homelessness policy at the federal level and being regarded as an effective, evidence-based policy to what was termed "chronic" homelessness was also important to the idea being noticed by European policy makers (USICH, 2010).

Criticism of Variation in Housing First

There have been many criticisms of Housing First in the United States. It has been argued that Housing First is reductive, using a crude construct of homelessness and providing a solution that is an equally crude construct, based on a restricted idea of what constitutes reliable evidence (Stanhope & Dunn, 2011). Housing First has been viewed cynically, as focusing on a very specific group that will visibly reduce public expenditure if they leave homelessness, while at the same time setting itself a relatively easily achieved goal of just keeping this high-need group of financially costly people housed, rather than really meeting all of their needs (Kertsez, Crouch, Milby, Cusimano, & Schumacher, 2009; Kertsez & Weiner, 2009). There have, conversely, also been claims that Housing First works with people with lower needs than the step-based models it was designed to replace, appearing to be more effective only because it handles less complex cases. More generally, the quality and veracity of the evidence base for the pioneer model of Housing First has been repeatedly questioned (Groton, 2013; Rosenheck, 2010; Waegemakers-Schiff & Schiff, 2014).

Arguments have also been raised that Housing First, when looked at carefully, is not really achieving consistently positive results beyond high levels of housing sustainment. While there are improvements, rates of severe mental illness and problematic drug and alcohol use do not always decrease among Housing First service users, nor is greater social integration consistently achieved (Edens, Mares, Tsai, &

Rosenheck, 2011; Greenwood, Schaefer-McDaniel, Winkel, & Tsemberis, 2005; Johnson, Parkinson, & Parsell, 2012; McNaughton-Nicolls & Atherton, 2011; Pleace & Quilgars, 2013). Gaps in evidence about the effectiveness of Housing First in helping to promote social integration and health and well-being remain at the time of writing (Johnson et al., 2012; Pleace & Quilgars, 2013).

From some European perspectives, Housing First can be seen as falling short of the genuine empowerment of homeless people with high support needs. This is because there is still a clear focus on seeking behavioral modification among homeless people, which is clearly central to having a recovery orientation, the use of a harm reduction framework, and the emphasis on active engagement within Housing First (Hansen Löfstrand & Juhila, 2012). Whether this means that Housing First constitutes reductive processing of homeless people is debatable (Stanhope & Dunn, 2011). Some European ideas do focus more on getting the mix and level of support correct, seeing an end to homelessness more in terms of what needs to change to help an individual out of homelessness, rather than how the individual needs to change in order to leave homelessness (Pleace, 2011).

From some European perspectives, the emphasis on consumer choice, person-centered planning, and harm reduction were not revolutionary; in Northern Europe, these ideas are mainstream (Pleace, 2011). This made the narrative of Housing First as being a "revolutionary" change much harder to sustain, and advocates of Housing First could struggle to be perceived as offering something that was significantly different from existing homelessness services (Pleace & Bretherton, 2013a).

Sustaining a critique that the evidence for Housing First is still unreliable, or that the approach is inherently flawed, is still possible (Waegemakers-Schiff & Schiff, 2014), but it is arguably becoming increasingly difficult. Criticisms from within Europe, centered on Housing First being too North American in conception, or as not representing a meaningful change in homelessness service design, have also become muted in light of evidence that Housing First is often more effective than existing services at ending homelessness.

European and North American research has produced results that are both very positive and strikingly consistent; good examples are the experimental evaluations of the Canadian *At Home/Chez Soi* and the French *Un chez soi d'abord* Housing First programs (Estecahandy, 2014; Goering et al., 2014). There is also a growing amount of observational research from Europe showing the same high degree of success (Bretherton & Pleace, 2015; Busch-Geertsema, 2013; Pleace & Bretherton, 2013b). The successes of Housing First are not universal; there are still inconsistent results in relation to mental health, drug and alcohol use, and social integration. However, almost every European Housing First experiment has ended homelessness among people with high support needs, including those with sustained and recurrent experience of homelessness, at very high rates.

There is still however the issue of variation in Housing First services. A key argument deployed against Housing First is that it is not one service model that can be clearly shown to be effective, but is instead an assemblage of only loosely connected services that have only a limited—and variable—resemblance to the pioneer model established in New York in 1992 (Pleace, 2011). Housing First does not, according to this argument, represent a coherent model around which either service delivery or wider homelessness strategies should be planned (Tabol, Drebing, & Rosenheck, 2009; Waegemakers-Schiff & Schiff, 2014).

Equally, advocates of the pioneer model of Housing First argue that services with a lower fidelity to the pioneer model have poorer results than would be delivered if the pioneer model were replicated. The successes achieved by the different versions of Housing First are, according to this argument, being diluted by insufficient fidelity to the pioneer model (Gilmer et al., 2014; Greenwood, Stefancic, Tsemberis, & Busch-Geertsema, 2013; Tsemberis, 2011). The opponents of the pioneer model of Housing First and those who champion it find themselves, in a limited sense, on the same side, as both argue that the implementation of Housing First is too inconsistent.

Philosophical Coherence and Operational Diversity in Europe

There are, on the face of it, a lot of different kinds of Housing First programs in Europe. There is a high-fidelity program in France, which reflects the pioneer model of Housing First as closely as the Canadian At Home/Chez Soi Housing First program (Estecahandy, 2014; Goering et al., 2014), and the pioneer model is also clearly very influential in Ireland (Pleace & Bretherton, 2013a) and in Denmark (Benjaminsen, 2013). There are, however, also Housing First services that use congregate housing–dedicated large apartment blocks, in which only Housing First service users live– in Finland (Kaakinen, 2012; Pleace, Culhane, D.P., Granfelt, R., & Knutagård, 2015), just as there are congregate models of Housing First in the United States (Collins et al., 2011; Collins et al., 2012; Greenwood et al., 2013; Larimer et al., 2009; Pearson, Montgomery, A., & Locke, 2009). There are also models of Housing First that do not have an ACT team, or an equivalent, relying instead entirely on case management (Bretherton & Pleace, 2015; Busch-Geertsema, 2013; Pleace & Bretherton, 2013b).

There are European models of Housing First that take levels of person-centered planning and personalization of support services *beyond* the point established by the pioneer model of Housing First. The pioneer model of Housing First requires service users to sign a subtenancy or lease, while the organization providing Housing First holds the actual contract with the landlord, exercises financial controls to ensure 30% of income is paid toward rent and requires a weekly meeting with a support worker in a Housing First service user's home. These requirements may hardly seem stringent compared with some of the services that Housing First has replaced in North America, but there are European Housing First services with no such requirements (Bretherton & Pleace, 2015; Busch-Geertsema, 2013).

Housing First is also not delivered in a consistent way in Europe. Finland, France, and Denmark have national homelessness strategies incorporating Housing First or dedicated Housing First programs organized at the national level (Benjaminsen, 2013; Estecahandy, 2014; Pleace et al., 2015). Sweden and the UK are also using Housing First, but their services are being developed and run at local level on an improvisational basis, in the absence of a clear national strategy or focused funding program (Knutagård & Kristiansen, 2013; Bretherton & Pleace, 2015).

As the first experiments in Housing First began to spread out across Europe and the results of initial evaluations started to be available, a pattern did start to become evident. There is a tendency for Housing First services that are successful in ending homelessness among people with high support needs to share a set of core principles, summarized as follows (Pleace & Bretherton, 2013b):

- housing is a human right;
- service users must have choice and control;
- housing and treatment are separated;
- services must follow a harm reduction framework;
- there is a recovery orientation;
- support must be flexible in nature; and
- support must be provided for as long as is needed.

Alongside evidence from Europe, there is also evidence that American Housing First services that show consistency in following these core principles of Housing First reduce homelessness among people with complex needs at very high rates (Bretherton & Pleace, 2015; Busch-Geertsema, 2013; Collins et al., 2012; Kaakinen, 2012; Kresky-Wolff, Larson, O'Brien, & McGraw, 2010; Larimer et al., 2009; Pleace, 2012; Pleace & Bretherton, 2013b; Pleace & Quilgars, 2013; Pleace et al., 2015). Clearly, these services are all following core principles that very closely reflect the core philosophy of the pioneer model of Housing First (Tsemberis, 2010a, 2010b). Yet while it can be argued, on current evidence, that European Housing First services that are philosophically close to the pioneer model all appear to be effective at ending homelessness (Busch-Geertsema, 2013; Pleace & Bretherton, 2013b), these European services often do not replicate the detailed operation of the pioneer model and can have marked operational differences, not least because these services can be operating in a radically different context to that found in North America.

There is the argument that closer fidelity, moving beyond the concepts that underpin the pioneer model and replicating the operational detail of the pioneer model of Housing First, would generate still better results (Greenwood et al., 2013). However, at present, there appear to be two problems with this assertion.

The first problem centers on what exactly is meant when a Housing First service is described as having an acceptable level of fidelity with the pioneer model of Housing First. High fidelity with the pioneer model of Housing First can work in European contexts, as pilot services in France and Ireland show (Pleace & Bretherton, 2013b). Yet, the French and Irish experiments were also tests, pilots operating under special conditions, different from the realities of working homelessness services integrated into wider strategic responses and administrative structures. For Housing First to work in varied European contexts it will almost certainly need to be adapted to those contexts, to work within existing social protection and health systems, within existing policies and strategies, and within cultural norms that are not the same as those of the United States. Simply transferring American Housing First without any modification to another country would not be a practical, indeed even a possible, approach (Johnson et al., 2012).

The question of how much variation from the pioneer model is acceptable could quickly become difficult to answer in the European context, because the multiply varied contexts across the European Union will require varying modification. Policy transfer can never be a matter of simply copying, nor setting a detailed, predetermined limit on what can and cannot be changed. Arguing in favor of high fidelity to the detailed operation of the pioneer model of Housing First is all very well, but can that model really be used in the same way in every European context, and if, in reality, Housing First has to vary in operational terms, can there really be a clear, fixed set of limits as to what the extent of that operational variation should be?

The second problem centers on successful European versions of Housing First that have varying levels of fidelity with the pioneer model. To reiterate, successful European examples of Housing First appear to have a high fidelity with the core principles of Housing First listed above, but often differ in their operation. These differences, in how housing is provided and how support is organized, while still consistent with the core principles of Housing First, often do not closely reflect how things were done in the pioneer model. As noted, there are European Housing First services that use congregate housing, have no ACT team, have no ICM team, and set fewer requirements for their service users than even the pioneer model of Housing First.

European Housing First services appear to be as successful as the pioneer model and some appear to be more successful. This does raise questions about how important detailed fidelity (i.e., near-replication) actually is for reducing homelessness among people with high support needs. True, the pioneer model of Housing First could achieve housing sustainment levels of 88 per cent (Tsemberis, 2010b), but at 1 year, the rates in European Housing First services, varying from the pioneer model in the detail of their operation, were 97 per cent in the Netherlands, 94 per cent in Denmark, 93 per cent in Scotland, and 80 per cent in Portugal (Busch-Geertsema, 2013). In England, five Housing First services kept 74 per cent of a very high need group, almost all of whom had severe mental illness, housed for a year (Bretherton & Pleace, 2015), using a case-management-only model of Housing First.

Adapting Housing First to different contexts may be the approach that makes the most sense in Europe. As in Canada, high fidelity to the pioneer model can deliver good outcomes (Goering et al., 2014), but philosophically consistent, operationally divergent examples of Housing First in Europe that are equally or more successful, do suggest that success may be a question of shared core principles, more than of replication. Reusing existing homelessness services by turning them into dedicated apartment blocks, using a Housing First support model, very quickly provided the necessary housing in a highly stressed housing market in Finland and appears to have worked. Long-term homelessness, a condition characterized by severe mental illness and other high support needs, fell in Finland by 1,200 people between 2008 and 2014, whereas it had hitherto been growing (Pleace et al., 2015). Using case- management only for Housing First, working alongside the relatively extensive health and welfare systems that are available to any citizen in the Netherlands and the UK, also seems effective (Busch-Geertsema, 2013; Bretherton & Pleace, 2015).

Fidelity in European Housing First Services and Social Integration

In the European sense, the social integration that Housing First seeks to achieve can be broken down into three main components. The first is positive personal relationships: The friends, family, and partner who provide informal social support and boost mental health and well-being by giving someone the sense they are valued and respected. The second component is community participation: Being part of a neighborhood and extending into political participation. The final component is economic integration: This might in some cases mean structured activity that is individually rewarding, such as some forms of arts-based or informal learning activity, but it also includes participation in formal education, training, job-seeking, volunteering, and securing and maintaining employment (Pleace & Quilgars, 2013; Tsemberis, 2010a, 2010b).

Some of the variation evident in European Housing First might potentially undermine promotion of social integration. Congregate Housing First services are found in the United States and in Finland (Collins et al., 2011; Collins et al., 2012; Kaakinen, 2012; Larimer et al., 2009; Pleace et al., 2015). The objection to using this form of housing, rather than the scattered housing advocated for in the pioneer model of Housing First, is that it physically separates people using Housing First from the communities in which they are supposed to be participating. There is also the possibility of stigmatization: a Housing First service user moving into a rented apartment could be just another tenant; someone moving into the "Housing First" apartment block is potentially marked as something other than normal. There are also the potential management difficulties in an apartment block populated entirely by people with high support needs (Busch-Geertsema, 2010; Kettunen & Granfelt, 2011; Tsemberis, 2011).

Yet, at present, arguing that using single-site housing will necessarily produce a negative outcome in social integration is problematic on three levels. First, the evidence suggesting that pioneer models of Housing First consistently achieve successful community participation for service users is patchy and the mechanism by which scattered housing helps deliver community participation is arguably quite vaguely defined (Johnson et al., 2012; Pleace & Quilgars, 2013). Second, the idea of community as necessarily being a nurturing and supportive place is not always accurate. There can be marked cultural differences in this regard, but the possibility of an often highly vulnerable person placed in scattered housing by a Housing First service becoming isolated or perhaps being persecuted by neighbors also exists. Third, Finnish experience suggests that internal and external relationships in congregate models of Housing First can be managed successfully and raises the possibility that emotional support might come from those with shared experiences living in a congregate service (Pleace et al., 2015).

Finding Meaning in Housing First

Existing evidence shows that Housing First can effectively reduce homelessness among people with severe mental illness and other high support needs. This evidence is not always consistent in quality; there are a lot of observational and quasi-experimental studies of Housing First sitting alongside the robust experimental evaluations carried out in Canada and France (Groton, 2013; Waegemakers-Schiff & Schiff, 2014). However, it is notable that almost all of the existing evidence points the same way. Housing First services following the broad philosophy of the pioneer model tend to be successful in a wide range of contexts.

This success is not absolute, in that where there is strong evidence of sustainably ending homelessness, outcomes in terms of health, well-being, and social integration can, as noted, be more mixed (Pleace & Quilgars, 2013). It is also important to note that, for the most part, a lot of the existing Housing First services are still relatively new at the time of writing. It may be that the apparent successes will not be sustained over time, although there is some evidence from the pioneer model showing it is able to maintain exits from homeless for years (Padgett, 2007; Tsemberis, 2010a). There is also the possibility that the homeless population who are engaging successfully with Housing First may undergo change. Finland's successful use of a congregate Housing First model engaged with a disproportionately male, alcohol-using population. A younger population presenting with polysubstance use and containing more women might be less well suited to this particular approach (Pleace et al., 2015).

Housing First is also not the sole answer to homelessness among people with severe mental illness. While success rates are generally very high, there is a small element of the population for whom Housing First is not suitable and who might require alternative service provision. In some instances, this might include some use of step-based services, as there are examples of tolerant, flexible, and effective step-based services (Pleace, 2008; Rosenheck, 2010). There are also alternative housing-led models using mobile, lower intensity, case management services and ordinary housing, which again, can be effective for some homeless people, including those with severe mental illness (Busch-Geertsema, 2005; Busch-Geertsema, Edgar, O'Sullivan, & Pleace, 2010; Caton, Wilkins, & Anderson, 2007; Goldfinger et al., 1999; Hickert & Taylor, 2011; Lipton, Siegel, Hannigan, Samuels, & Baker, 2000; Lomax & Netto, 2008; Tabol et al., 2010).

Finally, there are limits around what Housing First can realistically achieve in Europe and elsewhere. Mental health, drug and alcohol use, and physical health may improve, but not in all cases. There are going to be people using Housing First services with conditions that are degenerative. Housing First may improve lives, but it may not be able to ever fully reverse the consequences of homelessness, nor fully address negative experiences, severe mental illness, and high support needs that may have contributed to becoming homelessness or arisen during homelessness (Pleace, 2008).

Yet while poverty, poor physical and mental health, limited life chances, and other problems may remain, homelessness—the unique distress of being without any settled accommodation—is often ended for people with complex and high needs by Housing First services. Europe has benefited from Housing First, even as it has adapted the model and started to build European, rather than North American, versions of Housing First services. As Padgett (2007) notes when describing the outcomes achieved by the pioneer model of Housing First, "Having a 'home' may not guarantee recovery in the future, but it does afford a stable platform for re-creating a less stigmatized, normalized life in the present" (p. 1934).

Note

1. Also known as linear residential treatment (LRT), community housing, continuum of care approaches, and staircase model services.

References

Bretherton, J. & Pleace, N. (2015). *Housing First in England: An evaluation of nine services.* York: University of York.

Benjaminsen, L. (2013). Policy review up-date: Results from the Housing First based Danish homelessness strategy. *European Journal of Homelessness, 7*, 109–131.

Busch-Geertsema, V. (2005). Does re-housing lead to reintegration? Follow-up studies of re-housed homeless people. *Innovation, 18*, 202–226.

Busch-Geertsema, V. (2013). *Housing First Europe: Final report.* Retrieved from http://www.social-styrelsen.dk/housingfirsteurope/copy4_of_FinalReportHousingFirstEurope.pdf

Busch-Geertsema, V., Edgar, W., O'Sullivan, E., & Pleace, N. (2010). *Homelessness and homeless policies in Europe: Lessons from research*. Brussels: European Commission.

Busch-Geertsema, V., & Sahlin, I. (2007). The role of hostels and temporary accommodation. *European Journal of Homelessness, 1*, 67–93.

Caton, C.L.M., Wilkins, C., & Anderson, J. (2007). *People who experience long-term homelessness: Characteristics and interventions.* Unpublished Paper given at the National Symposium on Homelessness Research 2007, Washington, DC.

Collins, S.E., Clifasefi, S.L., Dana, E.A., Andrasik, M.P., Stahl, N., Kirouac, M., & Malone, D.K. (2011). Where harm reduction meets Housing First: Exploring alcohol's role in a project-based Housing First setting. *International Journal of Drug Policy, 23*, 111–119. doi: 10.1016/j.drugpo.2011.07.010

Collins, S.E., Malone, D.K., Clifasefi, S.L., Ginzler, J.A., Garner, M.D., Burlingham, B., . . . Latimer, M.E. (2012). Project-based Housing First for chronically homeless individuals with alcohol problems: Within-subjects analyses of 2-year alcohol trajectories. *American Journal of Public Health, 102*, 511–519.

Culhane, D.P. (2008). The costs of homelessness: A perspective from the United States. *European Journal of Homelessness, 2*, 97–114.

Edens, E.L., Mares, A.S., Tsai, J., & Rosenheck, R.A. (2011). Does active substance use at housing entry impair outcomes in supported housing for chronically homeless persons? *Psychiatric Services, 62*, 171–178.

Estecahandy, P. (2014). *First results of HF experimentation in France and next steps.* Presentation given at the FEANTSA 2014 Policy Conference, Confronting Homelessness in the EU: Seeking Out the Next Generation of Best Practices. Bergamo, 24–25 October 2014. Retrieved from http://www.slideshare.net/FEANTSA/pascaleestecahandy

Gilmer, T.P., Stefancic, A., Katz, M.L., Sklar, M., Tsemberis, S., & Palinkas, L.A. (2014). Fidelity to the Housing First model and effectiveness of permanent supported housing programs in California. *Psychiatric Services, 65*, 1311–1317.

Goering, P., Veldhuizen, S., Watson, A., Adair, C., Kopp, B., Latimer, E., . . . Aubry, T. (2014). *National At Home/Chez Soi final report.* Calgary, AB: Mental Health Commission of Canada.

Goldfinger, S.M., Schutt, R.K., Tolomiczenko, G.S., Seidman, L., Penk, W.E., Turner, W. & Caplan, B. (1999). Housing placement and subsequent days homeless among formerly homeless adults with mental illness. *Psychiatric Services, 50*, 674–679.

Greenwood, R.M., Schaefer-McDaniel, N.J., Winkel, G., & Tsemberis, S. (2005). Decreasing psychiatric symptoms by increasing choice in services for adults with histories of homelessness. *American Journal of Community Psychology, 36*, 223–238.

Greenwood, R.M., Stefancic, A., Tsemberis, S., & Busch-Geertsema, V. (2013). Implementation of Housing First in Europe: Successes and challenges in maintaining model fidelity. *American Journal of Psychiatric Rehabilitation, 16*, 290–312.

Groton, D. (2013). Are Housing First programs effective? A research note. *Journal of Sociology and Social Welfare, 40*, 51–63.

Hansen Löfstrand, C., & Juhila, K. (2012). The discourse of consumer choice in the Pathways Housing First model. *European Journal of Homelessness, 6*(2), 47–68.

Hickert, A.O., & Taylor, M.J. (2011). Supportive housing for addicted, incarcerated homeless adults. *Journal of Social Service Research, 37*, 136–151.

Johnson, G., Parkinson, S., & Parsell, C. (2012). *Policy shift or program drift? Implementing Housing First in Australia.* AHURI Final Report No. 184. Melbourne: Australian Housing and Urban Research Institute.

Kaakinen, J. (2012). Long term perspectives: From Housing First to ending homelessness. *Housing First: A Key Element of European Homelessness Strategies*, 23rd March 2012. Unpublished conference proceedings. French Permanent Representation, Brussels. Retrieved from feantsa.horus.be/code/EN/pg.asp?Page=1409

Kertesz, S., Crouch, K., Milby, J., Cusimano, R., & Schumacher, J. (2009). Housing First for homeless persons with active addiction: Are we overreaching? *Milbank Quarterly*, 87, 495–534.

Kertsez, S.G., & Weiner, S.J. (2009). Housing the chronically homeless: High hopes, complex realities. *Journal of the American Medical Association*, 301, 1822–1824.

Kettunen, M., & Granfelt, R. (2011). *Observations from the first year of the Finnish Name on the Door project: Recommendations for the long-term homelessness reduction programme for years 2012–2015*. Retrieved from www.housingfirst.fi/en/housing_first/reading_room/general_reading/observations_and_conclusions/

Knutagård, M., & Kristiansen, A. (2013). Not by the book: The emergence and translation of Housing First in Sweden. *European Journal of Homelessness*, 7(1), 93–115.

Kresky-Wolff, M., Larson, M.J., O'Brien, R., & McGraw, S.A. (2010). Supportive housing approaches in the collaborative initiative to help end chronic homelessness. *Journal of Behavioural Health Services and Research*, 37, 213–225.

Larimer, M.E., Malone, D.K., Garner, M.D., Atkins, D.C., Burlingham, B., Lonczak, H.S., . . . Marlatt, G.A. (2009). Health care and public service use and costs before and after provision of housing for chronically homeless persons with severe alcohol problems. *Journal of the American Medical Association*, 301, 1349–1357.

Lipton, F.R., Siegel, C., Hannigan, A., Samuels, J., & Baker, S. (2000). Tenure in supportive housing for homeless persons with severe mental illness. *Psychiatric Services*, 51, 479–486.

Lomax, D., & Netto, G. (2008). *Evaluation of tenancy sustainment teams*. London: Department of Communities and Local Government.

McNaughton Nichols, C., & Atherton, I. (2011). Housing First: Considering components for successful resettlement of homeless people with multiple needs. *Housing Studies*, 25, 767–777.

Padgett, D. (2007). There's no place like (a) home: Ontological security among persons with a serious mental illness in the United States. *Social Science and Medicine*, 64, 1925–1936.

Padgett, D. K., Gulcur, L., & Tsemberis, S. (2006). Housing first services for people who are homeless with co-occurring serious mental illness and substance abuse. *Research on Social Work Practice*, 16(1), 74–83.

Pearson, C., Montgomery, A., & Locke, G. (2009). Housing stability among individuals with serious mental illness participating in Housing First programs. *Journal of Community Psychology*, 37, 404–417.

Pleace, N. (2008). *Effective services for substance misuse and homelessness in Scotland: Evidence from an international review*. Edinburgh: Scottish Government.

Pleace, N. (2011). The ambiguities, limits and risks of Housing First from a European perspective. *European Journal of Homelessness*, 5, 113–127.

Pleace, N. (2012). *Housing First*. DIHAL. Retrieved from http://www.feantsa.org/IMG/pdf/housing_first_pleace.pdf

Pleace, N., & Bretherton, J. (2013a). *Finding the way home: Housing led responses and homelessness strategy in Ireland*. Dublin: Simon Community.

Pleace, N., & Bretherton, J. (2013b). The case for Housing First in the European Union: A critical evaluation of concerns about effectiveness. *European Journal of Homelessness*, 7(2), 21–41.

Pleace, N., Culhane, D.P., Granfelt, R., & Knutagård, M. (2015). *The Finnish homelessness strategy: An international review*. Helsinki: Ministry of the Environment.

Pleace, N., & Quilgars, D. (2013.) *Improving health and social integration through Housing First: A review*. DIHAL. Retrieved from http://feantsaresearch.org/IMG/pdf/improving_health_and_social_integration_through_housing_first_a_review.pdf

Ridgway, P., & Zipple, A.M. (1990). The paradigm shift in residential services: From the linear continuum to supported housing approaches. *Psychosocial Rehabilitation Journal*, 13, 11–31.

Rosenheck, R. (2010). Service models and mental health problems: Cost effectiveness and policy relevance. In I.G. Ellen, & B. O'Flaherty (Eds.), *How to house the homeless* (pp. 17–36). New York: Russell Sage Foundation.

Sahlin, I. (2005). The staircase of transition: Survival through failure. *Innovation*, 18, 115–136.

Stanhope, V., & Dunn, K. (2011). The curious case of Housing First: The limits of evidence based policy. *International Journal of Law and Psychiatry, 34,* 275–282.

Tabol, C., Drebing, C., & Rosenheck, R.A. (2010). Studies of "supported" and "supportive" housing: A comprehensive review of model descriptions and measurement. *Evaluation and Program Planning, 33,* 446–456.

Tsemberis, S. (2010a). Housing First: Ending homelessness, promoting recovery and reducing cost. In I. Ellen & B. O'Flaherty (Eds.), *How to house the homeless* (pp. 37–56). New York: Russell Sage Foundation.

Tsemberis, S. (2010b). *Housing First: The Pathways Model to end homelessness for people with mental illness and addiction.* Center City, Minnesota: Hazelden.

Tsemberis, S. (2011). *Observations and recommendations on Finland's "Name on the Door Project" From a Housing First perspective.* Housing First Finland. Retrieved from www.asuntoensin.fi/files/1242/Tsemberis_2011_-Observations_and_Recommendations.pdf

Tsemberis, S., & Asmussen, S. (1999). From streets to homes: The Pathways to Housing consumer preference supported housing model. *Alcoholism Treatment Quarterly, 17,* 113–131.

Tsemberis, S., Kent, D., & Respress, C. (2012). Housing stability and recovery among chronically homeless persons with co-occurring disorders in Washington, DC. *American Journal of Public Health, 102,* 13–16.

United States Interagency Council on Homelessness. (2010). *Opening Doors: Federal Strategic Plan to Prevent and End Homelessness 2010.* Washington, DC: USICH.

Waegemakers-Schiff, J., & Schiff, R.A.L. (2014). Housing First: Paradigm or program? *Journal of Social Distress and the Homeless, 23*(2), 80–104.

12

Housing for Australians with Serious Mental Illness

SHANNON MCDERMOTT

Australia began the process of deinstitutionalization in 1953. As large mental health institutions were systematically closed, funding for mental health services was predominantly directed toward acute care provided in general hospitals. Consequently, the responsibility for finding appropriate housing in the community fell to people living with mental illnesses and their support systems (Rosen, 2006). In the early years of deinstitutionalization, people exiting institutions could afford to live in boarding houses and hostels that provided low-cost private housing, but changes to the availability and quality of this type of housing in the 1980s and early 1990s made it increasingly difficult for people with serious mental illness to locate suitable housing options. The multitude of barriers to accessing appropriate housing was systematically documented for the first time by the Burdekin Report in 1993 (Burdekin, 1993).

To address these barriers, the Australian state and territory governments have focused their attention on two key areas. First, all Australian states and territories have implemented scattered-site housing approaches that provide access to permanent social housing as well as recovery-based, in-home support services for people with mental illness. The second area of focus is on providing appropriate housing and supports for people who are homeless or who are at risk of becoming homeless. With the release of the White Paper on homelessness, *The Road Home*, in 2008, the Australian government devoted significant resources to providing both scattered-site and single-site housing to people with the highest risk of becoming homeless, including those with serious mental illness.

I begin this chapter with a brief history of deinstitutionalization in Australia and an overview of the mental health system in Australia before discussing the current housing options for people with serious mental illness. I conclude by examining some of the ongoing challenges in ensuring that all Australians with mental illness are able to access their right to appropriate housing.

A Brief History of Deinstitutionalization in Australia

Australia was colonized by the English and was, at first, a destination for criminals and other undesirables from the homeland, including people with mental illness (Singh, Benson, Weir, Rosen, & Ash, 2001). The first asylum specifically for people with mental illness opened in 1811 in New South Wales and, by 1900, 16 similar institutions across Australia had been built (Willis, Reynolds, & Helen, 2009). Initially, there were no criteria for being admitted into an institution other than unusual social behavior (Shea, 1999) but, as the profession of psychiatry gained legitimacy, mental illness began to be classified as a medical disease rather than a social disorder and entry into asylums was regulated by the profession (Department of Health and Ageing, 2010; Willis et al., 2009).

Australian asylums were intended to be modeled on the "ideal" institution developed in the UK; the original aim was to provide an environment that supported a patient's well-being through good building design, including light, ventilation, and views (Biggs, 2003). State and territory governments were responsible for funding institutions for mentally ill persons, but planning did not drive funding decisions made in this sector. Rather, new institutions opened when state governments were pressured by advocacy groups, buildings quickly filled to capacity, and funding returned to a maintenance level until the next wave of pressure (Singh et al., 2001). Over time, increases in the country's population led to overcrowding in existing asylums. The economic impact of operating large numbers of institutions, along with concerns about the custodial practices employed within them, paved the way for deinstitutionalization, which began in earnest in 1953 (D. Richmond, 1983; Rosen, 2006). Although institutions began to close in most states and territories at this time, the policy of deinstitutionalization was not explicitly adopted by governments until the 1980s (Doessel, 2009).

By 1992, the majority of long-stay institutional residential mental health beds (approximately 22,000) had been abolished (Department of Health and Ageing, 2010; K. Richmond & Savy, 2005). Some of the money saved by closing institutions was redirected by states into the general hospital sector, where additional acute and nonacute (e.g., short-term rehabilitation) beds specifically for people with mental illness were established; few funds were devoted to developing services in the community and to establish alternative housing arrangements for people leaving institutions.

People who returned to the community after being institutionalized moved to a variety of places depending on income and the availability of familial support.[1] The most common housing options for people leaving institutions during the early stages of deinstitutionalization were unlicensed boarding houses, licensed hostels, and family accommodation (Andrews, Teeson, Stewart, & Hoult, 1990; Greenhalgh et al., 2004; K. Richmond & Savy, 2005; Rosen, 2006). Unlicensed boarding houses were small, family-run businesses established to provide low-cost, temporary accommodation to single people moving into cities. Accommodation comprised a single bedroom with shared bathroom facilities, and board was often inclusive of all meals. As deinstitutionalization gained pace, unlicensed boarding houses became a repository for people with mental illness because of the afford-ability and widespread availability of these accommodations (Andrews et al., 1990; Greenhalgh et al., 2004). Until recently, tenants in boarding houses did not have the same level of tenants' rights as in other forms of rental accommodation; they could be evicted and subjected to unregulated rent increases with few avenues of appeal (Carmody, 2008).[2] Licensed hostels were similar to unlicensed boarding houses in design, but differed in that they were registered with the government as providing services for people with disabilities (Australian Government, 1994). Licensed hos-tels controlled residents' meals and finances, but otherwise offered low levels of on-site support (Drake, 2010).

Since the 1980s, the amount of available accommodation in unlicensed board-ing houses and licensed hostels has dramatically decreased due to gentrification, rising property costs, and decreasing profit margins for operators (Carmody, 2008; Greenhalgh et al., 2004). The diminishing availability of low-cost private accom-modation, as well as the broader impact of deinstitutionalization on people with serious mental illness and their carers, was not widely understood in Australia until a national inquiry into the human rights of people with mental illness, the Burdekin Report, was published in 1993. The report documented thousands of consumers' experiences of institutional care and care in the community and, at its completion, resulted in a number of nonbinding recommendations of changes to state and com-monwealth legislation.

The inquiry uncovered that access to housing was one of the most problem-atic gaps in the service system, and that people faced barriers accessing almost all forms of housing. Consumers reported being precluded from public housing due to long waiting lists, the lack of suitable and safe housing options in some areas, and the lack of coordination between housing and health services (Burdekin, 1993). Consumers were highly dissatisfied with affordable housing options such as board-ing houses and hostels due to their poor maintenance; living with family was also problematic because of the high toll on carers and because consumers found it dif-ficult to become independent. Temporary accommodation provided by homeless-ness services was reported to do little to stop people from cycling through hospital services. Another crucial barrier identified by the Burdekin Report was the shortage of support services available to assist people to maintain their housing; at the time there were few accommodation options outside of boarding houses and services available to assist people to build independent living skills (Burdekin, 1993).

The process of deinstitutionalization resulted in a sharp division between the provision of care and housing for people with mental illness. The majority of mental health funding remained with general hospitals and acute hospital-based services, while the housing component of people's care became the responsibility of the person with mental illness and their support system (Rosen, 2006). The decoupling of these two elements was abrupt, and it was not until the 2000s that the two sectors began to work in partnership again (Battams & Baum, 2010).

Overview of the Current Mental Health System

Since the early 1990s, the Australian mental health system has gone through a process of change and reform led by the Commonwealth Government; the first broad-based system reform was announced in Mental Health Strategy in 1992, into which is subsumed the National Mental Health Policy, which lays out the vision of mental health service reform, the National Mental Health Plan, and the Mental Health Statement of Rights and Responsibilities (Commonwealth of Australia, 1992, 2009, 2012). The overall vision of reform in the mental health sector, according to the National Mental Health Policy, includes health promotion, least restrictive practices, early intervention and, more recently, recovery-focused care in the community (Commonwealth of Australia, 2009; Ramon, Healy, & Renouf, 2007; Whiteford & Buckingham, 2005). The implementation of this vision in recent National Mental Health Plans has focused on prevention, early intervention, and achieving better coordination between the health, housing, and other service sectors (Daniels, 2011).

The current mental health service system in Australia is composed of health, residential, and nonresidential services. Direct spending on mental health services in Australia totaled $7.6 billion in 2012–2013 (Australian Institute of Health and Welfare, 2014). The Commonwealth Government contributed $2.8 billion to this figure, and the majority of these funds (approximately 65%) were directed to mental health services provided under Medicare, Australia's national healthcare system (Australian Institute of Health and Welfare, 2014). Medicare was introduced in Australia in 1975 and provides universal access to general practitioners, psychiatrists, pharmaceuticals, and some allied health services (Biggs, 2003). The Commonwealth also provides funding for some nonresidential services such as the Personal Helpers and Mentors Service, and the Day2Day living services, both of which assist people with mental illness to increase their independence and improve daily living skills. In addition to direct mental health expenditure, the commonwealth is also responsible for providing general income support, employment services, and rent assistance, which equaled approximately $4.4 billion in additional expenditure in 2008 (Department of Health and Ageing, 2010).

The majority of direct mental health funding ($4.5 billion, 60% of total funds) is provided by state and territorial governments, which manage the operation of mental health services provided in stand-alone psychiatric hospitals; acute and nonacute mental health services provided through general hospitals; and community mental health services (Australian Institute of Health and Welfare, 2014). They are responsible for a wide range of accommodation options including public housing, licensed boarding houses and hostels, group homes, and temporary accommodation services (Australian Institute of Health and Welfare, 2012). Funding for mental health services provided by states and territories has increased by 110% since the first National Mental Health Plan in 1993, but the funding levels per capita vary substantially across the states: New South Wales, Queensland, and Victoria (the three largest states) are below the national average in terms of overall spending per capita (Department of Health and Ageing, 2010).

Funding for nongovernment organizations to provide care in the community to people with serious mental illness has increased since the first National Mental Health Plan in 1993, but it still remains a small proportion of overall mental health-care expenditure (Department of Health and Ageing, 2010). Nongovernment providers offer some types of housing and accommodation, in-home support, and advocacy services. With the exception of the community housing sector, which recently began to explore more diverse options for building affordable housing, state and territory governments provide the majority of the funding for nongovernment mental health service provision (Gilmour & Milligan, 2012).

Types of Housing for Australians with Serious Mental Illness

The first systematic examination of the quality of life of people with serious mental illness in Australia occurred in 1997, with the first national survey of people with psychotic illnesses (Jablensky et al., 1998). Drawing on a representative sample of people with psychotic disorders, the study identified that people with psychosis lived in a variety of places in the 1 month prior to the survey, the most common of which were rented public or private housing (31%) and institutions (20%). Eight percent of the representative sample were homeless or did not have secure tenure (Jablensky et al., 1998). This study also confirmed the high levels of hospital and emergency service use and the prevalence of homelessness among this group (Jablensky et al., 1998).

Since this survey, two significant policy reforms have been implemented, both of which have impacted on the housing available for people with serious mental illness. First, most states and territories have implemented and expanded scattered-site housing programs specifically targeted at this group and, second, the focus of homelessness services has shifted from the provision of temporary accommodation to the provision of permanent housing. These policy changes, and their relevance to housing for people with serious mental illness in Australia, are explored in the following sections.

Recovery-Based Scattered-Site Housing

All state and territorial governments, with the exception of the Northern Territory (Bowden, 2010), now provide scattered-site housing to people with serious mental illness. These programs aim to assist people in their journey of recovery and to prevent people from becoming homeless or entering into hospital prematurely. These programs predominantly operate as partnerships between state-level Departments of Health, which provide funding for clinical care and recovery-based accommodation support, and state-level Housing Departments, which facilitate access to social housing. The housing itself is provided either by the state Housing Departments (i.e., public housing) or by community housing providers. These programs are set up to ensure that housing is provided separately from the accommodation support functions, so if people move or their support needs change, their housing or support is not jeopardized. An overview of the key programs is provided in Table 12.1.

A number of themes can be noted from this overview of scattered-site housing programs. First, approximately half of these programs (Victoria HASP, Queensland HASP, Project 300, Western Australian Individualised Community Living Initiative, South Australia HASPP) operate a Housing First approach by providing immediate access to long-term housing. The other five programs (NSW HASI, NSW Outreach, SA IPRSS, WA Independent Living Project, and Tasmania's rehabilitation packages) place people in social housing when it becomes available.

The second characteristic of these programs is that, while the homes are scattered throughout the community, the housing is predominantly provided by social housing providers. In the Australian context, the term "social housing" refers to housing stock that is managed and owned by both state and territory governments (public rental housing and Indigenous Housing programs) and community housing providers (community housing) (Australian Institute of Health and Welfare, 2010). Social housing continues to be in short supply in Australia due to decades of underinvestment (Berry, 2003). The extent to which these programs can provide a Housing First approach as well as choice for consumers can therefore be limited by the lack of available housing stock (Bullen & Fisher, 2015).

A third characteristic of these programs is their reliance on nongovernment organizations to provide recovery-based support services to mental health consumers in their homes. This sector has also been active since the early 1990s in promoting recovery care in the community (Ramon et al., 2007), and funding for this care is provided by state and territory governments. Recovery is a foundational concept in mental health service provision in Australia more broadly; it signals a shift away from the deficit model of mental illness to one that recognizes the process people go through to learn to live with mental illness with dignity and autonomy (Davidson & Roe, 2007). With the exception of the outreach support provided to people with serious mental illness in NSW, all programs provide support to consumers for as long as it is needed, meaning that the support itself is not time-limited.

Table 12.1 Overview of Scattered-Site Housing Programs in Australia

Program	State	Capacity	Eligibility	Housing	Support
Housing and Accommodation Support Initiative (HASI)	NSW	1,135 people	People with disability resulting from severe mental illness	Consumers are given priority access to permanent social housing	Supports provided are based on a recovery framework; support ranges from 24 hours/day, 7 days per week to 2–3 hours, 1–2 days per week
Housing and Support Program (HASP)	Victoria	1,200 houses	People with disability resulting from severe mental illness	Public housing provided	Support provided by the Home Based Outreach Support Program, which provides support 5 days per week, 52 weeks per year. One-on-one support with daily living and other activities
Outreach support	NSW	655 people	People with mental illness who require a range of support. Run by local area health services, so there is no common program or eligibility criteria	Transitional accommodation provided for 42 people	In-home support that is operated at local health district levels; some people receive only clinical support
Housing and Accommodation Support Partnership Program (HASPP) (South Australia Department of Health, 2008)	South Australia	84 houses	People with mental illness and significant functional impairments, homeless, and connected with Community Mental Health	A range of permanent housing types are provided in metropolitan Adelaide	Support ranges between 24 hours/day, 7 days per week to 15 hours, 2–3 days per week

Program	State	Number	Target population	Housing	Support
Individual Psychosocial Rehabilitation and Support Services (IPRSS) (Health Outcomes International, 2011)	South Australia	936 people	People with severe mental illness and psychiatric disability	Housing is not provided in the program, but assistance to access permanent housing is provided	Partnership program between NGOs and government Mental Health Services. In-home support is based on a philosophy of recovery
Housing and Support Program (HSP) (Meehan, Madson, Shepherd, & Siskind, 2010)	Queensland	194 houses	People unable to leave mental health facilities due to lack of housing and support	Provided with social housing and given priority housing assistance	Support services funded and provided by the Disability and Community Care Services
Project 300 (Edwards, Fisher, Tannous, & Robinson, 2009)	Queensland	40 people per year	Long-term residents of psychiatric hospitals	Provided with social housing	In-home recovery care and support provided by NGOs. Support was approximately 23 hours/week
Individualised Community Living Initiative	Western Australia	150 houses	People with mental illness who are homeless or at risk of homelessness, and are leaving inpatient facilities	Permanent housing provided via social housing providers	Person-centered planning and supports provided by NGOs
Independent Living Program (Mental Health Commission, 2012)	Western Australia	1705 people	People who are homeless, at risk of homelessness, or living in unsuitable accommodation	Linked with a multiplicity of permanent accommodation options	Accommodation support provided by NGOs
Non-Clinical Rehabilitation packages	Tasmania	62 people	People with mental illness requiring support	Not stated	Recovery-based care provided by NGOs

Only three independent evaluations of scattered-site housing programs for people with serious mental illness in Australia have been published: the NSW Housing and Accommodation Support Initiative (Bruce et al., 2012; Muir, Fisher, Abello, & Dadich, 2010), the Queensland Project 300 (Meehan, Stedman, Robertson, Drake, & King, 2011), and the Queensland Housing and Support Program (Meehan et al., 2010).[3] Both the HASI and HAP evaluations found a significant decrease in the number and length of consumers' hospital admissions after joining the program (McDermott et al., 2016; Meehan et al., 2010). All three evaluations found small improvements in consumer functioning, high levels of consumer satisfaction with housing quality and support, and improvements in community participation (Bruce et al., 2012; Meehan et al., 2011). While the evaluations demonstrated mostly positive outcomes for consumers, there remain some concerns about the limited capacity of the programs to assist people with higher needs as well as the lack of availability of long-term housing options (Ombudsman of New South Wales, 2012).

Reforming Homelessness Services

The second set of reforms that have altered the type and availability of housing for people with serious mental illness are those occurring in the homelessness sector. Services specifically targeted at homeless people, or Specialist Homelessness Services emerged in Australia in 1985 to provide short-term accommodation options and other types of support such as financial planning, case management, and drug and alcohol services (Limbrick, 2006).[4] The predominant aim of homelessness service provision was to prepare people for permanent housing; to this end, people were provided with shorter-term housing options and additional support to make people ready to maintain more permanent housing (Bullen, 2011).

In 2008, the Australian government signaled a shift in philosophical foundations of homelessness services. This vision was outlined in *The Road Home*, a White Paper on homelessness, in which the government set high-level targets of reducing overall levels of homelessness, rough sleeping, and homelessness among Aboriginal people across Australia. The system reform outlined in *The Road Home* is multipronged. Its three aims are to prevent people from becoming homeless through the provision of appropriate tenancy support; reform the system so that it is more responsive to people who are homeless or at risk of becoming homeless; and reduce current levels of homelessness through the provision of permanent housing and support (Australian Government, 2008). The government provided matching funds to the states in order to expand provisions of homelessness services and, in addition, provided $6.2 billion in additional housing assistance and investment in social and public housing under the National Affordable Housing Agreement (Australian Government, 2012).

As part of this national vision, state and territory governments have funded an array of new scattered-site and single-site housing programs that are targeted at people who are chronically homeless, many of whom have serious mental illness. Many programs have been implemented only in the last few years, and little information has been published apart from online reports and conference papers. Although not a definitive list of programs, Table 12.2 provides a snapshot of some of the new programs that have emerged since 2009 and provide support to people with serious mental illness who have also been homeless.

Although these programs do not specifically target people with serious mental illness, emerging evidence indicates that mental illness is a common concern among program participants (Johnson, Parkinson, Tseng, & Kuehnle, 2011; Parsell, Jones, & Tomaszewski, 2012). While all programs take a Housing First approach, housing is not technically provided in three of the programs; instead, support is provided to access existing housing stock in the community. Unlike the mental health-funded programs discussed in the previous section, which provide recovery-based services, the philosophy of support services provided in these homelessness programs is often not explicit. More research is needed to understand the type and amount of support that is provided in these models.

Perhaps the most interesting observation is that five Australian states have established organizations that are modeled on the Common Ground model from the United States, which aims to provide chronically homeless people with permanent housing and on-site support, located in a safe, high-density building with a diverse social mix (Haggerty, 2008). The programs provide permanent housing and on-site support for approximately 345 people who have experienced chronic homelessness; approximately half of the housing provided in these buildings is targeted at formerly homeless people, and the other half at low-income residents (Australian Common Ground Alliance, 2012). It is interesting that Common Ground has proliferated in Australia despite the lack of rigorous, independent evaluation analysis of similar models in the United States. Some independent evaluations of these models are underway in Australia, but the findings are not yet publically available.

Discussion

Since the first national survey of people with serious mental illness in Australia, the housing profile of people in this group has changed substantially (Harvey, Killackey, Groves, & Herrman, 2012, p. 845). The second national survey of psychosis in Australia, conducted in 2010, found an 18% drop in the number of people living in institutions, and an 8% drop in the number who were homeless or living in insecure accommodation (Morgan et al., 2012). There was a corresponding increase in people living in rented housing (15% increase), in supported accommodation (6% increase), and in the family home (3% increase). These figures suggest that policy reform has made some impact in improving the housing options for people with serious mental illness in Australia.

Table 12.2 Overview of Scattered-Site and Single-Site Housing Programs Targeting Chronically Homeless Australians

Program	State	Capacity	Target Group	Housing	Support
Way2Home (Parsell, Jones, & Tomaszewski, 2012)	NSW, Queensland	Approximately 200 people in Sydney, unknown in QLD	Vulnerable rough sleepers	Housing First approach; scattered-site permanent social housing sought but is not provided as part of the program	Assertive outreach, including support and peer support workers (provided by NGO); health outreach also provided (hospital-based)
Journey to Social Inclusion (Johnson, Parkinson, Tseng, & Kuehnle, 2011)	Victoria	40 people	Chronically homeless people	Housing First approach; scattered-site permanent social housing sought but is not provided as part of the program	Case management support is provided up to 3 years
Platform70	NSW	70 people	Chronically homeless people	Housing First approach; scattered-site private rental housing is sought for participants	Case management and support provided by Way2Home case managers

Project 40	NSW	60 people	Chronically homeless people	Housing First approach; scattered-site permanent social housing is provided by community housing provider	Support services provided by a range of organizations; case management provided by housing provider
Common Ground	NSW, SA, QLD, VIC, TAS	345 people	Vulnerable, long-term homeless people	Housing First, single-site housing; permanent housing is provided in a purpose-built building operated by a community housing provider, with mix of formerly homeless and low-income residents	Case management and a range of other support services are provided on-site

Even with these improvements, more can be done to ensure that Australians with serious mental illness can access their right to appropriate housing. Particular groups within Australia continue to be highly disadvantaged, none more so than Aboriginal people who, since colonization, have been systematically displaced, dispossessed, and discriminated against (Larson, Gillies, Howard, & Coffin, 2007). Aboriginal people remain culturally and economically disadvantaged, and continue to experience a life expectancy of 10–12 years less than the general Australian population (Parker, 2010; Trewin & Maddison, 2005). As a result of the compounding, cumulative effects of poverty, powerlessness, and disadvantage, this group is at higher risk than the general population of suffering from depression, though experiencing similar rates of schizophrenia and bipolar disorder (McKendrick, 2001). Some programs that specifically take into account the unique cultural heritage of Aboriginal Australians have been implemented, but closing the gap for this group remains an ongoing challenge (Hunter, 2007).

There are, furthermore, eligibility criteria and organizational boundaries that preclude access for people with mental illness from needed services. As a result, some people with mental illness who are well enough to live in the community are being kept in hospital beds because appropriate housing is not available in the community (Ombudsman of New South Wales, 2012). Furthermore, due to continuing deinstitutionalization, there is a growth in people with multiple, high-level needs entering the system, which presents unique challenges for both housing and support providers (Department of Human Services, 2007; Singh & Castle, 2007; Townsend, Pirkis, Pham, Harris, & Whiteford, 2006).

A final challenge regarding the provision of housing for people with serious mental illness is place. Australia is a large landmass with an overall population of 22.3 million; 66% (14.7 million) live in or near capital cities, and only just over 2% live in remote or very remote areas (Australian Bureau of Statistics, 2011). People in rural and regional areas have good access to general practitioners but limited access to specialist mental health services (Parslow & Jorm, 2000). The Better Access to Mental Health Care program, implemented by the Australian government in 2009, provides Medicare funding to allied health providers such as social workers, psychologists, and occupational therapists. It is possible that this will assist with better access for people in regional and rural areas (Bambling et al., 2007; Morley et al., 2007). However, the specialist housing programs reviewed above are predominantly targeted around urban areas, limiting the amount of specialist recovery-based support and support for chronically homeless people in regional and remote areas.

Conclusion

Australia has proceeded with implementing large-scale reform in both the mental health and homelessness systems, which has resulted in changes to the availability of appropriate housing and support for people with serious mental illness. As a result, fewer Australians with mental illness are living in institutions and are homeless than 2 decades ago, and more are receiving access to the housing and support that they need. While Australia has made some progress in ensuring that all Australians can access their right to appropriate housing, more needs to be done to ensure equity for particularly disadvantaged groups, including Aboriginal Australians, people with high support needs, and those in rural and remote areas.

Notes

1. Little has been written in Australia about the income support available to people leaving institutions. It is likely that people with serious mental illness were eligible to receive the Invalid Pension, an income support payment implemented by the Commonwealth Government from 1909 for people with a disability who were permanently unable to work and who met a means and residence test (Daniels, 2011). Although people with mental illness technically qualified for the pension, it is likely that many people had trouble meeting eligibility requirements due to medical officers' focus on the degree to which a person was medically impaired rather than on a person's capacity to work (Kirkwood, 1984). It is also important to note that some groups were excluded from receiving the Invalid Pension, including people with Asian backgrounds (until 1941), Aboriginal Australians (until 1960; nomadic Aboriginal people were excluded until 1966), and other groups of immigrants (until 1966) (Daniels, 2011).

2. In 2012 NSW implemented the Boarding House Act, which requires, among other provisions, that all boarding houses with two or more people with disability be registered; that the premises are to be kept in a reasonable condition; and that landlords are to enter into a written agreement with tenants. So while boarding house tenants still do not have the same rights as tenants in private rental accommodation, the situation is improving. The situation does, however, vary depending on the state.

3. None of these studies used an experimental or quasi-experimental method, so the results should be treated with caution. The HASI evaluation used longitudinal administrative data collected over a 10-year period to understand changes in hospital service use and mental health scores before and during the program; the Queensland HAP evaluation was able to access longitudinal information and consumer functioning before and during consumer involvement in HAP; Project 300 collected data from consumers at 6 weeks prior to entering the program, and then at 6, 18, 36, and 48 months after being discharged from hospital.

4. Specialist Homelessness Services in Australia were formerly known as the Supported Accommodation Assistance Program, or SAAP.

References

Andrews, G., J., Teeson, M., Stewart, G., & Hoult, J. (1990). Follow up of community placement of the chronic mentally ill in New South Wales. *Hospital and Community Psychiatry, 41,* 184–188.

Australian Bureau of Statistics. (2011). *Regional population growth, Australia, no. 3218.0.* Canberra: Australian Bureau of Statistics.

Australian Common Ground Alliance. (2012). *About Common Ground: State by state.* Retrieved December 10, 2012, from http://www.commongroundaustralia.org.au/index.php/state-by-state.html

Australian Government. (1994). *The First National Mental Health Report 1993*. Canberra: Commonwealth of Australia.

Australian Government. (2008). *The road home: A national approach to reducing homelessness—An Australian government white paper*. Canberra: Australian Government.

Australian Government. (2012). *National affordable housing agreement*. Canberra: Australian Government.

Australian Institute of Health and Welfare. (2010). *A profile of social housing in Australia Cat. No. HOU 232*. Canberra: Australian Government.

Australian Institute of Health and Welfare. (2012). *Mental health services in Australia—Residential mental health care*. Canberra: Author.

Australian Institute of Health and Welfare. (2014). *Health expenditure Australia 2012–2013 CAT. no. HWE 61*. Canberra: Author.

Bambling, M., Kavanagh, D., Lewis, G., King, R., King, D., Sturk, H., . . . Bartlett, H. (2007). Challenges faced by general practitioners and allied mental health services in providing mental health services in rural Queensland. *Australian Journal of Rural Health, 15*, 126–130. doi: 10.1111/j.1440-1584.2007.00866.x

Battams, S., & Baum, F. (2010). What policies and policy processes are needed to ensure that people with psychiatric disabilities have access to appropriate housing? *Social Science and Medicine, 70*, 1026–1034.

Berry, M. (2003). Why is it important to boost the supply of affordable housing in Australia—and how can we do it? *Urban Policy and Research, 21*, 413–435.

Biggs, A. (2003). *Medicare—Background brief*. Canberra: Parliament of Australia.

Bowden, J. (2010). *A report on housing and support for people with a psychiatric disability living in Alice Springs*. Alice Springs: Mental Health Association of Central Australia.

Bruce, J., McDermott, S., Ramia, I., Bullen, J., Fisher, K. R., & ARTD Consultants. (2012). *Evaluation of the Housing and Accommodation Support Initiative (HASI)*. Sydney: Social Policy Research Centre.

Bullen, J. (2011). Where does Street to Home fit within past and present homelessness and housing policy settings? *Parity, 24*(1), 9.

Bullen, J., & Fisher, K. R. (2015). Is Housing First for mental health community support possible during a housing shortage? *Social Policy and Administration, 49*, 928–945, doi: 10.1111/spol.12104.

Burdekin, B. (1993). *Human rights and mental illness: Report of the national inquiry into the human rights of people with mental illness*. Canberra: Human Rights and Equal Opportunity Commission, Australian Government.

Carmody, D. (2008). *Boarding houses, owners and tenants: The demise of an old form of working-class housing*. (Masters of Philosophy), Australian Catholic University, Melbourne. Retrieved from http://dlibrary.acu.edu.au/digitaltheses/public/adt-acuvp246.21012011/02whole.pdf

Commonwealth of Australia. (1992). *National mental health policy*. Canberra: Commonwealth of Australia.

Commonwealth of Australia. (2009). *National mental health policy 2008*. Canberra: Commonwealth of Australia.

Commonwealth of Australia. (2012). *Mental health statement of rights and responsibilities*. Canberra: Australian Government. Retrieved from http://www.health.gov.au/internet/main/publishing.nsf/Content/E39137B3C170F93ECA257CBC007CFC8C/$File/rights2.pdf

Daniels, D. (2011). *Social security payments for the aged, people with disabilities and their carers 1901–2010*. Canberra: Parliament of Australia.

Davidson, L., & Roe, D. (2007). Recovery from versus recovery in serious mental illness: One strategy for lessening confusion plaguing recovery. *Journal of Mental Health, 16*, 459–470.

Department of Health and Ageing. (2010). *National mental health report 2010: Summary of 15 years of reform in Australia's mental health services under the national mental health strategy, 1993–2008*. Canberra: Commonwealth of Australia.

Department of Human Services. (2007). *An analysis of the Victorian rehabilitation and recovery care service system for people with severe mental illness and associated disability*. Melbourne: Victorian Department of Human Services.

Doessel, D. P. (2009). A historical perspective on mental health services in Australia: 1883–84 to 2003–04. *Australian Economic History Review, 49*, 173–197. doi: 10.1111/j.1467-8446.2009.00254.x

Drake, G. (2010). *The privatisation of the back wards: The accommodation of people with intellectual disability and people with mental illness in licensed boarding houses in Sydney*. (PhD), Curtin University, Perth.

Edwards, R., Fisher, K.R., Tannous, K., & Robinson, S. (2009). *Housing and associated support for people with mental illness or psychiatric disability*. SPRC Report 04/09. Sydney: Social Policy Research Centre.

Gilmour, T., & Milligan, V. (2012). Let a hundred flowers bloom: Innovation and diversity in Australian not-for-profit housing organisations. *Housing Studies, 27*, 476–494.

Greenhalgh, E., Miller, A., Minnery, J., Gurran, N., Jacobs, K., & Phibbs, P. (2004). *Boarding houses: Government supply side intervention*. Brisbane: AHURI Final Report No 54.

Haggerty, R. (2008). Common Ground: Ending homelessness, one person at a time. *Parity, 21*(2), 39.

Harvey, C., Killackey, E., Groves, A., & Herrman, H. (2012). A place to live: Housing needs for people with psychotic disorder identified in the second Australian national survey of psychosis. *Australian and New Zealand Journal of Psychiatry, 46*, 840–850. doi: 10.1177/0004867412449301

Health Outcomes International. (2011). *Evaluation of the individual psychosocial rehabilitation and support services program*. Adelaide: South Australia Health.

Hunter, E. (2007). Disadvantage and discontent: A review of issues relevant to the mental health of rural and remote Indigenous Australians. *Australian Journal of Rural Health, 15*(2), 88–93. doi: 10.1111/j.1440-1584.2007.00869.x

Jablensky, A., McGrath, J., Herman, H., Castle, D., Gureje, O., Morgan, V., & Korten, A. (1998). *People living with psychotic illness: An Australian study 1997–1998*. Canberra: Commonwealth of Australia.

Johnson, G., Parkinson, S., Tseng, Y.-P., & Kuehnle, D. (2011). *Long-term homelessness: Understanding the challenge—2 months outcomes from the Journey to Social Inclusion pilot program*. St. Kilda: Sacred Heart Mission.

Kirkwood, J. (1984). Medical Assessments for the Invalid Pension. *Legal Service Bulletin, 9*, 32.

Larson, A., Gillies, M., Howard, P. J., & Coffin, J. (2007). It's enough to make you sick: The impact of racism on the health of Aboriginal Australians. *Australian and New Zealand Journal of Public Health, 31*, 322–329. doi: 10.1111/j.1753-6405.2007.00079.x

Limbrick, D. (2006). Some reflections on the SAAP and homelessness in Australia. *Parity, 19*(10), 4.

McDermott, S., Bruce. J., Muir, K., Ramia, I., Fisher, K.R., & Bullen, J. (2016) Reducing hospitalization among people living with severe mental illness. *Australian Health Review, 40*, 124–128, doi: http://dx.doi.org/10.1071/AH15073.

McKendrick, J. (Ed.). (2001). *The mental health of Australia's Indigenous populations*. Melbourne: Oxford University Press.

Meehan, T., Stedman, T., Robertson, S., Drake, S., & King, R. (2011). Does supported accommodation improve the clinical and social outcomes for people with severe psychiatric disability? The Project 300 experience. *Australian and New Zealand Journal of Psychiatry, 45*, 586–592.

Meehan, T. J., Madson, K., Shepherd, N., & Siskind, D. (2010). *Final evaluation report of the Queensland Government's Housing and Support Program*. Warcol: Queensland Government.

Mental Health Commission. (2012). *2011/12 Annual Report*. Perth: Government of Western Australia.

Morgan, V. A., Waterreus, A., Jablensky, A., Mackinnon, A., McGrath, J. J., Carr, V., ... Saw, S. (2012). People living with psychotic illness in 2010: The second Australian national survey of psychosis. *Australian and New Zealand Journal of Psychiatry, 46*, 735–752. doi: 10.1177/0004867412449877

Morley, B., Pirkis, J., Naccarella, L., Kohn, F., Blashki, G., & Burgess, P. (2007). Improving access to and outcomes from mental health care in rural Australia. *Australian Journal of Rural Health, 15*, 304–312. doi: 10.1111/j.1440-1584.2007.00905.x

Muir, K., Fisher, K. R., Abello, D., & Dadich, A. (2010). "I didn't like just sittin'around all day": Facilitating social and community participation among people with mental illness and high levels of psychiatric disability. *Journal of Social Policy, 39*, 375–391.

Ombudsman of New South Wales. (2012). *Denial of rights: The need to improve accommodation and support for people with psychiatric disability.* Sydney: Author.

Parker, R. (2010). Australia's Aboriginal population and mental health. *Journal of Nervous and Mental Disease, 198*(1), 3–7.

Parsell, C., Jones, A., & Tomaszewski, W. (2012). *Service users: A baseline report on Sydney's Way2Home program.* Brisbane: Institute for Social Science Research, University of Queensland.

Parslow, R. A., & Jorm, A. F. (2000). Who uses mental health services in Australia? An analysis of data from the National Survey of Mental Health and Wellbeing. *Australian and New Zealand Journal of Psychiatry, 34*, 997–1008. doi: 10.1046/j.1440-1614.2000.00839.x

Ramon, S., Healy, B., & Renouf, N. (2007). Recovery from mental illness as an emergent concept and practice in Australia and the UK. *International Journal of Social Psychiatry, 53*, 108–122. doi: 10.1177/0020764006075018

Richmond, D. (1983). *The Richmond Report: Inquiry into health services for the psychiatrically ill and developmentally disabled.* Sydney: NSW Department of Health.

Richmond, K., & Savy, P. (2005). In sight, in mind: Mental health policy in the era of deinstitution-alisation. *Health Sociology Review, 14*, 215–229. doi: 10.5172/hesr.14.3.215

Rosen, A. (2006). The Australian experience of deinstitutionalization: Interaction of Australian culture with the development and reform of its mental health services. *Acta Psychiatrica Scandinavica, 113*, 81–89.

Shea, P. B. (1999). *Defining madness.* Sydney: Hawkins Press.

Singh, B., Benson, A., Weir, W., Rosen, A., & Ash, D. (Eds.). (2001). *The rise and fall of the institution in Australia.* Melbourne: Oxford University Press.

Singh, B. S., & Castle, D. J. (2007). Why are community psychiatry services in Australia doing it so hard? *Medical Journal of Australia, 187*, 410.

South Australia Department of Health. (2008). *A review of community mental health services in South Australia.* Adelaide: South Australian Government.

Townsend, C. E., Pirkis, J. E., Pham, A. T. N., Harris, M. G., & Whiteford, H. A. (2006). Stakeholder concerns about Australia's mental health care system. *Australian Health Review, 30*, 158–163. doi: http://dx.doi.org/10.1071/AH060158

Trewin, D., & Maddison, R. (2005). *The health and welfare of Australia's Aboriginal and Torres Strait Islander Peoples.* Canberra: Australian Bureau of Statistics; Australian Institute of Health and Welfare.

Whiteford, H. A., & Buckingham, W. J. (2005). Ten years of mental health service reform in Australia: Are we getting it right? *Medical Journal of Australia, 182*, 396–400.

Willis, E., Reynolds, L., & Helen, K. (2009). *Understanding the Australian health care system.* Sydney: Elsevier.

SECTION IV

VIEWS FROM THE FRONTLINE

13

Tenants' Reflections on Housing

KEN WIREMAN

Housing that would work for me cannot include some of the trappings of my past living arrangements. At the very least, I need a key to my home and enjoy the rights and responsibilities afforded any rent paying tenant. I need to have my own apartment or my own private bedroom with only a few roommates. My home needs to be a place I can call my own, a place where I have ownership of my responsibilities of living independently. Where I get my mental health services should not depend on where I live. I'm talking about permanent, affordable, safe, and comfortable housing where I can live independently and focus on my health issues.
—Excerpts from On Our Own Maryland Summer Conference (Wireman, 2012)

Though much has been written about housing for people with psychiatric disabilities, understanding how someone with a mental health disability sees housing is relatively simple at its core. What consumers want from their housing is simply the same as for anyone else in the community. The one difference is the availability of mental health services that they choose. It is notable that the title of this chapter is "tenants' reflections," rather than "patients' reflections" or even "consumers' reflections." The focus on tenancy reflects a fundamental shift in how we are looking at housing for people with mental health needs. This shift is the result of almost a half-century of progress from institutional care toward true community integration. And importantly, including the consumer's perspective in this book, written by a consumer, is still in many circles novel and unique.

The statement at the outset of this chapter comes from a consumer of mental health services participating at a forum on the future of housing for persons with psychiatric disabilities. This forum took place at one of North America's most successful conferences for consumers, hosted by Maryland's statewide consumer-run organization, On Our Own of Maryland, Inc. (OOOMD). Each year, this conference brings together approximately 400 consumers from across the state to learn about wellness activities, the state of affairs in the mental health service delivery system, peer support, and any other innovative consumer-run programming.

Importantly, this conference honors leaders in Maryland and throughout the United States in their efforts to help consumers lead better lives focused on recovery. Uniquely, OOOMD has a subsidiary housing development corporation, Main Street Housing, Inc. (MSH). I founded MSH in 1999 and have been its executive director since then. Main Street Housing provides affordable, independent, rental housing for people with psychiatric disabilities, across the state of Maryland. It purchases good quality properties across the state to provide permanent rental housing for individuals and families. One of our guiding principles is supportive accountability, which means establishing clear expectations for tenants' rights and responsibilities, but also providing support to meet those expectations.

This chapter is informed by my experiences and those of my colleagues and our tenants at MSH. I highlight the emergence and significance of MSH by discussing it in the context of what is commonly called the consumer/survivor movement. I begin by outlining the progression and movement of housing for people with mental health needs from institutions to the community, and also examine how policy at a national level has shifted from promoting an institutional/maintenance system of care to a system that is working to embrace the delivery of consumer-centered/directed services. This means services that are provided, minimally, with input from consumers, and in growing cases such as MSH, services that are actually directed by people who have faced the same challenges as those receiving the services.

The chapter is also informed by the recognition that, however far we have come, there is much distance to travel. The US Supreme Court's 1999 decision concerning the Americans with Disabilities Act, typically titled the *Olmstead* decision, stipulated that less restrictive community alternatives were preferred over institutional options. This Supreme Court decision led to the movement of thousands of residents in adult care homes with serious mental illness into community housing. Yet, as recently as 2014, the state of New York "agreed in July to settle a decade-long lawsuit allowing up to 4,000 individuals with mental illness to move out of adult group homes and into their own apartments" (Levin, 2014).

Further, a recent lawsuit against the state of North Carolina resulted in the North Carolina Department of Health and Human Services releasing a plan to provide an additional 3,000 beds for more independent housing. Similar steps have been taken in recent years in Florida; Mississippi; Texas; Washington, DC; Alabama; Pennsylvania; Rhode Island; and other states. These lawsuits were brought against these states for failing to comply with the *Olmstead* decision over a decade after the *Olmstead* decision was made.[1] Throughout North America, it may be the right of people with mental health disabilities to live in the least restrictive setting, but it has taken a multitude of lawsuits for people with lived experience to have the chance at living a more independent life in the community. In towns up and down the New Jersey shores, there remain flophouse board-and-care facilities that sprang up when Bedlam in New York mass discharged over 60% of its residents in a 2-year period during the 1970s. From the perspective of consumers, this history is still felt.

A progressive move to the community for consumers did not happen successfully over the past 50–60 years. For many consumers, this fight continues.

The Consumer Movement and On Our Own Maryland

The consumer movement has its roots in the mass deinstitutionalization from psychiatric hospitals during the 1960s and early 1970s in North America. The beginnings of the modern consumer movement are rooted in a shift in public policy that moved consumers from institutional settings to the community. Until this time, institutional care had been the standard for housing persons with psychiatric disabilities. The movement was initiated by people who were discharged from these hospitals but who recognized how they were denied basic rights while in the institutions and access to the support and opportunities they needed to live as citizens once they were discharged. These activists worked together to fight for change in how they and others like them had been treated. Consumers would form groups that met regularly, often in basements of churches or people's homes. These groups acted as what we know today as peer support groups (Frese & Davis, 1997). During the early 1960s and 1970s sit-ins were a common type of activity that challenged the traditional mental health hospitals.

One of the early leaders in the consumer movement, Joseph Rogers, chained himself to Philadelphia State Hospital's gates to protest the inhumane treatment there and to demand that it be closed. Mr. Rogers and other consumers got their message across. In 1987, the decision to close Philadelphia State Hospital in Pennsylvania was made, and in 1989 its doors were closed forever (Webster, 2013). Another early pioneer of the consumer movement, Judi Chamberlin, wrote the book *On Our Own* (Chamberlin, 1977), from which the organization where I work was named. The book focuses on consumer-run alternatives to the traditional mental health services of her time. Although she has passed away, her contribution to the consumer movement and her ability to give voice to persons with lived experience continues to reverberate throughout the consumer movement today in North America and throughout the world. What began as a cry for rights and fair treatment has become a movement to improve traditional mental health services and work to provide consumer-run alternative services such as drop-in centers, fellow consumers providing peer support, and in fact MSH. Throughout MSH's history, we have regularly received calls from throughout the country asking questions about our operations. Many times, these calls resulted from Judi Chamberlin talking about our program.

Gradually, the consumer movement shifted its focus from outcries against the system of care that had done its members damage to a movement that sought to provide alternatives and to provide input to work on changing these systems. Importantly, one of the first alternatives that a group of consumers in New York came up with was called Fountain House. It began as an excellent example of a consumer-run program. It evolved into what is currently called the clubhouse model (Mandiberg & Warner, 2013). Another important creation wrought from the consumer movement is Wellness and Recovery Action Planning (WRAP), founded by Mary Ellen Copeland (2002). This is a consumer self-directed plan for wellness, and has reached the level of an evidence-based practice (SAMHSA, n.d.). Peer-led groups have become increasingly popular within the traditional mental health delivery system. Providers have seen the immense value in hiring peers to help the consumers who are served at their organization. In Maryland, there has been a conscious effort to ensure that the state hospitals have peer support specialists in place. Such a presence diminishes the stigma attached to being a patient in an inpatient hospital bed and gives people hope after talking with someone who has experienced what they are going through.

At this same time, in the United States, the National Institute of Mental Health created the Community Support Program (CSP; McLean, 2003). By 1984, CSP had adopted several of the consumer movement's beliefs to include "self-determination" and "consumer empowerment" (McLean, 2003). In essence, there had been a shift from a consumer movement that came about as a result of major policy change to a consumer movement that was gaining influence in decision-making at federal policy levels. Through the work of early pioneers in the consumer movement by people such as Joseph Rogers, Daniel Fisher, Judi Chamberlin, Michael Finkle, and others, the consumer voice began to be heard. In the early days of the movement these were angry voices shouting at the system of care that many thought did more harm than good. Yet, as time progressed, consumers fought to gain a seat at the table and to voice an opinion from a consumer's perspective. This has progressed such that when US President George W. Bush created the President's New Freedom Commission on Mental Health, Dr. Daniel Fisher, a psychiatrist with lived experience was appointed to be a member. The Commission's report (New Freedom Commission on Mental Health, 2003) spoke of system transformation and encouraged developing systems of care focused on mental health recovery rather than simply the historical medical model of care.

During the 1980s, there was a move to fund the alternative services that were being developed by consumer groups. Since that time, funding for consumer-run services has expanded throughout the United States (Van Tosh & del Vecchio, 2000). The expansion of these groups and services led to the dramatic increase in the presence and credibility of consumers in development of policy at the state level (Van Tosh, Ralph, & Campbell, 2000). This presence, and the effectiveness of this voice, reinforced the belief that persons with psychiatric disabilities can recover from mental illness and become prominent players in the service delivery world.

Among the sectors that were greatly influenced by these developments was community-based housing. In Maryland, as well as throughout the United States, there was a dramatic shift from the development of large group homes, considered by many to be mini-institutions, to smaller residential settings. A particular turning point was after Paul Carling's landmark book *Return to Community*: Building Support Systems for People with Psychiatric Disabilities (1995) was published. Carling as well as others, such as William Anthony, were professing that it is not enough to leave state mental institutions and be maintained in the community, but rather that an integrated life in the community was the impetus. Importantly, studies show that more independent housing helped people remain stably housed (for a review, see chapter 2, this volume). Independent housing is much less expensive than group homes and other more restrictive residential settings (see chapter 4, this volume). As with deinstitutionalization, the marriage of the idea of greater independence with budgetary constraints was again present and positioned many people to move to more independent settings.

By then, the mantras of "empowerment" and "recovery" had taken on significant importance in policy and program development. Evidence of the impact of these concepts in the United States was the introduction of a federal mandate through the Substance Abuse and Mental Health Service Administration (SAMHSA) that consumers be involved in policy and program development (Van Tosh & del Vecchio, 2000; Van Tosh, Ralph, & Campbell, 2000).

On Our Own Maryland

In existence since 1992, On Our Own Maryland (OOOMD) is Maryland's statewide consumer organization that is dedicated to advocacy and education that works to change and improve the mental health system in Maryland. Composed of persons who have experienced mental illness, it is an organization that understands and embraces a belief in mental health recovery, and takes steps to enhance the chances of true recovery for Marylanders who have psychiatric disabilities. It is an outgrowth of several consumer organizations that came into existence as an alternative to traditional mental health services. At the time, each of the local On Our Own organizations operated drop-in centers, where consumers ran the organization as a place where fellow consumers could come to share their experiences and be around other consumers who were involved in bettering their lives and sharing their experiences with others who had gone through similar life experiences.

As OOOMD grew and became more involved in systems change, it took part in one of the first state-level class action suits against the State of Maryland in an effort to forward the rights of individuals confined to Maryland's state psychiatric hospitals. The work of OOOMD has traditionally been focused on the rights of fellow consumers both in the hospital and in the community. The OOOMD has worked to change laws and toward creating a level playing field where consumers have a say in their lives through self-advocacy and statewide advocacy in order to ensure that the mental health system is well funded and driven by the need to help consumers recover. The OOOMD works each year to ensure that state laws are enacted in such a way as to protect the rights of consumers and fund programs that help consumers' recovery.

The OOOMD worked tirelessly to ensure that a consumer-run organization was operational in every county throughout Maryland. These local consumer organizations worked to better the lives of the folks who attended their programs, and worked to help change regulation and service delivery at the local level. Currently in Maryland there are 18 consumer-operated organizations affiliated with OOOMD that engage fellow consumers in wellness and recovery activities to help people lead fuller lives and integrate into the community. The OOOMD provides everything from groups that allow a platform for consumers to tell their story, to activities that enhance their chance to lead a full life. In that light, in the late 1990s, Maryland's Mental Hygiene Administration saw fit to support OOOMD's move to make efforts to change the way housing is delivered. At that time an important shift to "supported housing" began to occur (Carling, 1995), from a programmatically-based residential housing model, where mental health services and housing are linked and are provided through a traditional mental health provider, to a model of more independent housing that seeks to provide a fundamentally sound basis for the person to recover and lead a fulfilling and integrated life in the community. The OOOMD's beliefs in these principals led to the funding and eventual existence of MSH.

Main Street Housing

Main Street Housing is a consumer-run housing organization that purchases property and rents to persons with psychiatric disabilities. Founded in 1999 and incorporated in 2001, MSH owns 31 properties that provide housing for 94 tenants. Our organization emphasizes many of the principles of a Housing First approach, including seeing housing as a fundamental right and that there should be no preconditions to acquiring housing (Tsemberis, 2010). However, our approach emphasizes peer support in the service of tenancy, rather than therapeutic goals. Our approach is informed by the history of the consumer movement, which emphasizes a respect for autonomy and choice, a focus on human rights, and peer support. In the following sections I outline our approach and some of our successes.

An Emphasis on Normal Housing

A central assumption at MSH is that our behavior and our conception of ourselves are intrinsically tied to our environments. In essence, whereas institutional settings beget institutional behavior, independent and empowering settings beget independence and self-determination. Some forms of housing, by virtue of size and regulations of behavior are clearly institutional. Such settings deny residents real choice, real freedom, and the ability to integrate into the surrounding community. The characteristics of an institutional setting can be present in settings with even few residents when there is a strong presence and requirement to use services, the regulation of behavior through restrictive rules, and features that prevent the property from fitting into the neighborhood or from providing the residents with their own autonomy. Such settings promote passivity, listening, and following instruction irrespective of personal wishes or desires, and a general sense of apathy and nonbelonging in the community.

It is not hard for a community to discern an institutional setting. There are "visitors" that come to the property, oftentimes never knocking on doors to gain entrance but instead walking right in or opening the door with their own key. Such "give aways" influence how the residents in the community are perceived and how they feel about interacting with the neighbors. When it becomes obvious to the community that the residents are not acting independently, it makes it almost impossible for the resident to assimilate. It is analogous to a mother who attends their child's high school dance and wonders why no one is dancing with their child.

In contrast, when a house or apartment has only one or two residents in a unit, the community does not see this as an anomaly. Importantly, this kind of housing is no different from any other rental in the community. As such, the residents have the ability to feel comfortable getting to know their neighbors. Residents are seen as any other renter in the community, which allows the resident more easily to take on the role of neighbor. It is far more desirable to introduce oneself as a tenant in the community rather than a resident in a program. Importantly, as a resident of independent housing, the activities of the property are not different from the surrounding properties. The resident has the ability to be someone who is independently living in the community, shopping at the local grocery store, taking walks to a nearby park, inviting friends over to their home, and other activities that are normalizing. Not only does this change the perception of others in the community, but importantly, the resident begins to make actual integration and begins to see themselves as a bonafide member of the community with all of its benefits and responsibilities.

Supporting Recovery and Community Integration

An important aspect of MSH's endeavor to help people become real members of the community involves our expectations. One major difference between MSH and traditional mental health providers who offer housing is that we have high expectations of our tenants. We expect the tenants of MSH to fulfill all the requirements of tenancy as would anyone else in the community. As a consumer-operated organization, we understand that these expectations are not unrealistic. Importantly, we believe that having high expectations makes a difference in the lives of the people we serve. It is clear that if we have low expectations, so will our tenants for themselves. Moreover, the staff of MSH has a greater litmus test than simply high expectations. The tenants of MSH understand that the staff members have been through the very same struggles, both with mental health and housing alike. Such an understanding many times can provide hope for an individual who may not feel that they can accomplish independent living. Leading by example is more than a mantra at MSH, it is an axiom.

Our Housing and Support Approach

The MSH approach separates housing and mental health services with the goals of removing barriers for consumers to move into regular housing and empowering them as tenants. Peer support provided to consumers as tenants is key ingredient to accomplishing these goals.

Support for Tenancy, Not Treatment

Perhaps the greatest difference that MSH exemplifies is that there is no mental health service requirement for MSH tenants. It is not part of the lease the tenant holds with MSH, nor is the expectation of MSH's staff to have any level of control regarding what mental health services, if any, the tenant chooses to receive from mental health providers in the community. This represents an entire paradigm shift from traditional thought and practice. The MSH staff members do not provide any mental health services. We offer support during times when a tenant may need support in selecting a community mental health provider, but we do not force treatment on any of MSH's tenants. Nevertheless, MSH staff members are very knowledgeable about what mental health services are available in the community, and during regular inspections, peer support in a limited fashion occurs. It is limited to peer support in the service of the resident's tenancy only focused on three basic issues: paying rent on time, keeping the unit in good order, and being a good neighbor. We do not provide in-depth peer support for any issue whatsoever, as we believe that MSH staff function first and foremost as the tenant's landlord; albeit a benevolent landlord that goes above and beyond the call when the tenant is having difficulty.

Some may have predicted that providing housing without any service requirement at all would lead to failures for tenants. However, the average length of stay of a MSH tenant is over 4 years. This supports MSH's belief that recovery does not happen in a vacuum. People do not get well and recover without a reason to do so.

Reducing Barriers to Housing

Historically, people with mental health issues have been told over and over: *"When your mental health symptoms subside, it will be time for you to get a job, a significant other, live independently, etc."* In reality, people in general do not operate that way. Real rewards come from our own accomplishments. They are not granted by others because we have met their goals for us. Whether it is going to college, becoming involved in a relationship, getting a job, or keeping housing, we cannot wait until we are deemed a better person by somebody else to be rewarded. We must stand to meet the challenge and become better for working through it.

In the vocational rehabilitation world, this concept has been shown through research. Historically, job readiness training has been the benchmark of preparation for a person with a disability to get a job. Paradoxically, numerous studies show that direct placement in work settings with appropriate support produces the best employment outcomes (Campbell, Bond, & Drake, 2011).

We believe this also applies to housing. There is ongoing discussion regarding "readiness" for independent housing. At MSH we have regularly accepted applicants directly from an inpatient psychiatric facility despite the hospital's staff feeling that the person should reside in a group home or live in a service provider's housing.

Our Successes

For the past 15 years, MSH has continued to be an example of what is possible. It is housing that is not service-linked, nor is it based on the notion that housing should come first and then the person should have services wrapped around them. It is housing that is based on the simple belief that people with mental health issues deserve housing that is no different from anyone else in the community. As a consumer-operated organization, MSH has purchased over six million dollars worth of housing and has offered these units to fellow consumers throughout Maryland with great success. We offer the opportunity for real community integration through a genuine tenant role. Each person residing in MSH holds their own lease, which comes with the rights and responsibilities that everyone who has ever rented an apartment or house has experienced.

Main Street Housing is an important testament to the belief that it is not sufficient to "sit around on a sofa and be symptom free." People need a reason to be, to exist, something to strive for and achieve. Being symptom free rarely happens anyway. What keeps a person going? It is having a goal and some hope, a direction in which to head, a way to make sense of the world. Main Street Housing has developed a program that provides a platform for true recovery. A platform from which a person can rightfully say, "I am a part of the community. I have responsibility I need to attend to. I am a good neighbor. I have a life."

Reflecting on Where We Have Been and Where We Are Going

Main Street Housing was developed by OOOMD, a statewide consumer-operated organization that was an outgrowth of the consumer movement—a movement that has been and still is involved in furthering the rights of those who have mental illness. Moreover, it is a movement striving to help fellow consumers through advocacy, education, systems change initiatives, and creating services that further their recovery. As such, MSH works to promote the well-being of the consumers we serve, and more importantly stands as an example of what is possible. In just over 50 years, people with mental illness have gone from being shut away in institutions to being given the chance at living in the community as full citizens. Main Street Housing is contributing to this struggle to reform our systems of care and support people with mental illness to live more hopeful and fulfilling lives, to be treated with respect and dignity, and to enjoy their rights and meet their responsibilities in society.

Achieving these goals starts and ends with where a person lives. If a person resides in an institution, that person will become an institutionalized patient. If a person lives in a group home, that person will be inclined to lead a life as a second-rate citizen. If a person lives in the community like everyone else, that person has the chance of living a fulfilling life; one that has community at the forefront and that includes being a neighbor, a friend, and a responsible and productive person in the community. We see it at MSH every day. We see it in the lives of the tenants, the change that it has made in the mental health system of care, the difference it makes to those who work in the system to see the people they serve moving forward, the way that people's beliefs change in the communities where we have our properties.

We have never experienced NIMBYism in its most serious form. No one has ever lived or owned a property beside one of MSH's properties and reported to us that they have "had enough." In fact, we regularly interface with neighbors of the properties we own, and the reports are consistent. We hear, "I never knew folks with mental illness could do this," "He is a good neighbor," and similar comments that indicate acceptance. Main Street Housing is raising the bar and moving the ball down the field. We have worked to change the lives of the folks we serve, and in doing so, we have seen movement in the system of care and the beliefs that people have about persons with mental illness.

Regretfully, MSH is only one organization. Although we are embraced with open arms from the systems of care that fund us, further development of similar housing is needed. Mental health administrations need to continue to put forth the belief that though housing and services should be separate, housing is a critical and important part of a person's recovery. In doing so, more efforts can be made to produce more housing similar to that of MSH: housing for housing's sake. At a time when there has been a great backlash from other advocates who would see a return to more hospitalizations and forced treatment, we need to stand fast to the belief that people can and do recover from mental health issues. We will continue to try, and hope that MSH stands as an example of what is possible in the lives of people with mental health needs.

Note

1. A full account of the *Olmstead* decision, and the laws that have been enacted can be found at the website of the United States Department of Justice, Civil Rights Division (http://www.ada.gov/olmstead/index.htm).

References

Campbell, K., Bond, G.R., & Drake, R.E. (2011). Who benefits from supported employment? A meta-analytic study. *Schizophrenia Bulletin, 37*, 370–380.

Carling, P.J. (1995). Return to Community: Building Support Systems for People with Psychiatric Disabilities. New York, NY: Guilford Press.

Chamberlin, J. (1977). *On Our Own: Patient-controlled alternatives to the mental health system.* Lawrence, MA: National Empowerment Center, Inc.

Copeland, M.E. (2002). Wellness recovery action plan. *Occupational Therapy in Mental Health, 17*, 127–150.

Frese, K., & Davis, W.W. (1997). The consumer-survivor movement, recovery, and consumer professionals. *Professional Psychology: Research and Practice, 28*, 243–245.

Levin, A. (2014, October 10). Settlement will move thousands to community housing. *Psychiatric News.* http://psychnews.psychiatryonline.org/doi/full/10.1176/appi.pn.2013.9a27

Mandiberg, J.M., & Warner, R. (2013). Is mainstreaming always the answer? The social and economic development of service user communities. *The Psychiatrist, 37*, 153–155. doi: 10.1192/pb.bp.112.040659

McLean, A. (2003). Recovering consumers and a broken mental health system in the United States: Ongoing challenges for consumers/survivors and the New Freedom Commission on Mental Health: Part I. Legitimization of the consumer movement and obstacles to it. *International Journal of Psychosocial Rehabilitation, 8*, 47–57. http://www.psychosocial.com/IJPR_8/Recovering-McLean.html

New Freedom Commission on Mental Health. (2003). *Achieving the promise: Transforming mental health care in America. Final Report.* Washington, DC. Department of Health and Human Services. Available at http://govinfo.library.unt.edu/mentalhealthcommission/reports/reports.htm

Substance Abuse and Mental Health Services Administration. (n.d.). http://nrepp.samhsa.gov/ViewIntervention.aspx?id=208

Tsemberis, S. (2010). *Housing First: The Pathways model to end homelessness for people with mental illness and addiction.* Center City, MN: Hazelden.

Van Tosh, L., & del Vecchio, P. (2000). *Consumer-operated self-help programs: A technical report.* Rockville, MD: US Center for Mental Health Services. http://akmhcweb.org/Docs/selfhelp.pdf

Van Tosh, L., Ralph, R.O., & Campbell, J. (2000). The rise of consumerism. *Psychiatric Rehabilitation Skills, 4*, 383–409.

Webster, J.R. (2013). *The Philadelphia State Hospital at Byberry: A history of misery and medicine.* Mount Pleasant, SC: History Press.

Wireman, K. (2012). Notes from a workshop at the On Our Own of Maryland Summer Conference, Rocky Gap, MD.

14

Reflections on Providing Single-Site Supportive Housing

LORRAINE BENTLEY AND JOHN SYLVESTRE

Since deinstitutionalization, a variety of approaches to housing people with serious mental illness have been advanced. This chapter builds on the 15 years of experience of the first author in the provision of single-site supportive housing by Options Bytown Non Profit Housing Corporation and as a member of the Ottawa Supportive Housing Network in Ottawa, Ontario. The chapter covers a range of issues, including a description of this approach to housing and a dispelling of some misunderstandings about it. The chapter also highlights the everyday issues that are associated with providing housing and offers some suggestions for improving practice.

Understanding Single-Site Supportive Housing

In this section, we begin by examining what we mean by single-site supportive housing. In keeping with the terms adopted for this book, we use the term "single-site supportive housing" to refer to housing in which people with a variety of challenges in maintaining their housing live in a single building within which is also located professional support. We restrict the use of the term to those housing programs in which people hold leases for their own self-contained units with their own bathrooms and kitchens, as well as to programs offered by nonprofit agencies.

Single-site supportive housing approaches emerged in the 1970s as a response to the poor housing options that were then available. In contrast to custodial housing approaches that replicated many of the features of institutions in the community (Parkinson, Nelson, & Horgan, 1999), single-site supportive housing approaches sought to combine good quality social housing, offered by nonprofit community-based organizations, with a variety of forms of support. Like other forms of social housing, a number of people are housed in a particular building or complex. All tenants have their own units, though they may also have access to common spaces to meet, to socialize, or for programming. Space is also available in the complex for on-site support providers and administration. In the past this may have included group homes in which people may have shared rooms, kitchen facilities, and bathrooms. Our observation is that the popularity of this type of housing, at least in Canada, is diminishing, though they still exist. Like other forms of social housing, single-site supportive housing is government funded; it is social housing with support provided on-site to individual tenants, based on their needs and interests, including counseling, life skills, and crisis support. The staff to tenant ratio varies from site to site. Support is offered through planned formal sessions and meetings as well as through unplanned interactions between staff and tenants. Additionally, there is group-based support, in the form of leisure or arts activities, and group decision-making. A final important feature is the routine opportunities for peer to peer support among neighbors in the housing in addition to professional support.

Tenants of single-site supportive housing may have access to a variety of amenities (such as telephone, computers, Internet, food, and arts and crafts supplies) offered by the program that they may not be able to afford on their own, even with subsidized rent. Their housing provides a foundation for participating in the community, volunteering, making use of local resources, and patronizing local businesses. Tenants can contribute to and make decisions with respect to their housing, the services they receive, and the operations of nonprofit housing providers. This occurs through tenant-directed support, tenants' associations, and the common practice of tenants participating on boards of directors.

The nonprofit agencies can themselves be important advocates and resources in their communities. The agencies and their staff members can be repositories of expertise in matters of housing, local services, mental health issues, program development, and other areas. The agencies should also be well integrated in their communities through networks and partnerships with a range of other local services and providers. This represents an important shift from an earlier era in which the focus of agencies tended to be more inward. Agencies can advocate for increased community access and services for tenants. For example, Options Bytown has advocated for participation of tenants in the local neighborhood watch program, and has negotiated with a local service provider for the on-site services of a nurse practitioner, because a number of tenants required these services. Finally, many agencies have active members of their boards of directors and volunteers who act as ambassadors for agencies and their tenants with other community groups, with funders, and with local politicians.

Understanding single-site supportive housing requires dispensing with some common misconceptions or assumptions associated with past practices. Single-site supportive housing is not a single or fixed approach (see chapter 2, this volume, for a discussion of the varying approaches). Since its introduction in the

1970s, the delivery of this form of housing has evolved. Some of the innovations have come from experience of providers and the drive to continuously improve. Some have been inspired by developments in the field such as the recovery movement, and other approaches such as scattered-site supportive housing and Housing First.

Most critically, it is important to understand that single-site supportive housing is permanent housing, that tenants sign their own leases, and that agencies and tenants abide by local applicable laws regulating tenants and landlord relationships. Second, this type of housing is not equivalent to the "staircase" or "continuum" model in which residents graduate to housing with lower levels of support as they gain increasing capacity for independence (Ridgway & Zipple, 1990). It is unlikely that many jurisdictions created a continuum of housing (Ridgway & Zipple, 1990), and leases and tenancy laws in most jurisdictions would make it impossible to move tenants along a continuum, if it existed.

Over the years, we have observed single-site supportive housing increasingly favoring the independence of their tenants, doing away with mandatory participation in programs offered by the agency, with compliance with medications or treatment, and the requirement that tenants not use drugs or alcohol. To the extent that these programs have removed these barriers to housing, they have adopted key principles of Housing First. Another area of progress has been the introduction of portable support. Whereas in earlier examples of single-site supportive housing all support was provided by the housing agency, increasingly tenants have individualized support provided by case managers or assertive community treatment teams employed by outside agencies. Some agencies, like Options Bytown, also offer case management to clients who are housed directly from shelters into social housing apartments throughout the city. At the same time, there can be limits on choice. In Ottawa, individuals on a centralized waiting list can indicate where they want to live, though choices are limited to the available affordable housing options.

Unfortunately, we know very little about how this type of housing is currently offered in Canada, the United States, and elsewhere. As other chapters in this book show, this housing model is rarely described in detail, and rarely studied using more sophisticated research designs such as randomized controlled trials (see chapter 2 and chapter 5, this volume). There are few widely agreed on best practices, beyond the standards and requirements set forth by local funders or regulating bodies. Whereas scattered-site housing and more recently Housing First have been the subject of considerable research focus, including the development of standards and fidelity measures, the same has not been the case for single-site housing. Whereas there has been great enthusiasm for studying scattered-site housing, we know relatively less about this type of housing. This is a gap that must be addressed as single-site supportive housing will continue to be an important part of any housing system for people with serious mental illness.

The Need for Single-Site Supportive Housing

With the increasing interest in Housing First, the discussion often seems to focus on the favoring of this one approach over others. For example, in Canada, the federal government's 5-year Homelessness Partnering Strategy for 2014 to 2019 focuses exclusively on the Housing First approach. There is a need, however, to think about the different housing approaches from a systemic perspective. Simply, scattered-site and single-site supportive housing approaches are each important parts of local housing systems that must collaborate to ensure that people have dependable access to high-quality housing and support that meets their interests and needs over the course of their lives.

The evidence for the need for single-site supportive housing approaches comes from a number of sources. For example, it appears that about 15% to 20% of people in Housing First programs do not retain their housing (e.g., Goering et al., 2014; Tsemberis & Eisenberg, 2000; Tsemberis, Gulcur, & Nakae, 2004) and may need access to more structured living situations, higher support, community involvement, or other options. In addition, studies of the housing preferences of people with mental illness consistently find that about 20% of people express a preference for single-site style housing (Aubry, Ecker, & Jetté, 2014). It is unclear whether there is overlap between people who do not succeed in Housing First and those who also prefer single-site living. In addition, there is no evidence that people who need or want single-site housing can and do access it. However, the implication is that a significant proportion of people may want or need single-site housing and the support it can offer.

It is also important to consider the need for access to single-site housing over the course of a person's life and how preferences for housing can change. For example, more collective forms of housing may be preferred by some people, and this is even normal at different stages of life (e.g., younger or older people). People who have experienced trauma or violence may fear living on their own and may also prefer collective options. For others, the social isolation that may accompany life in independent, scattered apartments may lead to a desire for collective living. Finally, for many, mental health may wax and wane over the course of a person's life, and there may be times when they might prefer living with support on-site.

The goal then is to provide choice and access to the housing that people need and want when they need and want it. In the province of Ontario in Canada, one of the challenges that we have faced is that people do not have access to housing they need. A study by Koegl, Durbin, and Goering (2004) estimated that only about 38% of people had access to housing that met their needs. In this study many people were assessed as capable of living in more independent housing but instead were living in housing with more support than they needed. A minority of people were found to be living in housing that provided less support than they needed. In Ottawa Ontario, we have also recognized the issue that tenants who are interested in moving on from

Options Bytown are stuck because of the shortage of housing subsidies or subsidized housing. Our local network has worked with the City of Ottawa to prioritize these individuals to provide quicker access to other social housing.

It is clear that social housing, like single-site supportive housing, provides a dependable housing stock that is unaffected by housing or economic trends. It is unclear how scattered-site or Housing First approaches may be affected by shifts in housing markets, such as the increases or decreases in vacancies, rising rents, or the willingness of the private sector to build more rental properties. Many jurisdictions have seen minimal growth in the private rental market, and the growth in scattered-site or Housing First approaches, particularly in smaller rental markets, might risk the displacement of tenants or the creation of a preferred group of renters backed by housing subsidies and professional support. An alternative argument, though, is that creating subsidized housing in the private market could take pressure off social housing, which has very long waiting lists in most municipalities.

Providing Single-Site Supportive Housing

Providing housing is complex. Housing providers must find innovative and creative ways to ensure they offer high-quality housing and support, often within the context of limited financial resources. In this section we reflect on this complexity and offer some suggestions for improving the delivery of this housing.

Public perceptions can create challenges for housing providers, particularly when the public does not distinguish between permanent housing programs and other services. There is an ongoing need for public education and for the agency to be active in the local community to dispel this confusion and to emphasize the tenancy and to promote the citizenship of the people who lease the units. One strategy has been to encourage tenants to become involved in local organizations and groups so that they are recognized themselves as neighborhood residents who share the same interests and concerns as other residents.

Housing providers must strive to ensure that tenants have a sufficient voice in their housing and in the direction and policies of the agency. Tenants' associations are one way for tenants to have more of a voice. The effectiveness of these associations can vary depending on the interest of tenants in participating and the strength of the leadership among the tenants. As in any other community, many people may simply elect to not participate, unsure of how the association is relevant, or wishing to spend their time and energy elsewhere. Other tenants may wish to play a role, but lack experience or confidence in their abilities. In some cases, agencies may provide staff assistance in running tenant meetings as part of a broader life skills training program.

It is clear that tenants require an effective voice in housing agencies. One avenue worth exploring to make these tenants associations more effective is leadership training. Leadership training is increasingly available in many communities and may help interested tenants to more effectively fill roles in tenants associations. Another possibility is to partner tenants associations with local consumer self-help initiatives. Through such partnerships, resources and expertise can be shared and tenants can be mentored in their leadership roles.

Ensuring that tenants have an effective voice also means including them on key decision-making bodies like boards of directors. The presence of tenants can sensitize board members to the experiences of tenants and to their needs and concerns. It is also important that board members are visible and members develop direct relationships with tenants and tenants associations. The board members must see themselves as advocates for tenants, as much as supporters of the agency.

Lack of sufficient funding is a constant challenge for housing agencies that manifests in a number of ways. Primarily, maintenance is an important and ongoing issue. It is essential that buildings and units be maintained for the well-being of the tenants and the perceptions of the community. Agencies must be resourceful to ensure that maintenance issues are responded to in a timely way. Tenants themselves can take the lead when they are provided with the means and support to maintain their units and common spaces. At one of Options Bytown's buildings, tenants have formed a gardening group that tends to a green space, grows their own food, and prepares it together. Another strategy has been to employ tenants themselves to do light maintenance, clean, and perform other functions in the buildings.

One common struggle for not only housing agencies but also other service providers in this sector is in the area of human services. Here lack of sufficient funding is expressed in the challenge in paying competitive wages. Simply put, most government funders fail to properly compensate these professionals who work to support people in their daily lives in the community. The challenge in paying a competitive wage can make it difficult to recruit new employees. Staff members may gain experience and move along to better paying positions in larger community mental health organizations or hospitals. Options Bytown has compensated for this by offering employees superior benefit packages.

Some agencies may experience difficulties in providing adequate professional development opportunities. Agencies in Ottawa have been able to benefit from many opportunities provided by the municipal government, through federal funding. Another way forward, already being implemented in Ottawa, is through networks and partnerships with other similar organizations. These partnerships or networks can be used to develop learning communities or communities of practice (Wenger, 1998) in which staff members from across agencies can regularly meet to exchange information and ideas, gain support, and discuss the best practice in the delivery of single-site housing. Alternatively, such networks can be sources of information sharing and a common platform for advocacy with policy makers and funders.

Agencies can also work with tenants to ensure that they have access to sufficient resources, activities, and meaningful roles in the community. Agencies cannot and should not do everything for tenants. Agencies must be as outward focused as they are inward focused. This means being an energetic player in the system, active in partnership development, and effective in managing relationships with neighbors and community groups. Agencies and, especially their boards, need to advocate to create opportunities for tenants, and to leverage new opportunities, or to identify new funding or resources. It also means connecting tenants to peer support organizations, consumer-run businesses, social enterprises, and employment support services.

More broadly, single-site supportive housing providers must work to ensure that the housing is sufficiently diverse or flexible to address a range of preferences and needs. The diversity or flexibility of single-site supportive housing required depends on the community, but may include options for people who wish for more support as well as for those who prefer to keep to themselves. It may mean flexibility in programming or more options for younger or older tenants as well as programming and housing that can address the safety concerns of vulnerable tenants. These options must all be linked together and working in partnership with independent housing programs, as well as other social housing programs, to ensure access and choice for tenants over the life course.

Finally, providers of single-site supportive housing can continue to work to dispel misunderstandings, demonstrate its effectiveness, and continue to evolve its practices. This requires active participation in research and program evaluation to identify issues in program delivery and act on evaluation findings. Providers must engage with researchers and the research literature to have a better understanding of the strengths and limitations of their programs, and be creative in developing innovations to continuously improve. At the same time, it is equally important for researchers to broaden their interests and engage more fully with all forms of housing. More important than privileging one form over another is paying attention to the development and evaluation of local systems that ensure choice over the life course and working in partnership with all providers to further develop and refine practices to best serve the needs and preferences of people who live in this housing.

Conclusion

Ultimately, housing programs are not just about buildings but more importantly about people. They are about the people who live in this housing as well as the people who work to provide this housing on a daily basis. Being a housing provider is not easy, but it is rewarding. Housing providers are witnesses to radical transformation in people's lives from having access to good quality housing and empowering support. It is critical for housing providers to continue to engage in new partnerships and to introduce innovative practices. It is clear that single-site supportive housing is an important asset in any housing system. For example, the City of Ottawa has recently included this type of housing in its 10-year plan to prevent and end homelessness and has committed to creating over 100 new units with on-site supports. Providers must work with all stakeholders, from tenants, to partners, to funders, so that all partners ensure that the provision of this housing continues to evolve, that tenants continue to have access and choice, and that communities are strengthened.

References

Aubry, T., Ecker, J., & Jetté, J. (2014). Supported housing as a promising Housing First approach for people with severe and persistent mental illness. In M. Guirguis, R., MacNeil, & S. Hwang (Eds.), *Homelessness and health in Canada* (pp. 155–188). Ottawa, ON: University of Ottawa Press.

Goering, P., Veldhuizen, S. Watson, A., Adair, C., Kopp, B., Latimer, E., . . . Aubry, T. (2014). *National At Home/Chez Soi Final Report.* Calgary, AB: Mental Health Commission of Canada. Retrieved from http://www.mentalhealthcommission.ca

Koegl, C., Durbin, J., & Goering, P. (2004). *Mental health services in Ontario: How well is the province meeting the needs of persons with serious mental illness?* Toronto, ON: Centre for Addiction and Mental Health.

Parkinson, S., Nelson, G., & Horgan, S. (1999). From housing to homes: A review of the literature on housing approaches for psychiatric consumer/survivors. *Canadian Journal of Community Mental Health, 18,* 145–164.

Ridgway, P., & Zipple, A. M. (1990). The paradigm shift in residential services: From linear continuum to supported housing approaches. *Psychosocial Rehabilitation Journal, 13,* 11–32.

Tsemberis, S., & Eisenberg, R.F. (2000). Pathways to housing: Supported housing for street-dwelling homeless individuals. *Psychiatric Services, 51,* 487–493.

Tsemberis, S., Gulcur, L., & Nakae, M. (2004). Housing First, consumer choice, and harm reduction for homeless individuals with dual diagnosis. *American Journal of Public Health, 94,* 651–656.

Wenger, E. (1998). *Communities of practice: Learning, meaning, and identity.* Cambridge: Cambridge University Press.

15

Frontline Practice in Housing First Programs

BENJAMIN F. HENWOOD AND EMMY TIDERINGTON

This chapter discusses the challenges and rewards that frontline providers experience when working with a Housing First (HF) approach from the perspective of frontline providers. These reflections are based on qualitative research on provider practice, the authors' in-depth knowledge stemming from real-world experience providing and supervising HF services, and the growing literature on HF models. This chapter explores central tenets of the HF model and the tensions that can arise as those tenets are implemented in day-to-day practice with an emphasis on harm reduction. In addition, core competencies required to provide HF services are identified and articulated through illustrative case examples.

Topics that emerged as central to this discussion include the importance of a values-based approach rooted in a recovery orientation, desire for social justice, and support of client self-determination. Examples are used to help illustrate the difficulty of embracing a harm reduction framework and supporting clients whose decisions cause them harm, the limits or restrictions on client choice, and the responsibilities (and ambiguity) of working in the community with individuals who may be actively using drugs or being disruptive or both. Such discussion highlights how supporting clients to make their own decisions and lead the treatment process, which are core competencies required to provide HF services, can be a new experience for many clinicians that requires training and flexibility, especially for those with experience in traditional public mental health settings.

HF is an evidence-based practice that has become increasingly adopted in the United States, Canada, and Europe (Busch-Geertsema, 2011; Goering et al., 2011; Greenwood, Stefancic, Tsemberis, & Busch-Geertsema, 2013; Keller et al., 2013). It represents an innovative approach to homeless services that is rooted in human rights by providing immediate access to housing with few strings attached. The evidence base and cost-effectiveness of HF for people who have experienced chronic homelessness has propelled its dissemination and endorsement among liberal and conservative parties alike (Stanhope & Dunn, 2011). Although HF can effectively end homelessness, for individuals who provide HF services, this ending marks the beginning of a challenging road to support recovery (Henwood, Stanhope, & Padgett, 2011).

A core emphasis of HF is promoting tenant self-determination and choice (Tsemberis, 2010). These have been central, organizing concepts of a recovery framework that have been associated with improvement in individual recovery outcomes (Calsyn, Winter, & Morse, 2000; Rapp, Shera, & Kisthardt, 1993). Although promoting self-determination and choice ideally results in the flourishing of human potential, it also may result in self-destructive behaviors that are often born out of a lifetime of cumulative adversity (Padgett, Smith, Henwood, & Tiderington, 2012). Further, delivering recovery-oriented care requires giving up a degree of control that is ostensibly ordained through schooling, training, and gaining employment as a provider of services. Embracing HF as a clinician is not easy, nor is it for everyone.

The Role of Frontline Providers

Frontline practice is often overlooked or deemed inconsequential to the bigger picture. Yet frontline providers often function as "street-level bureaucrats" (Lipsky, 2010), whose decisions and actions can ultimately account for how an intervention is implemented. Further, the way in which frontline providers interface with consumers can directly affect tenant outcomes. At its core, HF is a rights-based approach to ending chronic homelessness. The model was born out of the belief that housing is a human right, but it also presumes that every individual, regardless of ability level, has the right to choice, self-determination, and the pursuit of recovery from mental illness, substance abuse, and homelessness on his or her own terms. This rights-based orientation implies that HF also has a clear values base that informs frontline practice. Because chronically homeless individuals often experience a loss of control as a result of repeated psychiatric hospitalizations, housing instability, and struggles with addiction, this model is built on restoring consumers' control of their own lives (Tsemberis, Gulcur, & Nakae, 2004). A substantial body of evidence has demonstrated that not only are individuals with serious mental illness capable of making informed choices (Prager, 1980; Ridgway, 1988; Tanzman, 1990) but also they are far more likely to stay in housing programs that provide them with greater choice (Lipton, Siegel, Hannigan, Samuels, & Baker, 2000; Srebnik, Livingston, Gordon, & King, 1995). As such, the frontline practice of HF focuses on encouraging consumers to define their own goals and engage in treatment if and when they choose.

This radical departure from the prescriptive nature and heavy demands of traditional homeless services echoes a similar client-centered approach advocated for by supporters of the mental health recovery movement. This approach calls for individualized, hopeful, and empowering practices that support individuals in their recovery from mental illness and substance dependence, in which recovery is considered a unique journey rather than simply a functional outcome (Deegan, 1996). This new wave of choice and recovery is consistent with core HF principles and provides a framework for HF frontline practice. But what does it mean to provide recovery-oriented services? What does honoring client self-determination look like in practice? How do you offer and support a consumer's choice when that choice could potentially be harmful to the individual or the surrounding community?

These are the questions that frontline practitioners in HF programs grapple with during the delivery of these services. Because this approach is adapted to the particular goals and needs of an individual rather than dictated by a set of program rules and regulations, it is harder to specify an appropriate response to challenging behaviors (e.g., drug use, medication refusal, hoarding). A provider's response to a consumer whose stated goal is to maintain strict abstinence from substances would be different than a provider response to a consumer whose goal is to reduce substance use or who has no plans to stop using. This necessitates a flexible and creative approach.

Generally speaking, the response to most situations encountered in HF is to honor a person's right to self-determination and choice. Of course there are always limits to supporting a tenant's choice, such as when individuals have become an imminent danger to themselves or others or their choice begins to infringe on the rights of others. In such cases, HF providers may need to intervene through hospitalization or crisis services. Yet even in such cases, efforts can be made to provide choice and support empowerment when possible. Needing to limit choice in certain situations does not mean self-determination is not a value to uphold. It is also important to recognize that respecting choice is not equivalent to a hands-off libertarian approach. HF providers are there to provide support, resources, and linkages according to each consumer's desired goals and stated needs regardless of whether they are doing well (e.g., found a job, reconnected with family, maintained sobriety) or they are struggling (e.g., relapsed, evicted, arrested).

Maintaining a Housing First Approach Even After Accessing Housing

A values-based approach is critical to all phases of HF services, from engagement to active treatment to helping someone maintain their recovery to titrating service intensity and graduation from services. The beginning phase of engagement and retention in services can depend as much on how services are delivered as the type of services or programs being offered (Martin, Garske, & Davis, 2000; Padgett, Henwood, Abrams, & Davis, 2008). For example, an offer of a subsidized apartment with few strings attached can be a strong motivator for a person experiencing homelessness to engage with an HF provider. Yet if the offer is made without respecting individual autonomy and self-determination—presupposing acceptance or waiting impatiently for a response—even someone experiencing homelessness who wants housing may decline an opportunity to access housing. Of course, HF providers who offer housing in a sensitive way may also be turned down, often due to disbelief or questioning of the credibility of the offer. Yet an empathetic and curious response along with respect for a person's decision to stay in a familiar environment on the street can help keep a person engaged so that he or she will accept an offer of housing at a later point.

It is the offer of respect and dignity, along with housing, that sets the stage for engagement that must be maintained throughout an individual's tenure in a HF program. As Stanhope (2012) described based on a qualitative study of HF that examined the transition from homelessness to supportive housing, a tenant's narrative of recovery is often cocreated with HF providers, who are there to witness and support this transition. Respecting autonomy and self-determination therefore applies once someone has transitioned from homelessness into housing. HF providers who show up for a home visit unannounced with the expectation that they have an obligation and right to inspect an apartment will have more difficulty accessing that apartment compared with an HF provider who consistently respects a tenant's apartment as his or her home (e.g., asking permission to enter or scheduling home visits at a time convenient to the tenant). Although most tenants sign an agreement that acknowledges HF providers must conduct home visits or inspections, how providers approach those obligations can determine whether tenants uphold the agreement. It is the way in which these tenant–provider interactions take place and the underlying values motivating provider actions that make programs "Housing First" rather than "housing only."

Limited empirical research focused on HF frontline practices has shown that providers working in an HF setting articulate a different set of values than providers working in a traditional services setting (Henwood, Shinn, Tsemberis, & Padgett, 2013; Henwood et al., 2011). Both quantitative analysis of responses to structured, closed-ended questions and qualitative analysis of open-ended responses to semi-structured questions showed that providers working in an HF setting had greater endorsement of consumer values, lesser endorsement of systems values, and greater appreciation of the diversity and uniqueness of service recipients than providers in traditional services (Henwood et al., 2013). Comparing provider perspectives also revealed an implementation paradox in that providers adopting a traditional services approach were inhibited from engaging consumers in treatment and services without housing, whereas HF providers could focus on treatment needs and service delivery because housing was already secured (Henwood et al., 2013; Henwood et al., 2011). As programs increasingly adopt a HF approach, the existing workforce habituated to traditional services and values constitutes a significant challenge to effective implementation.

Incorporating a Harm Reduction
Perspective and Approach

As previously described, the HF model is predicated on client self-determination and consumer choice. This same orientation applies to how frontline providers address harmful behaviors (e.g., substance abuse, hoarding, or unprotected sex) in these settings. Unlike traditional housing programs, in which relapse can mean eviction and engagement in treatment programs is a requirement, HF takes a more flexible, client-centered approach. This model recognizes that individuals with serious mental illness often have co-occurring substance use disorders and other complex needs that can act as serious obstacles to maintaining housing. It also recognizes that forced sobriety and a more punitive approach is often not effective in helping people achieve long-term behavioral changes. Harm reduction, the framework used in HF, is a nonjudgmental, pragmatic approach (Marlatt, 1996) to addressing harmful behaviors focused on the reduction of harm rather than enforcement of abstinence from those behaviors. Originally employed in the context of public health through efforts to reduce HIV and hepatitis B transmission, harm reduction recognizes that incremental reductions of harmful behavior during the short term may be more realistic and obtainable than the giant leap to abstinence.

This approach is premised on the stages of change model, which recognizes that individuals' readiness to change harmful behavior often occurs in a nonlinear fashion, and treatment needs to be adapted to that specific stage of recovery (Prochaska, DiClemente, Velicer, & Rossi, 1992). As such, providers are tasked with "meeting the clients where they are" in this process, rather than demanding that the client meet the program. By incorporating a harm reduction approach in HF practice, providers are able to collaborate with consumers along the recovery path as they decide how and when to seek help, instead of policing consumers' behavior and enforcing abstinence. However, it also means additional work on the part of providers in that they must find creative and flexible ways to address and assist consumers in meeting these goals. It also means working with community stakeholders—landlords, family members, and neighbors—to help consumers stay in housing, even if they are actively engaging in harmful behaviors. This may involve educating stakeholders about the support available to the individual from the housing agency, brokering communication between parties, or linking stakeholders to outside resources (e.g., Al-Anon) as needed.

When it comes to working with the individual consumer, HF providers use the consumer–provider relationship as a vehicle for engaging consumers in discussions about their substance use (Tiderington, Stanhope, & Henwood, 2013). Employing creative approaches, such as engaging consumers in activities that the consumer enjoys (e.g., playing a game of basketball), and going beyond traditional case management duties, providers can build trust and facilitate open discussions about harm reduction. With the help of supervisors and agency-wide implementation efforts, motivational interviewing can also be used by providers as a concrete strategy to facilitate discussions about use and helping move consumers along the stages of change, from precontemplation to contemplation to preparation to action to maintenance (Miller & Rollnick, 1991). Motivational interviewing involves having service recipients articulate their goals and preferences, identify the ways in which they experience ambiguity, and consider how different methods of resolving their feelings align with their stated preferences. With these tools, providers are in a better position to address the challenges of working with harmful behaviors while helping consumers meet the legal obligations of tenancy.

In HF frontline practice, challenging situations can arise that may necessitate these skills and the use of astute clinical judgment. Generally, if a consumer discreetly uses substances in his or her apartment without causing disturbances to others in the building, there is not a problem. In these cases, motivational interviewing strategies can be used to engage the consumer on an ongoing basis while providing support and linkages according to the consumer's needs and respective stage of change. At other times, harmful behavior can affect the safety and security of those in the community and further action is needed. In many situations, HF's values-based approach and harm reduction perspective are two sides of the same coin.

Based on an aforementioned qualitative study (Stanhope, 2012), Tiderington et al. (2013) proposed a specific model of harm reduction in HF settings. The model recognizes the importance of being able to engage service recipients in a dialogue about their substance use, noting that an open dialogue is more likely to promote self-determination and improve public health whereas limited or no discussion can result in service recipients being unable to actualize self-determined and meaningful goals, which may lead to poorer public health. A key part of the model is that harm reduction can sometimes involve supporting service recipients who are actively using substances and making poor choices and who are not interested in changing these behaviors. In such a scenario, the provider relationship functions more as a holding environment (Winnicott, 1965), meaning a safe space for service recipients to take their time in deciding whether to acknowledge their use. Providing a safe space for ambivalence and for the consumer to initiate the conversation demonstrates a commitment to the consumer's right to self-determination that can open the door to further engagement.

Frontline Practice in Action

Although the majority of people who move into housing can succeed on their own with minimal but regular support, there are times when challenging situations can occur, including, for example, (1) nonadherence to medications; (2) substance use; (3) hoarding; (4) nonpayment of rent; (5) inability to maintain the apartment;

(6) medical disability; (7) client loneliness and vulnerability; and (8) mandated treatments. Serving a large number of people may result in such challenging situations becoming a regular part of frontline practice. The HF values-based and harm reduction approach provides a framework for addressing difficult situations that often can require creativity and an acceptance of differences. The following section describes several case examples of some of the more challenging situations an HF provider might face. These examples are based on actual cases that the authors have encountered; some details have been changed to safeguard the anonymity of the tenants.

Vignette 1

Paul was a 38-year-old man who had been diagnosed with schizophrenia, substance dependence, and mild cognitive impairment. He had been using crack cocaine for more than a decade and experienced frequent auditory hallucinations. Paul was also very enthusiastic about completing the equivalency of a high school diploma (GED) once he settled into his new apartment. Yet despite the toll it had taken on his health, Paul did not want to address his crack use when he first entered the program. He continued to smoke in his apartment and the landlord notified the HF team that Paul's smoke alarm had started to go off on a regular basis. Because of this the team checked in with Paul and discovered that he had been using his hot plate to ignite newspapers as a way to light his crack pipe. After some deliberation and clinical consultation with the team leader, the team brought Paul a lighter so that he no longer needed to use his hot plate. They also allocated more time during his weekly visits to help him explore and resolve his ambivalence about his crack use in relation to his stated goals of starting a GED program and decreasing his psychiatric symptoms. Once Paul decided he was ready to apply to the GED program, the team helped him locate a nearby program and complete the application. After starting the program, Paul said he felt proud of his accomplishment and found the schoolwork rewarding. His crack use slowly declined. After one relapse and a resulting hospitalization following the death of his mother, Paul reentered and completed the GED program. He is now pursuing a certificate in heating and cooling systems repair.

Analysis

In addition to the negative health effects of crack cocaine, its use can be highly stigmatizing. In traditional service settings, providers may have focused on Paul's substance use and overlooked other areas of his life, including goals that he wanted to pursue. The rationale for this focus may be that it is a waste of a provider's time to address education while a person is actively using. Yet engaging Paul in terms of both substance use and education enabled HF providers to highlight to Paul how his substance use may interfere with obtaining his GED, a technique used in motivational interviewing. This likely was more effective than lecturing Paul about crack's harmful effects.

The team's decision to provide Paul with a lighter may be viewed by traditional providers as enabling his substance use, yet HF providers are often faced with complicated assessments of risk, which in this case meant focusing on complaints from Paul's landlord. Paul's use of a hot plate to smoke crack not only risked eviction, but possibly an uncontrolled fire. Providing Paul with a lighter was the result of a more complex calculation of the risks involved given Paul's behavior and an assessment that Paul was not prepared to stop smoking crack. Had a traditional approach been employed, Paul would likely have been forced to leave his apartment and return to homelessness. In this case, the team was able to support Paul in maintaining his housing and reducing harm. As described in the vignette, such decisions are best made through consultation from multiple perspectives; implementing harm reduction in HF is difficult to do alone.

Vignette 2

Charles was a 48-year-old man with bipolar disorder and polysubstance abuse (alcohol being his drug of choice). Charles had spent many years homeless, including a period of time during which he lived in the park with other homeless friends. When he moved into an apartment he had difficulty telling his friends that they could not come to his home, and people at times stayed there with him. He had his friends over for parties, which would occasionally spill into the hallways or street and often end up in a violent altercation among his guests. The landlord informed the team that he was considering eviction. The team attempted to talk with Charles about his behavior during every visit, but he said drinking and hanging out with his friends was the only thing that made him happy. Despite being aware that the landlord was pursuing eviction and that he might be homeless again, his behavior did not change. Charles was eventually evicted from his apartment. He agreed to go to detox and rehab and to move to a new location where it would be harder for his friends to access him. Charles has now maintained that apartment for more than 2 years and has had two periods of sobriety lasting almost a year, with a relapse that lasted 2 months.

Analysis

The most frequent cause of failure in an HF program (about 10% to 15%) is related to excessive drug use involving people other than the consumer (Tsemberis, 2010). In this case Charles initially wanted to share his good fortune of having a place to call home with individuals he knew and who watched out for him while he was homeless. Yet it was not clear if Charles was unwilling or unable to ask his friends to leave when their presence and behaviors threatened his eviction. There is often no point for HF providers to force disruptive visitors to leave a tenant's apartment if the tenant will simply let his friends back in the next day. A client's apartment also may be taken over by drug dealers. Clients are given substances for free or reduced cost in exchange for the use of their apartment as a location for substance use or other illegal activities. These situations usually become quickly evident as neighbors complain of traffic. In some cases a tenant may ask or take HF providers up on an offer to "play the bad guy" and force unwanted visitors to leave. This can be done with or without assistance from local police. Charles did not express an interest in having his friends leave until he experienced being evicted. Rather than being viewed as a failure, Charles's eviction became a learning opportunity that allowed him to maintain a second apartment.

The vignettes described above are two examples of challenging situations that HF providers may face. Yet there are many others. When clients move into their own independent apartment, loneliness can be a significant problem (Hopper, 2012). Living alone in an apartment can make symptoms of loneliness more noticeable. Clients often do not know how to spend their time, especially due to extremely low rates of employment (Mueser, Salyers, & Mueser, 2001). One coping strategy is to allow others, such as strangers, family members, or friends, to spend time in their apartment with them. Visitors may stay longer than the client intended and take advantage of them. If the visitor causes problems in the building, the client could be at risk of losing his or her housing. Drugs are often but not always a factor. As noted in the vignettes, HF providers can play an active role in engaging unwanted visitors and maintaining communication with landlords to help resolve problems before they end in eviction.

Another situation that may occur is nonpayment of rent. This can occur for many reasons including paranoia, disorganization, impulsivity, substance use, and just not wanting to do so. It is important for HF providers to be aware that nonpayment is occurring, but it should only be the responsibility of a housing coordinator or designated representative payee to be involved in rent payment and collection. The HF providers can work with tenants to make clear the consequence of not paying rent; can offer that the program take charge of a tenant's finances or facilitate a third party taking charge of a tenant's finances (such as a supportive and trusting family member or professional representative payee service) to insure the rent is paid; and communicate with landlords on how best to resolve such issues. It is important to realize that landlords regularly face similar issues with tenants who are not affiliated with an HF program and often appreciate the responsiveness of HF providers who are working to resolve issues that arise.

Less frequently discussed within the HF literature is how physical illness and impairment can raise questions about the ability of clients to live on their own. Questions can arise regarding both terminal illnesses and chronic, poorly controlled illnesses such as diabetes. At the end of life, HF tenants often desire to die at home, which is consistent with societal preferences (Ballard et al., 2011). Housing First providers, in conjunction with existing community resources, must try to provide in-home services to help HF tenants age in place (Henwood, Katz, & Gilmer, 2015). At times tenants may reject service providers seeking to spend significant time in their homes or the existing community home care services because they do not feel comfortable due to lack of familiarity with mental health problems. If this happens, the team can encourage the client to move into a more assisted setting. These complex scenarios require frontline providers to draw on a variety of competencies.

Housing First Core Competencies

Core competencies can range from personal attributes to knowledge in a content area to a specific skill set. For example, when attempting to define an exhaustive list of competencies for community mental health support providers, Aubry, Flynn, Gerber, and Dostaler (2005) identified 59 core competencies, which included personal attributes, content knowledge, and specific skill sets, that were either absolutely necessary ($n = 46$) or desirable ($n = 13$) for effective service delivery. Due to the variety and complexity of challenges that HF providers face in the context of frontline practice, there is no amount of training that could cover all situations. For this reason, adopting a multidisciplinary team approach provides an added and sometimes necessary benefit. Nevertheless, there are general core competencies that all HF providers can develop that overlap with other community-based behavioral health providers (e.g., knowledge and skills related to developing a strong working relationship with clients, performing biopsychosocial assessments, providing treatment, integrating of cultural factors into care, and coordinating community resources and care). As discussed in this chapter, core competencies that are especially important to HF providers include: (1) engagement of consumers who have been homeless for months, years, and possibly decades; (2) responsiveness to key stakeholders including tenants, landlords, and employers; and (3) ability to implement harm reduction techniques that are specifically tailored (e.g., needle exchange programs for intravenous drug users, naltrexone for those with severe alcohol problems, etc.). Other core competencies include embracing a recovery orientation and supporting consumer self-determination, which require an ability to tolerate risk and failure. Rather than representing an exhaustive list of all possible core competencies, those covered in this chapter reinforce the underlying values-based approach that guide frontline provider practice in HF.

Conclusion

HF represents a radical departure from traditional programs designed to serve individuals experiencing homelessness and co-occurring psychiatric and substance use disorders that is consistent with mental health systems transformation to recovery-oriented care. In HF, providers work with and support tenants regardless of their symptoms, substance abuse, or whether they participate in formal treatment (Tsemberis et al., 2004). The notion of consumer-driven services cannot simply be jargon but must accurately depict the values, philosophy, and mission of clinicians working in the program who accept consumers' ability to be self-directive even when difficult at times. This does not entail, however, that anything goes. HF providers must recognize that tenants are accountable for their behaviors the same as other citizens.

Given the increasing dissemination of the HF model, it will be necessary to train more providers to work with this model, which raises important questions about whether and how providers habituated to traditional services can be reoriented toward an HF framework (Henwood et al., 2013). HF demands that provider expertise be minimized for tenant expertise to flourish. Yet this is not a zero-sum game, because frontline providers are critical to the success of HF. The rewards of adopting HF, however, are not easily measured as the number of people who move into housing. Frontline providers are rewarded by developing core competencies, which are guided by HF's values-based and harm reduction approach and ultimately allow for the possibility of recovery.

References

Aubry, T.D., Flynn, R.J., Gerber, G., & Dostaler, T. (2005). Identifying the core competencies of community support providers working with people with psychiatric disabilities. *Psychiatric Rehabilitation Journal, 28*, 346–353. doi:10.2975/28.2005.346.353

Ballard, S.M., Jenkins, C., Savut, N.Y., McKinnon, W.H., Carroll, K.E., & Escott-Stump, S. (2011). Innovative and complementary approaches to aging in place. *Journal of Family and Consumer Sciences, 103*, 24–34.

Busch-Geertsema, V. (2011). Housing First Europe: A "social experimentation project." *European Journal of Homelessness, 5*, 209–211.

Calsyn, R.J., Winter, J.P., & Morse, G.A. (2000). Do consumers who have a choice in treatment have better outcomes? *Community Mental Health Journal, 36*, 149–160. doi:10.1023/A:1001890210218

Deegan, P. (1996). Recovery as a journey of the heart. *Psychiatric Rehabilitation Journal, 19*, 91–97.

Goering, P.N., Streiner, D.L., Adair, C., Aubry, T., Barker, J., Distasio, J., . . . Zabkiewicz, D.M. (2011). The At Home/Chez Soi trial protocol: A pragmatic, multi-site, randomised controlled trial of a Housing First intervention for homeless individuals with mental illness in five Canadian cities. *BMJ Open, 1*, e000323. doi:10.1136/bmjopen-2011-000323

Greenwood, R.M., Stefancic, A., Tsemberis, S., & Busch-Geertsema, V. (2013). Implementations of Housing First in Europe: Successes and challenges in maintaining model fidelity. *American Journal of Psychiatric Rehabilitation, 16*, 290–312. doi:10.1080/15487768.2013.847764

Henwood, B.F., Katz, M.L., & Gilmer, T.P. (2015). Aging in place within permanent supportive housing. *International Journal of Geriatric Psychiatry, 30*, 80–87. doi:10.1002/gps.4120

Henwood, B.F., Shinn, M., Tsemberis, S., & Padgett, D.K. (2013). Examining provider perspectives within Housing First and traditional programs. *American Journal of Psychiatric Rehabilitation, 16*, 262–274. doi:10.1080/15487768.2013.847745

Henwood, B.F., Stanhope, V., & Padgett, D.K. (2011). The role of housing: A comparison of front-line provider views in Housing First and traditional programs. *Administration and Policy in Mental Health and Mental Health Services Research, 38*, 77–85. doi:10.1007/s10488-010-0303-2

Hopper, K. (2012). Commentary: The counter-reformation that failed? A commentary on the mixed legacy of supported housing. *Psychiatric Services, 63*, 461–463. doi:10.1176/appi.ps.201100379

Keller, C., Goering, P., Hume, C., Macnaughton, E., O'Campo, P., Sarang, A., . . . Tsemberis, S. (2013). Initial implementation of Housing First in five Canadian cities: How do you make the shoe fit, when one size does not fit all? *American Journal of Psychiatric Rehabilitation, 16*, 275–289. doi:10.1080/15487768.2013.847761

Lipsky, M. (2010). *Street-level bureaucracy: Dilemmas of the individual in public services* (30th anniversary ed.). New York: Russell Sage Foundation.

Lipton, F.R., Siegel, C., Hannigan, A., Samuels, J., & Baker, S. (2000). Tenure in supportive housing for homeless persons with severe mental illness. *Psychiatric Services, 51*, 479–486. doi:10.1176/appi.ps.51.4.479

Marlatt, G.A. (1996). Harm reduction: Come as you are. *Addictive Behaviors, 21*, 779–788. doi:10.1016/0306-4603(96)00042-1

Martin, D.J., Garske, J.P., & Davis, M.K. (2000). Relation of the therapeutic alliance with outcome and other variables: A meta-analytic review. *Journal of Consulting and Clinical Psychology, 68*, 438–450. doi:10.1037/0022-006X.68.3.438

Miller, W.R., & Rollnick, S. (1991). *Motivational interviewing: Preparing people to change addictive behavior*. New York: Guilford Press.

Mueser, K.T., Salyers, M.P., & Mueser, P.R. (2001). A prospective analysis of work in schizophrenia. *Schizophrenia Bulletin, 27*, 281–296. doi:10.1093/oxfordjournals.schbul.a006874

Padgett, D.K., Henwood, B., Abrams, C., & Davis, A. (2008). Engagement and retention in services among formerly homeless adults with co-occurring mental illness and substance abuse: Voices from the margins. *Psychiatric Rehabilitation Journal, 31*, 226–233. doi:10.2975/31.3.2008.226.233

Padgett, D.K., Smith, B.T., Henwood, B.F., & Tiderington, E. (2012). Life course adversity in the lives of formerly homeless persons with serious mental illness: Context and meaning. *American Journal of Orthopsychiatry, 82*, 421–430. doi:10.1111/j.1939-0025.2012.01159.x

Prager, E. (1980). Evaluation in mental health: Enter the consumer. *Social Work Research and Abstracts, 16*, 5–10. doi:10.1093/swra/16.2.5

Prochaska, J.O., DiClemente, C.C., Velicer, W.F., & Rossi, J.S. (1992). Criticisms and concerns of the transtheoretical model in light of recent research. *British Journal of Addiction, 87*, 825–828. doi:10.1111/j.1360-0443.1992.tb01973.x

Rapp, C.A., Shera, W., & Kisthardt, W. (1993). Research strategies for consumer empowerment of people with severe mental illness. *Social Work, 38*, 727–735. doi:10.1093/sw/38.6.727

Ridgway, P. (Ed.). (1988). *Coming home: Ex-patients view housing options and needs: Proceedings of a national housing forum*. Burlington: University of Vermont, Center for Community Change through Housing and Support.

Srebnik, D., Livingston, J., Gordon, L., & King, D. (1995). Housing choice and community success for individuals with serious and persistent mental illness. *Community Mental Health Journal, 31*, 139–152. doi:10.1007/BF02188763

Stanhope, V. (2012). The ties that bind: Using ethnographic methods to understand service engagement. *Qualitative Social Work, 11*, 412–430. doi:10.1177/1473325012438079

Stanhope, V., & Dunn, K. (2011). The curious case of Housing First: The limits of evidence based policy. *International Journal of Law and Psychiatry, 34*, 275–282. doi:10.1016/j.ijlp.2011.07.006

Tanzman, B. (1990). *Researching the preferences of people with psychiatric disabilities for housing and supports: A practical guide.* Burlington: University of Vermont, Center for Community Change through Housing and Support.

Tiderington, E., Stanhope, V., & Henwood, B.F. (2013). A qualitative analysis of case managers' use of harm reduction in practice. *Journal of Substance Abuse Treatment, 44,* 71–77. doi:10.1016/j.jsat.2012.03.007

Tsemberis, S. (2010). *Housing First: The pathways model to end homelessness for people with mental illness and addiction.* Center City, MN: Hazelden.

Tsemberis, S., Gulcur, L., & Nakae, M. (2004). Housing First, consumer choice, and harm reduction for homeless individuals with a dual diagnosis. *American Journal of Public Health, 94,* 651–656. doi:10.2105/AJPH.94.4.651

Winnicott, D.W. (1965). *The family and individual development.* London: Tavistock.

16

Landlords and Scattered-Site Housing

TIMOTHY MACLEOD, TIM AUBRY, GEOFFREY NELSON, HENRI DORVIL,

SCOTT MCCULLOUGH, AND PATRICIA O'CAMPO

The literature on landlords in scattered-site housing is surprisingly sparse, given that landlords are fundamental to the coordination and provision of housing for participants in programs like Housing First. The population of individuals served by Housing First programs have complex treatment and support needs and typically have had difficulty getting and keeping housing (Ridgeway & Zipple, 1990). Landlords are important stakeholders in housing programs because they directly impact program participants' ability to get and keep housing. Additionally, landlords represent novel stakeholders in housing and services for program participants insofar as they are "normal" community members contractually related to participants through tenancy agreements, but with no clinical role.

In the context of scattered-site housing, "landlord" refers to individuals renting commercial rental units in addition to their site staff including roles like caretaker, site manager, and superintendent. Landlords take on novel positions in scattered-site housing because they bridge services (clinical teams like assertive community treatment [ACT] or intensive case management [ICM]) with community resources (housing), facilitate the development of relationships among community members and people with mental illness (Trainor, Pomeroy, & Pape, 1999), and encourage new directions in mental health in which participants are treated as valued citizens and tenants, as opposed to clients or patients (see Sylvestre, chapter 7, this volume).

Participants in scattered-site housing have mental health challenges, which landlords will likely encounter and which will draw them at times into the unfamiliar territory of delivering informal support and crisis management. Issues related to participants' behaviors, contact with their social networks, social isolation, potential eviction, and their relationships with case managers are commonly faced by landlords who rent housing to people with mental illness. Therefore, it is important to understand the motivations, roles, experiences, and needs of landlords in the coordination and maintenance of participants' housing tenure, as well as the informal care functions they might fulfill with respect to tenants with mental illness.

In this chapter, we review the roles, experiences, and needs of landlords in scattered-site housing. We begin with a brief review of literature on landlords and scattered-site housing highlighting findings to date. Next, the main body of the chapter presents original research with landlords in four sites of the Canadian At Home/ Chez Soi Housing First initiative. We conclude with lessons learned from the At Home/Chez Soi experience and implications for practice.

Literature on Landlords and Scattered-Site Housing

The limited literature on landlords and scattered-site housing for people with mental illness has focused on four areas: (1) discrimination, (2) landlords as a source of informal support, (3) support for landlords, and (4) landlord experiences with tenants with mental illness.

Discrimination

While there is little research on discrimination in housing for people with mental illness, the available research clearly shows problems of discrimination by some landlords. Page (1977, 1983, 1996) conducted several studies of landlords' discrimination against people with mental illness in southern Ontario and Detroit, from the 1970s to 1993. The methodology of these studies employed deception, in which a researcher phoned a landlord who had advertised accommodation and inquired about the availability of the unit. In half of the phone calls, the researcher claimed to be in the hospital for mental health issues and was looking for a place to live following discharge. In the other half of the calls, the researcher made no mention of a mental illness label or experience. Page consistently found statistically significant differences in landlords' reports of availability of the rental unit for people identified with and without mental illness. When the researcher mentioned that individuals had recently experienced mental illness, landlords were twice as likely to report that the rental unit is unavailable (Page, 1996). Moreover, the level of discrimination exhibited by landlords did not change over a 20-year period.

In a study of people with mental illness who participate in a consumer-run organization, Corrigan et al. (2003) inquired about specific areas of discrimination. More than half of the sample reported some experience of discrimination. Of those who reported some experience of discrimination, 30% related an experience of discrimination regarding housing.

Landlords as a Source of Informal Support

There is also evidence that landlords can play an important role in providing informal support to tenants in mental health housing programs. In a qualitative study,
Flanagan and Davidson (2009) interviewed community members, including landlords, who had considerable experience with people with mental illness. They found
experiences of benevolence and feelings of compassion by some landlords toward
people with mental illness.

Foust et al. (March, 2013) conducted a study that linked consumers' relationships with landlords and property managers with consumers' self-reported functioning. After controlling for demographic and housing variables (e.g., age, sex, race,
type of housing), the relationship with one's landlord or property manager was significantly positively associated with measures of recovery and adaptive functioning
and significantly negatively associated with perceived stress and psychiatric stress.
The researchers suggested that landlords might be important partners in recovery
who can enhance consumers' well-being through supportive relationships.

Similarly, Townley, Miller, and Kloos (2013) examined the role of distal supports—casual community contacts—in facilitating recovery and community integration largely through the provision of tangible support (e.g., information sharing,
material supports). Hierarchical regression revealed that distal supports uniquely
predicted community integration and recovery after accounting for traditional
support networks. While this study focused on distal supports like employees of
pharmacies and coffee shops, as opposed to landlords, it highlights the importance
of casual social contacts and the potential of informal support from acquaintances
in recovery that landlords may provide to individuals in scattered-site housing
programs.

Support for Landlords

While landlords can provide support to people with mental illness, they also need
support themselves as they navigate the complex needs of tenants with mental illness. Kloos, Zimmerman, Scrimenti, and Crusto (2002) presented the New Haven
Landlord-Service Provider Forum as a model for working with landlords and property managers to promote successful scattered-site housing. They conceptualized
landlords as "natural supports" who can help tenants integrate into the neighborhood by directing them to local resources. Natural supports are people who are
"regular" community members who facilitate integration or help out but are not
paid to do so.

The Landlord-Service Provider Forum emerged out of scattered-site housing
training sessions for landlords and clinical teams in which clear tension and confusion regarding the overlapping roles and responsibilities of clinical teams and
landlords were identified. The forum met four times a year and had five principal

objectives: (1) to clarify the responsibilities, rights, and roles of landlords, service providers, and tenants; (2) to facilitate communication and shared problem-solving; (3) to increase housing stability; (4) to retain cooperative landlords; and (5) to recruit new landlords and expand known housing stock.

From the forum, Kloos et al. (2002) identified three challenges in the relationships between landlords and service providers. The first challenge was the fundamental differences in the perspectives of landlords and service providers (e.g., discrepancy of goals and different responsibilities with regard to tenants, property, and support). The second challenge was practical in nature, involving the difficulty of engaging and communicating with busy landlords who were often occupied during the day. The final challenge was role-based in which the goals related to tenants/consumers differed between landlords and service providers. An important dimension of this difference was the concern of landlords to pursue tangible outcomes related to their rental of their properties (i.e., payment of rent, resolution of property damage), while clinical teams were more concerned with ways to prevent problem tenancies in the future. Finally, there was an enduring role difference related to the legal system in which service providers are positioned largely as advocates concerned with rights, whereas landlords are positioned as businesspeople concerned with profits.

Landlord Experiences with Tenants with Mental Illness

In a recent qualitative study in Sweden, Bengtsson and Hansson (2014) explored 16 landlords' experiences with tenants with severe mental illness and identified three broad themes. The first theme is being confronted with difficult circumstances. This included consumer mismanagement of the apartments and premises (e.g., damage to apartments) and provocative behaviors (e.g., verbal and physical threats). Dealing with these difficulties required sensitivity to behaviors associated with disability on the part of the landlords, was time-consuming, and was something for which landlords felt ill-prepared. A second theme was providing assistance. This involved being helpful and offering security and was akin to the notion of landlords as a source of informal support or partners in recovery noted previously. The third theme was that landlords felt neglected when they needed help. Landlords sought collaboration and support from professionals, but were largely unsuccessful in obtaining this assistance from them. They desired something similar to the landlord-service-provider forum that Kloos et al. (2002) developed in New Haven.

In another recent study, MacLeod, Nelson, O'Campo, and Jeyaratnam (2015) compared landlord and clinical and housing teams perspectives on people with serious mental illness in two different scattered-site housing arrangements: head lease (agency holds the lease) and rent subsidy (tenant holds the lease). Based on qualitative interviews with 16 landlords and 24 clinical and housing team staff, they found that there was less contact between landlords and tenants in the head lease arrangement, where housing teams tended to address tenancy problems. As well, landlords tended to scrutinize tenants with mental illness more in the head lease arrangement. In head lease programs the agency as opposed to the tenant holds the lease and tenancies tend to be managed more closely by housing teams who tend to play the role of "surrogate landlord."

Finally, Aubry et al. (2015) conducted qualitative interviews with 23 landlords who rented to tenants in a scattered-site housing program. The authors found that landlords were motivated to rent to these tenants for financial and prosocial reasons. The landlords perceived the program tenants to be similar to other tenants and held a range of positive, neutral, and negative views of program tenants. Problems with tenants included disruptive visitors, upkeep of units, conflict with neighbors, and constant presence in their apartments.

At Home/Chez Soi—A Canadian Experiment in Housing First

Overview of the Project

At Home/Chez Soi is a Canadian research demonstration project that examined the effectiveness of the Housing First approach (Tsemberis, Gulcur, & Nakae, 2004) for people with mental illness who are homeless. Health Canada provided $110 million for 4 years (2009–2013) for both the services and research for this project. The Mental Health Commission of Canada (MHCC) administered the project in five cities across Canada. The Vancouver program was aimed at individuals living in the Downtown Eastside, with a high proportion of participants with co-occurring substance use disorders. The majority of participants in Winnipeg were Aboriginal, while the majority of participants in Toronto were immigrants from diverse ethnoracial backgrounds. Montréal is home to a large French-speaking population and Moncton, in the eastern province of New Brunswick, contains a mixed French-English population in a small city.

Housing First, modeled after the Pathways to Housing program in New York City, provides housing shortly after intake to homeless people with mental illness rather than waiting for individuals to be "ready" for housing through abstinence from alcohol and compliance with treatment (Tsemberis et al., 2004). Housing First is based on consumer-driven services, including choice over one's housing, separation of housing and clinical treatment, a recovery orientation, and an emphasis on community integration (Nelson, Goering, & Tsemberis, 2012). Rent supplements that reduce the financial barrier to obtaining housing are a key element of Housing First. Controlled outcome evaluations of Housing First and other permanent independent supportive housing approaches have demonstrated their effectiveness in improving housing stability and reducing use of hospitalization and emergency services (Aubry, Ecker, & Jetté, 2014; Rog et al., 2014).

At Home/Chez Soi was a randomized controlled trial (RCT) of Housing First in comparison to a treatment as usual (TAU) condition (Goering et al., 2011). Nested within each of these two experimental conditions were two groups of participants: those with high needs, who received ACT in the Housing First condition, and those with moderate needs, who received ICM in the Housing First condition. Additionally, sites had the option of developing a "third intervention arm," or an intervention that was tailor-made to local conditions and needs. All Housing First participants also received a rent supplement that enabled them to afford rental housing in the private market. Between October 2009 and June 2011, more than 2,200 participants were enrolled in the At Home/Chez Soi research.

Context of the Four Sites

Moncton

The Moncton site was unique in terms of the relatively small size of its population (130,000), and landlords differed in character from larger cities like Toronto, where rental management companies were the norm. The small size of Moncton meant that there was a relatively small pool of landlords who were in regular social contact and the maintenance of positive relationships between the program and landlords was particularly important. Housing was procured through a housing worker from the United Way of Greater Moncton and South Eastern New Brunswick. Members of the research team interviewed 23 landlords, who included building owners ($n = 13$) and property managers ($n = 10$) during the second and third years of implementation. In the second year, 12 landlords were interviewed, while 11 were interviewed in the third year.

Montréal

In Montréal, At Home/Chez Soi participants rented from both property management firms and individual landlords. Researchers from the At Home/Chez Soi project in Montréal conducted a total of 12 interviews that included six with property managers, two with individual landlords, and four with building superintendents (Dorvil & Guèvremont, 2013). The interviews focused on the perception and attitudes of these individuals concerning people with severe and persistent mental illness with a history of homelessness, the relationship between At Home/Chez Soi tenants and landlords, and the perceptions of landlords concerning their involvement with the At Home/Chez Soi program.

Toronto

Toronto was the largest city included in the At Home/Chez Soi program. Large rental management companies dominate the rental housing market in Toronto, making it difficult to speak about an individual landlord as individuals with personal involvement in particular tenancies. In Toronto, property managers and site staff tended to fill the role associated with that of a landlord. Housing for At Home participants was procured by the municipality through Toronto Community Housing that had existing relationships with large property management companies in the community to place tenants for other city-run programs. The existing relationships of the housing workers and landlords were an important facilitator in the procurement of rental units. During the second year of implementation, researchers at the Toronto site interviewed a convenience sample of 16 landlords (which included property managers but will be referred to as landlords hereafter) about their experiences with the program and identified what was working well and less well with At Home/Chez Soi (O'Campo, MacLeod, Minh, Borenstein, & Jeyaratnam, 2012).

Winnipeg

Compared with the other sites, Winnipeg had the lowest vacancy rate for rental housing (<1%), and the highest percentage (71%) of Aboriginal participants (Goering et al., 2014). Winnipeg was viewed as a particularly challenging context for the implementation of Housing First for several reasons. First, the Housing First approach and the introduction of innovative mental health services for Aboriginal people were new to Winnipeg, and efforts needed to be made to ensure that Housing First was culturally safe and responsive. Second, there was a view that systemic racism toward Aboriginal people, especially those who were homeless and had mental health and substance use problems, would make the procurement of rental housing challenging. The low vacancy rate was seen as exacerbating this challenge.

To partially address these problems, the Winnipeg Regional Health Authority (WRHA), which was responsible for housing procurement for the At Home/Chez Soi project, provided education to landlords regarding awareness of Aboriginal culture and mental health treatment. Additionally, the WRHA used a housing team to find and secure housing. Later, each of the Housing First teams had a housing specialist, whose role was to develop relationships with landlords and recruit new landlords. McCullough, Havens, Isaak, and Deboer (2012) reported on interviews with seven landlords from private companies, and five residence managers or tenant service coordinators from Manitoba housing, the largest supplier of housing units to the Winnipeg site, for a total of 12 interviews.

Overall

In Table 16.1, we present the average vacancy rates, the percentage of homes in core need, the average rents for a one-bedroom apartment, the number of landlords involved in At Home/Chez Soi, and the percentage of participants housed for 6 months or more at the end of the study. The vacancy rates across the four sites varied from a low of 0.7% in Winnipeg to a high of 4.1% in Moncton. In line with

Table 16.1 **Housing-Related Characteristics for At Home/Chez Soi Sites**

Variable	Moncton	Montréal	Toronto	Winnipeg	Average Across Sites
Vacancy rate	4.1	2.5	1.6	.7	2.2
% of homes in core need[1] (2009)	9	13.1	17.8	9.5	12.4
Average rent for 1-bedroom apt.	$583	$626	$969	$657	$709
Number of landlords	56	73	94	37	52
% housed for 6 months or more at study end	73	72	72	45	66

[1]Core housing need means housing does not meet one or more of the adequacy, suitability, and affordability standards (30% before-tax income to pay median rent including utilities (figures from the Canada Mortgage and Housing Corporation, 2012).

these rates, Winnipeg had the lowest percentage of participants (45%) who were consecutively housed for 6 months or more at the end of the 2-year study, while Moncton had the highest percentage of participants (73%) who were consecutively housed for 6 months or more at the end of the study. Both Toronto and Montréal had a similar level of participants (72%) being stably housed at the end of the study. Moncton had the lowest average rental rates ($583) for a one-bedroom apartment followed by Montréal ($626), Winnipeg ($657), and Toronto ($969). In line with having the highest rental rates of the four sites, Toronto also had the highest percentage of households in core need (17.8%), followed by Montréal (13.5%), Winnipeg (9.5%), and Moncton (9%). A total of 260 landlords across the four sites rented to Housing First service recipients in the study.

Research on Landlords in At Home/Chez Soi

Extensive qualitative research was conducted on the implementation of the programs, including landlord experiences with tenants (Macnaughton, Goering, & Nelson, 2012). Across sites, the Housing First programs achieved high levels of fidelity (Nelson et al., 2014) with the reliance on housing staff to assist consumers with finding and moving into housing and being available to resolve problems with them and their landlords as they arose. Moreover, a high level of housing stability was achieved by study participants receiving Housing First services, such that at the end of the 2-year study 62% of them had been housed for 6 months or more (Goering et al., 2014).

As part of the implementation evaluation, site researchers conducted qualitative interviews with landlords who rented housing to participants in the Housing First condition. Four broad questions were addressed in the landlord interviews:

1. What is their motivation for renting to Housing First tenants?
2. What are their views of Housing First tenants?
3. What worked well in their experiences with the At Home/Chez Soi project?
4. What worked less well?

The results presented below are drawn from At Home/Chez Soi Implementation and Fidelity Site reports from Winnipeg, Toronto, Montreal, and Moncton (Aubry, Cherner, Ecker, Jetté & Philander, 2011; McCullough et al., 2012; O'Campo et al., 2012; Dorvil & Guèvremont, 2013). The authors reviewed the above noted reports and synthesized how landlords viewed their participation in a scattered-site housing program. Themes representing factors associated with implementation of the program were coded using a matrix display (Miles, Huberman, & Saldana, 2014). Quotes representative of the themes were taken from the reports.

Findings

What Motivates Landlords to Rent to Housing First Participants?

Interviews with landlords across the four sites revealed *altruism* as a key motivator for landlords renting to participants of the At Home/Chez Soi project. For example, Moncton landlords talked about "giving back to the community" and "helping people find their feet" (Aubry et al., 2011, p. 40). In Toronto, landlords reported experiencing feelings of satisfaction associated with perceiving tenants from the program experiencing personal growth and positive outcomes as a result of their becoming housed. Some landlords in Montréal described themselves as sensitive and compassionate to the population served by the At Home/Chez Soi project, noting that they went beyond the usual landlord–tenant relationship in the support they provided to participants. Winnipeg landlords viewed renting to program participants as an opportunity to help them improve their lives. Landlords in both Moncton and Montréal explained their altruistic motives as the result of perceiving program participants as deserving of assistance because of the difficulties they had experienced as a result of their mental illness. For example, one landlord in Montreal stated the following:

"There are these people living on the street and they are ill; so you place them in their own apartment. I find this wonderful. It's very important that

a project like this one exists. I have no trouble with it. . . . I am for it 500%.
These are people who really need it." (Dorvil & Guèvremont, 2013, p. 86)

The fact that the *rent and payment for any damages were guaranteed* was identified by landlords in all of the sites as a central motivator for renting to tenants from the At Home/Chez Soi program. In particular, from a business standpoint, given these guarantees, they characterized renting to program participants as being of low risk compared with similar types of clients who are not associated with a program.

A landlord in Moncton described the attractiveness of having guaranteed rent:

"The rent is guaranteed pretty much. I mean they're subsidized and they're very proactive and you know with the rent and things like that, there's no delays . . . so I don't feel like I'm going to have to deal with . . . someone not paying the rent and then have to take action and things like that. So that is one of the benefits of it. . . .. The security of the income, the security of the payment of the rent." (Aubry et al., 2011, p. 40)

Finally related to the low-risk nature of program participants, landlords from all of the sites highlighted the fact that *the program assisted landlords* when problems arose as another motivating factor. In particular, they expressed appreciation for the potential assistance from housing workers and the clinical team that came with renting to tenants from the program. One landlord in Winnipeg said, "I wouldn't rent to them if it wasn't for the program; they wouldn't qualify for one of our apartments" (McCullough et al., 2012, p. 25).

What Are Landlords' Perceptions of Housing First Tenants?

Across sites, there was a theme of *close scrutiny and negative judgement*. For example, landlords in Winnipeg often mentioned that participants had "no housekeeping skills, no cooking skills, no bathing skills, no skills at all" (McCullough et al., 2012, p. 22). As well, Winnipeg landlords seemed to have little to no tolerance for solvent users. Some landlords tried to invoke "special provisions" in leases that banned visitors and required abstinence. These provisions not only go against the harm reduction philosophy of Housing First but also are illegal. This led staff to advocate with the Residential Tenancy Board to have these clauses removed from the leases. Other Winnipeg landlords expressed a desire for tenants to have a "compliant personality" or a "willingness to be medicated" (McCullough et al., 2012, p. 25). In Toronto, landlords indicated a preference for head leases—scattered-site housing programs where the agency holds the lease—in which the housing and clinical teams have a more involved role in managing the tenancies. In Montréal, landlords, for whom contact with At Home/Chez Soi tenants represented their first known exposure to people with severe mental illness, tended to characterize them as being different and having special needs. In one case, a landlord noted that At Home/ Chez Soi tenants presented with noticeably different behaviors. In another case, a landlord viewed them as being more demanding and lacking in experience with living in their own place.

These findings of close scrutiny and negative judgement did not characterize all landlords, but they are consistent with Page's (1977, 1983, 1996) survey research regarding stigma by landlords toward people with mental illness. Trying to invoke special lease clauses is clearly discriminatory and illegal and had to be addressed by clinical and housing staff. It should be noted that while some landlords treated some tenants differently in a negative way (i.e., discrimination) there were instances in which some landlords treated tenants differently in a positive way (i.e., tolerance of behaviors associated with disabilities).

A second theme was *screening for best fit*. Screening was a particular issue for Toronto landlords, who reported that some program participants were not a good fit or did not have an appropriate level of life skills for independent living. Some landlords indicated that some tenants "just do not belong" and should be housed in a "special place" where they might have more supervision.

> "Um, and everybody's interest was just keeping him safe, keeping him housed and not having to deal with the issues that he had originally, like, dealt with. So we did that to the best of our ability, but like I said, at the end of the day, it was still established that he needed to be in a more supervised environment." (O'Campo et al., 2012, p. 6)

As well, some Toronto landlords wanted more information about program participants' disabilities. While this is understandable and at times associated with landlords wanting to be helpful, there are clear privacy issues with disclosures about disability. In Winnipeg, landlords believed that solvent users needed some other type of housing, such as transitional housing, to deal with their substance use issues to become "ready" for independent housing. They wanted to screen people who use substances out of their housing. "You are just setting them up for failure by dumping them in apartments" (McCullough et al., 2012, p. 25). These findings are consistent with observations from the Toronto site, where landlords' desire to screen participants was common (O'Campo et al., 2012). Staff must work with landlords to disabuse them of the notion that they can serve a "gatekeeper" function. Moreover, staff members emphasize to landlords that participant tenancy is a right, not something that they can earn by passing some screening function imposed by landlords.

The third theme is that some landlords at each site stated they *viewed and treated At Home/Chez Soi participants like any other tenants*. In contrast to the previous two themes, some landlords recognized the need to treat At Home/Chez Soi tenants like any tenant, rather than subjecting them to special restrictions, judgments about their character, or perceived readiness for housing. In Montréal and Moncton, landlords who had had previous experience with homeless people with mental illness were more apt to describe At Home/Chez Soi tenants as regular tenants similar to other tenants, or even better in some cases.

> "There are not differences. You could pass for one of them. They present as ordinary tenants. There's no difference. They are normal. For me, they are mister or misses everybody." (Dorvil & Guèvremont, 2013, p. 92)

All of the interviewed Montréal landlords described treating At Home/Chez Soi tenants in the same manner as other tenants when it came to respecting their rights and responsibilities as tenants. When difficulties arose with At Home/Chez Soi tenants, they indicated that they followed the same set of formal procedures (e.g., verbal warning, letter) as other tenants. Similarly, in Toronto and Winnipeg, most landlords believed that they treated At Home/Chez Soi tenants just like they treated other tenants.

> "I try to develop a relationship to, to make them feel like they are not different than any other tenant, because I'm an individual who, you know, who has a good relation with all the tenants, you know, and communicates with them on a daily basis, and all of that." (O'Campo et al., 2012, p. 6)

These findings are similar to those reported in the study by Flanagan and Davidson (2009), who noted that landlords often experienced compassion for their tenants.

What Worked Well from the Perspective of Landlords?

Across sites there were clear themes in terms of what worked well in the implementation of At Home/Chez Soi from the perspective of landlords. First, *positive relationships and good communication between landlords and program staff* were prominent themes about what was working well across all four sites. Landlords in Toronto discussed positive relationships with housing and clinical teams whom landlords perceived as capable and professional. Additionally, landlords reported *having positive relationships with tenants*. Landlords in Moncton reported that program tenants were as good as or better than other tenants. A landlord in Moncton talks about program tenants in the following terms: "I would say most of the tenants that were part of the program were better than some of my regular tenants" (Aubry et al., 2011, p. 40). In Winnipeg landlords reported positive relationships with housing and clinical teams despite considerable tenancy challenges related to the unique implementation challenges of that site. The Winnipeg site faced unique housing challenges related to racism, substance use, and low vacancy rates. In both

Moncton and Montréal landlords reported that tenants assisted them with tasks in their buildings.

There were common themes regarding strategies adopted by project sites to appease landlords and smooth implementation when problems with participants as tenants were encountered. Landlords at all four sites reported that program staff were helpful and receptive when tenancy problems arose. One landlord in Toronto recounted, "We never had any issues getting in touch with anybody or getting things dealt with the way that they needed to be dealt with" (O'Campo et al., 2012, p. 5). Landlords particularly liked when program staff arranged cleaning and repair services for damaged units. This strategy served to intercede between the rights of landlords to property and the responsibility of tenants to maintain property. As program participants took on new social roles as tenants, a certain amount of difficulty associated with learning the responsibilities of these new roles is to be expected. Landlords in Moncton and Winnipeg talked very positively about this facet of the program while landlords in Toronto had mixed experiences with damages. The mixed experiences of these landlords were probably related to participation in other housing programs, notably head lease programs, where tenancies are closely managed by housing teams. A Toronto landlord framed head leases in the following terms: "The other agencies we deal with . . . they're the head tenant. . . . So they deal directly with everything so things move a little easier" (O'Campo et al. 2012, p.7).

A second strategy reported across sites was the *cooperation of program staff with housing unit transfers*. Landlords valued the willingness of program staff to intercede in tenancies that were troubled and not working well. Landlords reported that this cooperation was important because it helped to avoid time-consuming and costly eviction proceedings. While this is a positive finding in the context of program implementation, there is an associated risk that landlords might expect more from Housing First programs than they would from other tenants.

There were also instances of unique site-specific strategies that worked well during implementation. One example from Winnipeg was a roundtable with landlords that included both landlord education and a feedback mechanism, which landlords reported positive experiences with. Similarly, regular lunches between program managers and landlords in Moncton facilitated communication and assisted with problem-solving. In both Montréal and Toronto housing teams attended meetings with clinical teams in order to close information gaps between landlords and the program and between housing and clinical teams.

What Worked Less Well from the Perspective of Landlords?

There were some challenges associated with implementation from the perspective of landlords. One common challenge across sites was issues related to the *behavior of tenants* linked to the transition from street life to tenancy. Common issues with behavior included visitors who could be loud or disruptive, traffic in buildings, property damage, smoking, and drug use. In Toronto one landlord described a common scenario related to tenant behavior:

> "You know, they'd end up allowing him to take them back to the apartment, you know, they were doing drugs, they were drinking, you know, just raising chaos in the apartment, you know, really damaged his apartment, damaged his belongings." (O'Campo et al., 2012, p. 5)

In Winnipeg there were pronounced challenges with solvent use and "unit takeovers," reflecting the unique challenges at that site. Unit takeovers refer to instances when a tenant's visitors will not leave a unit and effectively take it over. Landlords in Moncton complained about some program tenants smoking heavily in their units. These challenges likely reflect the challenges of program participants transitioning into new social roles as tenants and the process of learning the social expectations associated with these roles. While these complaints are serious concerns for landlords that merit consideration, they represent a barometer of program success in the degree to which program participants are interacting with landlords and becoming increasingly involved in the mainstream housing market—a novel facet of the independent supportive housing model.

A substantive challenge from the perspective of landlords across sites was *communication*. There were two dimensions to this challenge: (1) communication in the buildings between landlords and program tenants and program tenants and other tenants, and (2) communication between landlords and housing and clinical teams. In Toronto and Moncton, landlords relayed instances in which noise and behavior disturbed the enjoyment of other tenants. Landlords across sites had issues with communication with housing and clinical teams. Across sites, getting in touch with housing and clinical teams was a concern. At times landlords believed that the program was unresponsive to *the support needs of tenants*. Landlords in Winnipeg, Montréal, and Moncton also noted that there were instances in which *program staff was not responsive*. There seemed to be a degree of confusion, for some landlords, about whom should be contacted for what, in addition to confusion about reaching both clinical supports and housing teams by phone. A landlord in Toronto suggested that it would be helpful to be provided with a list of numbers particular to a program participants housing and clinical contacts. The data suggested this might be an area in which concerns of landlords could be easily assuaged through the development of a communication protocol that includes the regular dissemination of clinical and housing contacts for program participants. Additionally, landlords in Toronto and Winnipeg indicated a desire for more frequent and regular check-ins with housing and clinical teams and increased support for program participants. One landlord in Winnipeg observed, "When it first started I found that the supports were magnificent but as the case load got heavier, they [the case workers] were spread thin and it was a lot harder" (McCullough et al., 2012, p. 23).

Implications for Practice
Building on Landlords' Motivations

It is clear from the landlord interviews that having guarantees related to rent and any damages serve as significant motivators for landlords renting to Housing First tenants. As a result, it is important that these advantages be communicated up front during negotiations with landlords and property management companies. As well, it makes sense to highlight to landlords the level of success that Housing First programs have achieved in helping the majority of their participants to exit homelessness and begin to establish a life in the community. The other motivating factor that should be noted in negotiations with landlords around accepting Housing First tenants is the assistance available from the housing and clinical staff if problems are encountered. These findings mirror those of Aubry et al. (2015).

Addressing Landlords' Perceptions of Housing First Tenants

While many landlords are motivated by both altruistic and financial reasons, it is important to recognize that landlords' differ in how they view Housing First tenants. Some landlords, especially those with previous experience with this population, view Housing First tenants the same way that they view other tenants. This is desirable from our standpoint, because it is consistent with the citizenship focus of Housing First (Sylvestre, chapter 7, this volume).

On the other hand, there are some landlords who view Housing First tenants as different, judge them in stigmatizing ways, and believe that they require close scrutiny. Some landlords want background personal information that they might use to invoke special restrictive clauses in their leases or to screen some people out of their rental units. Probing tenants' personal backgrounds is an invasion of privacy, and adding special clauses in leases or screening people out of housing are discriminatory and illegal.

The implication of these findings is that Housing First staff members that work with landlords need to educate them both about mental illness and individual rights. Sometimes this will involve standing up to landlords and using legal channels if necessary to protect tenants' rights. The Landlord-Service Provider Forum, described by Kloos et al. (2002) could be one mechanism to educate landlords. The combination of education, personal contact with Housing First tenants, and the supportive helped provided by Housing First staff could go a long way in overcoming stigma and discrimination on the part of landlords (Corrigan & Penn, 1999).

Building on What Worked Well

Positive working relationships between landlords and housing and clinical service teams were central to what worked well from the perspectives of landlords in At Home. One positive innovation from both Winnipeg and Moncton were meetings where landlords had a chance to interact with housing and clinical service team members in line with the Landlord-Service Provider Forum described by Kloos et al. (2002). In addition to the educational component outlined above, these events—held as monthly lunches—were valuable opportunities for landlords to find support and connections within their own peer group as well as to interact with service teams. When initiating a forum for landlords, it is important to consider times and locations that are likely to attract landlords.

Building on What Worked Less Well

One widely reported challenge from the perspective of At Home landlords and Bengtsson and Hansson (2014) was program participant behavior—this included substance use, unit damage, unit takeovers, and smoking. It is important to normalize these challenges both within housing and clinical service teams and with landlords. Because Housing First participants have typically been homeless for long periods of time and have complex care needs, challenges associated with becoming housed and taking on new social roles should be anticipated. To this end, these challenges should be framed as tenancy learnings that are valuable to recovery.

It is important that housing and clinical service teams have well-developed protocols for supporting landlords who experience challenges with the behaviors of program tenants (Bengtsson & Hansson, 2014). These protocols should include contact sheets that make clear whom landlords should contact for particular issues and include phone numbers and scheduling details. Protocols should also include strategies around unit transfers when tenancies become troubled. This will help avoid costly and time-consuming evictions and protect relationships with landlords and program participants.

References

Aubry, T., Cherner, R., Ecker, J., Jetté, J., & Philander, K. (2011). *Implementation evaluation report for Mental Health Commission of Canada's At Home/Chez Soi project: Moncton site.* Ottawa and Moncton: University of Ottawa and Université de Moncton.

Aubry, T., Cherner, R., Ecker, J., Jetté, Rae, J., Yamin, S., . . . McWilliams, N. (2015). Perceptions of private market landlords who rent to tenants of a Housing First program. *American Journal of Community Psychology, 55,* 292–303.

Aubry, T., Ecker, J., & Jetté, J. (2014). Supported housing as a promising Housing First approach for people with severe and persistent mental illness. In M. Guirguis-Younger, R. McNeil, & S.W. Hwang (Eds.), *Homelessness and health* (pp. 155–188). Ottawa: University of Ottawa Press.

Aubry, T., Yamin, S., Ecker, J., Jetté, J., Albert, H., Nolin, D., & Sylvestre, J. (2012). *Final report on the findings of the second implementation evaluation for the Moncton site of the At Home/Chez Soi project*. Ottawa and Moncton: University of Ottawa and Université de Moncton.

Bengtsson-Tops, A., & Hansson, L. (2014). Landlords' experiences of housing tenants suffering from severe mental illness: A Swedish empirical study. *Community Mental Health Journal, 50*, 111–119.

Canada Mortgage and Housing Corporation. (2012). *Housing in Canada*. Online. http://cmhc. beyond2020.com/HiCODefinitions_EN.html#_Core_Housing_Need_Status

Corrigan, P.W., & Penn, D.L. (1999). Lessons from social psychology on discrediting psychiatric stigma. *American Psychologist, 54*, 765–776.

Corrigan, P., Thompson, V., Lambert, D., Sangster, Y., Noel, J., & Campbell, J. (2003). Perceptions of discrimination among persons with serious mental illness. *Psychiatric Services, 54*, 1105–1110.

Dorvil, H., & Guèvremont, S.B. (2013). *Le logement comme facteur d'intégration sociale pour les personnes itinérantes aux prises avec des problèmes de santé mentale participant au Projet Chez Soi à Montréal*. Montréal: Université du Québec à Montréal.

Flanagan, E., & Davidson, L. (2009). Passing for "normal": Features that affect the community inclusion of people with mental illness. *Psychiatric Rehabilitation Journal, 33*, 18–25.

Foust, P., Kloos, B., Townley, G., Green, E., Davis, B. & Wright, P. (March, 2013). *The role of landlords in the functioning of persons with serious mental illness living in supported housing*. Manuscript in progress.

Goering, P.N., Streiner, D.L., Adair, C., Aubry, T., Barker, J., Distasio, J., … Zabkiewicz, D.M. (2011). The At Home/Chez Soi trial protocol: A pragmatic, multi-site, randomized controlled trial of a Housing First intervention for homeless individuals with mental illness in five Canadian cities. *British Medical Journal Open, 1*, 1–18.

Goering, P., Veldhuizen, S., Watson, A., Adair, C., Kopp, B., Latimer, E., … Aubry, T. (2014). *National final report: Cross-site At Home/Chez Soi project*. Calgary, AB: Mental Health Commission of Canada.

Kloos, B., Zimmerman, S., Scrimenti, K., & Crusto, C. (2002). Landlords as partners for promoting success in supported housing: "It takes more than a lease and a key." *Psychiatric Rehabilitation Journal, 25*, 235–244.

MacLeod, T., Nelson, G., O'Campo, P., & Jeyaratnam, J. (2015). The experience of landlords and housing and clinical staff in supportive independent housing interventions. *Canadian Journal of Community Mental Health, 34*, 1–13.

Macnaughton, E., Goering, P., & Nelson, G. (2012). Exploring the value of mixed methods within the At Home/Chez Soi Housing First project: A strategy to evaluate the implementation of a complex population health intervention for people with mental illness who have been homeless. *Canadian Journal of Public Health, 103* (Supplement 1), 557–562.

McCullough, S., Havens, M., Isaak, C., & Deboer, T. (2012, August). *At Home/Chez Soi: Winnipeg site later implementation evaluation report*. Winnipeg: Institute of Urban Studies, University of Winnipeg.

Miles, M. B., Huberman, A. M., & Saldana, J. (2014). *Qualitative data analysis: A methods sourcebook* (3rd ed.). Newbury Park, CA: Sage.

Nelson, G., Goering, P., & Tsemberis, S. (2012). Housing for people with lived experience of mental health issues: Housing First as a strategy to improve quality of life. In C.J. Walker, K. Johnson, & E. Cunningham (Eds.), *Community psychology and the socio-economics of mental distress: International perspectives* (pp. 191–205). Basingstoke, UK: Palgrave MACMILLAN.

Nelson, G., Stefancic, A., Rae, J., Townley, G., Tsemberis, S., Macnaughton, E., … Goering, P. (2014). Early implementation evaluation of a multi-site housing first intervention for homeless people with mental illness: A mixed methods approach. *Evaluation and Program Planning, 43*, 16–26.

O'Campo, P., MacLeod, T., Minh, A., Borenstein, H., & Jeyaratnam, J. (2012). *At Home: A report on landlords' perspectives—At Home/Chez Soi research demonstration project, Toronto site.* Toronto: Centre for Research on Inner City Health, St. Michael's Hospital.

Page, S. (1977). Effects of the mental illness label in attempts to obtain accommodation. *Canadian Journal of Behavioural Science, 9,* 85–90.

Page, S. (1983). Psychiatric stigma: Two studies of behaviour when the chips are down. *Canadian Journal of Community Mental Health, 2,* 13–20.

Page, S. (1996). Effects of the mental illness label in 1993: Acceptance and rejection in the community. *Journal of Health and Social Policy, 7,* 61–68.

Ridgway, P., & Zipple, A.M. (1990). The paradigm shift in residential services: From the linear continuum to supported housing approaches. *Psychosocial Rehabilitation Journal, 13,* 11–31.

Rog, D.J., Marshall, T., Dougherty, R.H., George, P., Daniels, A.S., Ghose, S.S., & Delphin-Rittmon, M.E. (2014). Permanent supportive housing: Assessing the evidence. *Psychiatric Services, 65,* 287–294.

Townley, G., Miller, H., & Kloos, B. (2013). A little goes a long way: The impact of distal social support and community integration and recovery of persons with psychiatric disabilities. *American Journal of Community Psychology, 52,* 85–96.

Tsemberis, S., Gulcur, L., & Nakae, M. (2004). Housing first, consumer choice, and harm reduction for homeless individuals with a dual diagnosis. *American Journal of Public Health, 94,* 651–656.

Trainor, J., Pomeroy, E., & Pape, B. (Eds.). (1999). *Building a framework for support: A community development approach to mental health policy.* Toronto: Canadian Mental Health Association/National Office.

SECTION V

CONCLUSIONS AND REFLECTIONS

17

Housing, Citizenship, and Communities for People with Serious Mental Illness

Reflections and Future Directions

JOHN SYLVESTRE

The chapters in this book testify to a field that is vibrant, growing, and making a significant contribution to bettering the lives of people with serious mental illness. Since deinstitutionalization, too many people with serious mental illness have experienced social isolation, marginalization, and poverty—problems that persist today. There are a number of causes including late, inappropriate, and ineffective treatment; stigma; and inadequate support. Other noteworthy causes have been the lack of, the inaccessibility of, or the poor quality of housing in the community. There is reason to hope that this is changing. In the following sections I summarize common findings and themes across the chapters in this book. Then I provide some suggestions for moving forward, in theory, research, practice, and policy.

Areas of Consensus

Across the chapters in this book there are notable areas of consensus. Below I highlight this consensus in theory and research, and policy and practice.

Consensus in Theory and Research

Across the various chapters on theory and research there were a number of areas of consensus. The first is that housing and support is effective for enabling people to keep their housing. In particular, when people with mental illness who have experienced homelessness are provided intensive forms of support (e.g., intensive case management, assertive community treatment) they are more likely to get and keep housing than people who receive less or no support. Housing and support programs that further reduce barriers to housing, such as expectations for sobriety or adherence to treatment, are among the most effective. Equally important are strategies to address affordability in the form of rent subsidies or supplements. Housing First, which incorporates these key features, is the most well researched of all the approaches examined in this book. The research conducted on Housing First clearly shows that it can help even those characterized as among the hardest to house, with long-standing histories of homelessness, to get and to keep good quality stable housing.

There are a number of reasons why Housing First has produced such a notable research base. Surely one reason is that the values that inform the approach, first articulated by Priscilla Ridgway and Anthony Zipple (1990) and Paul Carling (1995), coincide with the values articulated in the consumer/survivor movement as well as the recovery movement (see chapter 13). In addition, the emphasis on scattered-site independent housing reflects the preference of the great majority of people with serious mental illness (see chapter 1). Another reason, though, is that the theory of change and the model have been so well articulated and defined, such that it is easy to describe and communicate and replicate with a high degree of fidelity (see chapter 5). Despite the model being well defined, the term "Housing First" is increasingly being used loosely (see chapter 11), such as being applied to single-site housing approaches or housing that does not offer more intensive forms of support. There is a risk of confusion arising from the loose application of the term "Housing First." There is also risk of creating disappointment should inferior housing approaches branded Housing First not produce the expected outcomes. Alternatively, rigorous and careful evaluation may enable us to determine which adaptations for local contexts are detrimental to the impact of the intervention, and which are not.

In contrast to Housing First, there is no shared theory of change, model, or design, or any commonly agreed on best practices for single-site housing (see chapter 5). Consequently, there is the potential for significant variations among programs that provide single-site housing in terms of the amount and kind of support available, the role of tenants in decision-making in the housing, or the size of buildings and number of tenants. Though this approach has not received as much research attention, there are a number of reasons why it should. The first is that this form of housing currently constitutes a significant part of the housing stock of many local housing systems (a notable exception appears to be in Australia; see chapter 12). Equally important, it appears that a not insignificant number of people consistently express a preference for this type of housing, or may benefit from the additional structure and support this housing approach may provide (see chapter 14). It is noteworthy that, at present, there is not a lot of evidence that scattered-site approaches produce better outcomes over well-implemented single-site housing programs (see chapter 5) and single-site housing may in some cases provide the structure and support necessary for individuals who are unable to achieve housing stability in scattered-site programs. Finally, the absence of agreed on best practices means that there are no clear guidelines for housing providers or policy makers regarding the optimal implementation of this form of housing. It is possible that people are living in housing that is not only not optimal but also may be limiting them or even harmful to them.

It is also clear from the research literature that there are replicable and important outcomes that come from well-implemented and -resourced community-based housing programs, but that these outcomes are also limited (see chapter 3). The theory of change described in chapter 5 suggests a wide range of outcomes expected from the services and support that are part of Housing First, including reduced use of hospital and emergency services and involvement in the criminal justice system; improved community functioning; increased subjective quality of life; more positive consumer narratives; development of future-focused orientation; and improved clinical outcomes (i.e., reduced psychiatric symptoms and substance use). The research findings show that whereas good quality housing with intensive support enables people to get and to keep their housing, it is not sufficient (at least in the 1-year to 2-year window that is typically studied) to produce this broader range of outcomes that would support community participation and citizenship (see chapter 5 and chapter 11). Although people stay in their housing, many risk remaining socially isolated, with limited involvement in their communities, or in employment, educational, or leisure activities.

In part this may be due to the long process required to build a more positive life after having experienced a period of homelessness or substance abuse, as well as the result of the poverty that most will continue to experience. As some qualitative research shows (see chapter 8), housing provides an opportunity for people to begin to extricate themselves from social lives, behaviors, and identities linked to homelessness. However, this process is long, and people may require different kinds of support to achieve the other goals they hold for themselves.

It may also be that the focus of the support that is offered in these programs is insufficient to produce broader outcomes. Much of this support is focused on therapeutic outcomes, linking people to services, or assisting them with activities of daily living. To produce a broader set of outcomes, more specialized interventions may be required. The capabilities approach suggests two actions to improve functioning (or what people actually accomplish in their lives). The first is the creation of opportunities or capabilities (Rapp & Goscha, 2011) and the second is active support and accommodations so that people can take advantage of these increased opportunities (see chapter 6; see also Shinn, 2015). Promoting a broader set of outcomes may require targeted actions to identify and remove barriers and to create opportunities for participation as well as targeted support. Examples of programs that can provide such support are the Individual Placement and Support program (Drake & Bond, 2011) and Supported Employment (Bond, 2004). Examples also come from the consumer/survivor movement, in the form of alternative businesses and mutual support (see chapter 13). Despite these programs, poverty will remain a primary obstacle for many. Put simply, people on social assistance programs in most jurisdictions are very poor. They struggle to meet their daily needs. They do not have the economic power to gain access to settings or opportunities to substantially improve their lives. Whatever the strategies that are adopted, it appears that though housing is the foundation for community life, it is not sufficient. There will continue to be much work to be done to ensure the full enfranchisement of a substantial portion of people living with serious mental illness.

Consensus in Policy and Practice

The contributions in this volume point to the long road we have traveled from deinstitutionalization to provide good quality housing and support for people with serious mental illness. What is apparent in North America, Australia, and Europe is that following deinstitutionalization, there was no concerted or systematic effort to ensure that people with serious mental illness had adequate housing (see chapters 1, 9, 10, 11, and 12). Over the years, in response to the growing, yet predictable, homelessness crisis, a number of different approaches were tried, with no guidelines beyond good intentions. These approaches, whatever their value, were rarely sufficiently funded to fix the homelessness problem. Growing homelessness led to the growth of a social service industry to meet the immediate needs of the growing homeless population (e.g., homeless shelters, food banks, drop-in centers, street health or outreach teams; see chapter 9) rather than housing people. A number of factors appear to have turned the tide. One of these factors is the growing lack of tolerance for homelessness. Though this lack of tolerance may be attributable in part to compassion for homeless people, we cannot discount that the lack of tolerance was also related to aesthetic and safety concerns tied to an increasingly visible male homelessness problem.

This increasing concern coincided with the first strong research evidence of the effectiveness of Housing First. However, it is unlikely that this research evidence alone was sufficient to focus attention on not only the problem of homelessness but also the solution. Notably, the rise in Housing First coincided with the election of conservative governments in the United States and Canada, which looked favorably on private-sector partnerships with landlords over expenditures on social housing, and which may have also been swayed by the allure of significant cost savings (which have largely not been demonstrated; see chapter 4).

Whatever the reasons for the emergence of Housing First, it is clear that there is now some consensus on the elements of good housing and support to go along with the enthusiasm for addressing homelessness. Across Canada, the United States, Europe, and Australia (see chapters 9, 10, 11, and 12) Housing First is front and center in housing strategies. Key principles and assumptions of Housing First align with many of those of consumer-led housing (see chapter 13) and single-site housing (see chapter 14), though important differences remain. For those who have been working in this field, as practitioners, policy makers, or researchers, it must come as a remarkable and encouraging turn of events to see on the horizon the possibility that the levels of homelessness among people with serious mental illness we have witnessed for so long will be consigned to the past.

The Way Forward

The wealth of research, thought, experience, and expertise collected in this book shows that housing people with serious mental illness is no longer an insurmountable problem. The problem that remains is ensuring that the enthusiasm does not fade and that we build on and extend the gains that have been made. Though we are increasingly confident that we can enable people to get and to keep their housing, we must continue to be ambitious in seeking improvements in our practices, policies, and research in this area. This is imperative because the research evidence suggests that the strategies for housing people may not be sufficient to produce healthy and satisfying lives in the community. Second, it is imperative so that the enthusiasm and increased funding that we have seen not dissipate should longer term evidence show disappointing outcomes. To ensure that we continue to move forward, we offer the following suggestions.

A Clear Focus on Our Shared Goal

Despite our ability to house people, we have not yet demonstrated our ability to support people in becoming fully enfranchised as citizens (Hopper, 2012). Chapter 7 of this book outlines a citizenship agenda for housing for people with serious mental illness. This agenda envisions ensuring that people with serious mental illness are fully enfranchised as citizens and active participants in their communities, with housing as the foundation. It foresees not only ensuring access to housing, as a basic citizenship right, but also greater attention to everyday lives in community-based housing. It points to the need to be proactive in identifying barriers to citizenship from macro-level policies and laws to micro-level interactions in the very settings in which people participate every day.

Working toward full citizenship and community participation, requires temporal and ecological perspectives. Temporally, we must focus on the full life of people living in community housing. This means that we must (1) find housing solutions for people before they become homeless; (2) provide housing for younger people who cannot live with their families of origin earlier in their experience of mental illness; (3) offer greater availability and responsiveness of crisis and housing loss prevention services for people whose housing situations have become unstable; (4) recognize that it is normal for one's housing needs to change over time, and that staying in housing that does not meet one's needs leads to instability. Ultimately, it requires the ability to seek and obtain the housing that meets a person's needs at various stages of his or her life (Sylvestre, Ollenberg, & Trainor, 2009).

Working toward full citizenship requires an ecological approach. This means that the promotion of citizenship and community participation happens at multiple levels. Housing First has shown the way in this regard, with progress being made through changes in attitudes and expectations, through social policy at national, state/provincial, and municipal levels, and through active support and the provision of direct access to housing. As we refocus on lives in community housing, we will require concerted and complementary action at various ecological levels to ensure that people can work toward recovery and be fully enfranchised as citizens.

Though broader policy change is required, it is critical that we have good local housing systems. Good local housing systems will have (1) a mix of types of affordable housing that reflect the preferences of people with serious mental illness; (2) a sufficient supply of housing of various types that are linked so that people can make real choices about the housing that they want and can easily find new housing that meets their needs as their needs change; (3) housing options distributed in a variety of neighborhoods to support choice; and (4) a variety of supports that people in housing can access. Among these supports are not only individual professional supports for therapeutic needs, or linking to services, but also informal supports that promote community participation.

Good local systems are actively managed, and they grow and evolve as the profile of tenants changes over time. They have the capacity for local system monitoring, evaluation, and planning, so that when program standards are set, there is an ability to monitor the achievement of the standards and to support programs that fall behind (Sylvestre et al., 2007). It requires ongoing professional development and training for staff members. It requires partnerships with a broader range of stakeholders, including those who are not traditionally seen to be part of such systems, including private landlords, consumer/survivor initiatives, educators, urban planners, architects, and representatives from arts or leisure sectors. In short, good housing systems do not happen by accident. Good housing systems require the active collaboration of a variety of stakeholders to provide guidance and leadership.

A Renewed Theory and Research Agenda

Research has played an undeniable role in galvanizing attention both on the homelessness problem and on the solutions that good housing and support offer. Research can also point the way forward by continuing to adopt a broader focus that demonstrates the everyday challenges people living in housing face even after they are stably housed. To support this research we require better developed housing theory. Chapter 5 has shown that whereas there is a theory of change for the Housing First approach, no such theory of change is available for single-site housing approaches.

Though there is likely some overlap in the theory of change in these approaches, there are also likely some important differences that need to be documented (e.g., in the role of peer support in single-site approaches). A well-developed theory of change would support the assessment of whether the assumptions of either approach are supported by evidence. Theory must also evolve when research evidence does not appear support to support it. For example, whereas theory described in chapter 5 predicted improved community functioning and empowerment from the supports and services associated with Housing First, evidence to date does not strongly support these links. Though it may be that additional research will be successful in demonstrating these links, it may also signal an eventual need for the revision of theory.

Research that has received much of the attention over the past decade or so has focused on a 1- to 2-year window after formerly homeless people with serious mental illness have gained access to housing through programs such as Housing First. As we have noted, some of the research demonstrates that although people become stably housed they do not typically achieve a broader set of outcomes. Qualitative research described in chapter 8 suggests a slow process of disentangling oneself from a homelessness identity and social life prior to fully embracing a new identity and lifestyle. This research complements another line of research that has documented that people living in community-based housing are typically not as integrated in their communities as their neighbors (see for example Aubry & Myner, 1996) nor as active as citizens (see chapter 7).

There is a need for theory and research to support a citizenship agenda. At a broader level, as suggested in chapter 7, there is a need to identify and study indicators of citizenship among people with serious mental illness including social security, employment, housing, health, education, and community services; democratic process; legislation regarding access to services (Huxley & Thornicroft, 2003); and experience of discrimination and denial of rights that people may experience on a daily basis. It is also important to better understand the neighborhoods in which people live and the extent to which they afford or deny opportunities for participation. This understanding may come from drawing on a broader range of disciplines that also examine these issues, but that may not have scholars commonly examining the topic of housing. These disciplines may include geography, philosophy, leisure studies, political studies, sociology, and anthropology.

As has been shown, the range of options available for research has grown substantially over the years, in part by drawing on methods from a variety of disciplines (see chapter 8). We have also seen the growth of support for randomized controlled trials for examining the effectiveness of housing programs, as well as the exploitation of larger and larger data sets in research.

Finally, as we have suggested, research will continue to improve and become more relevant to the extent that it continues to become more engaged with other stakeholders including tenants themselves, providers of housing and support, and policy makers. Housing First research, such as in Canada's At Home/Chez Soi project, has demonstrated the value of multistakeholder collaboration in the conception and execution of intervention research. As has also been suggested, stronger research partnerships with tenants can point to previously overlooked research questions and novel findings that are directly relevant to the lives of people living with serious mental illness.

The Way Forward in Policy and Practice

As was noted earlier in this chapter, there is a need for more active management of local housing systems through system monitoring and evaluation. There is a need for systems with a range of types of housing and supports that evolve with the shifting needs and preferences of the users of the system. Beyond this monitoring, and in addition to system development and expansion, there is a need to promote local systems that are dynamic, open to innovation, contributing to research and evaluation, and able to absorb and implement new research findings.

Some effort can be made at the level of practitioners to be up on research and to find ways to implement innovations in their daily practices. Practitioners across a number of organizations can be supported in working together in communities of practice to challenge themselves to rethink and expand their practice beyond attending to solely therapeutic goals. There are a number of limitations to this approach. The first is the challenge that comes from sifting through a large body of research to determine which is the most relevant, or the strongest methodologically, or to determine common findings across a number of studies (Cooper, Levin, & Campbell, 2009). The second is that individual-level change is constrained by organizational and systemic factors (Hemsley Brown, 2004). Individual practitioners who may wish to make changes in their practice may be limited by job descriptions, organizational policies, system-level gaps, or other factors. A final challenge is that research findings may simply be irrelevant to or are not easily translated into practice innovations. The preoccupations of researchers may not be the same as those of practitioners who are seeking ways to continuously improve how they house and support people in the community.

According to Cooper (2014), systems are improved through "iterative, social processes involving interactions among two or more different groups or contexts (researchers, policy-makers, practitioners, third party agencies, community members)" (p. 29). According to Cooper (2014), one approach for ensuring an ongoing interaction among these parties is through the promotion of research-brokering organizations. These organizations are third-party intermediaries who play an active role in linking research producers and users in order to promote research use (Cooper, 2014, p. 29). One example is the Canadian Homeless Hub (www.homelesshub.ca), which produces a variety of resources on homelessness including a series of reports, e-books, research summaries, and blogs and supports researcher question and answer sessions.

These intermediaries perform a variety of functions to link research or researchers to potential end users. As Cooper (2014) notes, these research-brokering organizations can focus their attention at a number of levels and to different stakeholders, from practitioner to organizations, to systems, or to policy makers. There is likely a need for intermediaries to play different roles for these different end users. For example, in policy-making environments the timeliness in the mobilization of knowledge may be more important (see for example Notarianni, Sundar, & Carter, 2015) than in practice environments, where adaptation of information is more important (Cooper, 2014). Their efforts can include the distribution of research information in forms that are more accessible to end users to increase awareness and eventual use. This may involve dissemination in nontraditional knowledge products such as infographics or videos. It may also involve efforts to increase the capacity of organizations or systems to access and use evidence. Finally, these research-brokering organizations can perform important linking functions among various stakeholders, including among researchers and end users, that may help to promote more relevant and actionable research or evaluation (Cooper, 2014).

Conclusion

The contributions in this book point the way forward. Curiously, to the best of our knowledge, there are few examples of prior comprehensive overviews of the field of housing for people with serious mental illness—despite the field being close to 40 years old. We have assembled in this book a diverse set of topics, perspectives, and voices to demonstrate the vitality and complexity of this area. We believe this book arrives at an auspicious time, as important areas of consensus are emerging—the most significant of which is that good housing and support make a big difference in people's lives. Nonetheless, there remains much for us to accomplish. We hope that the contributions in this book can spur further conversation, debate, research, and action toward ensuring the people with serious mental illness can live full lives as fellow citizens and neighbors.

References

Aubry, T., & Myner, J. (1996). Community integration and quality of life: A comparison of persons with psychiatric disabilities in housing programs and community residents who are neighbours. *Canadian Journal of Community Mental*, 15, 5–20.

Bond, G. (2004). Supported employment: Evidence for an evidence-based practice. *Psychiatric Rehabilitation Journal*, 27, 345–359.

Carling, P.J. (1995). *Return to community: Building support systems for people with psychiatric disabilities.* New York: Guilford Press.

Cooper, A. (2014). Knowledge mobilisation in education across Canada: A cross-case analysis of 44 research brokering organisations. *Evidence and Policy*, 10(1), 29–59. doi.org/10.1332/174426413X662806

Cooper, A., Levin, B., & Campbell, C. (2009). The growing (but still limited) importance of evidence in education policy and practice. *Journal of Educational Change, 10*, 159–171.

Drake, R., & Bond, G. (2011). IPS supported employment: A 20 year update. *Psychiatric Rehabilitation Journal, 27*, 345–359.

Hemsley-Brown, J. (2004). Facilitating research utilization: A cross-sector review of research evidence. *International Journal of Public Sector Management, 17*, 534–552.

Hopper, K. (2012). Commentary: The counter-reformation that failed? A commentary on the mixed legacy of supported housing. *Psychiatric Services, 63*, 461–463. doi: 10.1176/appi.ps.201100379

Huxley, P., & Thornicroft, G. (2003). Social inclusion, social quality and mental illness. *British Journal of Psychiatry, 182*, 289–290. doi: 10.1192/bjp.00.675

Notarianni, M., Sundar, P., & Carter, C. (2015). Just in time: How evidence-on-demand services support decision making in Ontario's child and youth mental health sector. *Evidence and Policy*. Retrieved from http://www.ingentaconnect.com/content/tpp/ep/pre-prints/content-EvP_050. doi.org/10.1332/174426415X142988247320060

Rapp, C.A., & Goscha, R.J. (2011). *The strengths model: Case management with people with psychiatric disabilities 3rd edition*. New York: Oxford University Press.

Ridgway, P., & Zipple, A. M. (1990). The paradigm shift in residential services: From linear continuum to supported housing approaches. *Psychosocial Rehabilitation Journal, 13*, 11–32.

Shinn, M. (2015). Community psychology and the capabilities approach. *American Journal of Community Psychology, 55*, 243–253.

Sylvestre, J., George, L., Aubry, T., Durbin, J., Nelson, G., & Trainor, J. (2007). Strengthening Ontario's system of housing for people with serious mental illness. *Canadian Journal of Community Mental Health, 26*(1), 79–95.

Sylvestre, J., Ollenberg, M., & Trainor, J. (2009). A model of housing stability for people with serious mental illness. *Canadian Journal of Community Mental Health, 28*, 195–207.

INDEX

Page references for figures are indicated by *f* and for tables by *t*.